Ezra and Nehemiah

David J. Shepherd &
Christopher J. H. Wright

WILLIAM B. EERDMANS PUBLISHING COMPANY
GRAND RAPIDS, MICHIGAN

Wm. B. Eerdmans Publishing Co.
2140 Oak Industrial Drive NE, Grand Rapids, Michigan 49505
www.eerdmans.com

© 2018 David J. Shepherd and Christopher J. H. Wright
All rights reserved
Published 2018

ISBN 978-0-8028-6432-1

Library of Congress Cataloging-in-Publication Data

Names: Shepherd, David J., author. | Wright, Christopher J. H., 1947- author.
Title: Ezra and Nehemiah / David J. Shepherd & Christopher J. H. Wright.
Other titles: Nehemiah
Description: Grand Rapids : Eerdmans Publishing Co., 2018. | Series: The Two Horizons Old
   Testament commentary | Includes bibliographical references and index.
Identifiers: LCCN 2017030776 | ISBN 9780802864321 (pap)
Subjects: LCSH: Bible. Ezra--Commentaries. | Bible. Nehemiah—Commentaries.
Classification: LCC BS1355.53 .S54 2018 | DDC 222/.707—dc23
   LC record available at https://lccn.loc.gov/2017030776

Unless otherwise noted, Scripture quotations in chapters by Wright are from the Holy Bible, New International Version®. NIV®. Copyright ©1973, 1978, 1984, 2011 by Biblica, Inc.™ Used by permission of Zondervan. All rights reserved worldwide. www.zondervan.com

Scripture quotations marked NRSV are from the New Revised Standard Version of the Bible, copyright © 1989, by the Division of Christian Education of the National Council of the Churches of Christ in the United States of America. Used by permission. All rights reserved.

The Two Horizons Old Testament Commentary

J. GORDON MCCONVILLE and CRAIG BARTHOLOMEW, *General Editors*

Two features distinguish THE TWO HORIZONS OLD TESTAMENT COMMENTARY series: theological exegesis and theological reflection.

Exegesis since the Reformation era and especially in the past two hundred years emphasized careful attention to philology, grammar, syntax, and concerns of a historical nature. More recently, commentary has expanded to include social-scientific, political, or canonical questions and more.

Without slighting the significance of those sorts of questions, scholars in THE TWO HORIZONS OLD TESTAMENT COMMENTARY locate their primary interests on theological readings of texts, past and present. The result is a paragraph-by-paragraph engagement with the text that is deliberately theological in focus.

Theological reflection in THE TWO HORIZONS OLD TESTAMENT COMMENTARY takes many forms, including locating each Old Testament book in relation to the whole of Scripture—asking what the biblical book contributes to biblical theology—and in conversation with constructive theology of today. How commentators engage in the work of theological reflection will differ from book to book, depending on their particular theological tradition and how they perceive the work of biblical theology and theological hermeneutics. This heterogeneity derives as well from the relative infancy of the project of theological interpretation of Scripture in modern times and from the challenge of grappling with a book's message in Greco-Roman antiquity, in the canon of Scripture and history of interpretation, and for life in the admittedly diverse Western world at the beginning of the twenty-first century.

THE TWO HORIZONS OLD TESTAMENT COMMENTARY is written primarily for students, pastors, and other Christian leaders seeking to engage in theological interpretation of Scripture.

*This book is dedicated to
all those who, like Ezra and Nehemiah,
give their lives, restoring and rebuilding broken communities,
making the waste places burst into songs of joy (Isa 52:9).*

Contents

Preface	ix
Introduction	1
Commentary on Ezra	11
Commentary on Nehemiah	49
Reading Ezra-Nehemiah Canonically	111
Who Is This God?	113
Who Is This People?	133
Reading Ezra-Nehemiah Theologically Today	158
Leadership and Ezra-Nehemiah	188
Bibliography	212
Author Index	219
Subject Index	222
Scripture Index	231

Preface

Despite the authors having plowed largely lone furrows in their respective academic work prior to their collaboration on this volume, the prospect of working together on this book was a welcome opportunity to resume a friendship that had begun in the mid-90s in Northern Ireland. While there can be little doubt that our common academic interest in the Old Testament has made our shared yoke a lighter burden to bear, what was also shared was the belief that our distinctive interests as much as the views we shared would allow us to write a better volume together than either of us might write on our own.

David's meaningful interest in Ezra-Nehemiah dates from his first years of teaching these books on the Canadian Prairies at Briercrest Seminary—an experience that would in turn prompt his occasional musings on various topics that have been published since and will be discernible in the commentary at various points. However, if specialist interest of some sort in Ezra-Nehemiah seemed indispensable to the task of producing this volume, the particular aims of the Two Horizons Old Testament Commentary series—not least its ambition to widen the ambit of theological reflection beyond the books themselves—seemed also to call for specialist interest of a rather different sort. Chris's earlier work on wider theological, ethical, and missiological themes within and beyond the Old Testament and his ongoing leadership within a global organization, the Langham Partnership, offered him a quite different vantage point from which to view Ezra-Nehemiah and its theological relevance—a vantage point that will itself be discernible in his essays. Indeed, while such differences have undoubtedly shaped our respective contributions to this volume and the flavor of them, it is almost certainly also true that our common experience in leadership (as principals of Belfast Bible College and All Nations Christian College respectively) has inevitably shaped this volume's interest in what Ezra-Nehemiah does (and doesn't) have to say about leadership.

Preface

We, of course, gratefully acknowledge each other's contributions to this collaborative process, along with the wisdom of others, including Joe Blenkinsopp, Lester Grabbe, and the members of Princeton Theological Seminary's Old Testament Research Colloquium, all of whom offered constructive feedback on the last chapter of this volume.

Translations of Scripture in the sections written by David are his own unless otherwise noted. Translations of Scripture in the sections written by Chris follow the NIV (with "Yhwh" substituted for "the Lord"). Verse numbers follow those in the English Bible.

David J. Shepherd and
Christopher J. H. Wright
November 2016

Introduction

BY DAVID J. SHEPHERD AND CHRISTOPHER J. H. WRIGHT

> *In the first year of King Cyrus of Persia, in order that the word of Yhwh by the mouth of Jeremiah might be accomplished, Yhwh stirred up the spirit of King Cyrus of Persia so that he sent a herald throughout all his kingdom, and also in a written edict declared: "Thus says King Cyrus of Persia: Yhwh, the God of heaven, has given me all the kingdoms of the earth, and he has charged me to build him a house at Jerusalem in Judah. Any of those among you who are of his people—may their God be with them!—are now permitted to go up to Jerusalem in Judah, and rebuild the house of Yhwh, the God of Israel—he is the God who is in Jerusalem."* (EZRA 1:1–3 NRSV MODIFIED)

The books of Ezra and Nehemiah offer an account of the Judahites' return to Judah in the sixth century BCE and their efforts to restore Jerusalem and Judah, socially, religiously, and physically in the face of significant opposition from various quarters. However, perhaps the best way to make the acquaintance of the books of Ezra and Nehemiah is to allow them to introduce themselves. Indeed, the first few verses of the first chapter of Ezra hint at what is to follow by offering important indications of not only the setting of Ezra-Nehemiah, but also its dependence on various sources and indeed its character as theological historiography.

Settings of Ezra-Nehemiah

Places

The significance of location within Ezra-Nehemiah is signaled in the opening verses by the reference to going "up to Jerusalem in Judah" (Ezra 1:3). This and

Introduction

the subsequent notices of departure from Babylonia and Susa to Jerusalem in relation to Zerubbabel (2:1–2), Ezra (7:1–8), and Nehemiah (Neh 2:11; 13:6–7) serve to structure Ezra-Nehemiah as an episodic account of "return migration" from Mesopotamia to the Persian province of Yehud.[1] Beyond these notices, the narrative is punctuated by the flow of goods (Ezra 1:6, 9–11), people (Ezra 2; 7; 8), and correspondence (Ezra 4:6–6:12) that reinforces the umbilical connection in Ezra-Nehemiah between the heart of the Persian/Achaemenid Empire and its provincial periphery in the west. While various towns and settlements in Yehud are mentioned by name (Ezra 2 and Neh 3), they are themselves largely peripheral—both narratively and geographically—to Jerusalem and referenced primarily in relation to the rebuilding of the temple and the wall and the repopulation of Judah's preexilic capital, which serves as the setting for the bulk of the books.

Times

When precisely the various parts of Ezra-Nehemiah were originally composed and then subsequently compiled remains a matter for scholarly debate. However, the question of when the events narrated in Ezra-Nehemiah are themselves set is answered more easily by references within the books, beginning with the mention in the very first verse (Ezra 1:1) of the edict of King Cyrus of Persia in the first year of his reign (in Babylon), 539/538 BCE. The narration of the edict that follows (1:2–4) serves to identify the beginning of the story of Ezra-Nehemiah with the return from Babylonia, where the Judahite elite had been exiled following Nebuchadnezzar's decimation of Judah and Jerusalem and the destruction of the temple (2 Kgs 24–25). While the dedication of the altar and the initial phases of the return are set during the reign of Cyrus the Great (538–529), the brief tenure of his successor, Cambyses (529–522), has already passed unmentioned by the time the temple begins to be rebuilt (Ezra 5–6) under Darius I (522–486). Some argue that Ezra is presented as arriving and working in Jerusalem (Ezra 7–10; Neh 8) during the reign of Artaxerxes II (404–358), but it is more probable for a variety of reasons that Ezra-Nehemiah associates Ezra's ministry with the reign of Artaxerxes I (465–424) and nearer to the beginning of this king's rule (458) than the end (438/428).[2] If, as may be

---

1. For a recent discussion of Ezra-Nehemiah in light of anthropological studies of migration, see Southwood, *Ethnicity and the Mixed-Marriage Crisis*, 41–55, 191–212.

2. For a clear and concise evaluation of the evidence and an argument for the superiority of 458 BCE as the date implied by the text for Ezra's return, see Williamson, *Ezra and Nehemiah*, 55–69.

fairly assumed, Nehemiah's own initial arrival occurred in 445 under the same Artaxerxes, then his second return to Jerusalem narrated in Neh 13 seems to be set some fifteen years later (430). While Ezra-Nehemiah as a whole thus covers approximately the first century of the Achaemenid Empire, the events narrated in these books occur at the beginning (538–515) and the end (458–430) of this hundred-year period, leaving a gap of more than fifty years about which Ezra-Nehemiah remains largely silent.[3]

Sources of Ezra-Nehemiah

Proclamations and Letters

The initial verses of Ezra-Nehemiah hint at its dependence on a wide variety of sources by referring to a pronouncement of Cyrus (1:1) that commissions the return to Judah and rebuilding of the temple (1:2–4; cf. also 5:13–15; 6:13). Given the language used and the probable echoes of Exod 12:35–36 in Ezra 1:6, it is likely that we have here a version of an authentic Persian source, now lost. In addition to the edict of Cyrus, the first six chapters of Ezra include letters associated with his successors on the Persian throne. While the authenticity of these letters between local leaders and the Persian court (occupying the bulk of 4:6–6:12) is doubted by some, their presentation not in Hebrew, but in Aramaic, the political lingua franca of the Achaemenid Empire, is certainly intended to buttress their claim to be actual correspondence. That they may in fact be authentic is suggested by comparison with contemporary Aramaic letters, though it is not impossible that what we find in Ezra are versions or re-creations of the latter.

Lists

In addition to sources associated with the Persian court, Ezra-Nehemiah includes a number of lengthy lists. While these may make for less exciting reading then other parts of Ezra-Nehemiah, they are important for any assessment of Ezra-Nehemiah's purpose and approach to presenting the past. The linguistic character of the list of temple paraphernalia to be returned to Jerusalem (Ezra 1:9–11; cf. 8:26–27) and its similarity to other lists suggests that it has been drawn

---

3. For an excellent summary of the sociopolitical context of Yehud and the Persian Empire during this period, see Blenkinsopp, *Ezra-Nehemiah*, 60–69. For a more extensive treatment, see the essays collected in Lipschits, Knoppers, and Oeming, *Judah and the Judeans in the Persian Period*.

Introduction

from Aramaic sources available to the author/editor. Another much longer list of returnees supplied in Ezra 2 (cf. Neh 7) seems also to have been appropriated from an existing source, though for what purpose it was originally compiled is unclear. It is possible that this latter list served or perhaps was even composed as a roster of those (returnees or those associated with them) who were eventually permitted to rebuild the temple. Still another list in Neh 10:1–27, preserving the names of those who affirmed a pledge to observe the requirements of the law, clearly seems to have been added to the narrative from another source, as has the presumably authentic list of names of those who repopulated Jerusalem found in the following chapter (11:3–20). Finally, in Neh 3, the reader is presented with a list of those who participated in the reconstruction of the wall around Jerusalem associated with Nehemiah and his associates. That this list has been incorporated here from elsewhere is suggested by its differing at various points from Nehemiah's own recollections.

Recollections of Nehemiah

The figure of Nehemiah looms large in the latter half of Ezra-Nehemiah, which is dominated by what appear to be recollections of the man himself. For the most part these recollections are presented in the first-person (Neh 1–2; 4:1–7:5; 12:31–43; 13:6–31), inviting the common characterization of these passages as reflecting a "memoir" of Nehemiah, largely focused on his efforts to rebuild the wall of Jerusalem.[4] Encouraged by the observation that the first-person prayers that season Nehemiah's account reflect his desire to be remembered not for the wall, but for the community reforms he implemented on his return visit to Jerusalem (cf. Neh 10 and 13), it is plausibly suggested that these prayers were added along with the quite different prayer in Neh 1 by Nehemiah himself in producing a second edition of his memoirs to ensure that his efforts as a whole were properly appreciated.[5] Indeed, that not all the recollections of Nehemiah are presented as his own memories, but are sometimes presented as others' memories of him (see the third-person references to Nehemiah in 10:1; 12:26, 47) suggests that an editorial hand subsequent to Nehemiah's incorporated his recollections into the book as a whole.[6]

---

4. See Boda, "Redaction in the Book of Nehemiah," 25nn1–2, for a recent survey of opinions on the existence and extent of the Nehemiah memoir.

5. Williamson, *Ezra, Nehemiah*, xxiv–xxvii and the sections of the commentary referred to there.

6. For a recent treatment of the genre of the Nehemiah memoir, see Burt, *Courtier and the Governor*.

Recollections of Ezra

Less extensive than those of Nehemiah, the recollections of Ezra focus on his confrontation of mixed marriages among the community of returned exiles (Ezra 7–10) and his involvement in the reading and teaching of the law (Neh 8). As is the case with those of Nehemiah, some of these recollections are presented as first-person remembrances by Ezra of his own work (Ezra 7:27–9:15 except for 8:35–36), while others are recollections of him recounted in the third person (Ezra 7:1–11; 8:35–36; 10; Neh 8). While the prevalence of the latter and the paucity of first-person passages causes some to question the existence of an Ezra memoir comparable to Nehemiah's, there seem no obvious or compelling reasons to doubt its existence, if it is allowed that the first-person source was subjected to a thorough editing either before or as it was included in Ezra-Nehemiah. This editing may well have coincided with the editorial dislocation of Ezra's reading of the law (now to be found in Neh 8) from its original and historically more intelligible position between Ezra's arrival in Jerusalem (Ezra 8) and his confrontation of the mixed-marriage issue (Ezra 9).

Prayers

While it seems likely that Nehemiah's prayers for remembrance and the one found in Neh 1:5–11 belong to a second edition of his memoirs, the latter prayer may also be grouped with the two longest prayers found in Ezra-Nehemiah (Ezra 9:6–15; Neh 9), given the features they share with the tradition of penitential prayer seen in Dan 9 and elsewhere. Recent and extensive study of these penitential prayers highlights shared elements, including praise, supplication, confession, historical summary/review, and commonality of theme and purpose.[7] While the provenance and dating of these prayers remains a matter for scholarly debate, such elements point toward these prayers being offered up to God by a person or group seeking forgiveness for past sins with a view to improving their current situation.[8]

---

7. Boda, *Praying the Tradition*, 29.

8. For a thorough explanation of these prayers, their social situation, and their subsequent impact, see the three volumes edited by Boda et al., *Seeking the Favor of God*.

Introduction

Theological (Hi)stories of Ezra-Nehemiah

If, as we have seen, the books of Ezra and Nehemiah contain much more than merely the recollections of Ezra and Nehemiah, the centrality of their respective contributions within the books is nevertheless readily apparent. That what Ezra and Nehemiah offer are stories is evidenced by the presence of characters, setting, and plot,[9] but begs the question: what sort of stories do Ezra and Nehemiah offer? Most obviously, these are stories not about the future (as for instance may be found in apocalyptic literature), but rather stories about the past. Indeed, as seen above, Ezra's and Nehemiah's contributions are stories of a quite particular past, set in particular times and places within the history of the Persian Empire. Various questions may remain about how precisely Ezra's and Nehemiah's stories relate to other evidence of Achaemenid history (discussed only in passing in this commentary), but the fundamentally historiographical interest of Ezra and Nehemiah is patently clear.[10] Unlike historiographical accounts of David and many others in the Old Testament that were evidently written by others, however, Ezra's and Nehemiah's stories of the past are presented as their own stories. The autobiographical nature of Ezra's and Nehemiah's stories foregrounds a quality of all historiography, namely, that accounts of the past are of necessity perspectival and selective. Indeed, the recurring "I" of the memoir material in Ezra-Nehemiah is a persistent reminder of the "eye of the beholder"—the historiographical eye that beholds the beauty of some things and not others, but cannot possibly see everything in any case and must therefore of necessity attend to particular events and the relationship between them in order to allow them to form a (hi)story.[11] While scholars helpfully view the events seen and reported by Ezra and Nehemiah through a variety of sociological and other critical lenses, Ezra's and Nehemiah's recognition of their God's involvement in these events and the recording of their own and the people's response to divine initiative and instruction make clear the theological interest of their respective historiographies.

Yet, if the theological interests and assumptions of Ezra's and Nehemiah's recollections alone offer ample justification for further reflection on these books, it should be clear from the discussion of the various sources above that their memoirs by no means enjoy a monopoly on matters theological within Ezra-Nehemiah. For instance, the numerous prayers contained within Ezra

---

9. For a useful introduction to Hebrew narrative, see Walsh, *Style and Structure in Biblical Hebrew Narrative*.

10. For an overview of late biblical historiography, see Japhet, "Postexilic Historiography."

11. For a discussion of the analogy between representational art and historiography, see Long, *Art of Biblical History*, 63–87.

and Nehemiah reflect a plurality of voices and a variety of circumstances and indeed theological emphases—related in various ways to those of Ezra's and Nehemiah's memoirs. The inclusion of these prayers alongside the memoirs points toward a further and perhaps still more crucial source of theological interest, namely, the editor responsible for adding these and other elements and for giving the books of Ezra and Nehemiah the form in which we have inherited them.

While the editor of Ezra and Nehemiah may or may not also have been responsible for the books of Chronicles, with which they share some features,[12] there seems little doubt that he should be credited with Ezra-Nehemiah's original fusion. The antiquity of this unity is witnessed by a variety of factors, including especially Josephus's counting of Ezra and Nehemiah as one book and the lack of division between the two in either the earliest Hebrew or Greek manuscripts.[13] The most persuasive proof of Ezra-Nehemiah's unity, however, is the editorial interweaving of the ministries (and memoirs) of Ezra and Nehemiah.[14] Despite sharing various important theological assumptions with the memoirs of Ezra and Nehemiah, the editor's shaping of Ezra-Nehemiah as we now have it reflects and results in a rather different theological appraisal of their ministries than might be gleaned from their respective memoirs alone or indeed from other ancient accounts of Ezra's and Nehemiah's ministries.[15]

If our own historical sensibilities may be offended by the editor's incorporation—and, frankly, adaptation—of Ezra's and Nehemiah's own theological historiographies for his own purposes, we have no evidence that ancient readers would have felt the same sense of opprobrium. Indeed, whenever the final editor produced Ezra-Nehemiah as we now have it, the passage of time and the benefit of hindsight will have allowed him to offer a critical judgment on the ministries of Ezra and Nehemiah that would have been quite impossible without the benefit of working at some distance.[16] Accordingly, while we will attend to the theological interests of Ezra's and Nehemiah's accounts and other

---

12. For a balanced discussion of the degree of unity and uniformity between Ezra-Nehemiah and Chronicles, see Ackroyd, "Chronicles-Ezra-Nehemiah."

13. For further, see Williamson, *Ezra, Nehemiah*, xxi.

14. Following the interpretation worked out in detail by Williamson, ibid.

15. For recent scholarship on the character of 1 Esdras and its relationship to Ezra-Nehemiah, see Fried, *Was 1 Esdras First?* While the balance of the evidence weighs in favor of 1 Esdras as a whole being a later redaction of the Ezra-Nehemiah traditions, the occasional use of readings from 1 Esdras in this commentary reflects its witness to a more original Hebrew at certain junctures.

16. For more on the historiographical advantages of critical distance see Long, *Art of Biblical History*, 73.

Introduction

sources in their own right, our recognition of the historiographical principle that "time will tell" means that the lion's share of attention in this volume will be given to the (hi)story that the editor in his time felt called to tell. If this history (i.e., Ezra-Nehemiah)—told in the fullness of time—does not agree entirely with Ezra's and Nehemiah's own accounts, the differences should, however, not be exaggerated. Most importantly for our purposes, the degree of theological interest remains largely constant and both prompts and frames our own treatment of Ezra-Nehemiah as a story of God's involvement with his people.

Our Approach to Ezra-Nehemiah

If beginning our theological treatment of Ezra-Nehemiah with a commentary on the text itself requires either apology or *apologia*, we might recall von Rad's conviction that "retelling remains the most legitimate form of theological discourse on the Old Testament."[17] Admiring von Rad's intuition and conviction, we would prefer to insist only that retelling remains the most legitimate *starting point* for theological discourse on Old Testament *narratives*. We are not alone in this conviction, judging by various commentaries written on Ezra-Nehemiah, including most notably those of Kidner, Williamson, and others on whose shoulders this commentary especially stands. Our commentary follows Williamson (and others) in recognizing that the theological interests of the text cannot be discerned properly without at least some attention being given to relevant historical, but especially literary and indeed compositional issues.[18] Readers wishing to give more attention to such issues than may be afforded here will be referred to appropriate commentaries and other works at the relevant junctures.

  A great advantage of beginning one's theological reflection on narratives like Ezra-Nehemiah with a close reading of the text itself is that it offers the opportunity to attend to, in Goldingay's words, "the portrayal of the specificity of life with God." For Goldingay, and for us, these stories are about (and, we would add, written by):

> people facing the challenges, potentials, questions, achievements, ambiguities, puzzles, disappointments, demands and failures that are intrinsic

---

17. Von Rad, *Old Testament Theology*, 1.121.
18. On this point, we find ourselves in greater agreement with the approach of Williamson, *Ezra, Nehemiah* than for instance, Goldingay, *Israel's Gospel*, 41, whose assessment of scholarly vicissitudes regarding historical and compositional processes leads to a reluctance to offer any theological inferences on them.

to life with God. They thus invite their hearers to reflect on the equivalent specificities of their own lives in light of the stories' implicit convictions about who God is and what human life is. Such reflection needs the help of narrative with its concreteness and specificity.[19]

If such specificities highlight the importance of attending to the theological interests of Ezra-Nehemiah in their own right, the reference to Jeremiah in the very first verse of Ezra is the first but not last reminder that an appreciation of these theological interests also requires attention to resonances with other parts of the Old Testament, including especially the Pentateuch and the Latter Prophets. If the commentary and the first essay ("Reading Ezra-Nehemiah Canonically") dwell at some length on those resonances at the expense of casting the canonical net over the New Testament as well, it does so with, we hope, both justification and mitigation. Our justification for doing so relates to the observation that Christian theological reflection sometimes gives short shrift to Ezra-Nehemiah's own theological interests and rushed rather too quickly on to those of the New Testament and subsequent Christian tradition.[20]

Mitigation for our initial focus on Ezra-Nehemiah within the context and story of the Old Testament is supplied by the second essay ("Reading Ezra-Nehemiah Theologically Today"), in which Ezra-Nehemiah is situated within a wider canonical and overtly Christian context, reflecting the interest of this commentary series in locating this story within the wider Christian story, via the New Testament. In doing so, we draw encouragement from the recent and ongoing recovery of narrative theology, with its recognition of the centrality of "story" as a genre within Scripture and its potential for framing Christian theological reflection on the Bible as a whole.[21] Indeed, it was Israel's memory of its own story, and the future to which that story pointed, that preserved them as a community that could play their part—small though it must have seemed—in the unfolding story of the mission of God that drives the whole biblical narrative. From that perspective, this attention to the narrative for its own sake coheres well with a missional hermeneutic of these texts within a wider missional approach to reading Scripture as a whole. This in turn yields rich dividends as we reflect on what these texts from the tiny postexilic com-

---

19. Goldingay, *Israel's Gospel*, 36–37.
20. When these tendencies are combined with a less developed interest in historical and literary matters, the results seem less satisfying to us. See, for instance, Levering, *Ezra-Nehemiah*, for a rather different approach to theological reflection on Ezra-Nehemiah than the one offered here.
21. See, for instance, Bartholomew and Goheen, *Drama of Scripture*; and N. T. Wright, *New Testament and the People of God*.

munity might have to say to the missional life and witness of the multinational people of God today.

Finally, aware as we are that Ezra-Nehemiah continues to be a resource for those seeking to conform their stories to the wider Christian story of which these books are a part, we conclude this volume with a third essay ("Leadership and Ezra-Nehemiah") that builds on an initial treatment of Ezra-Nehemiah and leadership by offering a more lengthy worked example of how reflection on the representation of leadership within Ezra-Nehemiah may facilitate the church's deeper engagement with and understanding of the text itself.

Commentary on Ezra

BY DAVID J. SHEPHERD

Ezra 1

1:1 Not surprisingly, the beginning of Ezra commences with the beginning of Cyrus, whose arrival in Babylon in 539 BCE and proclamation in 538 offered both powers and pretenders conclusive evidence of his meteoric rise from the provinces of Media. While the first verse of Ezra begins and ends with Cyrus, the syntactical heart of 1:1 is profoundly theological: "Yhwh moved." Crucially for the book of Ezra, the word that Israel's God moves Cyrus to put into writing and publish is a fulfillment of the word that Israel's God has put into the mouth of Jeremiah. Precisely which word of Jeremiah Ezra here has in mind has long perplexed students of both books. While Jer 51:11 promotes Cyrus as Yhwh's instrument of judgment, it depends on supplementary passages in Deutero-Isaiah to adequately predict the consequent rebuilding with which Cyrus is associated here at the beginning of Ezra.[1] Much the same might be said of Jer 25:11–12, which focuses entirely on the punishment of the Babylonians (rather than their Persian successors' return of the exiles) despite its mention of the seventy years of exile. This latter emphasis is also found in 29:10–11, which is perhaps the most likely (but still not entirely convincing) candidate: "For thus says Yhwh: 'When seventy years are completed for Babylon, I will visit you, and I will fulfill to you my promise and bring you back to this place. For I know the plans I have for you,' declares Yhwh, 'plans for wholeness and not for evil, to give you a future and a hope.'"

---

1. For a variation on the same theme, see Williamson, *Ezra, Nehemiah*, 10. In their search for likely passages, some commentators (e.g., Batten, *Ezra and Nehemiah*, 56–57) abandon Jeremiah altogether in favor of Deutero-Isaiah's promotion of Cyrus (Isa 41:2, 25; 44:28; 45:1, 13), but such proposals, in failing to adequately account for the confusion between the prophets, fail to persuade at all.

1:2 While the tradition strongly associates Israel's God with sovereignty over the heavens (e.g., Genesis, Deuteronomy, Psalms), it is suggested that the use of the specific title "the God of heaven" within the edict of Cyrus reflects Persian usage. If so, it will be a reflection of either the mastery of the Persian's own deity Ormazd over the heavens or a calculated effort on the part of the Persians to employ terminology that would not offend, but rather allow for the religious sensibilities of their diverse subjects.[2] The use of this terminology among the returnees (cf. Ezra 5:12; 6:9–10; Neh 1:4–5; 2:4, 20 etc.) may then reflect an accommodation to imperial expectation, rather than a novel and original use of the title by the exiles. That Yhwh has given Cyrus "all the kingdoms," however, confirms that this heavenly God has earthly interests and intentions, while his charge to build Yhwh a house in Jerusalem illustrates the conviction of the returnees, not only that their God has the power to move the "powers that be," but also that his own worship is his chief priority.

1:3–4 Within the context of the Babylonian cult, the edict's reference to "may their God be with them" conjures up images of physical idols of the sort whose fabrication and transport the book of Isaiah delights in mocking (Isa 44:9–20; 46:1–7). However, for Jews about to embark upon a journey to a land that was once promised, this invocation of their God's presence "with them" might find a resonance rather in the exodus generation's hope that their God would go with them on their own journey out of a foreign land (cf. Exod 34:9; Num 14:8–9). The edict's suggestion that their God might be both "with them" and "in Jerusalem" poses no difficulty for those who conceived of their God in incorporeal terms in any case, though the association of the divine presence with Jerusalem will be expressed regularly in the early chapters of Ezra (e.g., 4:24; 5:2). That the Jews should return with more than "their God" is made explicit in 1:4, which encourages material support for the returnees and especially the temple, even if it is unclear whether such support should be expected from those Jews who were not willing or able to make the journey or from Gentile neighbors, on the pattern of the despoiling of the Egyptians found in the exodus tradition.[3]

1:5–6 While in the prayer of Neh 9, it is the divine spirit's tutelage of the exodus generation (Exod 9:20) that is remembered, here special note is made of the power of God's spirit to stir up the people to embrace the opportunity to return to Jerusalem. That this spiritual encouragement was necessary may suggest that the journey was perceived to be a daunting one and may also im-

---

2. See Andrews, "Yahweh the God of the Heavens."
3. For the former interpretation, see Williamson, *Ezra, Nehemiah*, 16; for the latter, see Blenkinsopp, *Ezra-Nehemiah*, 75–76; and Clines, *Ezra, Nehemiah, Esther*, 38–39.

ply that not all of the "heads of Benjamin and Judah, priests and Levites" were willing to make the trip. However, the emphasis here is laid very much on the receptivity and spiritual sensitivity of those who did so and the divine initiative of Yhwh, who stirs up or rouses, not only the "powers that be" like Cyrus (1:1) but also the people themselves. Whether the edict itself (see commentary on 1:3-4) reflects the exodus motif of plundering the Gentiles, the latter is unmistakable in the response to the edict in 1:6 confirmed especially by the addition of the word "vessels" (כֵּלִים/kēlîm), which emphasizes the resonance with the exodus traditions (כְּלִי/kəlî "vessel" also appears in Exod 3:21-22; 11:2; 12:35-36).[4]

1:7-11 That it is the Persian king himself who brings out the temple vessels (1:7) and then releases them into the charge of a royal treasurer, Mithredath (1:8), is further confirmation of the divine Spirit's stirring of Cyrus, while the mention of Nebuchadnezzar's plundering of the temple (2 Kgs 24:13; 25:13-16; 2 Chr 36:10) invites the reader to reflect on the ultimate sovereignty of the God of heaven over even the greatest sovereigns of the earth. The writer's attention to the facts and figures (Ezra 1:9-10) of the temple vessels reflects the importance of the return of what was taken and the notion of careful (ac)counting reflected also in 1 Chr 9:28,[5] which relates the practice of counting the vessels when they were brought into the temple for use and again when they were taken out. Having been taken out of the temple by Nebuchadnezzar in the most traumatic of circumstances, this precious paraphernalia is now "counted" out of the house of Cyrus's gods to ensure that all that should return to the temple does so. The apparent concern for a full accounting makes it all the more odd that the total of the individual items (2,499) does not tally with the overall total (5,400 in 1:11). The lack of a round figure (5,469) in 1 Esdras 2:10-14, and this number tallying with the total of the individual items noted there, may suggest that at this point, 1 Esdras has a more original text. However, it is not impossible that the discrepancy in Ezra arose because some items and numbers may have dropped out of the list offered here and/or because Cyrus did not return all the vessels at this time.[6] However many of the vessels there were, their importance is underlined by the note that they were entrusted to and transported "care of" one Sheshbazzar, who is mentioned as "governor" in 5:14 and here referred to as "the prince of Judah" (1:8). This otherwise unprecedented expression seems to have been less a designation than a description, perhaps added under the influence of Num 7:84-86, where the "princes" of

---

4. See Williamson, *Ezra, Nehemiah*, 16.
5. As noted by Blenkinsopp, *Ezra-Nehemiah*, 78.
6. Ibid., 8.

the tribes are mentioned in connection with a number of vessels associated with the worship of Yhwh.[7]

Summary of Ezra 1

The opening chapter of Ezra offers a revealing insight into the way in which some exiles made sense of the rise of Cyrus and the extraordinary opportunity that arose for them to return to the land that was "promised" (Jer 29:10). Viewed through the eyes of faith, this opportunity is seen by the Jews as arising not because of Cyrus's own pragmatism or opportunism, but because Yhwh, their God, is God of not only the heavens but also the earth. Ezra 1 insists that, despite appearances to the contrary, the return from exile was Yhwh's idea and his doing, the gracious initiative of a God who is in the habit of remembering and redeeming his people. Evidence for God's habit of redemption is found in Ezra's identification of the exiles' situation with that of their exodus ancestors, whom God returned to the land in fulfillment of the patriarchal promise. Indeed, just as the exodus narrative consciously invites remembrance of the God of Abraham, Isaac, and Jacob, so too Ezra 1 evokes recollections of the God of the exodus who led their ancestors through the wilderness to the promised land. The mechanics and means of redemption are explained, not in economic, social, or political terms, but in spiritual ones—it is God's spirit who stirs both the powers of this earth and his own people into action, and he does so for one purpose: so that worship of him may be restored.

Ezra 2

2:1-2 The mention again of Nebuchadnezzar and the circumstances of exile signals a reemphasizing of the continuity of the returnees with the original exiles.[8] That it was their own towns to which they returned reflects and depends on the divinely sanctioned division and allocation of the land described in Numbers and Joshua. Whether intentional or not, the listing of twelve leaders (not including Sheshbazzar) would likely have offered early readers an echo of the twelve sons of Jacob and the eponymous tribes that descended from

---

7. So Williamson, *Ezra, Nehemiah*, 18.
8. For the reasons adduced by Williamson, ibid., 29-30, the list here is likely dependent on the one in Neh 7. Because of the composite nature of the list and Sheshbazzar's not being mentioned, it is likely that the list reflects a series of returns that took place over the years following Cyrus's edict; ibid., 30-31.

them.[9] Though not emphasized here, Zerubbabel's Davidic ancestry may well have reminded ancient readers of the hope of royal restoration (and thus the fulfillment of God's promise to David in 2 Sam 7) that would wax and wane in the years following the return.

2:3-20 While the narrative has emphasized (2:1) and will again emphasize (2:70) the return of people to their appropriate places, the focus of the first portion and indeed the bulk of the list here is to establish the returnees' kinship and family association.[10] This choice of presentation here ("sons of") is unsurprising when it is remembered that the enumeration of the people on their original journey to the land that was promised likewise focused on parentage (Num 1:20-45).

2:21-35 Beginning in 2:21 the focus of the list seems to shift from parentage to place.[11] Given the overriding concern with the capital city, it is not surprising that most of the places mentioned are found in the neighborhood of Jerusalem, in Judah and historic Benjamin, though Lod, Hadid, and Ono (2:33) are more westerly. The significance of some being "sons" and others "men" of particular places continues to elude scholars, especially given that the genealogies of all are secure (2:59-63). The interest in connecting the returning people to particular places reflects the historic concerns with (re)securing the land that had been promised by God in ancient times. If the people are listed by place name because they are "the poor of the land" (2 Kgs 25:12) who do not hold title to any ancestral property, the list reaffirms the community's inclusion of those on the margins who might otherwise have fallen by the wayside on their return.

2:36-39 As in Numbers, where the priests and Levites are listed (Num 3-4) following the others (Num 1-2), so too here in connection with this new "exodus," the attention moves from laity to priests and functionaries—the comparatively sizeable numbers of the latter offer a further indication that worship is not incidental, but remains central to the plans of God and his people.

2:40-42 As Ezra would himself eventually discover (8:15), comparatively few Levites made this journey (2:40). While singers and gatekeepers would later (1 Chr 6) be incorporated into the Levite ranks and classified according to

---

9. Ibid., 32. The total of twelve depends on the addition of Nahamani, supplied through comparison with Neh 7:7.

10. For details of the specifics relating to the names in this list, see Blenkinsopp, *Ezra-Nehemiah*, 85-92.

11. Those names that can be positively identified in 2:21-28 refer to places, which suggests the probability that those that cannot be identified may do likewise. The parallel list in Neh 7 and the place names suggest that the Hebrew (Ezra 2:21, 24-26) should read "men of" rather than "sons of"; Williamson, *Ezra, Nehemiah*, 25-26.

descent (Asaph, Heman, and Jeduthun), here they are reported separately. Collectively, they are further testimony to the cultic ambitions and commitments of the returning community.

2:43–58 It is very likely that the temple servants, the נְתִינִים/*nətînîm* (lit., "given/devoted"), and the sons of Solomon's servants were responsible for assisting the Levites with some of the most basic tasks relating to worship and the temple. If, as some of the names suggest, this group included foreigners[12] (including, potentially, prisoners of war), their inclusion as full members of the community (as we see in 2:64) suggests that the community continued to be inclusive within the limits of the tradition as they understood it.[13]

2:59–63 The limits of the community's inclusivity appear to have had implications for those who belonged to specific communities in exile but were unable to establish their genealogical credentials and/or connection to a traditional location in the ancestral land. While the implications remain unclear for the laity, the priests are excluded from facilitating the worshiping community.[14] Given the emphasis on ensuring continuity with the community of origin, such a position, while appearing severe, would certainly have been understandable. Indeed, while the situation here differs in significant ways from Korah's outright usurping of the priestly office in Num 16, the concern for ensuring the legitimacy and authority of the leaders of the worshiping community, in anticipation of reentering the land, is perhaps comparable. In any case, the enumeration of both laity and priests in spite of genealogical uncertainties suggests their participation and inclusion at some level within the returning community.[15]

2:64–67 The total sum of the preceding numbers is considerably lower (by some 11,000) than the total given in 2:64. While it is possible, as in 1:9–11, that something has been lost in the preceding list, the more likely suggestion is that women have been included in the latter total, but not in the preceding numbers.[16] Both men and women are included in the figures for servants/slaves (2:65), who are included along with the animals (2:66)—a notion that is as anathema to modern sensibilities as it was apparently unremarkable to ancient ones.

2:68–69 While in Ezra 1, the returnees' Gentile neighbors gave voluntarily to support the restoration, the narrative here focuses on the generosity of the exilic leadership itself toward the rebuilding efforts. It is difficult to assess the

---

12. Zadok, "Notes on the Biblical and Extrabiblical Onomasticon."
13. Williamson, *Ezra, Nehemiah*, 36.
14. For references to the consecrated food, see Num 18:9–10. For the association of the priesthood with the Urim and Thummim (an ancient Israelite method of divine discernment), see Exod 28:30; Lev 8:8; Num 27:21.
15. Williamson, *Ezra, Nehemiah*, 37.
16. Ibid., 38.

ancient market value of the gifts themselves, but it seems unlikely that they would have been included here had they not been substantial or indeed "offered willingly" (*hithpael* נדב/*ndb* in 2:68; used also in relation to the original building of the temple in 1 Chr 29:6).[17]

2:70 Given that some of the priests and temple functionaries clearly (and of necessity) settled in Jerusalem (Neh 3:26, 31; 11:21), why does the text here make a point of suggesting that both they and the rest of the people settled in their towns? By reiterating the same point at the end of the chapter, which he had made at the beginning (Ezra 2:1), the editor/narrator perhaps wishes to emphasize that the return was not merely a symbolic but also quite literal (re)settlement of the land as evidenced by the repopulation of not just Jerusalem, but also the wide variety of cities and towns that are indicated at great length in the lists found in Josh 15:21–62; 18:21–28.

Summary of Ezra 2

In recounting the people of the return and the places to which they returned, the compiler of the list appears to evoke the ancient pattern of exodus and settlement, the ancient antecedent and archetype of the return from Babylon and reestablishment in the land. As in the ancient past, this list includes not merely the covenant people, but also those specifically appointed/anointed to facilitate the people in worship (priests, Levites, and other cultic functionaries). On one hand, the possibility that some foreigners were incorporated into the general ranks of the returnees cannot safely be excluded. On the other hand, a concern for the continuity of the exilic community with its forebears leads to the exclusion of some from priestly leadership whose ancestral connections cannot be confirmed—proof, if any were needed, of the seriousness with which leadership in the cultic realm is taken. What is made perfectly clear is that the layleaders too took very seriously their responsibility to contribute to the rebuilding of the temple, with the list here careful to note what was "freely given" and by whom.

Ezra 3

3:1 That the returnees gathered in the seventh month is the first of several indications in this chapter that the community is devout and, in this case, at-

---

17. For similar generosity in relation to the construction of the tabernacle, see Exod 25:2–7; 35:21–29.

tentive to the cultic calendar (Lev 23:23–25). Having reemphasized here the localized resettlement ("in their towns") described at the beginning and end of the previous chapter, the text now uses typical Hebrew language ("like one man"; e.g., Judg 20:1; 1 Sam 11:7; Neh 8:1) to emphasize the unity and solidarity of the returnees.

3:2 The writer is keen to demonstrate not only that the restoration of the altar was done under the aegis of the appropriate religious (Jeshua et al.) and civic (Zerubbabel et al.) authorities, but also that it was done "according to what was written in the law of Moses, the man of God" (Exod 20:25). As others note, the latter phrase is applied to David (2 Chr 8:14; Neh 12:24, 36) and Moses (1 Chr 23:14; 2 Chr 30:16), particularly in contexts where Torah observance is emphasized, thus allowing the writer here to not only establish the contemporary continuity with the cultic past, but also the care with which the commandments were kept in the process of restoration.

3:3 The emphasizing of the restoration of the altar on the "(original) site" (or "foundations" if the plural of the Hebrew is read) and the reinstating of the appropriate daily sacrifices (as stipulated in Exod 29:38–42) appear to be a further reflection of the writer's persistent concern to emphasize continuity with the past. Most striking of all, however, is the writer's insistence that the returnees' first recorded response to their "fear of the peoples" was to prepare for and recommence worship of their God. Prophecies around this time (see Hag 2:1–9) were keen to prescribe cultic restoration as a reassurance of God's presence and as an antidote to anxiety.

3:4–6 Just as Solomon celebrates the Feast of Tabernacles (3:4) hard on the heels of the dedication of the first temple (1 Kgs 8:2) so too here the "harvest" festival originally associated with the exodus generation (Lev 23:33–36, 39–43) is celebrated by the returnees as worship recommences. That this takes place "as is written" and "by the numbers" specified in Torah, day by day, reaffirms the faithfulness of the returnees and specifically their care and attention to the worship life of the community. Indeed, Ezra 3:5 goes on to establish the restoration of the full cultic calendar (see Lev 23) as well as reiterating (Ezra 2:68) the generosity of the returnees in going above and beyond what was required in the provision of "freewill offerings." While emphasizing the cultic correctness and personal investment in their worship, 3:6 also reflects the incompleteness of the restoration and paves the way for the account of the construction of the temple (whose foundations may not have needed laying, but only repairing).[18]

3:7 Although some suggest that this description of the laying or repairing of the foundation of the temple is to be located historically in the reign of

---

18. "To establish the foundation" (יָסַד/yāsad); Gelston, "Foundations of the Second Temple."

Darius (520 BCE),[19] in the absence of any notice of the passing of time, the securing of supplies and the abortive attempt to build (3:7-11) are probably meant to be understood by the reader as taking place shortly after the initial arrival of the returnees as indicated in 3:6 (539-538 BCE).[20] As others note, the writer's description of, in this case, the gathering of supplies for the building of the temple appears to be influenced by the description in Chronicles of the building of the Solomonic temple (1 Chr 22:2-4; 2 Chr 2:7-15).[21] Some returnees (and later readers) will have been aware of the prophetic word of Isa 60:13 to those exiled or returned: "The glory of Lebanon will come to you, the pine, the fir, and the cypress together, to adorn the place of my sanctuary; and I will glorify the place of my feet." For them, the arrival of building materials will have been a reassurance that the God who had promised to restore was beginning to do so.

3:8-9 Just as Solomon began the original temple in the second month (2 Chr 3:2), so too the returnees commenced their repair work in that same month.[22] As others note, the wording here in relation to the Levites "to supervise the work on the house of YHWH" is identical to that found in David's division of labor in anticipation of the construction of the original temple. Again, as we have seen, the emphasis is on the appropriateness and legitimacy of those involved in resurrecting the temple.

3:10-11 Rather than dwell on the mechanics of the reconstruction, the text is primarily interested in the character and intensity of the celebration that accompanies it. While we would expect such celebrations on momentous occasions, the similarity of the language here to that associated with the first temple (2 Chr 7:6) seems to reflect an attempt to evoke those festivities. Just as the sacrifices are performed according to the law of Moses (so Ezra 3:2-6), so the Levites' work is done according to David (cf. 1 Chr 15-16; 23-26) again to reemphasize not only that all has been done correctly, but also that all has been done the same way it always had been. The formulaic feel of this passage should not, however, obscure or diminish its significance within the book thus far. While Ezra 2 emphasized the sacrificial involvement of the people themselves, this passage here—with its multiple mentions of praise and adoration of God (3:10, 11 [twice])—reflects and resonates with the remembered reality of God's

---

19. For discussion of the later dating of this passage, see Williamson, *Ezra, Nehemiah*, 47.
20. See, e.g., Clines, *Ezra, Nehemiah, Esther*, 68-69.
21. Williamson, *Ezra, Nehemiah*, 47.
22. Clines, *Ezra, Nehemiah, Esther*, 69, notes that this is not entirely surprising given that the spring season was better suited than others to building. Williamson, *Ezra, Nehemiah*, 47, instead suggests that the writer's drawing of typological comparisons includes not only the point of the commencement of the work, but also its duration (some seven years).

initiative and action in Ezra 1. Indeed, the psalmic refrain that is sung (3:11) leaves no space for self-importance among the returnees: it is not their piety or preservation of Torah and tradition that endures forever; rather it is God's goodness and love that do so, and in their enduring, they make possible the repair, restoration, and renewal.[23] That they endure "forever" is thus not only cause for gratitude, but also cause for hope.

3:12–13 Having duly noted the corporate liturgical celebration (3:10–11) of the progress that had been made, the writer now adds color to the scene by recounting the range of emotional responses among those gathered. Given the effort expended by the writer to illustrate the continuity of the new with the old, if the tears of those who had seen the former temple were ones of sadness (given the contrast drawn in 3:13 and perhaps Hag 2:3), they are at least confirmation that there were some who were able to assess and guarantee a sufficient degree of similarity. The writer's curious insistence on emphasizing the impossibility of differentiating between joy and sadness suggests that the point is less the particular emotion expressed than the intensity and volume of their expression and their testimony to those beyond the community.

Summary of Ezra 3

The notice of the leaders' gifts for the house of Yhwh at the end of Ezra 2 anticipates the events narrated in Ezra 3, where the returnees move quickly to reestablish worship. Indeed, that they are encouraged and motivated to rebuild the altar by "the fear of the nations" suggests a clear sense of their own vulnerability and weakness and a corresponding dependence on the God whose worship the rebuilt altar will facilitate. The relative priority of worship is suggested by the commencement of offerings (before the construction of the temple) and embracing of the cultic calendar at the earliest possible opportunity, while the conformity of the practices with ancient patterns and the invoking of traditional requirements suggest a concern for continuity with the past already typical of the book thus far. If a similar note is sounded as the rebuilding and then celebration of the temple are recounted, there is also a consciousness of the losses of the past, as it becomes clear that the new cannot be precisely the same as the old. Yet, this does not prevent the community from engaging in still more worship as a means of celebrating the reconstruction of the temple as a very tangible sign of their God's enduring graciousness.

---

23. For other occurrences of this refrain, see the initial verses of Ps 106, 107, 118, 136.

Ezra 4

4:1-2 While the offer of help in building the temple appears to be genuine, the writer's characterization of those offering it as "enemies of Judah and Benjamin" is clarified by their "self-identification" in 4:2.[24] According to 2 Kgs 17:24, Sargon was responsible for the partial foreign repopulation of Israel after the fall of Samaria (722 BCE), but Esarhaddon did likewise in Sidon, and so the story is not unlikely.[25] Whatever the truth of the matter, the basis for their offer is neither ethnicity nor politics, but religious solidarity, and their claim is couched in terms that seem plausible (i.e., seeking God and sacrificing to him).[26] Second Kgs 17 confirms that some of the immigrants had become worshipers of Yhwh, and according to Jer 41:5 religious pilgrims continued to make the journey down from the north to Jerusalem to sacrifice during the exile.[27]

4:3 While the allusion to the Persian imperial edict is the explicit grounds for the returnees' rejection of cooperation, their emphasis on "our God" (cf. "your God" in 4:2) suggests that religious perceptions may lie at the root of their refusal. If this is the case, the problem may well have been the perception (or indeed reality) that even after two centuries, the practices of the immigrants' ancestors had continued (2 Kgs 17:41a notes that while these people were worshiping Yhwh, they were also serving their idols).[28] If so, given the Israelite tradition's insistence that it was the worship of gods alongside Yhwh that was instrumental in the fall of both the northern and southern kingdoms, the returnees' reluctance is understandable, especially if involvement in rebuilding would have been understood to offer a precedent for involvement in (and perceived corruption of) the cult.

4:4-5 While we may assume that the people who set out to discourage (lit., "weaken the hands") and frighten off the returnees include those already mentioned, 4:5 suggests that others may have been added to their number over an extended period of time. The motif of external intimidation met here for the first time will be a recurring one in Ezra-Nehemiah. Having dwelt at length on

---

24. The use of "Judah and Benjamin" by the writer here again confirms the identity of the returnees with the preexilic community; see 2 Chr 11:1, 3, 10, 12, 23; 2 Chr 15.

25. Pritchard, *Ancient Near Eastern Texts*, 291.

26. The Hebrew must originally have read "sacrificing to him" rather than "not sacrificing" as it currently does.

27. See 2 Chr 11:16, where however the verb used to refer to "seeking" is בקשׁ/*bqš* rather than שׁדר/*drš* as here.

28. 2 Kgs 17:41b: "To this day their children and grandchildren continue to do as their fathers did."

the initial progress of the returnees, the writer here offers a justification for the temple remaining unfinished until the time of Darius.

4:6-7 That opposition continued long after the reign of Darius is indicated first by the note regarding a charge or accusation made many years later (486/485 BCE) as Darius's successor, Xerxes, was coming to the Persian throne.[29] Slightly more information is furnished regarding the opposition during the reign of the latter's own successor, Artaxerxes (465–424 BCE)—that it took the form of a letter written in Aramaic, the lingua franca of the empire, by a group that included at least one person of Aramaic extraction ("Tabeel": God is good).

4:8-11 A second letter is sent during the reign of Artaxerxes (this time specifically "against Jerusalem") by another group, including Rehum and Shimshai (4:8) as well as various other district authorities (4:9). The latter clearly retained their association with their homelands (Tripolis, Persia, Uruk, etc.) despite being resettled in Samaria and elsewhere in the Persian satrapy, perhaps specifically by Ashurbanipal (669–633 BCE), but certainly by the Assyrians. Having introduced the senders more fully (after a false start [4:8: "as follows"]) the writer is now happy to cite the letter itself in Aramaic, beginning with a salutation in which the senders identify themselves to the king as "your servants."

4:12-13 While it is not clear precisely which group of returnees is being referred to or when they returned, that the foundations of the walls are still being repaired (4:12) indicates a time prior to the walls' completion in Nehemiah's time. Eventually the returnees themselves will confess their own wickedness and that of their predecessors (9:13). Here however the wickedness being alleged is clearly less theological than it is political, as may be seen from 4:13's rehearsal of the potential threats to the financial interests of the crown posed by the city's restoration.

4:14-16 The previous allegation is contrasted with and authenticated by the writers' insistence that the sole reason for their correspondence is the protection of the king and his interests.[30] Aware of the need to substantiate such serious allegations, the correspondents encourage the king to uncover for himself the proof that they themselves cannot supply. The political nature of the wickedness alleged in 4:12 is now amplified in 4:15, where Jerusalem's rebellious character is emphasized twice over in specifically anti-imperial terms. As the inheritor of both Babylon's interests and influence and its archives, the Persian king is presumably being encouraged to review the circumstances surrounding

---

29. Whether or not this accusation had anything to do with Judean support for the Egyptians against Xerxes is impossible to ascertain.

30. The reference to "the salt of the palace" will have been a reference to either the royal payroll or perhaps a pledge of loyalty to the king; see Williamson, *Ezra, Nehemiah*, 56.

the fall of Jerusalem at the hands of Nebuchadnezzar ("that is why this city was destroyed"; 4:15). The potentially negative financial consequences to the crown of the city's reconstruction as outlined in 4:13 now give way to a much larger (and surely even less credible) claim that Jerusalem's imagined independence will lead to the loss of the Persian district as a whole.

4:17-20 Having offered greetings to his addressees (4:17) and confirmed receipt of their correspondence (4:18), the king reports his investigations and confirms their allegations (4:19). While some suppose that 4:20 might refer to Judean kings' own historic hegemony over and exploitation of what was now the Persian district, the tradition does not remember David—nor even Solomon in all his splendor—exercising authority over this entire region. Instead, the king reasons that if Jerusalem has paid taxes, tribute, and duty to his imperial predecessors in Babylon, then any activity that has the potential to reduce or eliminate Jerusalem's contribution to his own coffers should be actively discouraged.[31]

4:21-24 Royal investigation now gives way to instruction as the addressees are authorized to order the work to be stopped until the king decides otherwise (4:21). What might persuade the king to allow such work is unclear, but this final phrase may betray an awareness (or anticipation perhaps) of the sending of Nehemiah and the work that was eventually concluded under his supervision. Given that the obvious intention of the initial correspondence from Rehum and others was to halt the work, the king's warning in 4:22 has a slightly ironic ring about it. We are thus not surprised when the writer of Ezra informs us (4:23) that the king's instructions are acted upon "immediately" (בְּבְהִילוּ/*bibhîlû*) and with "full force" (בְּאֶדְרָע וְחָיִל/*bəʾedrāʿ wəḥāyil*, lit., "with power and strength").

Summary of Ezra 4

Armed with an awareness that a rebuilt Jerusalem did not in fact rebel against Persian authority, it will be quite clear that the accusations of the threat posed were false or at least greatly exaggerated. Presented as basically slanderous, this correspondence invites comparison with other Old Testament texts and traditions in which deception is deployed against the purposes and people of God. Chief among such texts are the Psalms (e.g., Ps 109:2: "For wicked and deceitful mouths are opened against me, speaking against me with lying tongue."). While previously the fear of the enemies of God prompts worship (Ezra 3), here the community and its building activities are immobilized by intimidation (4:4) long before the official order to cease and desist. At such

---

31. Following Williamson, ibid., 64; contra Clines, *Ezra, Nehemiah, Esther*, 81.

moments, the community is in need of the reminders of Ps 2 ("Why do the nations conspire, and the peoples plot in vain?") or, indeed, those of David to Solomon when the latter was about to embark upon his building of the very temple that the returnees were seeking to replace: "Be strong and of good courage, and act. Do not be afraid or dismayed; for Yhwh God, my God, is with you. He will not fail you or forsake you, until all the work for the service of the house of Yhwh is finished" (1 Chr 28:20). In the absence of such encouragements and in the face of local opponents with imperial backing, the building grinds to a halt.

Ezra 5–6

5:1–2 Having described the frustration of the returnees' later efforts to rebuild the city and the walls, the book of Ezra resumes the story of the temple, the reconstruction of which was, according to 4:5, halted until the time of Darius. According to Hag 1:15, which seems to have been known to the writer, building was resumed in the second year of Darius, on the twenty-fourth day of the sixth month (September 21, 520 BCE). It may be that upheaval in the early years of Darius's reign facilitated a resumption of the building project in Yehud, but in any case, such explanations find no place in the book of Ezra, which instead finds the impetus for the renewed building work in the support of the prophets Haggai and Zechariah. While not all prophetic voices will be legitimated or appreciated within Ezra-Nehemiah (cf. Neh 6), the text here validates and explicates the contribution of Haggai and Zechariah by noting that the prophecies were "to/for the Jews in Judah and Jerusalem" rather than for the "enemies of Judah and Benjamin" (Ezra 4:1) who wished to join with them and/or the "people of the land" who sought to discourage them (4:4). That the community of returnees continues to receive prophecies also reaffirms its identification with the people of the past and their prophets—not least those prophets who had promised that Judah and its people would be rebuilt.[32] Moreover, these prophecies here are also "in the name of the God of Israel" and more specifically "Yhwh," already identified as the God of Israel (4:3), rather than the God of those whose cultic claims to being identified with Israel have been found wanting by the community of returnees. Finally, whether it is God or his name that is "over/upon them" and whether "them" refers to the prophets or the people or both, the text here seizes the opportunity to re-

---

32. Cf. Jer 30 and Ezek 36:10, 33–36; 48:15–35; Isa 44:26–28; 49:16–26; 61:4, which evoke the image of repopulation.

emphasize that the resumption commences under the aegis of the God whose house they are rebuilding.[33]

While the "enemies of Judah and Benjamin" sought to "build with" the golah community (4:2), the text now makes it clear that when the building was resumed (5:1) it was rather the "prophets of God" who were "with them and supported them" (5:2), whether this assistance was limited to the sharing of prophetic words or included other practical contributions.[34]

5:3–5 The news that those beyond the community approach the returnees "at the same time" as building recommences prepares the reader for opposition of the sort encountered later (but described already in Ezra 4). While there is nothing obviously malicious or malevolent about the enquiries, the querying by the district governor[35] and his associates of who has authorized the work (5:3) and who is undertaking it (5:4) is clearly seen as potentially if not actually obstructive ("they did not stop them").[36] It is quite plausible that a list of the sort found in Ezra 2 may have been compiled by the returnees in answer to an actual request for names, but the writer of Ezra records no response at this point on the part of the returnees. Rather, 5:5 reports the archival investigation, which the writer sees as a reflection of the "eye of their God on the elders of the Jews." While the "eye" of the king was apparently a Persian royal functionary, here the writer has in mind the "eye" of Israel's God—attentive sometimes for worse (Mic 7:10) but often, as in this case, for better (Ps 33:18; 34:15) and specifically for blessing.[37] The Chronicler (2 Chr 7:16) recounts the divine promise to Solomon that his "eyes" will always be at the temple, but in the context of the return from exile, perhaps most relevant of all is God's word through Jeremiah (24:6): "I will set my eyes on them for good, and I will bring them back to this land. I will build them up, and not tear them down; I will plant them, and not uproot them." Whether it is God's "hand" (Ezra 7:6, 9; etc.) or his "eye," the image of divine attention and tangible support is clear.

5:6–10 Not for the first time, the compiler of Ezra-Nehemiah furnishes his narrative with documentary evidence, this time in the form of correspondence

---

33. Indeed, in Haggai, the prophet upbraids the returnees for their interest in their own accommodation at the expense of the house of God (Hag 1:4), a situation that is not incompatible with and indeed may have been encouraged by the experience of external opposition to the rebuilding of the temple portrayed thus far in the book of Ezra.

34. Williamson, *Ezra, Nehemiah*, suggests the latter.

35. That Tattenai was governor at this time is confirmed by extrabiblical sources; see Olmstead, "Tattenai, Governor of 'Across the River.'"

36. The sense of the passage requires this to be Tattenai's question rather than that of the returnees, as is suggested by the Hebrew ("then we spoke to them").

37. For the Persian "eye," see Balcer, "Athenian Episkopos," and Oppenheim, "Eyes of the Lord."

from Tattenai and his associates to their Persian overlord, Darius. The introduction to their investigation of the rebuilding of the house of "the Great God" (Persian theological nomenclature found also in the Persepolis fortification tablets) is perhaps the basis of the report in 5:3–4, but is here merely prefatory to the returnees' *apologia* for rebuilding that lies at the heart of the report.

5:11 Given that Rehum and others introduce themselves as "servants" of the Persian crown (Artaxerxes) in correspondence from a later period (included, however, already in 4:11), the returnees' self-identification as "servants of the God of heaven and earth" is a bold beginning. While Cyrus's edict and the returnees themselves (cf. 5:12) refer to the "God of heaven" (see commentary on 1:2), the allusion to the original construction of the temple by Solomon ("a great king of Israel") may explain the returnees' recognition of their God's sovereignty over not merely heaven but "the earth" as well. After all, the opening verses of Solomon's prayer of dedication in 1 Kgs 8 (to which Neh 1 is perhaps also indebted) are not only replete with "servant" language,[38] they also consider the question of God's presence on earth as it is in heaven.[39] In alluding to Solomon's earlier building, the returnees yet again underline the continuity of their own building with that of the past.[40]

5:12 The note of continuity is sounded again as the returnees explain the exile in terms of the failings of their "fathers." The focus on the sins of the previous generation (rather than the present one; cf. Neh 1:5–7) likely reflects the official purpose of the correspondence rather than the lack of contrition or sense of responsibility, given what we see elsewhere among the exiles (cf. Ezek 18). The phraseology and indeed theology of the people being "given by God into the hand of Nebuchadnezzar" are attested in Chronicles (1 Chr 6:15; 2 Chr 36:17) but most importantly in Jeremiah (21:7; 22:25; 27:6, 8; 29:21; 32:28; 44:30; 46:26). Evidently, for the exiles, God's sovereignty is to be seen in both the ruin and the restoration. Of course, as we have seen, it is crucial for the exiles that the same people who were "carried" off to Babylon are now doing the rebuilding.

5:13–17 That it is Cyrus, Nebuchadnezzar's (eventual) successor as "king of Babylon," who initiates the rebuilding of the temple has been emphasized

---

38. For instance, in 1 Kgs 8:23–30 singular and plural forms of the verb "to serve" (עָבַד/ʿbd) appear in each verse apart from 8:27.

39. Solomon stands on earth and spreads out his hands "toward heaven" (1 Kgs 8:22) and declares that no one is like Yhwh "in heaven above or on earth below" (8:23). At the same time as Solomon acknowledges the deity's heavenly home—"But will God really dwell on earth? The heavens, even the highest heaven, cannot contain you. How much less this temple I have built!" (8:27)—he pleads that God will "hear from heaven, your dwelling place" (8:30).

40. Cf. also the references to God's sovereignty over the earth and heaven in the roughly contemporary prophecies of Hag 2:6, 21.

already (1:2–4) and will be again (6:3–5), but it is reiterated here, being crucial to the returnees' case.[41] The report here that Sheshbazzar laid the foundation of the temple soon after the return is compatible with the report in Ezra 3[42] and substantiates the suggestion that the building had begun, even if the bulk of it still remained to be done. The conclusion of the returnees' reply prompts the provincial authorities' request for confirmation of the authorizing edict of Cyrus and the wishes of the current regime in relation to the rebuilding (5:17).

6:1–5 Eventually located in the summer capital of Ecbatana rather than Babylon (6:1–2), the edict of Cyrus is included again in a slightly different and fuller form (see commentary on 5:13–17 and footnote there). The edict's specification of the building materials and physical footprint is perhaps to be explained by the crown's funding of the reconstruction, which is not, however, incompatible with Haggai's appeal for the community itself to contribute (1:1–11).[43] The explicit linking of the building site to "the place where sacrifices were offered" (Ezra 6:3) and the emphasis on the restoration of the temple vessels "each to its place" offer further comfort to a community concerned with its continuity with the past.

6:6–12 Having supplied the requested confirmation of the edict from Cyrus's time, the reply of Darius now further obliges by providing the current king's directives to the governors: "keep away" (6:6) being practically explained in terms of noninterference with the building activities of the Jewish leadership (6:7). Darius's confirmation of the crown's renewed or continuing financial support for the rebuilding (6:8) is specified in terms that must have satisfied the returnees and frustrated the governor of "Beyond the River" in equal measure (i.e., "in full," "without delay" from "Beyond the River's" provincial funds). While some query the plausibility of Darius's release of further resources in support of the temple sacrifices (6:9), the well-known interest of Darius II in the details of the cult in the Jewish colony at Elephantine in Egypt and the imperial motivation to facilitate provincial prayers for the preservation of the Persian crown (6:10) should not be underestimated.[44] The challenges of interpreting 6:11 make the precise nature of the punishment for altering the decree difficult

---

41. While 6:3–5 preserves a more straightforward ordering of the edict, in the version here the initial mention of the restoration of the paraphernalia (which establishes the cultic continuity) allows the final emphasis to fall on the reconstruction itself, which is, after all, the proper subject of the returnees' reply.

42. See commentary on 3:10–11 and Japhet, "Sheshbazzar and Zerubbabel."

43. For further discussion, see Williamson, *Ezra, Nehemiah*, 81.

44. See the Cyrus Cylinder in Pritchard, *Ancient Near Eastern Texts*, 316. The encouragement to the exiles to pray for the prosperity of their adopted city (in Jer 29:7) suggests that such practices were already being promoted before the return.

to determine. While the measures seem draconian by modern standards, they are broadly characteristic of the Persians' approach as it appears in their own documents (Behistun Inscription §67) and Jewish literature (e.g., Dan 2:5; 3:29).

The detailed knowledge of the daily offerings (cf. Exod 29:18, 40; Lev 1:3, 9, 10) and the Deuteronomic flavor of Darius's invocation "may the God who has caused his name to dwell" (Ezra 6:12) may or may not reflect an enhancement of the Jewish flavor of some original correspondence. Be that as it may, Darius's invocation of the returnees' God and his official recognition of and tangible support for his worship in the final form of the correspondence serve to reaffirm that the divine superintending of Persian power that had begun with Cyrus (1:1) continues under the current regime.

6:13–15 The due execution of Darius's orders ("with all diligence") by Tattenai and his associates leads to a notice of the successful completion of the building (6:14). In the preface to the resumption of the building (5:1–2), the focus is solely on the initiative of the returnees' God and his prophets (Haggai and Zechariah). Here, at its conclusion, pride of place is still given to these same prophets (6:14a) and to the decree of the God of Israel, but now alongside the decree of the Persian kings, including Artaxerxes, whose later involvement (7:15–24, 27) is here likely anticipated. The date of completion is carefully noted (6:15) and falls in the sixth year of Darius, 515 BCE—seventy-two years after the destruction of the first temple and thus at least an approximate fulfillment of the Jeremianic prophecy (29:10) that Cyrus's edict may well have begun to fulfill (see commentary on 1:1). While the absence of any explicit fulfillment notice argues against a firm conclusion, an allusion to the completion of both the temple and the time allotted for the exile does not seem out of place.

6:16–18 In the days of Zerubbabel and Jeshua, the rebuilding of the altar was marked by the offering of sacrifices (3:3–6), and the laying of the foundation stone of the temple led to corporate celebration (3:10–11). Now with the temple completed, it is not surprising that the dedication includes both celebration and sacrifice, just as Solomon's dedication of its predecessor did. The emphasis at this point is clear: the priests, Levites, and the rest of the returnees are, as in both Solomon's day and Zerubbabel's (3:1), nothing less than a reconstituted "people of Israel" (6:16) experiencing something of the same joy (6:16; 3:12–13; 1 Kgs 8:66) and offering the requisite sacrifices (Ezra 6:17; 3:3–6; 1 Kgs 8:63; 2 Chr 7:5). While the returning community's "twelve tribes" may be implied in Ezra 2:2, they are fully visible here in the twelve goats offered for the sins of "all Israel" (6:17)—a pattern paralleled precisely by the tribal leaders' dedication of the altar of the tabernacle in the days of Moses (Num 7).[45] The latter is cited

---

45. See Blenkinsopp, *Ezra-Nehemiah*, 130, for further discussion of resonances with the

explicitly as the source for the organization of the cultic personnel (Ezra 6:18), perhaps with passages such as Exod 29 and Lev 8 in mind.

6:19-22 While the similarities between the returnees' celebration of the Passover and those recorded in connection with Hezekiah (2 Chr 30) and Josiah (35:1-19) are widely observed and cannot be gainsaid, the allusions to the exodus tradition in the book of Ezra alert us to the importance of Numbers in the account found here. For instance, though the Passovers of Hezekiah, Josiah, and the returnees all follow varying levels of renovation and rededication of the cultic precincts, only in Ezra and Numbers do we find the specific tribal pattern of dedication noted above. Moreover, whereas mention is made of the consecration (*hithpael* קדשׁ/*qdš*) of temple personnel (2 Chr 30:15; 35:3, 6) in the Hezekian and Josian Passovers, the insistence on the purity of the Levites in Ezra's account (טָהוֹר/*ṭāhôr*; 6:20) resonates specifically with the extensive instructions for the cleansing (טָהַר/*ṭihar*) of the Levites in Num 8:6-26.[46] The insistence too in Ezra that the Passover was celebrated only by those outsiders who had separated themselves from uncleanness (6:21; in keeping with Num 9:14) stands at odds with Hezekiah's practice of relaxing the pertinent regulations (2 Chr 30:17-20).[47] Finally, the specific sequence of the (re)dedication by the tribal leaders (Ezra 6:17; Num 7), purification of the Levites (Ezra 6:20a; Num 8), and celebration of the Passover (Ezra 6:20b-21; Num 9) that appears in both Ezra and Numbers seems unlikely to be accidental.

As in the Passovers of Hezekiah (2 Chr 30:13) and Josiah (35:17), here the Feast of Unleavened Bread follows (see Num 28:17), and as in Hezekiah's time, the emphasis of the report falls on the emotion of the celebration (cf. 2 Chr 30:21). Here, however, alongside the narration of emotion there is explanation: they celebrate "with joy, for YHWH had made them joyful." That this joy is related to what has been accomplished is not syntactically explicit in Ezra 6:22, but is suggested by the reminder in this verse that YHWH had enlisted the royal might of Mesopotamia (lit., a turning of the king's "heart")[48] in completing the

---

Torah. If the special noting of the sin offering is significant, it may reflect the perception that expiation was long overdue and/or was perhaps particularly necessary in advance of the Passover.

46. Following Blenkinsopp, *Ezra-Nehemiah*, 131, Ezra 6:20b and 1 Esdras 7:11 suggest that the Levites were the sole focus of attention in Ezra 6:20.

47. Here again (as possibly in Ezra 2) we recognize the lines of inclusion/exclusion being drawn in religious terms, with the openness to outsiders contingent upon the manifestation of purity as defined by the community.

48. The unexpected allusion to the king of "Assyria" here may be explained by an accidental slip and/or the influence of Hezekiah's time (so Blenkinsopp, *Ezra-Nehemiah*, 133), or it may even be a historical and quite generic reference to the region at the heart of the Persian Empire.

restoration of his "house"—a fitting recapitulation of the theme introduced at the outset of the book and visible at various points in the chapters that have followed.

Summary of Ezra 5–6

The prophets of God initiate a new phase of development (5:1–2) in which the eyes of their God (5:3–5) are on the servants of the God of heaven and earth (5:11). The same God who had given his house into the hands of Nebuchadnezzar (5:12) now restores it in compliance with his own decree by his own people under the aegis of the Babylonians' Persian successors (both Cyrus and Darius). The focus on God in both the dedication (6:16–18) and the celebration of the Passover (6:19–22) that follow confirms the community's perception of the instrumental role that God has played in the full restoration of the cultus and a worshiping community that is both purified and full of praise for him.

Ezra 7

7:1–6[49] Having recounted the completion (and celebration) of the restored temple in Darius's time, the book of Ezra skips forward to the time of Artaxerxes. On the assumption that this is indeed Artaxerxes I (465–424 BCE) rather than Artaxerxes II (404–358 BCE), the book's silence regarding the intervening almost sixty years is unexplained, but the attention given to Ezra marks out his contribution as the next key development in the community's restoration. Ezra's own name (perhaps an aramaized form of Hebrew "Azariah"—"Yhwh has helped") neatly underlines one of the themes evident in the book thus far. It is, however, the names that follow that serve to legitimate the role and activities that Ezra will be commissioned to undertake.[50] While comparable to the high priestly genealogy in 1 Chr 6:1–15, the list here (Ezra 7:1b–5) passes over several names, likely by accident; "Seraiah" (7:1) may well have been Ezra's actual father or an ancestral one (perhaps through a collateral line) if the preexilic Seraiah of 1 Chr 5:40 (6:14) is here intended. As with previous lists (cf. Ezra 2), the paramount concern is to establish continuity with the past—extending in this

---

49. For discussion of the composition and literary history of Ezra 7:1–10, see Williamson, *Ezra, Nehemiah*, 89–90; and Pakkala, *Ezra the Scribe*, 23–32.

50. While not a high priest himself (contra Koch, "Ezra and the Origins of Judaism," 190–93), Ezra's association with the high priests can only have enhanced his reputation and claim to authority.

case back to Aaron the chief or first priest of Moses's time.[51] Irrespective of its provenance, the length of the genealogy requires the narrative to resume by clarifying that it was "this Ezra" (7:6a) who came back from Babylon. Whatever else a "scribe" may be equipped and called upon to do (7:12, 21), the emphasis here in the description of Ezra is on his proficiency in the "Torah of Moses, which Yhwh, the God of Israel, had given." While the text notes that Artaxerxes too is generous ("giving all for which Ezra asked"), it is at pains to clarify that the gift of Persian royal favor and provision derives ultimately from the "hand of Yhwh his God which was upon him [i.e., Ezra]."

7:7–10 Having introduced Ezra, the text now details the rest of Ezra's traveling party.[52] The particulars of this group of returnees will be supplied in Ezra 8, but here, in keeping with some other lists (cf. Ezra 2), the writer refers to the laypeople first and includes the singers and the gatekeepers. While there was evidently a delay in their departure (see commentary on 8:21–34), the plan to leave Babylon on the "first day of the first month" is taken by some as signaling an intention to associate this "going up" from Babylon with Exodus's archetypal "going up" from Egypt following the first Passover.[53] Whether or not this return to Yehud is to be understood as a second exodus of the exiles, the group's departure in the first month and safe arrival in Jerusalem in the fifth month is seen to be no less a reflection of the ("gracious") hand of the heavenly king (7:9), than the favor of the earthly king in sending them (see commentary on 7:1–6). The notion that the presence of God's hand on Ezra is in turn a reflection or result of his engagement with Torah is not widely observed, but is in fact suggested by the Hebrew particle כִּי/kî that introduces 7:10 ("for Ezra had set his heart," i.e., "committed himself").[54] The tasks to which Ezra had committed himself include first "to seek" the Torah (דרשׁ/drš, suggesting a greater degree of care than בקשׁ/bqš). If, as Neh 8 will suggest, Torah should be understood here as a written text, equivalent to some or all of the Pentateuch, then Ezra joins a relatively small group of texts in the Hebrew Bible where the verb "to seek" (דרשׁ/drš) is governed by the word of God (Isa 34:16). In 1 Chr 28:8, David charges the leaders of Israel to not merely "observe" but also "seek" the commandments of Yhwh your God "that you may possess this good land and leave it for an

---

51. The latter is suggested by Japhet, "Supposed Common Authorship," 344.

52. Although not always reflected in modern versions, the switch from singular (7:7) to plural (7:8) and back to singular (7:9–10) is perfectly intelligible (cf. RSV).

53. The further suggestion of Koch, "Ezra and the Origins of Judaism," 190–93, that the text portrays this "exodus" plan as arising from Ezra's own engagement with Torah is possible but not likely, given that the plans appear to be related first and foremost to the provision of divine favor (7:9).

54. As translated by Williamson, *Ezra, Nehemiah*, 88.

inheritance to your children after you forever." The notion that "seeking" then involves more than merely obedience to, but rather deep engagement with, the written word is reinforced by the instructive references found in Ps 119. In 119:155, salvation is far from the wicked because "your statutes they do not seek," which then finds its positive counterpart in the psalmist's own affirmation, "your ordinances I have sought" (119:45, 94). Ezra's commitment to a searching enquiry of Torah is accompanied by a conviction (Ezra 7:10) regarding his own practical application of it (עשׂה/ʿśh, "to do" it) and then finally to inculcate this same passion and process within the community through education (למד/lmd, "to teach" the statutes and ordinances in Israel). The veneration of Ezra within later Jewish tradition owes much to the resonance of his role with a comparable convergence of observance and education in the tradition of Moses: "Now this is the commandment, the statutes, and the rules that Yʜᴡʜ your God commanded me to teach [למד/lmd] you, that you may do [עשׂה/ʿśh] them in the land to which you are going over, to possess it" (Deut 6:1).

7:11–20 Once more, what appears to be official correspondence is furnished by the editor (and again in Aramaic) to support the commission of Ezra just described in 7:1–10.[55] Ezra 7:11 portrays Ezra in familiar terms, specifying him to be not merely "the priest" and "the scribe," but more particularly (and more literally in the Hebrew than some English versions might suggest) "the scribe for matters relating to the commandments of Yʜᴡʜ and his statutes for Israel." Whether this constitutes, as some assume, a formal office within the Persian administrative hierarchy is unclear, but it does serve to establish official recognition of Ezra's role in both cultic and judicial terms, as does the reiteration of this dual role in 7:12.[56] As conventional as both phrases are for the Persian crown, that the "king of kings" acknowledges the "God of heaven" must have been a significant encouragement for a community of returnees attempting to reconcile the unlimited sovereignty of Yʜᴡʜ with the undeniable precariousness of their position. Also encouraging is Artaxerxes's ability to draw the distinction between laity and priests and between the latter and the Levites (7:13)—though the probability of Jewish influence here (perhaps of Ezra himself) either in the writing or perhaps later editing of the letter seems strong. Despite the absence in 7:13 of the singers and gatekeepers mentioned earlier in the chapter (who must now be included in "the people"), Artaxerxes follows Cyrus in opening the doors to a return for any among the wider community who volunteer to go.

---

55. While the commentary will note particular issues as they arise, for general discussion of the authenticity of this passage, see Williamson, *Ezra, Nehemiah*, 97–100.

56. For discussion of Schaeder's theory in *Esra der Schreiber* relating to Ezra's role in the Persian court, see Blenkinsopp, *Ezra-Nehemiah*, 136–37.

Yet the focus soon returns to Ezra's role, now explained in terms of inquiring concerning Jerusalem and Judah in/with the "law of your God, which is in your hand" (7:14). If this is meant to license Ezra's involvements in the following chapters, perhaps the sense here is of a simultaneous survey (now בקר/*bqr*) of the commandments and the existing cult and culture with a view to ensuring eventual compliance. Like his royal predecessor, Artaxerxes clearly permits the canvassing of the Jewish community (7:16; 1:4, 6), and despite the fact that or perhaps because the original temple vessels themselves have been returned by Cyrus, the Persian court commits itself to a further contribution (7:15). The emphasis in all cases is on the voluntary nature of the gifts (7:15, 16 [twice]) but as the letter continues, this generosity is colored by a clear concern that the resources be efficiently used (the purchasing of animals should be done "expeditiously" (אָסְפַּרְנָא/*'osparnā'*;[57] 7:17) for the benefit of "your God."[58] So too remaining funds may be disposed of at Ezra's discretion, but only according to the "will of your God" (7:18), and it is also emphasized that the vessels that have been given for the service of "your God" (7:19) must be delivered before "the God of Jerusalem." Even the final carte blanche from the crown lays special emphasis on royal support for all that is required for the house of "your God" (7:20). As we will see in 7:23, however, the Persian crown's seemingly enlightened concern for the returnees' God is far from disinterested.

7:21–24 That the royal check is not entirely blank and that even Persian largesse has its limits is made clear by what appears to be a separate decree addressed now to provincial treasurers. When compared to Herodotus's estimates (*Histories* 3.91) of the provincial revenue (350 talents), one hundred talents of silver seems improbably generous and may be a mistake, but any erroneous exaggeration of Persian generosity must be set in the context of a decree in which the emphasis is very much on maximizing supply (7:21: "whatever Ezra ... requires ... let it be done expeditiously"; and note 7:24's prohibition of taxing of cult personnel), rather than limiting demand. However much these decrees are colored by Jewish influence in their composition or redaction, 7:23 confirms that like Darius (Ezra 6) and Cyrus before him, Artaxerxes's desire to support the Jewish cult in Yehud ("let it be done with zeal") stems from a calculated and pragmatic piety that seeks to cultivate loyalty among the elite of the religious establishment and appease the gods whose "wrath" he fears might otherwise destroy the empire.[59] In Exodus, while Pharaoh likewise so-

---

57. Although the precise meaning of this adverb (used frequently in Persian correspondence; cf. 5:8) is unclear, it seems likely to have the connotation of urgency and/or thoroughness.

58. That the sacrifices to be purchased include grain and wine offerings (cf. Num 15:1–16) seems again to presuppose the influence of someone with expert knowledge of the Jewish cult.

59. קֶצֶף/*qeṣep* is characteristically used to refer to divine wrath; e.g., 2 Kgs 3:27.

Ezra 7

licits Hebrew prayers to ward off divine judgment (e.g., Exod 8:8), this motif is unconnected to the theme of the despoiling of the oppressors, which may well be present in the account of the first return (cf. Exod 12:35; Ezra 1) but cannot be discerned as clearly here.

7:25-26 Having outlined and authorized Ezra's priestly responsibilities (and what they entail for others), the letter of Artaxerxes now specifies Ezra's scribal role and its legal and juridical implications. That Ezra is equipped to proceed according to the "wisdom of your God, which is in your hand" suggests an equation of "wisdom" with "the law of your God," which the letter has already specified is also "in your [i.e., Ezra's] hand" (7:14).[60] Such an equation is anticipated already in Deut 4:6, which also provides a precedent (1:16-17; 17:8-13) for the appointing of judges (שָׁפְטִין/*šāpaṭîn*; Ezra 7:25; cf. Deut 16:18) — itself a development anticipated earlier within the exodus narrative by Moses's devolution of judicial responsibility in Exod 18:19-24.[61] That Ezra's jurisdiction is limited to the Jewish community/ies within the province is suggested by the mention of "all the people ... who know the laws of your God" (7:25), but the specification of comparable punishments, listed here in descending order of severity, for the violation of this law and "the law of the king" (7:26),[62] is an indication of both the significance of Ezra's authority and the importance of his role in educating the local communities (7:25: "you shall teach").[63]

7:27-28 The first words of Ezra himself encountered in the book that bears his name offer a blessing of Yhwh of the sort found in the Psalms (e.g., 28:6; 31:21) and indeed elsewhere on the lips of Israel's past leaders (e.g., 1 Kgs 8:15). Like Jehoshaphat in 2 Chr 20:6 (after his own reformation efforts), Ezra also invokes the "God of our fathers" (Ezra 7:27; elsewhere only Deut 26:7) and recognizes the "hand" of God (Ezra 7:28; cf. 7:6, 9) as the stimulus for his strengthened resolve and invitation to others to "go up" (cf. 7:9) with him to Jerusalem. The specific catalyst for Ezra's blessing is, first, his conviction that the same God who "turned the heart" of Darius to complete the temple in Je-

---

60. If so, this marks a stage in the development of an identification that is eventually embraced in Sirach 24. Given the resonance with Ezra 7:14, it is more likely that the "wisdom" of Ezra is here equated with the law, rather than additional to it; cf. Williamson, *Ezra, Nehemiah*, 105.

61. For the antecedents in Deuteronomy and 2 Chr 19 (in Jehoshaphat's time), see Blenkinsopp, *Ezra-Nehemiah*, 151.

62. Though these need not be equated, contra Bowman, "Book of Ezra and the Book of Nehemiah," 954, 630.

63. How this letter and the one included in Ezra 4 could have both originated from the royal desk of Artaxerxes may be illustrated with reference to the "taxes" mentioned in both. While Artaxerxes's concern might be expected if the rebuilding of the wall were to stem the flow of taxation revenue from Yehud (4:13), ensuring tax relief for the religious establishment in Jerusalem (7:24) will ensure that both the *pax persica* and the *"tax persica"* endure.

rusalem (6:22), also "placed in the heart" of Artaxerxes the impulse to glorify/beautify it.[64] The second stimulus is his belief that the same "loving-kindness" (חֶסֶד/*ḥesed*) of God that was celebrated at the completion of the altar in the early days of the return (3:11) has persuaded the Persian king to allow Ezra to play his part in the further restoration of worship in Jerusalem.[65]

Summary of Ezra 7

The introduction of Ezra at this point resumes some of the themes already detected in the book, but also announces new ones. The concern, ever present in Ezra to this point, to establish the returnees' continuity and indeed identity with the people and traditions of the past may be seen in the inclusion of Ezra's genealogy. So, too, the furnishing of documentary evidence of the authorization and encouragement of the Persian crown for a Jewish mission to their homeland sounds a similar note to that heard in relation to the first wave of returnees. Nevertheless, while the Persians' earlier concern for and contribution to a fully functioning "house of God" are also seen here again in Ezra 7, the advent of Ezra reflects a significant explicit interest in the law of God and its interpretation, application, and enforcement. That it is the divine author of this law who is both impelling the Persians and propelling Ezra himself on the way of Torah is regularly reinforced in this chapter, both by the words of the narrator (7:6, 9) and those of Ezra himself (7:27).

Ezra 8

8:1–14 As is the case in the first return (Ezra 1–2), authorization is again here followed by enumeration. It is difficult to imagine why the name "Artaxerxes, the king" would need to be reiterated in 8:1 if the list that is found here was composed in concert with the previous chapter, but this is no reason to doubt its authenticity.[66] It is entirely plausible that the return in Ezra's time was much smaller (approximately 1,500 men, entailing a total of 5,000) than the earlier

---

64. As we shall see, the specific form of Ezra's words "to set in the heart" (נתן + בְּ + לֵב/*ntn + bə + lēb*) finds its closest correspondence in those of Nehemiah (2:12; 7:5).

65. The prayer's focus on the cult at the expense of other aspects of Ezra's work (as outlined in the present chapter) creates an inescapable sense of the former's importance in Ezra's own memory.

66. For a helpful discussion regarding the authenticity of the list, see Williamson, *Ezra, Nehemiah*, 108–10.

one and primarily populated by a selection of the same families.[67] Presumably the bulk of enthusiasts will have departed in the first wave, with others leaving later to join family members already established in Yehud.

Unlike Ezra 2, where the laypeople head the list, here the priests are given precedence. Also unlike that list, where the priests are apparently of the Zadokite line, here Gershom and Daniel are descended from Phinehas and Ithamar respectively and are thus of the Aaronic line, as is Ezra himself (7:5). This may be a reflection of a shift in authority among the priestly houses in Babylon between the time of the first return and that of Ezra's time.[68] Hattush son of Shecaniah,[69] the sole descendant of David mentioned by name in the second return, is subordinated to the priests but given priority over the other heads of families—presumably a reflection of the relative, residual status of the royal house in Ezra's time. The rounded numbers of the returnees may suggest that the source document had access only to numbers that were estimated (and therefore approximate), but one family for each of the twelve tribes can hardly be accidental given the pattern already established (2:2; 6:17), nor is the appearance here (8:1) of the verb "to go up" (עלה/'lh) accidental, given its earlier use (1:3, 5; 7:9) to describe the return in exodus-like terms.

The leaders of the house of Adonikam may well have been "the last/later ones" (אַחֲרֹנִים/'aḥărōnîm; 8:13) in Ezra's party to arrive in Jerusalem (or perhaps the last of their family to leave Babylon), but as we will see they will not be the last exiles to make the journey. Indeed, the overtones of this "going up" and the resonances with the earlier journey in Zerubbabel's time confirm the archetypal status of the exodus within the Judaism of this and other periods—unrepeatable in its essence but infinitely inspiring for a people inexorably drawn to the land from which they have been exiled. As in Ezra 2, the list included here is a tangible expression of the author's insistence that God's purposes were being fulfilled and that those who returned were truly Israel, in every sense.

8:15–20 After the provision of the list (8:1–14), Ezra's first-person account picks up where it left off with a reiteration of "I gathered" (8:15; 7:28). The precise location of Ezra's staging point near an unnamed river flowing to an otherwise unknown "Ahava" is impossible to pinpoint, but the region has an abundance of rivers, and the Jewish exiles were clearly no strangers to them (Ezek 1:1: "by the river Chebar"; Ps 137). Ezra's mention of camping (חנה/ḥnh) resonates

---

67. The common families are all drawn from the first portion of the list in Ezra 2.
68. Myers, *Ezra, Nehemiah*, 69.
69. Assuming an original "son of" (בֶּן/ben) as per 1 Esdras 8:29 instead of "from the sons of."

with the frequent use of this term in the exodus tradition (esp. Numbers), and the period of three days' preparation may well be an intentional evocation of the same length of time taken by Joshua and the Israelites before crossing the Jordan and entering the land (Josh 1:11; 3:2). If, however, a period of three days' preparation is conventional, its practical plausibility may suggest that the convention is somehow related to departures and arrivals (cf. also Ezra 8:32) rather than simply indicating a stereotypically brief period of time.

Reporting his review of those assembled, Ezra notes, but does not explain, the initial absence of the Levites (about which one may thus only speculate), but his immediate action to remedy the situation provides advance notice of their importance for his mission. The list of those sent to recruit Levites seems to include a suspicious number of "(El)nathans,"[70] but the importance of the embassy is underlined by Ezra's sending of those who are "leaders" (8:16) and "those who are wise" (or perhaps "those skilled in instruction").[71] Nothing is known of Casiphia, nor its leader, Iddo and his brethren, but the nature of the request, "send us ministers for the house of our God" (8:17), and the speedy compliance (8:18) suggest that Casiphia may have been a spiritual center for the exilic community (or at least some Levites), though one may only speculate regarding what worship facilities it may have offered. The returnees at the river are joined by three Levites and their kin: Hashabiah, Jeshaiah, and Sherebiah (8:18), the latter of whom is noted as a man of שֶׂכֶל/ śekel, a term used elsewhere in association with Levites (1 Chr 26:14; 2 Chr 30:22) and may connote "skill" or "ability" (so NIV and King James Version) rather than "discretion" (NRSV).

In keeping with the reduced enrollment generally in the second return, significantly fewer Levites (38) volunteer than in Zerubbabel's time but their descent from Merari (entrusted with the transport of sacred things; Exod 6:16; Num 3:17) may be relevant given the role that some of them will be asked to fulfill (8:24–30). The temple servants who will return (220) are also reduced in number in comparison with earlier times but are apparently still too numerous to mention by name in the context of Ezra's memoir (8:20).[72] Whether it is the provision of all of these or Sherebiah alone that is understood to betoken God's favor, Ezra voices his conviction that the Levitical addition to the traveling party is a sign that the specifically "good hand of God" (7:9; cf. 7:6, 28: "hand of God" *simpliciter*) is now resting not on him alone, but also "us."

70. For discussion of the textual issues, see Williamson, *Ezra, Nehemiah*, 113.

71. Reading מְבִינִים/*mabînîm* as implying pedagogical ability in light of 1 Chr 25:8 and 2 Chr 35:3; see Blenkinsopp, *Ezra-Nehemiah*, 165.

72. The explanatory note regarding David's institution of the "temple servants" is likely required to justify this innovation (unattested in the Mosaic tradition).

Ezra 8

8:21–36 Ezra's bold declaration to the king—offered in a couplet perhaps more appropriate to other occasions than this one[73]—is that the "goodness" of their God's hand would also ensure the safe passage of the "seekers" (בקשׁ/*bqš*) on their apparently dangerous road to Jerusalem (8:22). On one hand, Ezra's acknowledgment that he was embarrassed (*qal* בושׁ/*bwš*) to ask for the royal protection ("soldiers and cavalry") later afforded Nehemiah's mission (Neh 2:9)[74] may reflect Ezra's own admission that prudence has been preempted on this occasion by either his pride or his piety. On the other hand, and perhaps more to the point, the absence of such an escort offers an opportunity to solicit the protection of God himself. As elsewhere in Jewish literature and practice of the postexilic period (10:6; Neh 9:1; Esth 4:3, 16), the offering of prayer is enhanced by fasting (Ezra 8:21, 23)—a tangible expression of the community's humble hope for the "straight/smooth road" through the wilderness envisioned in Isa 40:3. Having proclaimed the fast (Ezra 8:21), Ezra then reports not only the community's prayer, but the divine protection afforded—visible of course only from the vantage point of the journey's end (8:31–32), but reported here to emphasize the efficacy of the community's petitionary faith.

Ezra's setting apart of twelve priests (8:24; cf. 2:2; 6:17; 8:3–13) is not likely to be accidental (though here all are members of a single tribe), nor is his listing of the donors and the careful accounting of their contributions (8:25–27); by doing these things Ezra celebrates yet again the support of the crown and the community for the worship of Yhwh. In emphasizing that both the Levites and their freight are "holy" (קדשׁ/*qōdeš*; 8:28), Ezra acknowledges the appropriateness of the descendants of Merari for the transportation of the sacred vessels. It is precisely because these and "the silver and gold" are for "Yhwh, the God of your fathers" (8:28) that Ezra provides clear instructions to ensure that they arrive safely, not merely in Jerusalem, but "within the rooms of the house of Yhwh" (8:29; cf. Neh 10:37–39; 13:4–9). Ezra's issuing of orders to "guard" and to "weigh" the treasure out on arrival will have been intended to protect both the precious goods against thievery and the porters (and Ezra himself) against any suggestion of personal profit or mismanagement.[75] Having reported the transfer

---

73. Divine "power and wrath against all who forsake him" is reminiscent of Ps 27:9; 119:53; and 2 Chr 34:25, but not obviously applicable to roadside raiders that the returnees may well have expected to encounter.

74. If a contrast unfavorable to Nehemiah is intended here, it is the work not of Ezra himself, but rather the editor who finally incorporated both memoirs in Ezra-Nehemiah.

75. The only amounts that strain credulity are the 650 talents of silver and 100 talents of gold, unless we are being asked to imagine the returnees bearing some twenty-five tons of precious metal overland from Babylon to Jerusalem. For varying estimates but a comparable assessment, see Williamson, *Ezra, Nehemiah*, 119; and Blenkinsopp, *Ezra-Nehemiah*, 169.

of the treasure into the custody of the porters (Ezra 8:30) and confirmed the date of departure from Ahava, Ezra reemphasizes (8:31) the positive answer to their prayer for safe passage by means of the familiar language of God's hand being upon "us" (8:22).[76]

The delay in their departure—likely due to the recruitment of the Levites—until the twelfth day of the first month (rather than the first day as intended; 7:9) facilitates their arrival some four months later on a Friday—the same day on which Joshua and the Israelites arrived in the promised land. This is a further encouragement to see Ezra's three-day pause (8:32) on arrival as a reflection of a comparable period recorded in connection with the arrival in Canaan (Josh 3:1).[77] Ezra confirms the heeding of his orders and the safe arrival of the transported goods the following day, recording both the names of the recipients of the donations and the appropriate processing of them (Ezra 8:33–34).[78] In 8:35 we find further confirmation, not now in the words *of* the returnees, but in words *about* them, that Ezra's party also complied with the other conditions of Artaxerxes's edict (7:17). In the record of the burnt offerings made on their arrival, the recurring appearance of twelve ("bulls for all Israel" and "male goats" as a sin offering) and its multiple (ninety-six rams) strikes that same chord of continuity with the distant past (Num 7) as was struck more recently in connection with the restoration of the temple (Ezra 6:17). It is probable that the sin being atoned for is that which had accumulated prior to the return, including but not limited to the impurity arising over the course of the four-month journey—the safe completion of which is also now marked by thanksgiving offerings to their God. The summary of the discharging of their responsibilities is completed with a note of the delivery of the royal instructions (7:21–24) to "the satraps" and, curiously, "the governors" (plural), of which a Persian province would normally have only one.[79] Finally, the news that these authorities accordingly "supported the people and the house of God" explicitly affirms the provincial leadership's faithful obedience to the king of Persia, but must also imply the efficacy of the God who had placed "this thing" into the royal heart (7:27).

---

76. It is not clear (nor apparently crucial) whether Ezra is suggesting that his party was protected *from* attacks altogether or *despite* them.

77. Jaubert, "Le Calendrier des Jubilés," 261.

78. The references to Meremoth (Ezra 8:33; Neh 3:4, 21) suggest to some that Nehemiah in fact preceded Ezra in coming to Jerusalem. Even if the respective "Meremoths" are one and the same (likely, but not certain), arguments for his demotion from or, alternatively, promotion to the priesthood are far from conclusive; see Williamson, *Ezra, Nehemiah*, 121.

79. Thus perhaps we should understand "local officials."

Summary of Ezra 8

The recurrence of the language of exodus in Ezra's account of his *aliyah* (lit., "going up") to Jerusalem invites comparison with that of the return in Zerubbabel's day. The reduced numbers and the initial nonappearance of the Levites contribute to the impression of these returnees as little more than reluctant "reinforcements" for the army of volunteers who poured enthusiastically into the initial breach opened during the days of Cyrus. Yet, in contrast to the absence of detail in Ezra 1–2, the abundance of detail offered by Ezra 8 provides—if not a greater awareness—then at least a far fuller illustration of both the conscientiousness of the community and its leadership (e.g., the recruiting of the Levites, the prayer and fasting for safety, the careful accounting of gifts) and their dependence at every point on the superintending hand of their God (8:18, 22, 31).

Ezra 9–10

9:1-2 While Ezra introduces his intervention regarding intermarriage in the community with the words "after these things were done," precisely how long after (four months) becomes clear only in 10:8–9. Given Ezra's official mandate to not only enforce but teach Torah (Ezra 7), it is plausible that the account of Ezra doing the latter (Neh 8) may have originally intervened at this point, thereby explaining both the four-month delay and the people's otherwise unprompted crisis of conscience (Ezra 9:1). As the text stands, however, the emphasis is squarely upon the people's own awareness of the problem within the community and initiative to address it, while news of Ezra's solution proposed at some point prior to the eruption of the crisis is deferred until 10:3. The impression given by the present text then is of a portion of the community whose urgency is animated by outrage.

The problem voiced by the chiefs (9:1a) relates to the intermarriage of Israelites, including primarily or initially some of their fellow chiefs (9:2b) with the "peoples of the land" (9:2). That such a practice represents "faithlessness/sin" (9:2) in their own eyes is explained by their association of the "peoples of the land" (i.e., those who were not identified with the returnees) with the abominations of a list of nations that is generally familiar from the Pentateuch (e.g., Gen 15:19–20; Exod 3:8). The tradition assumed here seems to be drawing upon a combination of Deut 7:1–3, which proscribes intermarriage with the usual seven nations indigenous to Canaan, and Deut 23:2–7 which excludes from the community Edomites and Egyptians up to the third generation and Ammonites and

Moabites altogether.[80] The Deuteronomistic Historian's comparable (though not identical) indictment of Solomon (1 Kgs 11:1) further supports the notion that such a rigorist interpretation of the law had currency among the exilic communities. The "peoples of the land" are initially condemned by the chiefs for something (presumably religious practice) that is "like the abominations" of the proscribed peoples, rather than for being actual descendants of them.[81] However, while passages such as Ps 106:35 also confirm the practical religious consequences of such "mixing," the chiefs here finally focus on the miscegenation (*hithpael* ערב/*'rb*) of these peoples with the "holy seed"—a notion found elsewhere in Isa 6:13 and probably arising from an admixture of the biological denotation of זֶרַע/*zera'*, "seed" (e.g., the offspring of Abraham in Gen 15:3; 21:12; Ps 22:23; Neh 9:2) and the divine election of the "sons of Israel" as a holy people (e.g., Deut 7:6; 26:19; Isa 62:12; 63:18; Dan 12:7). While such an interpretation is neither inevitable nor particularly palatable to most modern sensibilities, the Levitical association of "holiness" with genetic purity in the biological realm (Lev 19:19) certainly makes it understandable.[82]

9:3-5 Ezra's reaction to this revelation may be compared to Job's (1:20) in the tearing of the cloak (and in Ezra's case even the "tunic" [בֶּגֶד/*beged*]), the removal of hair (plucked by Ezra to avoid violating the law against shaving in Deut 14:1) and in Ezra's sitting in silence (Job 2:13). If Ezra's response is, like Job's, one of mourning, it must be for the "death" of the community that will be assumed to follow if remedial action is not undertaken. If Ezra's response is not one of mourning, the similarities between the actions of Job and Ezra will simply reflect a comparable strength of response, which in turn underlines Ezra's depth of feeling regarding the seriousness of the situation. If he had offered instruction on the passages of which the chiefs seem to be aware, but was himself unaware of the scale or existence of the problem, Ezra's dramatic reaction here may well be intended to suggest the strength of his own personal shock and dismay. If, however, as is perhaps more likely, Ezra was already specifically aware of the problem, the strength of Ezra's response here will be primarily for the benefit of galvanizing the community into the appropriate response.[83]

Much like the term "Quakers" of the more recent past, "all who trembled at the words of the God of Israel" (Ezra 9:4; Isa 66:2, 5) evidently became a way

---

80. Reading "Edomites" with 1 Esdras 8:69 instead of the Masoretic Text's "Amorites." Williamson, *Ezra, Nehemiah*, 131, plausibly explains the otherwise surprising proscription of Egypt by means of Lev 18.

81. Most English translations inexplicably fail to translate the comparative -כ/*k-* ("like").

82. Williamson, *Ezra, Nehemiah*, 132, sees this as a clear "misapplication."

83. For a fuller discussion of the way Ezra 9 relates to the portrayal of Ezra's charismatic leadership, see the chapter "Leadership and Ezra-Nehemiah."

of referring to a party within the returnees distinguished by their particular reverence for and interpretation of the Torah (Ezra 10:3). Their sympathies may well have been wholly or partly prompted by Ezra's ministry, but their solidarity with him is unmistakably expressed here by their sitting "appalled" with Ezra, in much the same manner as Job's friends do (2:13). Having accompanied his fasting with a prayer for protection before the return from Mesopotamia (Ezra 8:21, 23), Ezra's fast now leads at the appropriate hour (3:00 pm) to a prayer of contrition and confession—an attitude emphasized by the spreading of the hands and the kneeling posture that was less common before the exile (1 Kgs 8:22).

9:6–7 Now that others have expressed their solidarity with him, Ezra commences his confession by identifying with the community's sin ("our iniquities") in spite of his own individual innocence. It is precisely because the community's sins and iniquities have "climbed to the heavens" (9:6) that Ezra is ashamed to "show [lit., lift] his face" (Job 22:26) to the God of the heavens (Ezra 1:2; 5:11–12; 6:9–10; 7:12, 21, 23). Ezra now admits that "our iniquities" (9:7) include those of "our fathers," and the resulting "great guilt" (בְּאַשְׁמָה גְדֹלָה/*bə'ašmâ gədōlâ*) has caused not only the community's destruction, dislocation, and despoiling, but also its dishonor at the hands of kings (i.e., those of Assyria and primarily Babylon). Far from denying Ezekiel's point (Ezek 18) that each generation must take responsibility for its own sin, Ezra here insists that the sins of his own generation have added height to the tower of trespasses already erected in the preexilic period.

9:8–9 The guilt of Ezra and his contemporaries is all the greater, he admits, because of the grace that the "remnant" (i.e., the community associated with the returnees) has experienced "for a brief moment" (i.e., since the edict of Cyrus). The "givenness" of this grace is expressed in the gift of "a stake" (NRSV; lit., "a tent peg") in the holy place, which likely intends a contrast to the nomadic transience of exile (see, e.g., Isa 33:20). This stability is in turn closely related to God's "brightening" of their eyes—a picture of restored vitality elsewhere associated with nourishment (1 Sam 14:29) and contrasted with potential death (Ps 13:3). While Ezra's prayer acknowledges that the "bondage" (Ezra 9:8–9) of exile is not ended, God's graciousness is seen in the extension of love to them, such that their Persian overlords (as in 7:28) have in turn allowed them a minirevival (9:8–9) defined in terms of restoring the ruins of the temple and setting up a "wall" (גָּדֵר/*gādēr*) in Judea and Jerusalem. Because this latter term is more commonly found around a vineyard (e.g., Isa 5:5) than a city (cf. חוֹמָה/*ḥômâ*; Neh 1:3; 2:8; 4:13, 15, 17, 19) and is here associated with not only Jerusalem but Judah as a whole, גָּדֵר/*gādēr* is not likely meant as a literal "wall," but rather as a metaphor for the protective and supportive measures authorized by the Persians.[84]

---

84. It may thus not be used as an argument for Ezra's arrival following the construction of

9:10–15 Having acknowledged that God has not forsaken them, Ezra answers his own rhetorical question ("what shall we say?") by admitting that they have "forsaken" God (9:10) by disregarding the words of the prophets (9:11). That Ezra's "prophets" must include Moses is indicated by the pastiche of primarily Pentateuchal phrases that Ezra sees as relevant to the case at hand. The uncleanness of the land (9:11) is owed to Leviticus, but the following make it clear that Ezra's primary debt is to Deuteronomy: "land which you are entering to take possession of it" (Deut 7:1), "abominable practices" (18:9), "do not give your daughters" (7:3), "do not seek their welfare" (23:6), "that you may ... eat the good things of the land" (6:11), and "inheritance of your children forever" (1:38–39). When Ezra considers their past transgressions, that even a remnant still exists is testimony to the triumph of God's mercy over their "great guilt" (Ezra 9:13, 7) and invites a rhetorical interpretation of Ezra's question: "Shall we break your commandments, again?" The subsequent question, however, suggests that an affirmative answer is not out of the question and will in turn invite the ultimate catastrophe: the extinction of the remnant that has escaped thus far (9:14). The very real possibility that the remnant's "escape" (9:15) has been thus far ("at this day"; 9:15), but will be no further, is raised by Ezra's words "you are righteous," which when addressed to God elsewhere (Ps 119:137) imply just judgments. The precariousness of their position is underlined by Ezra's acknowledgment that while they are still "before" God, they cannot "stand before" him, with this petitionary "posture" of the prayer's conclusion thus mirroring Ezra's adoption of a kneeling position at the outset of the prayer (Ezra 9:5).

Like the prayers of lament found in the Psalms, Ezra's prayer displays a profound awareness of the problem in the relationship between God and his people. While some laments focus on God's apparent neglect and the people's relative innocence, Ezra's exoneration of God and admission of sin/guilt mean that at a functional level, his prayer has more in common with psalms such as Ps 51 and of course especially penitential prayers such as may be found in Neh 9.[85] The homiletical aspects of Ezra's prayer are foregrounded by a comparison with the sermons found in the Chronicler's work.[86] Like these sermons, Ezra's prayer includes features such as a request for attentiveness, a historical recital/reflection, and rhetorical questions toward its conclusion. Given Ezra's role and activities as described earlier in his memoir, it is hardly surprising that

---

the wall erected by Nehemiah. For the use of the term to refer to the vineyard itself on stamped jar handles found at Gibeon, see Gibson, *Syrian Semitic Inscriptions*, 56.

85. For discussion of the genre of Ezra's prayer and its points of connection with the psalms of (communal) lament (though not Ps 51), the so-called levitical sermons, and Deuteronomy, see Bautsch, *Developments in Genre*, 80.

86. See Mason, *Preaching the Tradition*, 137–42.

even when praying, he is also preaching/teaching Torah (primarily as mediated by Deuteronomy).

10:1-2 The narrative resumes following the prayer, but it does so in the third person, perhaps due to ancient editorial considerations.[87] While Ezra's initial reaction attracts an inner circle of sympathizers who sit in silence (10:3-4), his subsequent—equally emotional—outburst of contrition now draws a large cross-section of the community ("men, women, and children") to the outer courts of the temple, where the people weep in solidarity with him (10:1).[88] The community's confession of marrying foreign women is voiced by Shecaniah, one of the sons of Elam from the first return.[89] He himself is not named as an offender (10:18-44), nor would the implication of Jehiel (10:26) necessarily implicate Shecaniah or exclude him from the community, even if this Jehiel was his father (10:2). While echoing Ezra's corporate confession of the community's "faithlessness" (so the chiefs in 9:2), Shecaniah also suggests that there may yet be "hope [מִקְוֶה/miqweh] for Israel."[90]

10:3-4 Shecaniah's proposed solution is to enter into a "covenant" (בְּרִית/ barît) with God (see, e.g., 2 Chr 15:8-15; 29:10) and to "send away" all the women and their children—terminology that is atypical of Jewish divorce and possibility pejorative (see footnote to commentary on 10:1-2). Only now is it made clear that at some point in the preceding four months, Ezra had evidently pointed the way toward this solution. That this solution is in accordance with the counsel of Ezra and "the (Torah) Tremblers" (הַחֲרֵדִים/haḥărēdîm) is thus less surprising than Shecaniah's insistence that it is also in accordance with "the law." There is no legal requirement to divorce foreign wives, but if Deut 24's provision for divorce in case of "something objectional" (24:1-4) is in view here, then the women might be eligible to marry again. If what is in mind is another more specific precedent or injunction instead, then this will be testimony to the evolution of the legal tradition within a particular stream of postexilic Judaism. In either case, while Shecaniah clearly hands the initiative back to Ezra (Ezra

---

87. Though one should not conclude from this change that these are therefore necessarily any less the words of Ezra.

88. While the mention of the people weeping at the end of 10:1 is likely a reference to the "men, women, and children" who eventually gathered (so NRSV: "the people also wept bitterly"), it is not impossible that they themselves were gathered because "the people [who had originally sat in silence with Ezra] wept bitterly" (RSV).

89. The terminology of "causing [foreign women] to dwell" (i.e., "living" with) found here and in Neh 13 is not typical marital idiom and may suggest that the relationships were being disparaged.

90. If this otherwise unique usage is meant to evoke the very similar Jeremianic divine epithet "the hope of Israel" (Jer 14:8; 17:13; cf. also 50:7), it will have served to underline the divine source of the returnees' hope.

10:4: "it is your task"), his additional encouragement ("we are with you") suggests that the community's continuing solidarity will be as important as Ezra's willingness to "be strong."

10:5–9 With Shecaniah's encouragement still ringing in his ears, Ezra strikes while the iron is hot by immediately securing the commitment of the leadership of the community (10:5). Ezra's subsequent withdrawal to continue his fasting and mourning of the community's "faithlessness" (10:6) through the night undoubtedly reaffirms Ezra's depth of feeling but also his awareness that the damage to the community's integrity has only begun to be undone.[91] The urgency of engaging the entire community in the process is underlined by the insistence not only that "all" the returnees should assemble within three days, but also that their failure to do so would lead to expropriation and excommunication from the assembly.[92] That both of these sanctions are included in those authorized by Artaxerxes's edict (7:26) would seem to require the presence of Ezra's own authority, but the issuing of the actual order itself by the "chiefs and elders" continues the pattern of emphasizing the initiative of the people (9:1).[93] The community's rapid compliance ("all the men of Judah and Benjamin assembled within three days"; 10:9) signals its recognition of Ezra's authority, while the people's apprehension ("shivering") seems likely to reflect in part the seriousness of the issue and also the inclement conditions ("heavy rain") that though not uncommon in Jerusalem in the winter ("ninth month") must have increased the people's sense of discomfort and foreboding.

10:10–11 Ezra begins by clarifying the accusation that was already expressed in his prayer, before insisting on a confession that follows the form of "giving thanks/praise" (תְּנוּ תוֹדָה/tǝnû tôdâ) found elsewhere only in Joshua's exhortation of Achan to confess his sin (Josh 7:19). This further resonance with the exodus/settlement/conquest tradition foregrounds the conviction that the returnees' sin, like Achan's, has the potential not only to compromise the divine intention to install his people in the land, but also, as Ezra's prayer indicates, to undermine the very existence of the community. That praise cannot be disconnected from—and indeed *must be* intimately connected to—practice

---

91. The frequent appearance of the names "Eliashib" (Ezra 10:6, 24, 27, 36; Neh 3:1, 20, 21; 12:10, 22, 23; 13:4, 7, 28) and "Jehohanan" (Ezra 10:6, 28; Neh 6:18; 12:13, 22, 23, 42) in Ezra and Nehemiah makes it difficult to determine the relationships between those so named.

92. While the Hebrew term used here for "expropriation" (יָחֳרַם/yāḥŏram) can refer to the devotion of people and property to God through their wholesale destruction (e.g., Deut 13:15), the law does make provision for this to take the form of permanent donation to the cult (e.g., Lev 27:21).

93. For a fuller assessment of this in the context of an assessment of Ezra as leader, see the chapter "Leadership and Ezra-Nehemiah."

is demonstrated by Ezra's clarification of the requirement that follows from this confession: "do his will"—defined here as the separation (*niphal* בדל/*bdl*) from the peoples of the land and, more to the point, in the case at hand, from "the foreign wives."

10:12-15 Like their forefathers at Sinai (Exod 24:3), the people respond (Ezra 10:12) clearly ("with a loud voice"), decisively ("we must do"), and apparently collectively ("all the assembly"). While they are conscious—and quite reasonably so—of the impracticality of a group so large trying to resolve the problem then and there, their awareness of the seriousness of the situation ("for we have greatly transgressed") leads them to an alternative proposal. Given that the leaders have been engaged from the beginning (9:1; 10:5), it is not surprising that they are commissioned to form a representative committee to adjudicate the cases of intermarriage brought before them by those concerned, in the company of local authorities who might speak on their behalf. Once completed, it is hoped that the process will be sufficient to assuage the divine wrath that it is assumed will otherwise destroy the community (cf. 8:22; 9:14). Special mention is made of four whose response was somehow distinct from the majority (10:15). That Meshullam and Shabbethai are mentioned after Jonathan and Jahzeiah suggests that these latter two (i.e., "them") received Meshullam and Shabbethai's support rather than the proposed plans. However, because none of the four are obviously implicated elsewhere in the marrying of foreign wives, it is unclear whether the men's opposition was to the separation proposed or rather to any delay in its implementation. While the paucity of dissenters may illustrate the otherwise overwhelming acceptance of the proposal (10:12) and the immediate implementation of it (10:16), the mention of them at all may also be intended to sow seeds of doubt regarding the recognition of Ezra's authority.

10:16-17 Precisely which "leaders" (10:14) will populate the adjudication committee is now made clear by the report of Ezra's appointment of the heads of the fathers' houses (Ezra 2 and 8), the names of whom may well have been listed at some point, but are not included in the text in its present form (cf. also 8:20). While the committee obviously began work promptly ("the first day of the tenth month"), without more information regarding its working practices, it is difficult to know whether the three-month duration of the enquiry is in any way remarkable. The point is perhaps rather that the hearings did not finish until the list of "all the men who had married foreign women" was exhausted.

10:18-19 As is common in Ezra, the book here includes a list apropos of the foregoing narrative. Like the list of Ezra's returnees, this one begins with the priests. Unsurprisingly, it is the sons of the house of Jeshua, listed in the first return (2:36), who are indicted, rather than the Aaronic priests who had only just returned to the province with Ezra. Also unsurprising, given the seriousness of the trespass, is that the sending away of the wives was accompanied by a guilt offering.

10:20-24 The offenders of the remaining cultic orders are now listed in much the same sequence as in 2:37-43.[94] While no mention is made here of the "sending away" of the wives or the guilt offering, it would be peculiar indeed if this absence was intended to indicate that the rest did not take the same action as the priests. Thus, whether or not an equivalent to 10:19 was originally repeated at appropriate points in the remainder of the list and subsequently deleted, the reader of the current list is presumably invited to assume that all those listed took the appropriate remedial action. The absence of temple servants from the list suggests to some that intermarriage was more prevalent among the upper echelons of the community, where both the temptation and opportunity to secure the societal advantages of such matches may have been greater (cf. 9:2). Alternatively, it may be that the problem among the upper classes was not more prevalent, but simply more relevant to the writer—on the assumption that once the practice was addressed and eliminated among the so-called leaders, the rest of the community would soon follow suit.

10:25-44 Whether or not the list of laity that follows was originally organized according to twelve family heads (as in 8:3-14) likely depends on the second Bani (10:34) being split into two phratries. If this second Bani is indeed to be read as Bigvai (2:14), then the only name that appears in Ezra 2 but not here is Binnui (itself textually questionable; cf. "Bunni" in Neh 10:15).[95] While there is thus significant, but not complete overlap between the list here and those of Ezra 2 and 8, the reasons for the absence of some names among the divorce list are unclear: some may not appear because they didn't take foreign wives in the first place, and/or others may not be listed because they did, but refused to send them away. A literal reading of the Hebrew text of 10:44 might mean something like: "And they had wives and they begat/bore children," but the banality and redundancy of such a conclusion encouraged emendation to "and they sent them away, wives and children together" following 1 Esdras 9:36. This may well be correct, but the textual confusion prevents this verse from adding much to our understanding of the preceding chapter.

---

94. Though the "sons of Harim" now follow the "sons of Immer," rather than the "sons of Pashur" (as in Ezra 2).

95. The Masoretic Text of Ezra 10:38 ("and Bani and Binnui") should be read as "and from the sons of Binnui" (so RSV). For discussion of other minor textual issues in relation to the list, see Williamson, *Ezra, Nehemiah*, 144.

Summary of Ezra 9–10

The prayer of Ezra (9:6–15) and the basic endorsement of it signaled by the community's response (10:2) furnish the reader with an insight into their shared understanding of God's character and his requirements of his people. Their interpretation and understanding of Torah suggests to them (and the reader) that God's passion for holiness and purity (in religious and increasingly racial terms) remains as fervent after the exile as before (and arguably more so). While their hermeneutics are not always transparent, their conclusion that this particular divine passion requires a ceasing and indeed reversing of the practice of intermarriage is not surprising and indeed may be seen as a reasonable (though far from necessary) deduction from the hard lessons of Israel's decline and eventual exile. The evocation of precisely these lessons from the past in Ezra's prayer testifies both to the fervency of this divine passion and—more importantly for the people—its potential to impede the gracious restoration that God has begun. Thus the recurring theme of the present community's continuity with the past is sounded again—not in terms of obedience now, but rather in terms of apostasy.

While it is Ezra and those especially sympathetic to him who identify the remedy, the text is also clear that it is the people who eventually recognize the seriousness of their situation, express a hope for a positive prognosis, and take the lead in seeking the prescribed treatment (confession and covenant). The people's initiative serves also to underline its recognition of Ezra's authority to assist them in dealing with the situation. The absence of some names from the list included here (and the very existence of this list) as well as the mention of those who apparently dissented may well hint that the community's acceptance of Ezra's position and embracing of his prescription were not as comprehensive or as permanent as he or others might have wished them to be. Given the social and emotional consequences of the familial disruption, this is perhaps not surprising, yet for Ezra and those who gathered around him, the focus is clearly not on those who refused the radical surgery, but on those who underwent it. For Ezra, it is these, however few, who constitute the restored community of "Israel" and who will ensure that the divine wrath is not revisited upon it. The abruptness of the conclusion of Ezra 10 and of the book of Ezra itself is mitigated somewhat by the knowledge that Ezra will eventually reappear later on in the second part of Ezra-Nehemiah (Neh 8).

Commentary on Nehemiah

BY DAVID J. SHEPHERD

Nehemiah 1

1:1-4 While many of the words that appear within Nehemiah are presented as those of the man himself, the introduction of them here—"the words of Nehemiah son of Hacaliah" (1:1a)—is likely to be the work of an editor. The similarity of this introduction to that found in Jer 1:1 (cf. Amos 1:1) may well reflect an editorial appreciation of Nehemiah's own identification with the purposes of this prophet. If Nehemiah's subsequent conversation with the king (Neh 2:1) takes place in Nisan, the first month of Artaxerxes's twentieth year, then one wonders how his conversation with Hanani could have taken place in Chislev (the ninth month) of Artaxerxes's twentieth year (1:1b). It may be that Nehemiah has accidentally got ahead of himself (in which case, we should read here "in the nineteenth year"), but a more plausible explanation has Artaxerxes I ascending the Persian throne in the late summer of 446 BCE. If so, Chislev would be the fifth month and Nisan the ninth of Artaxerxes's twentieth year.[1] The group of Jews Nehemiah meets (1:2) may have been an official delegation, but "Hanani, one of my brothers," appears likely to be the brother of Nehemiah mentioned in 7:2, in which case he may also have been visiting Susa on family business. Nehemiah's concern for "the remnant" (הַפְּלֵיטָה/*happəlêṭâ*) resonates with Ezra's prayer (Ezra 9:8, 13, 15) without differentiating between those who had returned to the land and those who had never been exiled in the first place. While the people and the province as a whole are not forgotten, Nehemiah's query clearly and significantly connects the fate of the people to the state of Jerusalem (Neh

---

1. Bickerman, "En marge de l'Écriture."

1:2). Judging from their response (1:3), it seems clear that Nehemiah's fellow Jews also closely connect the physical state of Jerusalem with the situation and reputation of the remnant: the "shame" of the latter is directly related to the shattered physical fabric of the city's walls and gates (cf. Nehemiah's own assessment in 2:17). That this sad state of affairs relates not to Jerusalem's original depredation in 586/587 BCE but a more recent setback—quite possibly the intervention of Rehum and his associates reported in Ezra 4:7–23—is suggested by the pious emotion of Nehemiah's response. Like Ezra, Nehemiah adopts a sitting posture (Neh 1:4; Ezra 9:3, 4, 15) and weeps (Neh 1:4; Ezra 10:1) in keeping with the practice of mourning (Neh 1:4; Ezra 10:6) while also embracing fasting (Neh 1:4; Ezra 8:23; 9:5; 10:6) and persistent prayer before the God of heaven (Ezra 1:2; 5:11–12; 6:9–10; 7:12, 21, 23).

1:5–11 As in Ezra 9, the description of appropriate and presumably heartfelt piety here gives way to a prayer of confession and petition (1:5–11).[2] The prayer opens by invoking again the "God of heaven" (1:5) but now in decidedly Deuteronomic terms: "a great and terrible God" (Deut 7:21), "who keeps covenant and steadfast love with those who love him and keep his commandments" (7:9).[3] The request for divine attentiveness (Neh 1:6) phrased in anthropomorphic terms ("ears attentive," "eyes open") and the petitioner's naming of himself and his community (1 Kgs 8:23, 32, 36) as "servants" are both familiar from the prayer attributed to Solomon (8:52).[4] The emphasis here on persistence in prayer ("day and night") also echoes the supplication of Solomon (Neh 1:6; 1 Kgs 8:59), but its more immediate resonance with Ezra's own pious endurance (Ezra 10:6) prepares the reader for the confessional tone that this prayer also shares with Ezra's.

While the identification with the sins of the forebears is not as developed here as in Ezra 9, it is worth noting that Nehemiah does implicate his "father's house" along with himself. Characteristically Deuteronomic again is the combination "commandments, statutes, and ordinances" (Neh 1:7; Deut 5:31) and the understanding of Moses as "servant" (34:5) but the use of the latter term as a means of identifying the contemporary community with an ancient authority finds its clearest parallel in 1 Kgs 8, where Solomon makes a point of referring not only to Moses (8:53) and David (8:26), but also to himself and his community as "servants." The exhortation for God to "remember" (Neh 1:8–9) the Mosaic covenant (1:5) is clearly paralleled (or indeed undergirded) by Lev

---

2. As will be clear from the commentary, it is far from impossible that this prayer originated with Nehemiah himself.

3. An almost identical form of words in Dan 9:4 demonstrates how widespread Deuteronomic language had penetrated the spiritual practices of the postexilic period.

4. Balzer, "Moses Servant of God and the Servants," also draws parallels to 1 Kgs 8 (for which cf. J. L. Wright, *Rebuilding Identity*, 14–17).

26:42, 45 and other priestly texts (e.g., Ezek 16:61–63). However, the only precise parallel to the prayer here for God to "remember" (זְכָר־נָא/zəkor-nāʾ; Neh 1:8) the Mosaic covenant is to be found in Jer 14:21, which likewise turns this language of promise into petition—insisting imperiously that God "remember" (זְכֹר/zəkōr) and "not break your covenant" (בְּרִיתְךָ/bərîtəkā) with us" (i.e., that covenant made with the people in the time of Moses).[5] The debt to Moses's magisterial proclamation in Deut 30:1–5 is suggested by the shared notions of faithlessness leading God to "scatter" the people (Neh 1:8; Deut 30:3), but willing too to "gather" (Neh 1:9; Deut 30:3–4) them from the farthest heaven (Neh 1:9; Deut 30:4) if only the people will "return" (Neh 1:9; Deut 30:2) to a keeping of the divine commands (Neh 1:9; Deut 30:2). Finally and typically Deuteronomic too is the understanding of Jerusalem as the place where God chooses to make his name dwell (Neh 1:9; Deut 12:11), even if in Neh 1:10, the echoes of "redeemed" and "strong hand" also suggest an awareness of the language of the exodus tradition (Exod 13:9, 13, 15, 16). Having confessed and "reminded" God of the conditions of restoration, the petitioner finally reiterates his request for divine attentiveness ("let your ear hear") to the supplications of God's "servants" (who fear God's "name") and more specifically to Nehemiah's request for "success" in soliciting a reversal of the previously obstructive policy (cf. Ezra 4:17–22) of the king of Persia.

Summary of Nehemiah 1

As the book opens, we hear in Nehemiah's voice a concern for the fabric and physical integrity of the city of Jerusalem that was not as overtly expressed in the book of Ezra. Nevertheless, Nehemiah's connection of this concern with the fate of the people and their restoration does resonate with the interests and priorities of the earlier returnees (including Ezra). Nehemiah's own account of his burden for his people and his homeland is more visceral and emotive than Ezra's account of the initiation of his ministry, and some sense a resonance of Nehemiah's "call" with those of the prophets (e.g., Moses, Isaiah, Jeremiah). The absence, however, of any explicit divine initiative or encounter, or indeed mediation of the divine word, here would seem to prevent the pressing of such comparisons.[6]

---

5. Boda, *Praying the Tradition*, 54n43, provides a helpful discussion of the numerous parallels between Jer 14:17–21 (1 Kgs 8) and esp. Lev 26; see also Jones, *Jeremiah*, 212–13. While the Chronicler's version of Solomon's prayer (2 Chr 6:42) also includes an exhortation to "remember," it is clearly the Davidic covenant that is in view.

6. See Shepherd, "Is the Governor Also among the Prophets?"

Nevertheless, the impression created by Nehemiah's self-presentation is undoubtedly one of a faith that is solicitous, serious, and above all sincere. In this respect, Nehemiah has much in common with Ezra, and indeed the flavor of their postexilic piety and the prayers attributed to them strike some of the same notes. Supplication for restoration is suffused with an awareness of sin, past and present, and an earnest confession of it. Even more than Ezra's prayer—or perhaps simply more explicitly so—Nehemiah's prayer is saturated in the traditions of his community's past—a feature that is itself a practical and very powerful expression of the kind of historical continuity that the wider narrative continues to reinforce.

Nehemiah 2

2:1-8 Whether Nehemiah awaits his turn to attend to the king, or perhaps awaits the return of the king himself from the royal winter residence in Babylon, some four months pass (see commentary on 1:1–4) before an opportune time arises for Nehemiah to disclose his concern to the king. Such an opportunity is afforded him due to his role as "cupbearer" (מַשְׁקֶה/*mašqeh*; 1:11), a position whose duties may well have included sampling the royal cup to prevent the poisoning of the royal person, but whose influence apparently extended far beyond this.[7] Nehemiah reports (2:1–2) that his sadness—whether heartfelt or artful—contrasted sharply with his usual demeanor, thereby piquing the curiosity of the king and prompting royal concern. Nehemiah's anxiety at this point ("I was very much afraid"; 2:2) may relate to the dangers of displaying anything other than a cheerful disposition in the Persian court (cf. Dan 1). However, Nehemiah's apprehension may well be prompted by the prospect of voicing a concern that is, on one hand deeply personal, yet on the other, directly related to Persian imperial interests and policy vis-à-vis Jerusalem (Ezra 4:21).

Nehemiah's apprehension does not prevent him from sharing his concern, but it may well account for the careful choice of words that follow. The conventional salutation formula "may the king live forever" (Dan 2:4; 3:9; 5:10) gives way to Nehemiah's rhetorical question, which invites the king to reflect on the emotional toll taken on his cupbearer by the unrepaired and unsecured

---

7. As attested by ancient Greek historian Herodotus (*Histories* 3.34) and the book of Tobit (1:22) in its characterization of the sage and scribe Ahikar, who as Esarhaddon's lieutenant held this same position in the Assyrian court. While some who held the position of cupbearer may have been eunuchs, there is no reason to assume that Nehemiah was one himself, particularly given the Israelite aversion for emasculation (Deut 23:1).

state of the city of his ancestors' graves. This touch was presumably calculated to evoke the maximum sympathy from any ancient audience, but especially a king whose own forebears' graves were so impressively commemorated and worthy of royal concern.[8]

While the king's invitation of Nehemiah's request may reflect the memory of a Persian proclivity for doing so on special occasions of feasting (Esth 5:3, 6; cf. Herodotus, *Histories* 9.110–11), Nehemiah's account emphasizes instead the responsiveness of the king to Nehemiah's situation. Before Nehemiah makes his request, he first notes his prayer to the God of heaven—most probably itself a request and if so perhaps similar in spirit (and also brevity) to the one he had been praying in the months previous (Neh 1:11): "Give success to your servant today, and grant him mercy in the sight of this man!" (NRSV).

Nehemiah's request itself—always at the pleasure of the crown he "serves" (2:5–7; cf. Esth 1:21; 2:4, 9)—is that he be sent to remedy the ruin of Jerusalem by rebuilding the city of his currently "restless" ancestors. While the king's questions regarding timescale (Neh 2:6) may seem perfunctory, they are in fact perfectly plausible and indeed eminently reasonable given Nehemiah's apparently important position in the royal court. Nehemiah thus obliges the king (though not the reader) by providing a satisfactory return date, and the required royal permission is granted.

It seems slightly fanciful to suppose that Nehemiah's parenthetical noting (2:6) of the presence of the royal "consort" (הַשֵּׁגַל/*haššēgal*) is intended to emphasize the king's attentiveness and compliance *in spite* of feminine distraction. In fact, the ancient suggestion that feminine influence was strong in the court of Artaxerxes (Ctesias, *Persica* 14.39) encouraged the supposition that Nehemiah may have been, on the contrary, the beneficiary of her support in the present case. While the historiographical credibility of Ctesias may be questioned, there seems no other more obvious reason why Nehemiah should mention her.[9]

In Ezra, a letter of royal authorization is quoted *in extenso* (e.g., Ezra 7:12–26). Here Nehemiah merely notes his request for comparable correspondence, guaranteeing safe passage to Judah through the province (Neh 2:7) and then authorizing the requisition of sufficient timber supplies for the restoration of the fortress, wall, and his own residence. In building the Second Temple, the first returnees had to content themselves with sourcing Lebanese timber from

---

8. See, for instance, the sepulchers of Darius and Artaxerxes himself carved into the rock face of Naqsh-i-Rustam and the so-called Tomb of Cyrus at Pasagardae.

9. The suggestion that Nehemiah's intent was to signal a shift at this point to a more private audience (so tentatively, Williamson, *Ezra, Nehemiah*, 180) depends on the assumption that the queen was initially absent—an assumption that may not be altogether safe given the impression offered by Dan 5 and indeed Esth 5 and 7.

the Tyrians out of their own pockets (Ezra 3:7; though note 1 Esdras 4:48); by contrast, Nehemiah's ability to draw directly from the resources of the Persian crown (i.e., the king's forest; Neh 2:8) may reflect his position within the court or perhaps the perceived strategic importance of the work. Nehemiah does, however, share with the book of Ezra not only the phrase the "good hand of my God" (e.g., Ezra 7:9; 8:18), but also the understanding of this divine agency as the sole motive force behind the Persian crown's authorization of the return(s) (7:6).

2:9–10 As in Ezra 8:36, Nehemiah here offers confirmation that the royal authorizations were delivered to the appropriate authorities, along with an additional note that his party had an armed escort. Given that the provision of such escorts was apparently standard practice, it is Ezra's earlier refusal of such protection that is remarkable, rather than Nehemiah's acceptance of it here. Precisely why, therefore, Nehemiah feels compelled to mention it is unclear, unless perhaps to suggest that the danger to life and limb on the way to Yehud was as real as that which would await him on his arrival (Neh 4:18; 6:10). In contrast to the official support recounted by Ezra on his arrival and his confirmation that the requisite authorizations were delivered (Ezra 8:36), Nehemiah reports (Neh 2:10) that news of their arrival to work for the "good" (טוֹבָה/*ṭôbâ*) of the "children of Israel" is taken very badly indeed by Sanballat and Tobiah (רָעָה גְדֹלָה/*rāʿâ gədōlâ*, "it displeased them greatly"). According to official correspondence between Yehud and the Jewish colony in Egyptian Elephantine, Sanballat would, in 408 BCE, become governor of Samaria, Jerusalem's chief rival and nearest neighbor; he may well have already taken up the post, or at least have been aspiring to it, when Nehemiah arrived in Jerusalem in 445 BCE. It is possible that "Tobiah the Ammonite" was in fact a governor of Ammon and thus a regional peer of Sanballat and Nehemiah, but the latter's probably pejorative reference to Tobiah as "the servant, the Ammonite" (2:10) and his association with Sanballat may suggest that Tobiah was a powerful but ultimately subordinate associate within the Samarian hierarchy.

2:11–16 A note of Nehemiah's arrival and pause for "three days" (2:11; see commentary on Ezra 8:21–36) sets the stage for a recounting of his own survey of "the walls of Jerusalem, which had been broken down, and its gates, which had been destroyed by fire" (Neh 2:13). The location of the gates named by Nehemiah depends not only on the identification of individual sites (easy in some cases, impossible in others) but also on whether the Jerusalem of the restoration included both the hills to the east ("City of David" along with some or all of the Temple Mount) and the west (i.e., modern "Mount Zion"). Rather than including the hill to the southwest enclosed by the late preexilic walls of Hezekiah and Manasseh, it seems most likely that Jerusalem was restored along the more limited lines of the earlier Davidic-Solomonic city.[10] Exiting the city through the westerly Valley Gate on either a horse or mule, Nehemiah circumnavigates the walls in a counterclockwise direction before apparently abandoning his mount (2:14) either due to the steepness of the ridge or quite possibly the scale of the rubble. Evidently, Nehemiah turns back without completing his circuit, suggesting that the northern and eastern stretches of the wall were either unreachable in this direction or perhaps—given that Nehemiah omits them from his reconnaissance altogether—did not require examination or at least not the sort that required such discretion. That Nehemiah felt such discretion was required for his "inspection" (2:13, 15) is suggested by his note that the journey was a nocturnal one (2:12, 15) and unaccompanied apart from "a few men" (2:12) and a solitary "animal" (2:12).

Just as Ezra sees the beautification of the temple as being "put by God in the hearts" of the Persian kings (Ezra 7:27), so too Nehemiah understands his plans as those that "my God had put in my heart" (Neh 2:12). The prospect of opposition to these divinely inspired plans—a prospect that 2:19-20 shows to be a very real one—is perhaps the most obvious explanation for Nehemiah's insistence that what God had told him "I told no one" (2:12). Indeed, one suspects that Nehemiah's reemphasizing of the completeness of his discretion—cataloged in some detail in 2:16b and celebrated in 2:16a—reflects his awareness of the potential damage that might be done if advance notice of his plans reached the opposition before they could be fully formed and communicated within the community.

2:17-18 Whatever the actual time that elapsed between Nehemiah's assessment of the walls and his call to rebuild them, the narration of the latter (2:17-18) hard on the heels of his nighttime survey only heightens the impression of a carefully constructed communication strategy designed to minimize the opportunity for obstruction and maximize the effectiveness of a call to action.

Having seen the situation for himself, Nehemiah's articulation of both the problem and the solution in the same terms used by the visitors to Susa (2:17; cf. "trouble/bad situation," "gates burned," "disgrace" in 1:3) must have been intentional. In addition to confirming and identifying with the community's own understanding of its plight ("you see the trouble we are in"; 2:17), Nehemiah reinforces his charismatic authority to lead by sharing his earlier awareness (2:8) of "the hand of God for good" upon him—manifest not only (but presumably not least) in the royal interest in and approval of Nehemiah's plans (2:18).

---

10. For further discussion of the detail, see Williamson, "Nehemiah's Walls Revisited"; Clines, *Ezra, Nehemiah, Esther*, 146; and Blenkinsopp, *Ezra-Nehemiah*, 239-42, all of whom favor a contracted Jerusalem in Nehemiah's time.

Nehemiah's report of the collective response of the people, "Come let us begin building!"—itself an enthusiastic endorsement of Nehemiah's approach—is followed by his own summary of their commitment. Nehemiah presumably sees it as no accident that his report of "God's good hand" upon him leads to the people's "strengthening of their hands for good"—a turn of phrase that elsewhere has the connotation of enablement (Ezra 6:22) and determination (Neh 6:9).

2:19-20 Confirmation of the importance of an expeditious and well-executed plan arrives in Nehemiah's report of further opposition from expected quarters (Sanballat and Tobiah) and a new adversary in the shape of "Geshem the Arab" (2:19).[11] Having initially noted his opponents' "great displeasure" at his mere arrival, Nehemiah now explicitly documents the expression of this displeasure—presumably to illustrate the escalation of opposition in response to Nehemiah's own progress toward concrete action. Their opponents' question, "Are you rebelling against the king?," seems an allusion to earlier allegations of rebellion (Ezra 4) and a very thinly veiled one at that. However, Nehemiah's reporting of their hectoring tone ("they mocked and ridiculed us") and especially his response (Neh 2:20) suggests he has seen through their bluff—armed as he is with the knowledge of Artaxerxes's own approval of Nehemiah's activities in the province. That this approval has been forthcoming from the earthly king is credited by Nehemiah to "the God of heaven," the same God who answered Nehemiah's prayers and is the ultimate guarantor of the project's success. In light of this seemingly inevitable success, and armed with the courage of his conviction, Nehemiah finally responds to what he feels is his opponents' real ambition by contrasting his own community's ownership of the rebuilding project ("we his servants") with his opponents' lack of any legitimate claim to or stake in Jerusalem.

Summary of Nehemiah 2

The piety, prayer, emotion, and introspection of Neh 1 give way in this chapter to a gripping self-portrait of Nehemiah in action. A moment's anxiety, a daring disclosure, a bold request, an apparently dangerous journey, a clandestine reconnaissance, and an uncompromising rebuttal of his opponents—all add

---

11. Evidence of Geshem's sphere of influence to the south and east of Jerusalem as ruler of Qedar is furnished by the appearance of his name in Egypt and Dedan (Dumbrell, "Tell el-Maskhuta Bowls"), though judging by his more occasional appearance in Nehemiah's narrative, Geshem's apparent interest in obstructing the reconstruction of Jerusalem was less profound than that of the city's nearer neighbors.

color to the self-portrait of a man of considerable intelligence, capability, and conviction. But to paint too sharp a contrast between the opening two chapters would be to ignore the theological current that flows from its source in Neh 1 and carries Nehemiah on his winding way from the splendor of Susa to the ruins of Jerusalem. After all, by Nehemiah's own account, his plans are not his own, but have been placed in his heart—that organ of intention and volition— by the hand of God himself (2:12). While Nehemiah doesn't explicitly attribute this divine inspiration to his own petitions, his report of his own preemptive prayer in 2:4 cannot but reflect both his belief in a God who hears and his desire to model this belief and practice for his readers. One might wonder what theological conclusions Nehemiah might have come to had the king not granted his request, but here as elsewhere Nehemiah's seeming success allows the causal connections between heaven and earth—between God's good hand on Nehemiah (2:8) and royal approval of the request—to remain unquestioned. That Nehemiah should choose to share his perception of God's favor, inspiration, and sanction with those whose assistance he requires (2:18) is hardly surprising in light of the community's ancient tradition of charismatic leadership (prophetic and otherwise). The question that it raises is whether Nehemiah feels the need to share this with the local leadership *despite* his position and authority as the authorized agent of the Persian crown or rather *because* of it. Convinced as he is, though, that his plan enjoys divine sanction, his conviction that God will guarantee its success (2:20) resonates clearly with a longstanding Israelite belief in God's sovereignty and the efficacy of the divine intention.[12]

Nehemiah 3

Nehemiah's report of planning and preparation is now followed by a detailed list of what was done by whom in relation to the rebuilding of the wall. It seems very probable for two reasons that this list was added later to an earlier version of Nehemiah's memoir, quite possibly by the man himself. First, the list details the hanging of doors (e.g., 3:1), which seem to remain unhung in Nehemiah's own narrative as late as 6:1. Second, the list seems to refer to Nehemiah in the third person ("their lord"; 3:5), which is at odds with the largely first-person presentation of the memoir. It is possible, though not provable, that the leaders' use of the same terminology ("my lord" [אֲדֹנָי/*'ădōnāy*]; Ezra 10:3) in referring to Ezra indicates that some of the same leaders were responsible for compiling

---

12. One thinks, for instance, of Job's belated admission (42:2): "I know that you can do all things; no plan of yours can be thwarted."

the list found here, perhaps to memorialize their own contribution to a successful project.[13]

3:1-2 Confirmation of the community's earlier commitment to the project (2:18: "Let us arise and build") is supplied by the report here that Eliashib the high priest and his confederates "arose and built" (בנה + קום/*qwm + bnh*; 3:1) the Sheep Gate. This may well have been of particular interest to the priests along with the stretch of wall between the towers of "Hananel" and "the Hundred" (cf. 12:39) because of their probable association with the temple complex (2:8) in the northeast of the city. It is possible that the dedication and purification of the walls mentioned in 12:27–30 is to be identified with the "consecration" of the building work here (3:1), though a separate process of sanctification for repairs to the sacred precincts cannot be ruled out. That the men of Jericho, Zaccur and others, build "alongside" (עַל־יָד/*ʿal-yād*) each other and are focused on the gates (3:1–15) may suggest that they are here following the line of a previous wall (Neh 2) before later adopting a different course (3:16–32).

3:3-32 The Fish Gate—built by the sons of Hassenaah (3:3)—was likely located in the northwest corner of the city and marks the point at which the focus of the work shifted from the late preexilic wall to the earlier one. While the Tekoites are represented in the work party, the list makes a point of noting the Tekoan nobles' lack of support and loyalty "to their lord(s)" (3:5). Whether or not their lack of support for Nehemiah's initiative reflects Tekoa's proximity to Qedar (and an allegiance to Geshem), this incidental note confirms that not all of those who might have been expected to contribute did so. The work on the Mishneh Gate[14] attracted the help of various members of the community from as far afield as Gibeon and Mizpah (3:7). Given its status as an imperial administrative center after the fall of Jerusalem (Jer 40:5–12; 2 Kgs 25:23) it is not surprising that those from Mizpah were under the jurisdiction of the governor and that their participation was therefore perhaps worthy of particular note (Neh 3:7). Others involved in this section include a perfumer and a goldsmith (3:8), who along with the merchants (3:31) may have been motivated by a vested commercial interest in this particular area of the city, much as Jedaiah and others worked opposite their own houses (3:10).[15] Among those engaged in

---

13. Williamson, *Ezra, Nehemiah*, 200. Moreover, the use of "nobles" (cf. also Neh 10:29) to refer to leaders within the community is quite uncharacteristic of Nehemiah (cf. 2:16).

14. Rather than "Old Gate," which reflects the Masoretic Text's הַיְשָׁנָה/*hayašānâ*, a text that is likely a corruption of מִשְׁנֶה/*mišneh*, if this is indeed the name of the quarter (Neh 11:9) to which this gate presumably gave entrance.

15. If עזב/*ʿzb* means "abandon" as it usually does in Biblical Hebrew, then it is likely that their abandonment of Jerusalem (contra NRSV: "they restored") is some kind of reference to the exclusion of some part of the former city from the circuit of the new walls.

repair work beyond the Broad Wall in the direction of the Tower of the Ovens were two responsible for the two subdistricts of Jerusalem, Rephaiah son of Hur (3:9) and Shallum son of Hallohesh (3:12). The specific mention of the latter's daughters simultaneously discloses Shallum's lack of sons and celebrates the commitment of his daughters to share their father's responsibilities.

Despite not being from the area, those with comparable responsibility for various subdistricts of Yehud appear to have taken on the renewal of various gates and sections of wall: Malkijah (Beth Hakkerem), the Dung Gate; Shallum son of Col-Hozeh, the Fountain Gate along with the wall of the Pool of Shelah (3:15; likely the King's Pool in 2:14) and in the vicinity of the city of David. The references here and in the remainder of the chapter (3:16–32) to city landmarks rather than existing gates signal the work parties' abandonment of the line of the old wall in favor of building a new wall nearer the crest of the eastern ridge. This change of tack is also signaled by the preference for noting that successive parties and individuals now work not "alongside" but "after" (אַחַר/'aḥar) each other (so 3:16–32 apart from 3:19, 26, 28)—though the specific impetus for adopting different terminology here remains unclear.

Others with leadership responsibility elsewhere (Nehemiah over Beth Zur [3:16]; Hashabiah and Binnui over half districts of Keilah [3:17–18]; Ezer over Mizpah [3:19])—some of whom were apparently Levites (3:17)—also make repairs on behalf of "their district" (3:17). The proximity of the work to the house of the high priest Eliashib (3:20–21)—already involved near the temple enclosure (3:1–2)—may well explain the involvement of the priests (3:22), whose number may have included Meremoth (Ezra 8:33). Others continue the pattern of working on the wall in the vicinity of their own houses (Neh 3:23). Moving northward, one Pedaiah son of Parosh (likely the Levite of 13:13) is charged with supervising the temple servants of the Ophel who are enlisted to work on the wall that passed above the old Water Gate and presumably the Gihon spring. Whether the Tekoans who carried out the work on the next section (3:27) were the same as those already mentioned (3:5), it is not impossible that the extra investment by the Tekoans was motivated by a desire to make up for the absence of their nobles.

While the Horse Gate is more likely to have given entrance to the city itself (Jer 31:40) rather than the sacred precincts, the nearing of the work to the temple will explain the involvement of priests with homes in the vicinity (Neh 3:28). The East Gate by contrast is likely to have been set within the wall of the temple enclosure; if so, Shemaiah, who seems to have been a gatekeeper, may well have been a Levite as well (3:29). Meshullam son of Berekiah—whose contribution near the Fish Gate has already been noted (3:4)—appears to have been involved in the work here as well, opposite his own "room" (נִשְׁכָּתוֹ/niškātô)—a term used to refer to the chamber in the temple courts illegitimately occupied by Tobiah (13:4–9) to whom Meshullam was, as it happens, related. That the temple servants who lived on the Ophel would have had some kind of accommodation along with merchants generally (3:32) and goldsmiths specifically (3:31–32) in this part of the city is not surprising given the need for manpower and cultic paraphernalia at the temple.

Summary of Nehemiah 3

Given the importance of physical reconstruction in both Ezra and Nehemiah, the extensive cataloging of who did what in rebuilding the wall in Neh 3 invites comparison with the book of Ezra's account of the reconstruction of the temple. While Ezra chronicles the political impediments to rebuilding the temple and the celebrations that followed its completion, there is within that book only a general and very passing interest in who did what: "So the elders of the Jews built and prospered" (Ezra 6:14 NRSV). By contrast, Neh 3 dwells at length on precisely these issues, furnishing the reader with every evidence of the community's commitment and, in only very exceptional cases, the lack thereof. While the language ("repair," "build," "set in place") is generic and formulaic, the sheer accumulation of verbs results in a picture of concentrated and concrete action and a vivid illustration of the willingness of the returnees to take a share in the actual physical building itself. If the "what" of Neh 3 is formulaic, the "who" is, by contrast, nothing short of encyclopedic: priests, Levites, temple servants, rulers and administrators, goldsmiths, perfumers, and other merchants all join in the work alongside others whose normal occupations remain unknown to us. Amid those not normally classed with the "great and the good" in Ezra-Nehemiah are the unnamed daughters of Shallum—mentioned despite the improbability of their participation, or perhaps indeed because of it. That this chapter celebrates and commemorates the obvious unity of purpose in building the wall despite such diversity can hardly be doubted. Indeed, while it seems evident that for some the motivation for improving their own neighborhood may have been at least partly self-interest—and indeed self-preservation—the involvement of others from further afield cannot be explained away in this fashion. What it does suggest is that whatever the status of Mizpah, Jerusalem continued to serve as a vessel for the aspirations and ambitions of those associated with the return who settled right across the province. At the same time, not all who could and should have participated did in fact do so (3:5); this acknowledgment serves—much as the note in Ezra 10:15 does—as a reminder that support and solidarity could not simply be assumed and that the project was still very much a partnership of the willing.

There is, however, one final contrast to Ezra's earlier tale of temple building worth observing. Ezra's note of the construction and completion of the temple (Ezra 6:14) comes precisely where we would expect it to—between preparations before and celebrations after. By contrast, while Nehemiah has barely begun his narrative account of the building of the wall, the picture presented in Neh 3 is one of not merely building commenced but, in fact, completed. The undoubted effect of this preemptive conclusion is to rob Nehemiah's account to come of a good deal of suspense, but evidently the loss of narrative momentum was felt to be a price worth paying for the opportunity to emphasize the full and final answer to the question of who built the wall. Nevertheless, it is also worth noting that if Neh 3 is manifestly and insatiably interested in documenting the community's contribution, Nehemiah's positioning of this evidence of the completed wall hard on the heels of his response to his opponents at the end of the preceding chapter suggests that the ultimate answer to the question of who built the wall should be sought from above: "The God of heaven is the one who will give us success" (2:20 NRSV).[16]

Nehemiah 4

4:1–3 Though the list found in the preceding chapter must have been compiled after the eventual completion of the wall, the resumption of Nehemiah's narrative in Neh 4 requires that Neh 3 be read as merely a beginning to the building, while the renewal of Nehemiah's enemies' malevolent machinations suggests that the success of the project is by no means assured. That this opposition is mounting is indicated by Sanballat's previous mockery (4:1; 2:19) being now fueled by a great rage. Sanballat's decision to vent his spleen in the presence of "his associates" (including Tobiah; cf. 4:3) and the garrison under his command may reflect his need to publicly justify his lack of intervention up to this point, but he may also have wished to send a message signaling his very real capacity to disrupt proceedings. Sanballat's earlier allegations of rebellion, easily dismissed by Nehemiah (2:19–20), now give way to a vitriolic questioning of the returnees' ability to complete the job. First, Sanballat casts aspersions on the possibility or efficacy of their pious dependence on God: "Will they leave it to God?"[17] Will

---

16. Such an answer provides yet another point of comparison with Ezra's account of the temple's construction: "They finished their building by command of the God of Israel" (Ezra 6:14 NRSV).

17. Assuming that the Masoretic Text originally read הֲיַעַזְבוּ לֵאלֹהִים/*hăya'azəbû lē'lōhîm* ("will they abandon [themselves] to God?") in the spirit of similar sentiments in Job 39:11 and Ps 10:14b; Williamson, *Ezra, Nehemiah*, 214.

Nehemiah 4

they sacrifice?" Then, by asking: "Will they finish in a day?" Sanballat scornfully calls into question either their own unrealistic expectations or their ability to expedite matters—or both. Finally, he queries the wisdom of salvaging burnt and thereby weakened stones for the rebuilding. Tobiah's own contemptuous contribution likewise focuses on the work on the wall itself, by suggesting that its fragility would be exposed by a scampering fox—a creature known to haunt the stones of ruined cities (Lam 5:18), but hardly sizeable enough to dislodge them in normal circumstances.

4:4-5 Unlike Neh 2, this explosion of mockery and criticism is merely reported by Nehemiah rather than addressed to him, so it is perhaps not surprising that his response is not to his enemies (as in Neh 2) but instead to his God. That his prayer lacks any introduction (e.g., "and we said") strengthens the assumption that it has been inserted into the narrative by Nehemiah himself, but within the narrative as it stands it also contributes to the impression of both extemporaneity and spontaneity. Nehemiah's awareness that news of their progress had caused their enemies to despise (בזה/*bzh*) them (2:19) leads naturally now to a plea that God would hear their prayer "for we are despised (בוּזָה/*bûzâ*)" (4:3). The plea for God to "hear" is of course common currency in psalmic prayers of petition generally (Ps 27:7; 30:10) while prayers for deliverance from an enemy (Ps 44; 74; 77) and those of an imprecatory spirit (Ps 137; 109:6-19) are also well represented among the Psalms. However, when Nehemiah declares, "Do not cover their guilt, and do not let their sin be blotted out from your sight" (Neh 4:5 NRSV), it is to Jeremiah and his prayers that he is specifically indebted. In fact, apart from minor adjustments,[18] Nehemiah's use of Jeremiah's words of imprecation extends even to the order in which they appear.[19] While Jeremiah's words are used by Nehemiah in his own context, the latter, like Jeremiah, unabashedly urges God to take action against those whom he perceives to be obstructing his purpose, invoking God's vengeance against those whose scornful rage (כעס/*kʿs*; 4:1)—apparently also expressed in the presence of the builders—is provoking God's own wrath (הִכְעִיסוּ/*hikʿîsû*).[20]

---

18. The more generic כסה/*ksh* employed by Nehemiah is used occasionally elsewhere with the meaning "forgive" (cf. Ps 32:1); whereas Neh 4:5 uses a passive construction אַל־תִּמָּחֶה/*ʾal-timmāḥeh* (*niphal* third-person feminine singular) meaning "let their sin not be blotted out," Jer 18:23 uses *hiphil* second-person masculine singular: אַל־תֶּמְחִי/*ʾal-temḥî* ("do not blot out [their sin]").

19. For Nehemiah's identification with the purposes and concerns of Jeremiah, see Shepherd, "Is the Governor Also among the Prophets?"

20. Following RSV's "for they have provoked thee to anger before the builders"; for similar uses of the verb in the context of divine provocation see 1 Kgs 21:22; 2 Kgs 21:6; Ps 106:29.

4:6–9 Nehemiah resumes his account with a progress report on the wall, emphasizing the completion of the circuit ("all the wall") up to half its projected height. Given that it was the community's lack of capacity to reconstruct the wall that was the object of their enemies' mockery, Nehemiah's progress report here confirms that his prayer that God would turn their enemies' taunts back on them (4:5) has been answered—thanks in no small part, he notes, to the commitment of the people who "had a mind to work" (4:6). Nehemiah furnishes further evidence that the opposition continues to mount as the wall climbs higher by once again reporting the reaction to the repair of the wall[21] and more specifically to the progressive "closing of the gaps." In addition to the usual suspects, Tobiah and Sanballat (2:10, 19; the latter at 4:1), the ranks of those ranged against Nehemiah are now swelled by the previously unmentioned "Ashdodites" to the west, as well as "Ammonites" to the east and "Arabs" to the south. That the latter two are mentioned without reference to Tobiah ("the Ammonite") or Geshem ("the Arab") suggests these figures may in fact have had little to do with their regions of origin, but also that bona fide opposition is now coming from quite literally all quarters, given the Samarian challenge from the north. Here as earlier (4:1) there is great anger, but instead of mockery, Nehemiah now reports a plot to "fight/make war" in or against Jerusalem and cause confusion (4:2). While the prospect of open military conflict seems rather unlikely given Persian hegemony in the region, it is certainly not difficult to imagine agents of opposition infiltrating Jerusalem to cause confusion—not least by spreading rumors of various and violent plots. Indeed, that such plots were sufficiently plausible to unsettle the community is demonstrated by Nehemiah's felt need to respond. As before (4:4–5), the response reported by Nehemiah includes an appeal to "our God" (4:9), and while the prayer itself is not included, it is—as before—offered up by the community ("we prayed") rather than merely by the leader. Just as Nehemiah himself had combined prayer with practical action in the throne room of Artaxerxes (2:4–5) so here prayer is accompanied by the very pragmatic posting of a protective guard round the clock (4:9).

4:10–13 It is not impossible that it is precisely this shifting of manpower to guard duty (and resulting understaffing of the building crews) that prompts the complaint from "Judah" about a lack of resources and an unworkable site (4:10). However, the erosion of the community's will to work (contrast 4:6) is also attributed by Nehemiah to more specific rumors suggesting that the impending enemy attacks will be not only unpredictable ("they will not know")

---

21. Lit., "healing went up [for the wall]"—a turn of phrase used in Jer 8:22; 30:17; 33:6 (cf. 2 Chr 24:13; Isa 58:8) in relation to the restoration of the nation and perhaps a pointed rejoinder to Tobiah's taunt that the wall would not bear even a fox "going up."

but also lethal ("[we will] ... kill them"; 4:11). That this campaign of (mis)information threatens to further undermine the builders' efforts is confirmed by Nehemiah's report of the reaction of those living in the vicinity of their "enemies" and thus most susceptible to such rumors: "They said to us repeatedly [lit., 'ten times'] from everywhere [i.e., various outlying regions]: 'Return to us!'" (4:12).[22] With Jerusalem inevitably destined to bear the brunt of any attack, it is only natural that families would want their loved ones home and out of harm's way. Nehemiah's response is, however, to rally the people, either in areas that were particularly vulnerable or more likely in a single space that was particularly visible,[23] mobilizing and arming the "people" in their relevant families to literally stand in the breach (4:13).

4:14–15 Nehemiah preserves here only an excerpt from what may well have been a longer speech, clearly designed to bolster sagging spirits. His indebtedness again to Deuteronomy (7:21) is evident not only in his evoking of YHWH as the "great and awesome" God (so also Neh 1:5) but also in his warning: "Do not be afraid" (4:14). Yet again, and even more clearly here, the specific rhetoric of remembering (cf. 1:5–11) is reminiscent of Jeremiah, which supplies the only other example in the Hebrew Bible of an imperative to specifically "remember YHWH" (Jer 51:50).[24] Interestingly, however, Nehemiah does not suggest here that the God they are to remember will fight their battle for them; rather, he encourages the returnees to "fight for" each other—with the mention of brothers, sons, daughters, wives, and houses presumably offering a catalog of things most worth fighting for. It is unclear whether the show of strength orchestrated by Nehemiah was more bluff than genuine brinkmanship, but it gives the impression that his enemies were made aware that the returnees would not be caught unaware themselves (cf. 4:11). Despite his own substantial contribution to the thwarting of their enemies' plans, Nehemiah heeds his own advice, remembering YHWH by attributing the frustration of the enemies' plot to God himself[25]—though one may doubt whether this particular interpretation of events would have been shared by Sanballat and his allies, as Nehemiah

---

22. Following the Masoretic Text's תָּשׁוּבוּ עָלֵינוּ/*tāšûbû ʿālênû* ("return to us"; cf. English Standard Version), with Williamson, *Ezra, Nehemiah*, 221–22, rather than the NRSV, which emends the text unnecessarily at this point.

23. For the former suggestion, see Clines, *Ezra, Nehemiah, Esther*, 163; for the latter, see Williamson, *Ezra, Nehemiah*, 222.

24. Though compare also Deut 8:18, where the force (if not the form) of the verb is imperative.

25. Nehemiah's reuse of עֵצָה/*ʿēṣâ* + פרר/*prr* ("to frustrate plans") here offers a neat counterpoint to the enemies' successful frustrating of the first returnees' efforts to build the temple (cf. a similar usage at Ezra 4:5).

perhaps innocently suggests (4:15). While the success of Nehemiah's tactic is signaled by the return of the people to their work on the wall (4:15b), he was evidently persuaded that sufficient threat remained to assign half of his own men to an armed security detail to provide reassurance to the workers on one hand and a visible deterrent and capacity for rapid tactical response to any attack on the other.

4:16-20 Whether the rulers of the people had ever been fully engaged in the manual labor on the wall (cf. Neh 3), they are now withdrawn from the front line and positioned "behind" the people doing the work (4:16b-17), in all likelihood to protect the fledgling community's small corps of leaders.[26] Given that they would form the bulk of any fighting force, even the workers themselves are armed—the basket carriers with a stone or other missile in their free hand (4:17) and the builders with swords on hips (4:18) to keep both hands free. Recognizing that "we are separated far from one another on the wall" (4:19 NRSV), Nehemiah's plan to muster the people by means of the trumpeter at his side draws on time-honored traditions of Israel's military history (Judg 3:27; 6:34; 7:18) as does his reassurance that "our God will fight for us" (Neh 4:20; cf. Deut 1:30; Josh 10:14).

4:21-23 Finally, Nehemiah reports taking measures to speed the completion of the project by extending the working day well beyond sunset and into the evening ("till the stars came out"; 4:21).[27] Such an extension may well partly explain (and may also have been used to justify) Nehemiah's requirement that the workers remain in Jerusalem. While a system of rotating watches will have allowed a workforce restricted to Jerusalem to "labor by day" having also stood "guard for us by night" (4:22), the more pertinent purpose of the restriction may well have been to prevent the leading figures and their servants from heeding the cries to "return to us!" (4:12), which may well have continued in outlying areas despite Nehemiah's efforts to quell them. Acknowledging the importance of setting an example, Nehemiah makes a point of noting the visible vigilance of him and his closest colleagues, with sentiments such as "never took off our clothes" and "weapon in our right hand" (4:23) being roughly equivalent to sleeping with one's boots on and a pistol under the pillow.

---

26. That this group was especially valuable and worthy of extra protection may well suggest that it was they who were pressuring Nehemiah to be allowed to return to the safety of the country (4:12) until Nehemiah confined the workforce to Jerusalem (4:22).

27. For the deletion of the erroneous "and half of them held the spears," which Nehemiah's men clearly did (4:16), but the rest did not, see Williamson, *Ezra, Nehemiah*, 223.

Summary of Nehemiah 4

In Nehemiah's account of the mounting opposition to the work, his enemies contemptuously question not only the builders' professed dependence on God, but also their endurance and even their technical knowledge. These queries—presented as the seeds of doubt that, if unchallenged, might blossom into full-blown fear within the community—set the tone for the verses that follow and shape Nehemiah's report of the community's response.

Faced with the scorning of his community's (in)capacity, Nehemiah makes a point of affirming the very reliance on God his enemies ridicule ("Will they leave it to God?") by appealing to God directly in prayer. If the imprecatory tone of the prayer seems at odds with the spirit of some other sentiments within the Hebrew and Christian Scriptures, it is by no means uncommon elsewhere in the Hebrew Bible (e.g., Jeremiah, Psalms) or indeed even elsewhere in Nehemiah, as we will see. While this tension raises questions requiring attention in the context of the wider canon and tradition, in the context of the narrative here, the prayer's invocation of God's action on behalf of the community against its enemies—and the forgoing of any preemptive response or even direct retort in favor of simply resuming the work—emphasizes a radical embrace of divine dependence.

As the opposition continues to mount, further prayer is accompanied by the taking of practical steps—to prevent the obstruction of the work—a combination seen already in Nehemiah's initial approach to the king in 2:4–5. Further opposition and the prospect of a fearful weakening of the collective will—a theme prominent in, for instance, Num 14 and elsewhere in the wilderness wanderings—leads to the report of Nehemiah's speech. On one hand, his focus is, of course, the divine deliverer, whose capacity and character the community is encouraged to "remember"—not least because, as the holy warrior of Deuteronomy, it is Yʜᴡʜ who will fight for them in this battle of nerves.[28] While the divine frustrating of the enemy plot is duly acknowledged, Nehemiah's portrayal of himself and his community is far from quietist. In much the same way that the book of Joshua's insistence on God's intervention does not preclude the community's own involvement (e.g., in Jericho, where divine assistance does not build a wall, but brings it tumbling down), so too Nehemiah's report displays a profound appreciation of the balance between divine responsibility and human activity. Thus as they remember the God who will fight for his people, Nehemiah also insists that the people must be willing to fight (if only

---

28. Compare also Isa 8:10: "Take counsel together, but it shall be brought to naught; speak a word, but it will not stand, for God is with us" (NRSV).

in self-defense) for each other and for the community that is being built as the wall itself takes shape.

Nehemiah 5

Nehemiah's account of the wall-building and his enemies' attempts to thwart it, which began in earnest at the end of Neh 3 and will resume in Neh 6, is here interrupted by an episode concerned less with external opposition than internal division. Yet, the continuing first-person voice of Nehemiah and the allusion to tensions within the community already in the previous chapter, where some were tempting their neighbors to return from Jerusalem to the safety of the countryside, suggest that the inclusion of Neh 5 at this point in the book is far from accidental.

5:1-5 While the prayer in 9:9 will recall the "outcry" (זְעָקָה/zəʿāqâ) of the Israelites at the threat of the Egyptians (cf. Exod 3:7, 9), the "outcry" of the people that Nehemiah hears and reports here in Neh 5:1 (צְעָקָה/ṣəʿāqâ) and 5:6 (זְעָקָה/zəʿāqâ) is instead voiced by the people against "their Jewish brothers" (5:1). As in Exodus, the threat of the sword (Neh 4:11) is accompanied now by the prospect of deprivation and indeed potential starvation, judging from 5:2. If Neh 3-4 suggests that those farmers drawn to Jerusalem to work on the wall have been productive, Neh 5 hints that in their absence some of their farms may have been less so, perhaps because those who might have worked them were required to stay in the city to guard during the night the wall they were building during the day. Whatever the plausibility of this suggestion, the complaints reported by Nehemiah prefer to attribute their suffering to the perennial problem of dwindling resources ("famine," so Gen 12:10; 26:1) and the unrelenting demands on these resources.

Nehemiah 5:2-5 appears to report separate complaints, but the increasing specificity of their presentation contributes to the cumulative rhetorical effect on the reader. Thus the articulation of the basic problem, an existential need for food for families (5:2), gives way to complaints regarding the consequent need to mortgage family holdings in order to meet the twin demands of feeding the family (5:3) and paying the crown (5:4). That even these practices were insufficient to alleviate the financial distress is indicated by the final complaint that, having lost financial control of their land, members of the community had to resort to the still more desperate (and certainly more emotive) measure of indenturing their children (5:5) without having the means of eventually freeing them. If Pentateuchal traditions contain provisions for the transfer of land and indeed for debt servitude as a means of staving off the extinction of families (e.g., Lev 25; Deut 15:1–18, esp. 15:12), it is clear that at this crucial juncture, the prospering of some at the expense of others by means of such practices was seen to pose a credible threat to the sense of community cohesion required by Nehemiah's project.

5:6-13 Indeed, while progress on the wall had prompted Sanballat and his allies to become "very angry" as recently as the previous chapter (4:7), the seriousness of this internal "outcry" is marked by Nehemiah's insistence that "I was very angry" (5:6). Nehemiah's accusation against the nobles and officials concentrates not on the lending itself but on the charging of interest on what was being lent. If, as seems likely, this refers to a particular Judean practice (rather than one associated with Babylon), Nehemiah may have in mind Pentateuchal traditions that effectively ruled out the charging of interest to members of the community who were impoverished and greatly restricted the practice of retaining property for the purposes of securing loans (Exod 22:25–26).[29] Evidently judging that certain sectors of the community had fallen into the category of needy and were therefore entitled to protection from those who would force them into an unrecoverable financial position, Nehemiah calls a meeting of the guilty parties to address the problem.

Yet, if Nehemiah does have particular or indeed even general legal traditions in mind, he begins instead by explaining how the abuse of the debt-servitude system is undermining the efforts of the community as a whole, not least because the community had been redeeming (cf. Lev 25) those indentured to Gentiles. That the community is redeeming their kinsfolk from Gentiles and, at the same time, enslaving others themselves is roundly criticized by Nehemiah in part because it would require the intervention of "us" (Neh 5:8), i.e., members of the community, including perhaps even Nehemiah personally. His condemnation of the offenders in no uncertain terms ("what you are doing is not right"), his invocation of "the fear of our God," and his raising of the specter of hypocrisy make it unlikely that he intends to include himself in the warning "let us stop this taking of interest"[30] (5:10 NRSV) and more likely that his own practice of lending (i.e., without interest or perhaps even pledge) is reported as an example to be followed, rather than as a confession.[31]

The twofold remedy Nehemiah prescribes in 5:11 may be seen to treat both elements of the commandment in Exod 22:25–26. Just as the cloak of the needy cannot be kept as collateral, so Nehemiah orders the return of the property

---

29. In light of the reoccurrence of "outcry" (5:1, 6) noted above, Exod 22:27 is noteworthy: "And if your neighbor cries out [יִצְעַק/yiṣ'aq] to me, I will listen, for I am compassionate" (NRSV).

30. Or pledges taken to secure loans; Clines, *Ezra, Nehemiah, Esther*, 169.

31. So, e.g., Blenkinsopp, *Ezra-Nehemiah*, 259–60; contra, e.g., Williamson, *Ezra, Nehemiah*, 240.

repossessed or held as security; and in keeping with Exod 22:25's injunction against charging interest to the impoverished, Nehemiah orders the renunciation and return of interest on loans already made.[32] Nehemiah records not only the nobles' and officials' agreement to his orders in Neh 5:12, but also his efforts to ensure that these practices are not repeated. First, cultic sanction is invoked by the witnessing of the leaders' oath by the priests, summoned for the purpose and perhaps included themselves, but Nehemiah also goes on to insist that noncompliance will be met with excommunication (5:13), much as Ezra does in response to the intermarriage crisis (Ezra 10:8). Whatever the origins of Nehemiah's "coat-shaking" exercise, its resemblance to the object lessons of prophets such as Ezekiel and Jeremiah suggests a general familiarity with such practices. Whether Nehemiah's final words in Neh 5:13 indicate that the congregation literally followed his symbolic lead or simply followed through on what they had agreed ("amen"), his mention of the praise of the people affirms a happy ending to his intervention, much as it marks such moments elsewhere in Ezra-Nehemiah (Ezra 3:10–11; Neh 12:24).

If this passage displays a general awareness of Pentateuchal legislation, Nehemiah's final prophetic flourish at the end points toward a more pronounced indebtedness to the prophetic tradition and, in particular, to Jer 34:8–22. Significantly, both here and there, political leaders address issues of debt servitude that pit the upper classes (Jer 34:10; Neh 5:7) against the people (Jer 34:10; Neh 5:1, 13). A certain amount of shared terminology might be expected in texts that take up a common topic, but these two texts' relationship to Deut 15:12 and to each other on the subject of the debt-servitude issue appears to suggest Jeremianic influence on Nehemiah.[33] While the terminology of the Deuteronomy passage, "your *Hebrew* brother" (אָחִיךָ הָעִבְרִי/*'āḥîkā hā'ibrî*), is followed in Jer 34:14 (אָחִיו הָעִבְרִי/*'āḥîw hā'ibrî*), Jeremiah earlier refers instead to "a *Jew*, his brother" (בִּיהוּדִי אָחִיהוּ/*bîhûdî 'āḥîhû*; 34:9). Significantly, the only other text in the Hebrew Bible in which this particular terminology is used is Neh 5:1, when it refers to "their Jewish brothers" (אֲחֵיהֶם הַיְּהוּדִים/*'ăḥêhem hayyəhûdîm*) in dealing with the same topic. Moreover, the terminology used by Nehemiah in describing the process of enslavement, "to indenture ... as servants" (כֹּבְשִׁים לַעֲבָדִים .../*kōbšîm ... la'ăbādîm*; 5:5) is again virtually unique to this text and Jer 34:11 (וַיִּכְבְּשׁוּם לַעֲבָדִים/*wayyikbəšûm la'ăbādîm*; cf. also 34:16).[34]

Even more striking are the parallels between the Jeremiah and Nehemiah

---

32. This seems more probable than the suggestion that Nehemiah here requires the return of the principal as well.

33. Reinmuth, *Der Bericht Nehemias*, 176–79.

34. The only other appearance of this terminology in the Hebrew Bible is found in 2 Chr 28:10, where it is used to describe the enslavement of Judahites by Israel in the time of Ahaz.

Nehemiah 5

passages that extend beyond shared topic and terminology to include the plot: in neither text is it merely a matter of confronting and condemning inappropriate indenturing of fellow community members; rather just as Jer 34:11 describes the prophet's confrontation of reenslavement following an initial manumission of slaves (34:9–10), so too Nehemiah's account describes his confrontation of the intramural indenturing of servants (5:5) after his own prior attempts to liberate these same people from debt servitude (in this case to non-Jews; 5:8a). When this parallel of plot is coupled with those of topic and terminology, it is difficult to escape the conclusion that here again Nehemiah's memoir reflects his own awareness of and identification with the prophetic purposes and actions of Jeremiah.[35]

5:14–19 While these verses cannot have been penned before the completion of Nehemiah's tenure as governor (in the "thirty-second year of King Artaxerxes"; 5:14), his use of "moreover" (גַּם/*gam*) and the references to the gubernatorial food allowance connect this passage with the initial concerns of the chapter (5:2) and explain its inclusion at this point in the book. Indeed, if Nehemiah's reflection on his own position vis-à-vis the debt crisis comes increasingly to the fore in the preceding verses (esp. 5:9), this passage here has very much the ring of a full-blown *apologia*. Nehemiah's mention of the food allowance to which he and his coterie were entitled (5:14) clearly facilitates his identification—in principle at least, if not in actual practice (5:18)—with those who have less food than they might have had (5:2). That Nehemiah has already presented his abstaining from usury as exemplary fits well with his favorable comparison here of his own personal restraint with what we are left to assume was the typically exploitative behavior of those who preceded him in his post (5:15). This personal restraint is motivated by the same "fear of God" (5:15) that Nehemiah exhorted the community's leaders to display in abandoning their ignoble pursuit of interest (5:9), suggesting the importance (to Nehemiah and his intended readers) of presenting this reform as theologically motivated. By offering the subsequent assurance that "I . . . acquired no land" (5:16), Nehemiah confirms his disinterest in—or better, disavowal of—the acquisitive practices of his predecessors. Not content to report his renunciation of the personal profit that might normally be extracted by men in his position, Nehemiah goes on in 5:17–18 to detail the extensiveness of his hospitality, in order to confirm that his declining of the food allowance required him to suffer personal financial loss by funding the supply of the governor's table out of his own means. Interestingly, whereas Nehemiah earlier reports his renunciation of his rights in terms of

---

35. For other examples of Nehemiah's indebtedness to the book of Jeremiah, see Shepherd, "Is the Governor Also among the Prophets?"

religious piety (5:15), he here credits his "sacrificial" generosity not to religious piety, but to his sensitivity to the difficult circumstances of the community to which he has come ("because of the heavy burden of labor on the people"; 5:18 NRSV).

The progressively sharper focus on Nehemiah's own situation and position culminates in the prayer found in the final verse of the chapter: "Remember for my good, O my God, all that I have done for this people" (NRSV). Whereas an earlier imprecatory prayer (4:4–5) was offered in the first-person plural, being voiced by the community and possibly situated within the diegesis of the narrative, the prayer at this point is voiced by Nehemiah himself and, in appealing to God directly, interrupts the flow of the narrative. Moreover, whereas Nehemiah has already resorted to imprecation—or at least the threat of it—in this chapter, here his prayer for his own remembrance reflects the focus of the chapter itself, especially from 5:7 onward, on what Nehemiah himself did for these people.[36]

Summary of Nehemiah 5

Whatever the historical sequence of the events chronicled in Neh 3–6, the positioning of the debt crisis and Nehemiah's response to it after Neh 4 offers a salutary reminder to the reader that sometimes the greatest threat to the restoration of a community is the community itself. That Lev 25 was (along with Exod 22) a crucial resource for Nehemiah in his response to this threat is made clear, not only by its attention to the very same issues of economic exploitation seen in Neh 5, but also by Nehemiah's insistence that it is the "fear of God" that motivates him (5:15) and must motivate others (5:9) to take responsibility for—rather than advantage of—those pressed on to the margins of society by circumstances beyond their control. Indeed, while this notion of the "fear of God" appears at various points in Lev 25's wide-ranging compendium of social concerns (25:17, 36, 43), one such moment is particularly apposite: "If any of your kin fall into difficulty and become dependent on you, you shall support them; they shall live with you as though resident aliens. Do not take interest in advance or otherwise make a profit from them, but fear your God [וְיָרֵאתָ מֵאֱלֹהֶיךָ/*wəyārē'tā mē'ĕlōhêkā*]; let them live with you. You shall not lend them your money at interest taken in advance, or provide them food at a profit" (25:35–37 NRSV). Leviticus's encouragement not to simply "fear YHWH," nor even "fear God," but specifically "fear *your* God" in addressing these issues

---

36. For other prayers for his own remembrance, see Neh 13:14 and 13:22.

finds an interesting resonance in Nehemiah's own insistence that some within his community are not displaying the "fear of *our* God" (בְּיִרְאַת אֱלֹהֵינוּ/*bayir'at 'ĕlōhênû*; Neh 5:9). Nehemiah's emphasis at this point—that the God who requires such compassion is not simply a God, but "our God," the very God worshiped by the community as a whole—is surely not incidental at the very moment when the community's cohesion is being tested so severely and the lines of fracture and faction announce the very real prospect of disunity.

While these fault lines appear in—and are exacerbated by—an economic environment parched by drought, it is not merely the Pentateuchal tradition that illustrates the awareness of the recurring temptation to take economic advantage of misfortune even when it occurs in the most close-knit communities. The undoubted parallels between Neh 5 and Jer 34 suggest that the latter may have offered Nehemiah both evidence of the perennial nature of the problem he encountered but also inspiration to tackle it in particular ways. Yet, such concerns are by no means limited to Jeremiah; indeed, of all the prophets, it is Isaiah who most vividly and vitally connects a mission to the margins with "the fear/reverence" of God. Isaiah describes one on whom "the spirit of knowledge and the fear of YHWH" (11:2 NRSV) rests and, moreover, one whose "delight shall be in the fear of YHWH" (11:3 NRSV). More to the point, it affirms that "with righteousness he shall judge the poor, and decide with equity for the meek of the earth; he shall strike the earth with the rod of his mouth" (11:4 NRSV). That Nehemiah's self-portrait in Neh 5 sits so comfortably alongside the messianic mission to the margins painted by Isa 11 may be mere coincidence. If so, it is made all the more striking by the rumors reported in the very next chapter that prophets are proclaiming (unhelpfully from Nehemiah's perspective), "There is a king in Judah" (Neh 6:7).

Nehemiah 6

With the internal quarreling finally quelled, Nehemiah's recollections turn in the first fourteen verses of Neh 6 to the increasingly extreme and quite personal measures resorted to by his enemies in what would become the last gasp of opposition to the wall building. The concluding verses of the chapter (6:15–19) then confirm the completion of the wall while continuing to elaborate on the complex network of local allegiances that had threatened to compromise Nehemiah's project entirely but ended up merely complicating it inordinately.

6:1–7 Nehemiah resumes his chronicling of the external opposition offered now by "Sanballat, Tobiah, Geshem the Arab, and the rest of our enemies" (6:1). News of Nehemiah's virtual completion of the wall apparently prompts Sanballat and Geshem to request a meeting with Nehemiah outside Jerusalem (6:2).[37] Whatever the full story may have been, Nehemiah is clearly of the conviction that his enemies' strategy now includes the tactical deployment of deception and that Sanballat and Geshem's desire for a meeting is less innocuous than it might seem (6:2). Following a note of his resistance to their repeated overtures, Nehemiah then records a change of tack on the part of Sanballat, whose request for a meeting is accompanied by an accusation, placed by Sanballat in the mouths of others and clothed by him in the guise of concern (6:5-7). According to Nehemiah, he stands accused not only of fomenting rebellion by rebuilding Jerusalem's wall but also of preparing to assume Judah's vacant throne (6:6) by setting up "prophets" to proclaim "about" or "concerning" (עַל/'al) himself: "There is a king in Judah!" These specific accusations are enveloped by Sanballat's claims regarding not only the source of the words ("it is reported among the nations—and Geshem also says it"; 6:6 NRSV) but also their probable destination ("and now it will be reported to the king according to these words"; 6:7 NRSV). In fact, Sanballat's emphasis on the potentially public nature of the letter's contents seems to be mirrored also by the letter's form (i.e., "open"), which would seem to encourage, if not promote, the dissemination of its contents.[38] By making use of an open letter and by openly revealing both the origins of "this report" and their threatened destination, Sanballat hints that if such rumors were not widely known before the writing of his letter, they would be or could be made known in short order. Indeed, if these words or rumors did not exist, or could not easily be disseminated, it is difficult to see why Nehemiah would go to the trouble of rebutting Sanballat's reporting of them.

The possible existence and probable effectiveness of rumors that Judah was rebuilding for the purposes of rebelling are of course suggested, as we have already seen, by the correspondence included in Ezra (4:6-24). Whether possible Davidic ancestry left Nehemiah particularly vulnerable to the more personally damaging allegations of coopting royal prophecy is unclear,[39] but it

---

37. See Williamson, *Ezra, Nehemiah*, 248, 254-55, for the significance of Ono's location as either neutral territory or on or near the provincial border.

38. While Ackroyd, *I and II Chronicles, Ezra, Nehemiah*, 287, suggests that Sanballat's open letter implies the employment of a "duplicate" system and therefore the existence of a closed or sealed counterpart to the open letter sent by Sanballat, Williamson, *Ezra, Nehemiah*, 255-56, rightly points out that there is little to suggest the use of such a system here. Brockington, *Ezra, Nehemiah, and Esther*, 154, rightly notes that an open letter would (at least potentially) be subject to the scrutiny of more than merely the primary intended recipient—which would of course not have been lost on either Sanballat or Nehemiah.

39. Kellerman, *Nehemia*, 156-59, 179-82, contends that Nehemiah became an object of royal restoration prophecy by virtue of his Davidic ancestry—an ancestry not noted explicitly in

does not seem improbable that prophets based in Jerusalem at this time may have been prophesying in much the same way that Haggai (2:20–23) and Zechariah (6:9–14) had done in the early days of the return.[40] Indeed, whatever the historical sequence, Nehemiah's self-presentation in dealing with the debt crisis (Neh 5) does little to dampen messianic enthusiasm.

6:8-9 Rather than refuting the existence of either "these words" or the prophets and prophecies that might advance royal claims on his behalf, Nehemiah apparently prefers to accuse Sanballat himself of purveying false information that he himself has fabricated or invented, from his own "heart," a notion known from elsewhere in the Hebrew Bible (6:8).[41] It is interesting to note that it is the "heart" too that is indicted in connection with false prophecy not only in the Torah, but also in the Latter Prophets.[42] Indeed, it is not impossible that Nehemiah's use of "fabricating/inventing from your own heart" is intended to invite comparison of Sanballat's actions with those of Jeroboam in 1 Kgs 12:33 where the radical and unauthorized expansion of the priesthood is followed by a liberty taken with the cultic calendar. There Jeroboam offers whole burnt offerings on the altar that he had made in Bethel "on the fifteenth day of the eighth month"—the month he had "invented from his own heart" (בָּדָא מִלִּבּוֹ/ bādā' millibbô). Given that this precise turn of phrase is used in the Hebrew Bible only in 1 Kgs 12 and Neh 6, it may be that Nehemiah is likewise accusing Sanballat of usurping the prerogative of, not the priests, but rather the prophets by "inventing from his heart" the prophets' words: "There is a king in Judah!"

Whereas in 6:8, Nehemiah's response is directed solely at Sanballat, his analysis of the situation in 6:9 implies Sanballat's involvement in a wider effort to intimidate him and the builders. By referring to "all [of them]" (כֻּלָּם/ kullām), Nehemiah broadens the scope of his accusation to include not only Sanballat—the suspected source of "this report"—but also the reported sources—Geshem and the *goyim* in the surrounding regions.[43] In light of the

---

Ezra-Nehemiah but perhaps alluded to in Neh 1–2. For discussion and, ultimately, a dissenting opinion, see Williamson, *Ezra, Nehemiah*, 256–57.

40. See, for instance, Becker, *Esra/Nehemiah*, 81–82.

41. While Fabry in *Theological Dictionary of the Old Testament*, 7.399–437, differentiates between voluntative and noetic functions of the Hebrew word usually translated "heart," he also admits that "the line between the rational function of the *lēb* and the activity of the will is blurred, because it is impossible pragmatically to distinguish between theory and practice."

42. We see in Ezek 13:2, for example, Yhwh commanding the "son of man" to denounce his prophetic competitors: "Say to those who prophesy out of their own hearts: Hear the word of the Yhwh!" and again fifteen verses later: "Now, son of man, set your face against the daughters of your people who prophesy from their own hearts." Note also the connection between false revelation and the heart in Num 16:28; 24:13; Jer 23:16, 26.

43. Noted by Batten, *Ezra and Nehemiah*, 254.

above discussion, however, it seems quite possible that Nehemiah's denunciation of "all [who] wanted to frighten us" is meant to include the prophets who have been set up to prophesy about (עַל/ʿal) him.[44] Aware of the danger of allowing himself to be intimidated by false prophets/prophecies designed to cause his "*hands* to drop from the work," Nehemiah reports yet another of his prayers, in which the request for God to "strengthen my *hands*" suggests a tighter integration of the prayer into the narrative horizon of the chapter than is the case with the prayer at the end of the last chapter (5:19) or the one toward the end of this one (6:14).

6:10–14 Following his steadfast refusal to be intimidated by his opponents' scare tactics, Nehemiah recounts his own visit to the house of one Shemaiah son of Delaiah. While the cause of Shemaiah's confinement is unclear, he loses little time in attempting to persuade Nehemiah to flee to the temple allegedly now in the interests of protecting him from imminent assassination (6:10).[45] The question of how Nehemiah arrives so quickly at the conclusion that Shemaiah is a false prophet, sent not by God, but by his enemies (6:12), is one that has long vexed scholarship.[46]

Nehemiah's initial rhetorical question, "Should a man like me flee/run away [יִבְרָח/yibrāḥ]?" (6:11a), seems to reflect the prominence of "fear/intimidation" already seen in this chapter and to establish the primary parameters for interpreting what follows.[47] By causally connecting (כִּי/kî) his conclusion that "God had not sent him" (i.e., that Shemaiah was a false prophet) with several other assertions, Nehemiah explains in 6:12b how he came to the conclusion arrived at in 6:12a. How Nehemiah's observation that "the prophecy he spoke was about/concerning me [עָלַי/ʿālay]" led him to the conclusion that Shemaiah had not been sent by God becomes clear when we remember that back in 6:7 the false prophecies were also "about" (עַל/ʿal) Nehemiah. Although this subsequent false prophecy (i.e., the governor is in mortal danger) is different in detail from the first (i.e., the governor has royal ambitions), their common focus on the

---

44. In fact, the "prophets" (נְבִיאִים/nəbî'îm) of 6:7 are the nearest plural antecedent of "all of them."

45. Williamson, *Ezra, Nehemiah*, 249, surveys no less than six distinct suggestions regarding the meaning and significance of וְהוּא עָצוּר/wəhû' 'āṣûr (often translated "but he was shut up/in") in the context of Neh 6.

46. See Shepherd, "Prophetaphobia," for a discussion of the strengths and weaknesses of various proposals and for a fuller discussion of the reading proposed here.

47. On this reading, the meaning of the two parallel questions might be paraphrased as follows: "Should someone like me be running scared? Indeed, what kind of man in my position could afford to be seen as so fearful that he needs to run for his life to the security and safety of the temple?"

person of Nehemiah evidently allowed him to perceive (*hiphil* נכר/*nkr*) that God had not sent Shemaiah.⁴⁸

If Nehemiah quite understandably infers that Sanballat has once again been hiring false prophets "to intimidate me," his further elaboration of his enemies' motives to "make me sin by acting in this way" is less transparent in meaning. While the common assumption has been that the "this/thus" (כֵּן/*kēn*) that Nehemiah is worried about "doing" is entering the temple, it seems more likely that Nehemiah's overriding concern is to avoid a display of fear. Given this, it is interesting to note that the immediately preceding clause (lit., "cause me to be afraid" [לְמַעַן־אִירָא/*ləmaʿan-ʾîrāʾ*]) offers an antecedent for "this/thus" that is not only more proximate but also more apposite in light of Nehemiah's familiarity with Deuteronomy (e.g., Neh 4:14; 1:6). Thus it seems likely that the sin that Nehemiah is keen to avoid doing is the sin that Deut 18:22 warns against—namely, fearing the false prophet. Despite being deprived of the opportunity to deploy Deut 18's "time-will-tell" test of true and false prophecy, Nehemiah nevertheless manages to recognize false prophecy when he hears it, not once but twice in Neh 6. Nehemiah also recognizes, however, that the true test of his convictions about the falseness of the prophets and their prophecies would lie in his reaction to them. In facing down the false prophets and prophecies ranged against him in Neh 6, Nehemiah recognizes that the real weapon of his enemies—the real danger posed by the false prophets—is the fear that they might induce in him. Moreover, if Nehemiah were to have responded fearfully to the false prophets by either scaling down the work on the wall or fleeing to the temple, 6:13 suggests that he would have seen himself as compromised in the eyes of the people.

If 6:1–13 offers ample evidence of Nehemiah's concern regarding prophetic attempts to induce fear and intimidate him, the prayer that follows (6:14) reflects this same concern. Nehemiah's indictment of "Noadiah and the rest of the prophets" offers little detail and prompts considerable speculation as to the nature of her (and their) activities.⁴⁹ As in 4:4, though with slightly less venom, Nehemiah prays for the divine remembrance of the community's opponents "according to these things that they did," yet the increasingly personal nature of their campaign here in Neh 6 appears to be reflected in the special place

---

48. Nehemiah's recognition of the connection may have been further aided by the recollection that like the first letter from Sanballat and Geshem (6:2), Shemaiah's prophecy begins with a first-person common plural invitation: "Let us meet" (6:10).

49. Kidner, *Ezra and Nehemiah*, 100, favors the suggestion that Noadiah and her anonymous comrades were involved in some sort of "prophecy-for-pay" scheme à la Shemaiah. Batten, *Ezra and Nehemiah*, 259, observing that Shemaiah himself would surely have been named in 6:14 if this were the case, improbably prefers a Greek text (Codex L of the Septuagint) that understands Noadiah and her fellow prophets to have been not scaring, but warning Nehemiah.

that Nehemiah reserves in his prayer for Noadiah and the rest of the prophets who wanted to "make me afraid." While it is not clear whether Noadiah was among those anonymous messianic prophets alluded to by Sanballat in his letter (6:5–7), there can be little doubt that Nehemiah's implacable opposition to her reflects his perception of her as a false prophetess.

6:15–19 Having explained why it was that he refused to meet Shemaiah at the temple (6:12–14), Nehemiah underlines the import of this decision (6:11) by noting the completion of the wall on the twenty-fifth of Elul (6:15). It is not unlikely that the reduced circuit of the wall and an emphasis on the speed rather than the standard of the work contributed to the pace of the rebuilding.[50] However, such considerations are of little interest to Nehemiah, who prefers to note that the news of the wall's completion—and perhaps the speed of it—strikes the very fear in his enemies' hearts (6:16) that they had been hoping to induce in him. Instead of his reputation being tarnished by a tactical retreat (6:13), Nehemiah reports that it is his enemies' own self-confidence that dropped perceptibly. Interestingly, on Nehemiah's view, this psychological setback for his opponents arose not as a result of their perception of the increased security of the community or the self-confidence derived from such an accomplishment—but rather their growing awareness that "this work had been done with the help of *our God*" (6:16), an appellation that serves to reinforce Nehemiah's insistent claim on God's identification with his community, but also his radical exclusion of his opponents in theological terms.

In keeping with the tenor of the chapter, Nehemiah concludes it in 6:17–19 by offering further evidence of the complexity of the opposition he faced. Having included Tobiah in his earlier accusations (6:1, 12, 14), Nehemiah notes that the latter's unhelpful influence was facilitated by his close connections to those within the community who were otherwise supportive of the project (cf. Meshullam in 3:4, 30). It is perhaps fitting that Nehemiah should conclude a chapter that begins with threatening messages (6:2, 4, 5) with a note that Tobiah too was guilty of not merely sending letters to the nobles of Judah (6:17) but of doing so "to intimidate me" (לְיָרְאֵנִי/ləyārʾēnî; 6:19).

Summary of Nehemiah 6

If the "fear of Yhwh" features prominently in Nehemiah's report of the debt episode in Neh 5, in this chapter we see the concern to be rather the "fear of

---

50. See Williamson, *Ezra, Nehemiah*, 260, for further discussion and comparable wall-building elsewhere in the ancient world.

man." Nehemiah previously acknowledged his own fear in the presence of the king (2:2) and exhorted the community to not fear those ranged against them (4:14), but in Neh 6 he feels the full force of his opponents' efforts to intimidate him into inactivity. The prominence of "false" prophets and prophecies (6:1–14) is noteworthy and reflects concerns about precisely this phenomenon in Deut 18:21–22. Unsurprisingly such anxieties also surface in the prophetic traditions found in, for instance, the book of Ezekiel, where the striking denunciation of those who prophesy "lies" resonates with Deuteronomy's denial that false prophecy comes from God (13:6–7) and insistence that its lack of fulfillment proves its falseness (13:6). Yet, Ezekiel is not the only prophet within the tradition to rail against others whom he sees to be false. Indeed, it is again Jeremiah and his encounter with Hananiah son of Azzur (Jer 28) that offers not only a comparable awareness of Deut 18, but also a narrative in which (a) false prophecy is confronted, (b) the Deuteronomic fulfillment criteria of "time will tell" is clearly and explicitly in view, (c) the prophecy is preemptively unmasked as false by other means, and (d) the Deuteronomic exhortation to resist the intimidation of the "false prophet/prophecy" is clearly demonstrated.[51]

Yet if Nehemiah's account here reflects further awareness of Jeremiah's ministry and the latter's own engagement with false prophecy,[52] it also bespeaks an approach that is typical of Nehemiah. Already in the second chapter, Nehemiah's fear (2:2) of the king's response to his show of sadness and his request regarding Jerusalem prompts a prayer (2:4). Here, too, when Nehemiah faces a temptation to fear (6:9), we find another prayer: that God would strengthen his hands. Evidence of such divine strengthening is furnished not only by Nehemiah's successful avoidance of the temple but also by the concluding of the building work—an achievement that Nehemiah explicitly reports as being accomplished by means of the help of "our God" (6:16). While Nehemiah will go on in Neh 7 to outline the practical consequences of the wall's completion for the community, the focus in 6:16 is rather on the theological implications for their opponents, whose recognition of the divine support enjoyed by the community induces fear in them. While it is tempting (and not entirely impossible) to see the object of this fear as YHWH, the possibility that the enemies may now

---

51. See Shepherd, "Is the Governor Also among the Prophets?"

52. Hossfeld and Meyer, *Prophet gegen Prophet*, 155–56, also highlight the awareness of and resistance to prophetic intimidation found in Deut 18:21–22 and Neh 6 and recognize the resonance of the latter with the Hananiah episode in Jer 27–28. While their suggestion that the fear to be resisted was being induced by postexilic prophets parroting the doomsday prophecies of the past is not impossible, it goes beyond the evidence of Deut 18:21–22 and could only be in the background in Neh 6, where the content of the false prophecies (including the allegations of Nehemiah's royal ambitions) is focused first and foremost on inducing fear in Nehemiah.

fear the golah community itself is far from unlikely if Nehemiah's awareness of Deuteronomy extends to passages such as 28:10: "All the peoples of the earth shall see that you are called by the name of Yhwh, and they shall be afraid of you" (NRSV).

Nehemiah 7

That Nehemiah's memoir continues into Neh 7 is confirmed by the continuity of subject and of first-person narration up to 7:5. After Nehemiah's reporting of the organization of operations within the newly completed fortifications, the reader is offered in the remainder of this chapter a list that is highly similar, yet not entirely identical, to the one encountered at Ezra 2. For various reasons, some of which have already been mentioned (see commentary on Ezra 2), it appears as if the list was included first here in Nehemiah before it (or one very like it) was subsequently introduced into Ezra by an editor.

7:1-4 Given their appearance in 7:45, it is most probable that the gatekeepers (7:1) mentioned by Nehemiah were normally associated with the temple and here stationed along with the other cultic guilds (singers and Levites) on a temporary watch. Perhaps more permanent is Nehemiah's appointment of his own brother, Hanani, who having lamented Jerusalem's ruined walls (1:2-3), now takes charge of the city around which they have been rebuilt (7:2a). Also mentioned by Nehemiah is the elevation of a certain Hananiah as commander of the citadel, though not on the basis of kinship nor even his particular military experience or expertise. Though the latter may well be presumed, Nehemiah makes a point of explaining Hananiah's appointment first and foremost on account of his virtuous character and his "fear[ing] God more than many." Having castigated some for lacking such a trait (5:9) and reaffirmed his own fear of God (5:15), it is perhaps understandable that Nehemiah would appoint someone who shares a quality that he himself so prizes.[53]

Whether uttered by Hananiah or Nehemiah himself,[54] the instructions found in 7:3 make most sense if they are understood as warning against the opening of the gates not "until" (NRSV) but rather "while" the sun is hot. That this is most probable is confirmed by ancient testimony that city gates were often vulnerable in the heat of the day, at which time potentially lethargic guards

---

53. For an analysis of these appointments in relation to Nehemiah's leadership see the chapter "Leadership and Ezra-Nehemiah."

54. "I said" follows the Qere (i.e., the vocalization of the Hebrew consonants found in the margin of the Masoretic Text).

should thus be encouraged to "shut and bar the doors" (7:3).[55] The further precaution of enlisting the general populace at particular strategic points and near their own houses—in whose defense they might be expected to be especially energetic—is a further measure of the continuing anxieties regarding the defense of the city and leads understandably to Nehemiah's subsequent observation that the city's people were few and its houses rather too far between (7:4).[56]

7:5 While, as we will see, Neh 11 will deal more directly and explicitly with the repopulation of the city, the gathering of the people by Nehemiah for the purposes of a census (7:5) is not unintelligible as a preparatory step to this repopulation. Thus it may well be that the list that follows (7:6–73a) did belong properly to the Nehemiah memoir.[57] In the present form of the book, in which the census list is immediately followed by the corporate reading of Torah (Neh 8), Nehemiah's reflection that God had "put it into my mind" (lit., "heart," לֵב/ *lēb*; so also 2:12) now appears as the divine impetus to a covenantal convocation rather than the city's repopulation. Indeed, it is syntactically possible (and not out of keeping with Nehemiah's character) that he means to attribute his archival explorations (7:5) and indeed the very discovery of the list itself to this same divine prompt.[58]

7:6–73 See commentary on Ezra 2.

Summary of Nehemiah 7

It is suggested somewhat speculatively that the production of a list totaling 42,360 (7:66) and divisible by twelve may reflect a type of realized eschatology in which the redeemed community's names are written in the book of Yhwh (Mal 3:16).[59] While such a supposition seems improbable, the theological significance of the list—especially where it appears here in Nehemiah—should not be underestimated. As it does in Ezra 2, the list—with its ancestral/genealogical cast—establishes the link between the returned exiles and their ancient ancestors of the preexilic past, who had historic rights and recognizable claims to the land to which they were returning. Moreover, in its context here in Neh 7, and

---

55. For examples of this vulnerability in antiquity, see Driver, "Forgotten Hebrew Idioms," 4.
56. The complete absence of houses (suggested by the NRSV) is unintelligible in light of 7:3 and is not required by the appearance of אֵין/*'ên*, which may simply mean "not sufficient" (7:4). Alternatively, and less probably, the reference in 7:4 may be to the absence of "houses" in the genealogical/dynastic sense.
57. Williamson, *Ezra, Nehemiah*, 269.
58. Ibid., 271.
59. Gunneweg, "Zur Interpretation der Bücher Esra-Nehemia."

with one eye on Neh 11, the list links the anticipated repopulation of Jerusalem with the more recent exodus of exiles from Babylon, which began with Zerubbabel back at the beginning of Ezra. Indeed, in its rehearsal of the settlement of the returnees in their towns (Neh 7:73), the chapter not only reminds the reader of the recent sacrifices of those who returned to complete the wall, but also the sacrifices that will be required when Jerusalem is to be repopulated on a permanent basis (Neh 11). Nehemiah's insistence that his archival exploration was not merely prompted by God, but facilitated by him, suggests that issues of continuity and identity with a remembered past and the practices of remembering themselves are—or at least may be—more than merely pragmatic ones. Instead it suggests that such recollection for the purposes of re-creation may be inspired and sustained by the God whose law will be heard anew in the very next chapter.

Nehemiah 8

With the narrative of repopulation in Neh 7 only resuming again in Neh 11, Ezra's reappearance here unannounced at the beginning of Neh 8, apparently to fulfill the mandate "to teach the statutes and ordinances in Israel" (Ezra 7:10 NRSV), persuades many that Neh 8 (and probably Neh 9–10) was originally associated with the memoir tradition of Ezra, before being transposed by an editor to their present location in Nehemiah.[60] In historical terms, this may suggest that the events described in Neh 8 took place well before Nehemiah arrived, but in literary terms, Ezra's extended absence from Nehemiah's narrative up to this point gives the impression of either narrative irrelevance or ineffectiveness or perhaps merely the absence of the man himself from Yehud for a time.[61] What can more surely be concluded, however, is that the theological necessity of reading and teaching Torah prior to the eventual repopulation of Jerusalem establishes the centrality and indeed theological primacy of this episode in the editor's understanding of how the community comes to be reconstituted fully.

8:1-8 Having described in great detail the diversity and distribution of the returnees in Neh 7, the narrative moves quickly to affirm in 8:1 the unity of ("all") the people and the singularity of their purpose. Indeed, given that the books of Ezra and Nehemiah are not slow to acknowledge the leadership of their protagonists, it cannot be coincidental and should not be overlooked that

---

60. So, for instance, Williamson, *Ezra, Nehemiah*, 275–86, who suggests that Neh 8 sat originally between Ezra 8 and Ezra 9.

61. For the latter, see Fensham, *Ezra and Nehemiah*, 7.

it is the people who prompt Ezra to produce the Torah and the people who also feature most prominently in Neh 8:1–12.[62] The emphasis on the people perhaps also explains why the Torah is not merely the "law of Moses" (תּוֹרַת מֹשֶׁה/*tôrat mōšeh*) commanded by the God of Israel (as at Ezra 7:6), but also the law that "YHWH had commanded *Israel*." The inclusiveness of the gathering is further emphasized by the mention of both "men and women" (Neh 8:3) and indeed "all who could understand (מֵבִין/*mēbîn*), a notion whose inclusiveness of children in 10:28 would seem to imply the presence of the latter here too.[63] That this audience in its entirety (again, "all") was especially attentive is explicitly emphasized by the narrator—and perhaps implicitly too by the note of how long Ezra read (six hours).

In describing parenthetically how this public reading was managed (8:4–7), the narrator emphasizes the pulpit or platform from which the Torah was proclaimed, noting that it was prepared for the purpose and afforded Ezra an elevated position (8:5). While audibility may have been one advantage of such a position, the emphasis in the narrative is rather on the ceremonial implications of the elevation of Ezra and the others. The specific significance of the individuals named with Ezra eludes us, but their physical presence with him is a first hint that this will be a reading not merely *for* the people but also *by* the people—and by laypeople no less.[64] Interestingly, Ezra's physical prominence facilitates the spectacle not of Scripture itself, but of the interpretation of Scripture—or at least the commencement of it (cf. the mention of the opening of the book/scroll in 8:5). Beyond these obvious practical advantages, the physical elevation of the act of interpretation (rather than the interpreter per se) fits neatly with the narrator's note of the audience's response—their rising en masse ("all" again; 8:5) signaling their solidarity with Ezra and the others in this act of reading (cf. 9:3). This solidarity with Ezra finds further expression when "all" the people answered "Amen, Amen" in response to Ezra's blessing (8:6) of YHWH[65]—an act that serves to qualify, though perhaps not all together eliminate, the impression of the veneration of the Torah itself.

That the Torah will be not merely venerated but taught becomes clear as the narrative shifts its attention from liturgy to pedagogy in 8:7–8. In light

---

62. Eskenazi, *In an Age of Prose*, 96–99. The people's initiative may well be highlighted here to emphasize the community's recognition of Ezra's authority (see the chapter "Leadership and Ezra-Nehemiah").

63. This inclusiveness is found also in Ezra 10:1. The teaching of the law to the younger generation is famously exhorted in Deut 6:7.

64. Assuming the lay status of those assembled with Ezra; see Blenkinsopp, *Ezra-Nehemiah*, 287.

65. Here worship apparently precedes the reading of Torah, whereas in Neh 9:3 it follows from it.

of the involvement of Levites later in the passage (8:9, 11, 13) and the specific identification of some here as Levites elsewhere (e.g., Jeshua, Bani, and others in 9:4–5), it seems likely that Levites were employed to assist the crowds in understanding what they heard, presumably by circulating among them in some fashion.[66] The technique of the "tutors" includes reading the text themselves, but extends also to some type of interpretation. Despite the insistence of later rabbinic witnesses (Babylonian Talmud, tractate *Megillah* 3a), the Hebrew term מְפֹרָשׁ/*məpōrāš* ("with interpretation"; 8:8) is unlikely to reflect the genesis of the "targumic" translations known from later Jewish tradition,[67] yet the hermeneutical impulse seen in these much later translations is unlikely to be entirely discontinuous from the emphasis seen here in Nehemiah (שׂוֹם שֶׂכֶל/*śôm śekel*, "giving insight" or "the sense") or indeed in Deut 1:5, where Moses does not merely read, but expounds or "explains" (בֵּאֵר/*bē'ēr*) the law. Given that those gathered evidently have the capacity to understand (Neh 8:3), it is unclear why they need further assistance in order to understand (8:8), especially when this is not required in other "readings" of the law (cf. Shaphan in 2 Kgs 22:8–9). Nevertheless, the interpretive limitations of the people are assumed rather than emphasized, and the narrative's greater interest is in affirming the hermeneutical legacy of the Levites, whose skills in the teaching of the law prior to the exile are acknowledged in 2 Chr 17:7–9. The insistence that the teaching of Torah too is being done now, as it was then, is yet another confirmation of the importance of continuity with the past.

8:9–12 As in Ezra 10, the emotional response of the gathering expresses itself in "weeping," a visible sign of mourning and emotional distress comparable (if not identical) to that found in 2 Kgs 22:11, where Josiah is convicted by the hearing of the law, as seems to be the case here. While such a report reaffirms both the power of the law and the tenderheartedness of the people, the admonitions first in Neh 8:9 and then twice in 8:10–11 ("do not be grieved") suggest a popular response quite out of keeping with the spirit that the leaders wished to cultivate on a day that was "holy" (three times in 8:9–11). The choice of the first day of the seventh month, announced already in 8:2, was evidently far from accidental, with Rosh Hashanah, the first day of the New Year, being a traditional day of "holy gathering" (Lev 23:24). While Levitical legislation (cf. also Num 29:2–6) notes the sacrificial requirements of the day, the encouragement here to "eat the fat and drink sweet wine and send portions" (Neh 8:10

---

66. It is difficult to be certain whether the omission of "and" before the Levites in the version of this verse in 1 Esdras 9:48 reflects the original text or suspicion of it.

67. For discussion of the improbability of this suggestion, see Van der Kooij, "Nehemiah 8:8."

NRSV) and the people's willingness to do so and "make great rejoicing" (8:12) finds its closest parallel in the conclusion of Esth 9:19–22. There too the specific encouragement to festal celebration (9:19) results in not merely consumption but also communal generosity/charity[68]—and in Esther, as here, the narrative context is one of grief giving way to joy. It is clearly not incidental to the narrator that joy has arisen specifically because the gathered crowd "understood the words that were declared to them" (Neh 8:12 NRSV). Perhaps it is the words of Nehemiah and the Levites (8:9–11) that persuaded them to turn their tears into laughter. If, as seems more likely, "the words" (דְּבָרִים/*dəbārîm*) that give rise to joy are to be taken as those of Torah (דִּבְרֵי הַתּוֹרָה/*dibrê hattôrâ*; 8:9) whose initial hearing caused the crowd to weep, then the narrator may be suggesting that the Levites had directed them toward other, less chastening, words of Torah more appropriate to the occasion.

8:13–18 That the community has been captivated by their engagement with Torah is suggested by the narrator's insistence that the very next day, a now more restricted group of laymen—the unnamed heads of the ancestral houses—together with the priests and Levites, take the further initiative of gathering around Ezra the scribe to "study" (לְהַשְׂכִּיל/*ləhaśkîl*; 8:13) the words of Torah. The similarity to the Levitical interpretive activities of the previous day (שׂוֹם שֶׂכֶל/*śôm śekel*, "gave the sense"; 8:8) may imply that they were now seeking to explicate the fresh relevance of the Torah in the community's own context, because the study on this second day leads to both textual encounter (8:14–15) and interpretive enactment (8:16–18). As at the outset of the chapter (8:1), emphasis is laid in 8:14 upon the law as divinely "commanded" and mediated by Moses, which in turn reaffirms the continuity of the community's interest with the traditions and practice of the past. References to the collecting of foliage of various sorts (e.g., palm) and the building of booths strongly suggests that the observance of Sukkot as laid down in Lev 23:33–43 was in some form or another considered to be part of the Mosaic law. If so, then the multiplication of the types of foliage for constructing the booths reflects the kind of interpretation of that law that would continue down through the centuries.[69]

While Neh 8:18 ("they kept the festival seven days"; NRSV) implies that the community proceeded to observe Sukkot more or less immediately, 8:16's focus is on where it was observed, namely, in both private homes and public spaces in Jerusalem, including within—and perhaps in proximity to—the

---

68. Indeed, the word used for charitable "portions" (מָנוֹת/*mānôt*) here is also used this way in Esth 9:19, 22.

69. Blenkinsopp, *Ezra-Nehemiah*, 291–92. It is not impossible that the four species were carried in procession here (as in 2 Maccabees 10:7) but if they were, the narrator clearly did not feel this information to be worthy of note.

temple. The pervasiveness of the celebrations is reinforced by the reminder that Sukkot was observed by "all the assembly of those who had returned from the captivity" (8:17 NRSV)—a turn of phrase found with some variation quite frequently in Ezra (e.g., 3:8; 6:21; 8:35; 10:8, 12, 14) but not often in Nehemiah. Rather than suggesting that the celebrations had not taken place at all since the time of Joshua (Neh 8:17), it seems more reasonable to take "like this" (כֵּן/*kēn*) as indicating that Sukkot had not been celebrated since Joshua in this fashion (cf. 1 Kgs 10:20; so NIV). Precisely which of the innovations were seen by the narrator as restoring the practice of Joshua's time is unclear, but this in no way impairs the point being made: the community that entered the land after the exile is, in matters of observance, equivalent to and therefore the legitimate successor to the community that did so after the exodus. The joyful character of the observance invites comparison not only with Hezekiah's restoration of festive practice from Solomon's time, but also the returnees' earlier celebrations (שִׂמְחָה גְדוֹלָה/*śimḥâ gədôlâ*; Neh 8:12; 2 Chr 30:25), both of which are outstripped by the intensity of joy recorded here (שִׂמְחָה גְדוֹלָה מְאֹד/*śimḥâ gədôlâ məʾōd*; Neh 8:17). Whether the daily reading of Torah throughout the festal week points toward the same practice associated with the year of release (Deut 31:10–13) or indicates an innovation on Ezra's part, the final verse captures neatly the dynamics of the chapter as a whole. On one hand, the "he" (singular) who is noted as reading (Neh 8:18) can only be Ezra, whose six-hour recitation of Torah was the starting point from which all else flowed. On the other hand, the mention of the now solemn assembly ("they") with which the observance concludes reflects the fundamental part played by the people themselves in responding to the Torah read by Ezra, but given by God.

Summary of Nehemiah 8

If the heart of the book of Nehemiah is Neh 8, then it is clear that Torah sits at the heart of both chapter and book. That Torah is for all the returnees (8:1, 2, 3, 5, 6, 9, etc.) is unsurprising given the emphasis on the unity of the golah community and those joined to it, seen in the narrative already. Nor is it unexpected that the Torah is presented in this chapter as an inheritance, one more strand in the cord that binds those returning from exile with both the ancestors (e.g., Joshua) and the God of the exodus whose greatness (8:6) is as visible now as it was then and not least in the giving of the eternal law (8:1, 14). This law is evidently meant to be revered but, more importantly, to be read. Yet according to the narrative, reading alone is apparently insufficient for the people at large, whose understanding of the law depends on interpretive assistance.

Such intervention undoubtedly accounts for the fact—ignored by the narrative, but inevitably implied by it—that Torah is itself evolving despite its apparent immutability. This evolution of Torah must be seen in turn to be a corollary of the need for the law to be observed in circumstances that themselves are ever changing—a point that the present chapter illustrates. At a visceral level, this purchase of the law on the life of the people, this experience of fulfilling the divine will that the Torah be heard and obeyed, unites the people in joy (8:10, 12, 17). But at a practical level, it also encourages the community toward a material generosity (8:10, 12) that stands in stark contrast to the grasping greed that had riven the community during the time of the debt-slavery incident (Neh 5).

Nehemiah 9

That Neh 9 has been relocated here from its original (or at least prior) setting in Ezra may be suggested not only by the similarity of the penitential tone and common notion of separation found here and in Ezra 9–10, but also by the seeming incongruity of mourning/penitence hard on the heels of rejoicing. Both of these issues will be taken up below, with the former being seen to carry more weight than the latter. The prayer that dominates Neh 9 draws extensively but also selectively on historiographical traditions found in the Pentateuch and beyond, not all of which, however, it will be possible to note.[70]

9:1–5 The narrator's mention of the "twenty-fourth day of this month" clearly implies that the characteristic acts of mourning performed by the reassembled people of Israel take place only one day after the joyful conclusion of Sukkot (Neh 8). While the later Jewish liturgical sequence of New Year followed by the Day of Atonement is not in evidence here, its survival in normative Judaism suggests that the sequence of celebration followed by self-reflection and penitence is not itself implausible, even if such a transition over the course of the seventh month in modern Jewish observance is rather more gentle than the seemingly abrupt change of "emotional" tone seen here. As in Ezra 10, the assembled people here manifest visible signs of mourning, and the Israelites separate themselves from those described as "foreign." While it is suggested that the Israelites' separation here is of a quite different sort from that recounted in Ezra—not from foreign women, but from all foreigners—the reading of Neh 9 with Neh 10 where marital separation is very much in view tends to encourage the interpretation of the intervention here in similar terms, whether or not it always had this meaning. As in Neh 8, an initial summary (9:2) is here followed

---

70. For a helpful and detailed analysis of these traditions, see Boda, *Praying the Tradition*.

by elaboration of the event (9:3) in which the reading of the law, now undertaken by the people themselves untutored, not only occupies the same period of time (six hours; 9:3) but also produces a similarly visceral, remorseful response. That their confession (9:3) is intimately bound up with their "worship" (i.e., the physical acknowledgment of the divine) accords with the narrator's emphasis on Yhwh as specifically "their" God (twice in 9:3). The Levites, released from pedagogical duties by the people's own engagement with Torah, are now elevated as Ezra was, not on a platform but on eponymous stairs, from which vantage point they cry out to one who is also "their" God (9:4). The first words they cry out ("stand up and bless Yhwh, your God") are addressed not to God, but to the people, and are thus merely preparatory to the Levites' own prayer to God that begins in 9:5b.

Heeding their own exhortation in the first half of the verse, the Levites begin their prayer with "blessed be your glorious name" (9:5b). That this name is invoked at the beginning of both the following two verses suggests that the assigning of the prayer to Ezra (9:6a: "And Ezra said"; cf. Septuagint and RSV/NRSV) is neither necessary nor probable. Indeed, it is more than likely that the prayer that commences in 9:6 predates the return of Ezra, though precisely how early in the postexilic period it is likely to have been written is impossible to determine.[71]

9:6-8 While the prayer in Neh 9 (including especially its historical scope) has most in common with Ps 106, it is only Ps 136 that begins as this prayer does with a eulogizing of God as creator of heaven and earth before proceeding with a full historical recital. While Ps 136 similarly notes the creation of sun and moon (cf. Gen 1), the heavenly hosts of Neh 9:6 are not only created by God, but worship him as well (cf. Ps 148:1-6). The repetition of "you are Yhwh" from Neh 9:6 invites the hearer to see the election of Abram too as an act of creation, and indeed throughout these verses, the subject, the active agent, is overwhelmingly God, who first chooses, brings out, and gives a new name to Abraham (9:7) and then finds him faithful and makes a covenant with him (9:8). While these verses disclose an awareness of traditions very like (but not identical) to Gen 15 and Gen 17, it is not the promise of progeny, but land—promised to one who had also come from Mesopotamia—that prompts the proleptic acknowledgment of its fulfillment and the expression of adoration ("you are righteous").

9:9-11 No less resonant for returning exiles was the exodus tradition, reduced here to God's climactic intervention against the Egyptian oppressors at the Sea (Exod 14-15). The repeated invocation of "our ancestors" (אֲבֹתֵינוּ/

---

71. Based on his thorough traditio-historical study of the prayer, Boda, ibid., 197, plausibly favors a date shortly before the ministries of Haggai and Zechariah.

'ăbōtênû; Neh 9:9–10) strengthens the identification of the returned exiles' own distress (9:9) and insolent treatment (9:10) with that of their ancient forebears, even as the name that God made for himself in those days remains an encouragement "to this day."

9:12–15 The recital of God's gracious agency on behalf of Israel continues into the wilderness wanderings, with the tradition of the pillar (9:12) and the giving of Torah at Sinai (9:13) invoked in terms of divine movement/presence ("you led" in 9:12; "you came down" in 9:13) and the gift of divine guidance ("the way they should go" in 9:12). Given the significance of Torah (suggested by Neh 8–9), it is hardly surprising that the value of the divine law as guidance is especially affirmed ("right," "true," "good" in 9:13), nor is an emphasis on the Sabbath commandment (9:14) unexpected given its prominence elsewhere in the book of Nehemiah (Neh 10 and Neh 13) and the postexilic period generally. The theme of divine gift (וַתִּתֵּן/*wattittēn*, "and you gave;" 9:13) is echoed in the reference to the giving (נָתַתָּה/*nātattâ*; 9:15) not only of the manna (Num 11) and the water from the rock (Num 20) but most importantly the land.

9:16–22 The arrival of the disjunction "but they, our ancestors"[72] sounds the note of rebellion characteristic of historical recitals within the penitential prayer tradition (Ps 106:13). The Israelites' emulation of the Egyptians' hubris (Neh 9:10) is accompanied by disobedience of the commandments (9:16) though the Israelites' initial refusal to enter into the land is not specifically mentioned. The persistent grace of Israel's God is reiterated in phrases drawn from and otherwise reminiscent of passages like Exod 34:6, before the prayer belatedly invokes that archetypal sin of the wilderness period, the idolatry of the calf (Neh 9:18). Yet such sin is juxtaposed with the mention again of God's provision of the pillar (9:19), the manna and water (9:20), as well as "the good spirit to instruct them" (cf. Ps 143:10, where "good spirit" is also related to instruction). The recapitulation of divine mercy in the wilderness is drawn to a close by references to Deut 8:4 ("clothes did not wear out and their feet did not swell") and gifts of territory (Heshbon and Bashan) in the Transjordan (Num 21)—gifts that in turn anticipate, both in the Pentateuch and in this prayer, the Israelites' entrance into and possession of the land (Neh 9:23–25).

9:23–25 While the prayer does now also invoke the divine promise of progeny (cf. Deut 1:8), the focus is again the gift of the land (Neh 9:23b–24a) and especially the defeat of its inhabitants, including the notion that the ancestors could do with them "as they pleased." This sentiment's emphasis on untrammeled license (cf. Esth 9:5 and Neh 9:37) may well reflect the aspirations of the

---

72. Rather than "they [and] our ancestors," which fails to understand the conjunction as explicative.

returnees more closely than the nuanced presentation found in Deuteronomy and Joshua. Descriptions of the land and its produce, also inspired by Deuteronomy (cf. 3:5), form the climax of the account that concludes with a note of the people's delight in the goodness of the divine giver (Neh 9:25).[73]

9:26-31 For the second time (cf. 9:16), a succession of blessings is interrupted by rebellion characterized especially by the rejection of Torah (so already 9:16) but now also by the killing of "your prophets," a tradition found relatively late in the historical consciousness (Jer 26:20-23; 1 Kgs 18-19). In Neh 9:27, the prayer presents the spiraling cycle of disobedience known from Judg 2 (disobedience, deliverance into hands of enemies, cry for mercy, and divine deliverance [by "saviors"; Neh 9:27]) and does so again in 9:28, noting for good measure that "many times you rescued them according to your mercies" (NRSV). A second invocation of the law and the people's disobedience of "your ordinances, by which a person shall live" (9:29) is again followed by a reminder of the rejection of "your prophets" inspired by "your spirit" (cf. 9:20). The prayer notes finally the Israelites' inevitable deliverance into the hands of not merely "enemies" but the "peoples of the lands" (עַמֵּי הָאֲרָצֹת/ʿammê hāʾărāṣōt)—a phrase whose application to those outside the golah community (Ezra 9:1, 2, 11; Neh 10:28) will have confirmed the contemporary relevance of the lessons of the past.[74] While the historical recital ends on a note of divine blessing despite previous rebellion, the transition to petition proper (9:32) is signaled by the prayer's note that the most recent mercy falls short of full redemption ("did not make an end of them"; 9:31 NRSV) and especially by the movement from historical reflection to present praise: "you are a gracious and merciful God" (9:31).

9:32-38 The move from past reflection to present exhortation is signaled by the provision of "now" and by the shift from "them" (i.e., our ancestors) to "us" in 9:32. Indeed, it is not incidental that the people (listed sequentially and inclusively: "all")[75] whose sufferings God is encouraged to remember in 9:32 are both "our ancestors" and "your people" given that "our God" is invoked as not only powerful but faithful to his covenant (9:32). The juxtaposing of this divine fidelity with the faithlessness of these same people in neglecting the law and ignoring (prophetic) "warnings" is acknowledged as full justification for "all that has come upon us" (9:34). If the prayer's owning of the past lapses briefly into further lament of ancestral ungratefulness ("they did not serve you" in 9:35), the continuing abundance of the divine generosity of the past ("great goodness"

---

73. While "becoming fat" in Deut 32:15 must be negative, the context here requires it to be interpreted positively, contra Clines, *Ezra, Nehemiah, Esther*, 196.

74. As suggested by Blenkinsopp, *Ezra-Nehemiah*, 306.

75. The inclusion of the "prophets" among the guilty is perhaps slightly curious given that prophets have largely been seen as "sinned against" in the preceding historical narrative.

in 9:35; "good gifts" in 9:36) down to the present day ("rich yield"; 9:37) makes the community's current status as "slaves" in a land that used to be their own (9:35) all the more painful ("in great distress" in 9:37). The voice of the selected Levites on behalf of the people, heard in the concluding verses of the prayer in Neh 9, is continued into 9:38, whose introduction "therefore" (lit., "with/in all this" בְּכָל־זֹאת/bǝkol-zōʾt) establishes an indissoluble link with what has gone before (Neh 8).[76] Before the wider community itself expresses its recommitment to the covenant obligations, the civic and religious leaders, as authorized representatives of the community, engage in the appropriate confirmation ritual. Ezra's name may be reflected in "Azariah" or omitted as unnecessary given his authorship of the agreement.

Summary of Nehemiah 9

The God on view in Neh 9 and especially in the prayer at its heart is one who not only creates the world, but also creates and chooses a people. The God of the prayer of Neh 9 binds himself to this people by means of a covenant whose generosity is expressed in the gifts of progeny, but especially promised land— land whose richness and goodness reflect the full extent of God's generous spirit. Yet the covenant also discloses a God of expectations, expressed in his law, which is seen to be no less good, right, and true. Indeed, God's revelation of himself is not limited to the law, but finds expression in the deployment of his equally "good" Spirit by which he sends warnings through his prophets. If the presence of these prophets and the sheer length of the history recited in Neh 9 is proof of the patience of God, his impatience with his people's rebellion is a corollary of his justice that, the prayer acknowledges, rightly demands that the sins of the people be punished in some way.

At the same time and indeed interwoven with the evidence of God's justice, the prayer furnishes still more evidence of God's mercy—a mercy sufficiently great to persuade him to relent and redeem not only in times past, but also (it is hoped) in the present circumstances. This God's expectation of his people, as attested by Neh 9 at least, is that they should, first and foremost, remember. While both the preparation for the prayer and the prayer itself obviously encourage a remembering of the ethical and cultic obligations of Scripture, the form of this prayer itself is (unlike Ezra 9) focused instead on the

---

76. As Blenkinsopp, *Ezra-Nehemiah*, 312, notes, 1QS i–ii suggests that at Qumran the Levites too recited the confession and pronounced the curses within the covenant-renewal ceremony.

remembering of the stories of Scripture.[77] In encouraging reflection on these narratives, the prayer is an invitation to reflect on divine mercies despite past infidelities as well as a call to own the latter in the hope of securing the former. Situated as it is hard on the heels of the public engagement with Torah in Neh 8, with which it is linked by its prologue (9:1–5), the prayer offers an invitation to not merely study and obey Torah, but to pray it as well.

Nehemiah 10

The origins of Neh 10 and its relationship to the chapters that precede it and the memoirs of Ezra are debated, without a consensus emerging. That the commitments of the people in Neh 10 correspond closely to their failings in Neh 13 and might easily be imagined as following them (rather than preceding them) historically and perhaps in some earlier narrative ordering can hardly be gainsaid. Nevertheless, it will be clear from the account given below that Neh 10's allusions to Sabbath (10:31, 33; 9:14) and separation (10:28, 30; 9:2) make its inclusion here at least intelligible, if not necessarily original.

10:1–27 The list of priests who apparently signed this covenant is almost identical to the one found in 12:1–7, 12–21 and may indicate the names of priestly families or courses. Ezra may thus have been included in Azariah (10:2).[78] Most of the Levites listed here (Jeshua, Binnui, Kadmiel, Hodiah, Kelita, Pelaiah, Hanan, Sherebiah; 10:9–12) were noted in connection with the reading of the law in 8:7, while others like Shebaniah appear in connection with the prayer of penitence (9:5). The list of laypeople closely resembles the lists in Ezra 2 and Neh 7. While the absence here of the leading names in these lists (Shephatiah, Arah, and Zaccai) is mysterious, the inclusion of new names (Neh 10:20–27) is perfectly understandable as existing family groupings grew and multiplied.

10:28–29 The listing of the cultic guilds (Levites, gatekeepers, singers, etc.) reflects the prominence and importance of these groups, while the emphasis on the agreement's wide subscription ("the rest of the people," "all," "wives, sons, daughters, and all who have knowledge") is accompanied by the predictable qualification: "who have separated themselves." That this differentiation is similar in kind to that mentioned in the previous chapter is suggested by the reuse here of the verb "to separate" (בדל/*bdl*; cf. Ezra 6:21; 9:1), with the "foreigners"

---

77. See Boda, *Praying the Tradition*, 30–87, who helpfully discusses Dan 9 in light of other instances of penitential prayer.
78. So Clines, *Ezra, Nehemiah, Esther*, 200–201.

Nehemiah 10

of that passage here referred to as "peoples of the lands"—a phrase that appears in the final stanzas of the prayer at the end of the previous chapter (Neh 9:30). While those who have been left behind are acknowledged, it is rather the renewed adherence to the law of God (10:28) that is unpacked at greater length and in quite Deuteronomic terms (10:29): the peoples' commitment—bound by a "curse" (cf. Deut 29:12–21)—is "to walk," "to observe," and "to do" not merely the "law," but "all the commandments," "ordinances," and "statutes" of a law that is mediated by Moses but given by YHWH.

10:30 Given the prominence of the theme of separation in the book as a whole (Ezra 9; Neh 9:2) and the aversion for intermarriage (Ezra 9), it is hardly surprising that this concern heads the list of covenant commitments. While some groups (cf. Neh 13:23: Ashdod, Ammon, Moab) may have been more prominently associated with the practice than others, the generic terminology of the "peoples of the lands" here resonates with usage in this chapter and Neh 9 and gives the impression of a wider proscription akin to Ezra 9. Here, as there (Ezra 9:2; Neh 13:26), the giving of both sons and daughters to those outside the community reflects the abiding suspicion of intermarriage as the inevitable prelude to religious infidelity. While the actual fate of any existing marriages with proscribed partners is unclear, the failure to mention their dissolution here gives the impression at least of a more lenient line than was taken in Ezra 9–10.

10:31 Here again, the commitment relating to Sabbath observance is anticipated in its present context by the mention of Sabbath in the penitential prayer of the preceding chapter (9:14). While the regulation of the Sabbath in the Torah did not specifically include commerce in its prohibition of work, Amos 8:5 suggests that selling on the Sabbath had already been restricted before the exile, and the extension of the proscription to buying here is an illustration of the progressive regulation of the Sabbath that had thus begun long before the return from exile and would continue long after it. That this commitment is made specifically in relation to again the "peoples of the land" may well have answered a legitimate query regarding the application of the law, but reflects in any case the consuming interest in maintaining the boundaries of identity and community.[79] This same interest will presumably also lie behind the further commitment that the seventh year should be both a year for leaving fields fallow and for the forgiving of debts. While the coinciding of such practices would seem to be implied by legislation that specifies that both be observed in the "seventh year" (Exod 23:10–11; Deut 15:1–18), if the novelty here is to make this

---

79. For an accessible discussion of the evolution of Sabbath in ancient Judaism, see McKay, *Sabbath and Synagogue*.

requirement of coincidence explicit,[80] then perhaps inspiration has been drawn from the practice of Jubilee in which both practices are explicitly incorporated (Lev 25). In any case, while this commitment lacks a correspondence in Neh 13, it clearly resonates with the concerns that gave rise to the debt crisis (Neh 5) and reflects something of the generosity seen in the observance of Sukkot (Neh 8).

10:32–33 While seen as supplementary (cf. "also") to their covenantal obligations, the community's commitment to support the temple resumes the interest in the cult that was seen especially in the early chapters of Ezra, but rarely in Nehemiah up to this point (though cf. Neh 13:30). Whether early imperial financial support (Ezra 6:9; 7:21) had subsequently waned or simply proved insufficient, the voluntary contributions of the community had always been encouraged and noted (1:4, 6; 2:69). Even if it was a one-off contribution (cf. Exodus and Joash's levy in 2 Chr 24:4–14), and all the more if it was a regular commitment akin to the later temple tax (Matt 17:24), such a voluntary subscription represented a significant step forward, both as a concrete expression of solidarity and as a tangible investment in the institution of the temple and the cultic establishment. The full extent of this investment and the scale of the cult is well illustrated by the range of activities to be supported (Neh 10:33) for the sake of "our" God (10:32–33).

10:34–39 The continuing reiteration of the community's relationship with "our God" (twice in 10:34) prompts the volunteering of wood for the altar—apparently in keeping with some law ("as it is written") now unknown but surely necessitated by the requirement to keep the altar alight (Lev 6:8–13). Considering the presumed dearth of wood in the area, this would have been provided at some cost, which perhaps explains why Nehemiah feels obliged to mention his part in securing this commitment (Neh 13:31).

The people's support of the temple cult is now pledged more specifically in terms of the gifts in kind required in general by the law. The gift of firstfruits (deconsecrated to allow for use of the rest) was mandated (e.g., Exod 23:19), but the further specification of "*all* the fruit of *every* tree" appears to be an example of rigorist extension of the law to cover additional cases. The firstborn males of family and flock also are required (and may presumably be redeemed; cf. 34:19–20) while only the clean animals will be offered to the priests (Neh 10:36). Nehemiah 10:37 completes the list with the mention of the first portions of foods produced, but not otherwise covered, with the repetition of the "fruit of every tree" justified now by that which it produces—"wine and oil." While the destination of all gifts to this point is specified as the temple under the ju-

---

80. Presumably at some considerable economic cost; see Blenkinsopp, *Ezra-Nehemiah*, 316; and Clines, *Ezra, Nehemiah, Esther*, 206.

risdiction of the priests, in 10:37b, the pledge now points toward the previously unknown and perhaps novel contribution of the Levites in collecting tithes outside Jerusalem. Even here, however, a priest is present, presumably to ensure that priestly interests are protected en route to their final destination (10:38). The final commitment of 10:39 ("we will not neglect [עזב/'zb] the house of our God") while certainly resonant with Nehemiah's accusatory question in 13:11 (also עזב/'zb), serves to sum up the pledge of support for the temple articulated toward the end of this chapter (10:32–39) and the theological motivation for offering it (i.e., "our God").

Summary of Nehemiah 10

While the account of Nehemiah's contribution to the restoration of Jerusalem may be seen to climax in the repopulated Jerusalem's celebration of its reconstituted walls (Neh 12), Neh 10 may reasonably claim to represent a kind of culmination of the ministries of Zerubbabel, Ezra, and Nehemiah. The commitment of the community here is often compared with that secured by Ezra in Ezra 9–10, not least because of the common interest in the thorny issue of intermarriage and the shared emphasis on the community's ready acknowledgement of the problem and commitment to take steps to remedy it. Yet to limit our appreciation of Neh 10 in this way is to seriously underestimate the ways in which its concerns extend well beyond that of Ezra 9–10. Certainly, Ezra's addressing of intermarriage in the interests of "separating" is repeated in Neh 10, but the use of בדל/bdl here to indicate a separation "from the peoples of the lands to adhere to the law of God" (10:28) hints at a broader differentiation from those who did not share this community's convictions. That the basis for this more general cultural differentiation is adherence to "the law of God"—including but not limited to its received wisdom on intermarriage—is made clear by the broader reference to separation (בדל/bdl) already in 9:2, where it follows the Torah study at Sukkot and is intimately related to the petitionary prayer that also emerges out of the reading of Scripture. Given the current position of the chapter, coming directly after first a rereading and then a praying of Scripture that is profoundly confessional in every sense of the word, it is unsurprising that the diverse practices by which the community pledges to differentiate itself are inextricably bound up with the continually evolving understanding of the "commandments of Yhwh, our Lord" (10:29).

As already discussed in the commentary on Ezra 9–10, the pledge here to avoid intermarriage (Neh 10:30) reflects the scriptural tradition's memory (Deut 7) of an apostasy of disastrous consequence and its recognition of the fundamental importance of marital relations in maintaining cultural and religious identity. While the pledge of a renewed and perhaps even rigorist Sabbath keeping (Neh 10:31) should be read in light of the praying of Scripture in Neh 9, the significance of Sabbath as a marker of identity is also reflected in its particular application to the sphere of commerce—where the community's boundaries were inevitably more visible and vulnerable. That the economic costs of the community's promised devotion are not limited to the loss of business on the Sabbath is made clear by the additional, scripturally inspired commitments to "rest" the land and forgive debts (the difficulty of which was signaled already back in Neh 5). Finally, the significant costs of the community's commitment are witnessed in their undertaking to support the temple cult with the first and the best of what they had produced, at least to the level obliged by Torah and perhaps beyond that legal minimum. In so doing, the community expresses its costly commitment to the ongoing worship of their God, which was of course the impetus for the initial wave of returnees documented in the early chapters of Ezra.

Nehemiah 11:1–12:26

The repopulating of Jerusalem was anticipated both at the beginning and the end of Neh 7, which may suggest that Neh 11 may have been found elsewhere in a version prior to (or at least different from) the one found in the Hebrew (Masoretic) text. Yet the positioning of the repopulating of Jerusalem—after the reading and penitential praying of Torah and the covenanting ceremony—has its own logic, paralleling for instance, the preface of the settling of Canaan with the Torah covenant in Deuteronomy.

11:1-3 Having recommitted themselves in the previous chapter to a giving of the firstfruits and tithes that would sustain the temple, the people now cast lots in order to "tithe" *themselves* in the repopulation of Jerusalem (11:1). That specific mention is made of the casting of lots serves to continue the echo of the settlement of the land, which was also done by lot according to Num 26:55-56 and Josh 14:2. Evidently, both there and here, the apportioning of unequal "shares" was seen to require divine impartiality (cf. Prov 16:33). This may also suggest that the relocation was seen to be a costly one, or unappealing at least, for families only recently returned to ancestral lands and keen to extract a living from them. Indeed, this costliness would seem to be confirmed by the note in Neh 11:2 that the people blessed those "who willingly offered to live in Jerusalem" (NRSV), though it may well be that this blessing was reserved for those who moved to Jerusalem without being compelled by the lot. However it has come to be, 11:3's seemingly curious supplementing of the mention of Jerusalem (11:3a) with a reference to those living in the towns of Judah "on their property" (11:3b) may be a further reflection of the ancestral settlement (Numbers/Joshua), but in any case prepares the reader for a chapter whose focus turns out to be first Jerusalem and then the towns.

11:4-9 Heading the list of those settling in Jerusalem are the laypeople, listed not by phratry or family (as in Neh 7) but by tribe and subdivision, continuing the resonance with the exodus/settlement. That the Manassehites and Ephraimites of the related list in 1 Chr 9 are passed over in the present list in favor of Judahites and Benjaminites is not surprising given the southern orientation of the account here. While the abiding interest in connecting the present with the past is reflected in the linear genealogies of Athaiah (Neh 11:4) and Maaseiah (11:5)—descended from Perez and Shelah respectively—the specific mention of Perez's descendants may well reflect the importance of their security contribution ("valiant warriors"; 11:6). That the Benjaminites were even more numerous (928) and held the top two positions in the city (11:9) may well reflect their greater proximity to Jerusalem, which was positioned within its tribal allotment.

11:10-18 The enumeration of the laypeople now gives way to the listing of the clerical ranks to be found in Jerusalem. If, as seems likely, the "officer of the house of God" (11:11) is the chief priest, then Jedaiah (11:10) is either previously unknown or an alternative spelling of Joiada (12:22), a contemporary of Nehemiah. A small cohort (128) again specified as "valiant warriors" evidently contributed to the garrison, but this number is predictably dwarfed by the 1,064 priests who did "the work of the house" (11:12). Note is also made (11:18) of those "over the outside work of the house of God," the Levites, far fewer in number, 284, with Mattaniah, a descendant of Asaph, receiving a special mention as one responsible for leading the prayer of thanksgiving (11:17).

11:19-24 Only two of the gatekeepers appearing in the corresponding passage in 1 Chr 9 are mentioned here, along with their brethren, totaling 172. If the passage in Chronicles may be taken as a reliable guide to the responsibilities implied here, then these men were responsible not only to keep "watch at the gates" of the temple (Neh 11:19) but also to act as custodians of its furniture and implements—garrisoning the temple itself by dwelling within its precincts. While the note of those dwelling in their inheritances in the towns reminds the reader that there is more to the province of Yehud than simply Jerusalem, it is as awkward here (11:20) as it is was in 11:3, for Jerusalem remains the focus in 11:21-24 and the towns do not receive attention until 11:25. Further evidence of the scale of the cult is furnished by the note of the temple servants on the Ophel (11:21) along with their overseers (unknown from elsewhere), while the oversight of the Levites by Uzzi, if he is the great-grandson of Mattaniah (11:17), may refer to a later period. Whatever the real cause for the mention of a royal warrant (11:23) for the support of the singers, the impression given of "a settled provision ... every day" for the descendants of Asaph (11:22) suggests that the musical contribution was no less important than any of the others. If Pethahiah's position (11:24) at the king's right hand in all matters concerning the people suggests the role of governor (as it could easily do), then he must have come sometime after Nehemiah (or in his absence), which may in turn explain the inclusion of so important a figure so late in the list.

11:25–36 The list of towns in which the tribes of Judah and Benjamin settled is now included, having been anticipated in 11:3 and 11:20. While Zanoah (11:30) is the only Judahite place name here to be included in Ezra 2/Neh 7, that virtually all the other place names (apart from Meconah; 11:28) are to be found in Joshua's list of Judahite settlements, and in largely the same order, strongly suggests that the tracing of the southern and western boundaries of Judah in the present list consciously mirrors the pattern of the ancient settlement of Canaan. The mention of Hinnom in summarizing the border (11:30) seems also to offer an echo of Josh 15:8 while the peculiarity of the insistence that "they camped" (וַיַּחֲנוּ/*wayyaḥănû*) may be at least partially explained by its prominence in Numbers and Joshua. The Benjaminite settlements listed serve to complete the northern circuit of settlements in the orbit of Jerusalem, while the reference in Neh 11:36 that "certain ... Levites in Judah were joined to Benjamin" (NRSV) nicely completes the picture of a Judahite-Benjaminite confederacy with the capital at its heart.

12:1–7 With the Judahite-Benjaminite settlement of Jerusalem and the region now documented, the account offers a supplementary list of clerical personnel extending across multiple generations. The list is headed by those associated with the high priesthood of Jeshua (12:1, 7) during the first return under Darius I, sixteen of which (in varying forms) are found in the list of signatories to the covenant in Neh 10. That these names appear as the patronymics here suggests that they also function as such in Neh 10 and 12:1–7, and that personal names were not known for some periods, or at least not used.

12:8–26 The resonance with the signatories of Neh 10 continues into 12:8, in particular in relation to the first four Levites listed (Jeshua, Binnui, Kadmiel, Sherebiah). Mattaniah, listed already in 11:22, is here again associated with music and specifically with songs of thanksgiving (cf. 11:17), as perhaps were their associates Bakbukiah and Unni (12:9). A special note regarding the high priestly succession from the beginning of the return concludes with Jaddua (12:11) though it seems probable that this list passes over some members of this line, perhaps because they were unavailable to the compiler/editor.[81] For the generation of Joiakim's high priesthood (early fifth century), both family names and personal names were evidently available (e.g., of Ezra [i.e., Azariah], Meshullam) and moreover the list includes six additional names (12:19–21) not found in connection with the signing of the covenant, which suggests that this list may depend on a different source. One name that is included is Zechariah of Iddo (12:16), which is most likely the Zechariah of prophetic fame (Zech 1:1), though Ezra 5:1–2 clearly locates the latter in the time of Jeshua rather than Joiakim. It is not impossible that Zechariah's ministry extended into the next generation or that the priest listed here was also of the family of Iddo, but named after the prophet. Notes concerning the recording of the Levites and priests (Neh 12:22–23) offer a further hint of the consuming interest (visible in these very lists) in documenting who did what in the days of the return, while 12:24 recollects those responsible not just for thanksgiving (cf. 11:17) but now also for "praise," both of which are seen to have a Davidic connection (cf. Chronicles). The gatekeepers, familiar from 11:19, remind the reader of just how treasured the newly rebuilt temple and its precincts were for the returnees, while the intention of the final verse (12:26) may well be to indicate that the service of the Levites referred to in the previous verse was associated with the days of Joiakim and those later days in which Ezra and Nehemiah are to be found together (when Eliashib was high priest).[82]

Summary of Nehemiah 11:1–12:26

In their own way, the great lists of 11:1–12:26 (and others within Ezra-Nehemiah) are as much about "remembering" as about the historical recital found in the penitential prayer (Neh 9). In taking their lead at various points from the pattern of the exodus-settlement (e.g., the casting of the lot), these chapters continue Ezra-Nehemiah's interest in legitimating the return of the recent past by identifying it with the archetypal redemption (Exodus-Joshua) that it regularly remembers. Yet if the recollection of, and resonance with, the patterns of the ancient past remain important, it is the more recent past that truly animates the remembering seen in these lists. While the land is far from incidental in this remembering—indeed Jerusalem and the towns are persistently present

---

81. For discussion and eventual rejection of Cross's alternative suggestion that the original list included multiple people bearing the same names that then led to haplography and a defective final product, see Blenkinsopp, *Ezra-Nehemiah*, 336.

82. So Clines, *Ezra, Nehemiah, Esther*, 227, who offers this and other suggestions for the resolution of this seemingly curious note.

in these passages—these chapters are in the final calculation overwhelmingly concerned with remembering the people of the return. In introducing the lists, the opening verses of Neh 11 seem intent on recollecting the people's sacrifice, as expressed in a willingness to settle in and revivify the rebuilt capital of Jerusalem—a willingness that prompts a blessing from the wider populace that is itself remembered. However it has happened, the heading of the list with the laity (though note the belated mention of the governor!) serves as an antidote to any assumption that clerical contributions were all that mattered. Indeed, in these chapters we see people remembered as contributing in various ways, including the securing of the city and the temple, the oversight of confreres, and not least the leading of praise and thanksgiving that themselves facilitate and depend on a remembrance of God and his gracious, saving acts. Finally, it is worth noting that these chapters remember people not by their role, but by their name and, in some cases, the name of the family to which they belong. It is the remembrance of these names—of individuals and of families—that constitutes the real contribution of these chapters to the larger narrative of the returnees' "resettlement" of "Benjamin," "Judah," and especially Jerusalem.

Nehemiah 12:27–13:3

The drawing together of cast and characters in 11:1–12:26 now gives way to the rededication of the wall whose completion was noted as far back as 6:15. If, as noted above, the account of the resettlement of Jerusalem originally followed Neh 7 but was later editorially displaced until after the reading (Neh 8) and praying (Neh 9) of Torah and the recommitment of the people (Neh 10), the reader has been made to wait still longer for what must be seen as the climax of Nehemiah's contribution to the restoration of Jerusalem—the dedication of Nehemiah's wall. Insofar as we now pick up the story left off in Neh 6, it is not surprising that the first-person singular voice of the Nehemiah memoir is resumed, though not explicitly until 12:31.

12:27–30 Given the numbers of Levites already in the capital (on the basis of the previous chapter), the summoning to Jerusalem of those from towns outside (12:27; cf. 11:3, 20) hints at the scale of the celebrations to come. Their distinctive contribution "rejoicing, with thanksgivings and with singing"—anticipated already in the foregoing lists (11:17; 12:24)—is elaborated upon here with the mention of musical instruments and indeed the recruiting of additional singers from the environs of the capital (12:28–29). That such preparations would include the purification of the Levites and the priests (12:30) is hardly unanticipated given the mention of this same practice in Ezra 6:20 at the

Nehemiah 12:27–13:3

dedication of the temple. Precisely what was involved in this purification of the clerical ranks is not specified, nor is it clear how the further purification of the people, gates, and wall itself were accomplished, though the appropriateness of sanctifying the latter is anticipated by the earlier qualification of the city as "holy" (Neh 11:1, 18).

12:31–39 The voice of Nehemiah resumes in 12:31 in the description of how the dedication of the wall itself unfolded. To facilitate the giving of "thanks," Nehemiah forms two great companies, the first of which, composed of leaders, priests, and musicians, is led by Ezra (12:36). Nehemiah by contrast (12:38) follows the other half of the people (also giving thanks), with the two parting company from their starting point, likely at the Valley Gate. If this was their point of departure, one may well imagine Nehemiah surveying with some satisfaction the progress that had been made since he passed through the very same gate to inspect the ruined walls in the dead of night on his arrival in Jerusalem (Neh 2). While it is not impossible that the two companies merely walked alongside the wall, archeological excavations suggest that the wall of Nehemiah's time was sufficiently wide to permit three to walk abreast. If they did, as seems likely, travel atop the walls (NRSV "up onto"; 12:31), the safe arrival of both companies at the Gate of the Guard (12:39) may be seen to provide an emphatic response to Tobiah's taunt back in 4:3 that "if even a fox climbed up on it, he would break down their wall of stones" (especially if Tobiah had been evicted prior to the dedication of the wall).

12:40–43 Proceeding on to the temple, the two companies take their places to give "thanks," with the presence of the priests noted as well as the trumpets (12:41) and singers (12:42). Here, as at the dedications of the temple (Ezra 6) and the altar (Ezra 3), mention is made of both joyful celebration and the offering of sacrifices (Neh 12:43). Whereas the dedication of the altar predictably betrays a greater interest in these sacrifices, here the emphasis is squarely upon the joyfulness of the celebration. The amplification of such joy is accomplished not only by means of repetition within the verse but also by mentioning that the noise was so loud that it could be heard at a distance, inviting comparison with the similar sentiment in Ezra 3:13. While there, in the early days of the restoration we see both rejoicing and regret; here in Neh 12, at the dedication of the wall, the sound is not a mixture of laughter and tears, but rather one of pure, unadulterated praise.

12:44–47 While the reader has already been informed of the people's commitment to offer the first portions (10:35–37) and to bring them to the storerooms (10:38–39), the oversight of these chambers and their contents is mentioned as being established "on that day"—that is, the day of the dedication (12:27–43). That it happened on this day is explained by the "rejoicing" of the wider populace (as represented by "Judah") over the priests and Levites, partly in keeping with the general atmosphere of joyfulness on this day (12:43) created in part by the clerical contribution of music and leadership ("who ministered"; 12:44). The recollection of the latter prompts a further note that serves to identify the reinstated clerical "service of their God" with the pattern established in the era of David and his son (12:45). With descendants of Asaph already noted as serving amid the cohort of the returnees (11:17, 22), 12:46 confirms the ancestral antecedents of the choirmaster and the songs of "praise and thanksgiving." Having also already detailed that the provisioning of the singers was royally mandated (11:23), a further note here describes the means of such provision (also for the gatekeepers), clarifying too the process of supplying for the needs of the clerical classes in terms of "hallowing or setting apart."

13:1-3 Perhaps prompted by the emphasis on purification (וַיִּטַּהֲרוּ/*way-yiṭṭahărû*; 12:30; cf. 12:45) and sanctification (מַקְדִּשִׁים/*maqdišîm*; 12:47), a final note also concerning "that day" (13:1) resumes the earlier theme of exclusion (Ezra 9:2; Neh 9:2). Here as earlier, the separation is justified in relation to Torah observance, now explicitly in connection with a public reading of Deut 23:3-5—with its references to Ammonite and Moabite exclusion on the basis of an association with Balaam. As in Ezra 9-10, this exclusion (וַיַּבְדִּילוּ/*way-yabdîlû*; Neh 13:3) is articulated in rigorist terms as applying to those of foreign descent generally. If, as we tentatively suggest below, this invocation of Deut 23 and commitment on the part of the community reflect their own diagnosis of the problem during Nehemiah's return visit to Jerusalem but prior to the dedication of the wall, the events narrated in these verses report the final acts of the community in Nehemiah's narrative, even if those narrated in Neh 13 are the final ones to be reported.

Summary of Nehemiah 12:27-13:3

Amid the many notes (musical and otherwise) sounded in connection with the day of the wall's dedication, it is perhaps that of joy that echoes loudest of all—initially in 12:27, but especially in 12:43, which seems scarcely able to contain it. While the cultic expression of gratitude is acknowledged, the greatness of the joy is expressed not only in terms of its comprehensiveness (wives and children also) but its ability to be heard beyond the community. That such joy on the part of the people would be appreciated and indeed celebrated by Nehemiah is entirely understandable, given his investment in the restoration of Jerusalem's people and its wall—that final, potent symbol of the resurrection of the city. That it is the people rather than Nehemiah who are foregrounded in the festivities is also worth noting. Indeed, it is only in 12:31 that Nehemiah's voice is disclosed as that of the narrator, and even then it is only to note that I "brought" the leaders up onto the wall and indeed "followed" (12:38) the company and "stood with" (12:40) them. If Nehemiah's voice is thus almost elided in the narration, the same cannot be said for the voices of the people. That their joy is expressed is not surprising, nor is it unexpected (though no less worthy of note) that this expression is facilitated by means of song—a pattern that the narrative specifically and typically associates with its ancestral past (e.g., David). What is still more noteworthy perhaps is that this unbridled joy is articulated so consistently in terms of thanksgiving (תּוֹדָה/tôdâ; e.g., 12:27, 31, 38, 40, 46). That this is so reflects the claim of the community's fundamental orientation toward the God whom it understands to have superintended not only the community's return to the physical city of Jerusalem, but also its return to a cultic, social, and ethical life rooted in Torah, whose requirements are now so radically reembraced.

If the people naturally express their joy in thanksgiving to God, it should not be forgotten that they take joy too in the contributions and giftedness of the priests and Levites who lead (12:44) and that this rejoicing prompts the community to take very practical steps to ensure that they are provided for. The understanding that this radical reembracing of Torah also obliged a concern for sanctifying the community by means of separation from those deemed to be "foreign" to it resumes this theme sounded already in Ezra 9–10. Indeed, the presentation of the people's application of Torah here invites the suggestion that the earlier separation in merely marital terms (Neh 10:30) is here being superseded by an even more broadly based cultural and religious separation (cf. 10:28).

Nehemiah 13:4–31

While it is commonly assumed that the events chronicled in Neh 13, including Nehemiah's reported return trip to the Persian court, cannot have taken place before the dedication of the wall,[83] this requires an understanding of the opening words of 13:4 ("before this") that is diametrically opposed to their obvious meaning in the text as we now find it. If these words are understood instead as an indication that Eliashib's desecration of the temple precincts during Nehemiah's sojourn in Babylon took place at some point prior to "this" (i.e., the dedication of the temple narrated in Neh 12), the question is how much prior

---

83. So, for instance, Clines, *Ezra, Nehemiah, Esther*, 239.

to the dedication did they take place?[84] While it does seem probable that the lapses narrated by Nehemiah in Neh 13 took place before (historically speaking) and gave rise to the covenantal undertaking now recorded in Neh 10, in the final form of the book, these lapses (Neh 13) are presented as taking place not only after Nehemiah had secured the community's covenantal undertaking recounted in Neh 10 but also after the resettlement of Jerusalem (Neh 11), which must have taken place over the latter years of his tenure.

According to the presentation of the book as it now stands, it would appear that Nehemiah departs for Babylon only after securing the covenant (Neh 10) and seeing the resettlement of Jerusalem finally or largely accomplished (Neh 11). When reports of the lapses arrive in the Persian court, just as news of the ruins of the wall had originally reached him in Neh 1, Nehemiah then returns to Yehud from the east. Concerned at the speed with which his rebuilding of the community was being undone, Nehemiah is presented as redressing what he could (13:4–31) and then with these reminders of the fragility of his gubernatorial legacy fresh in his mind, he proceeds to preside over the rededication of the wall (12:27–13:3).

13:4–9 Nehemiah's account of the problems that he found on his return and the actions he took begins with his eviction of Tobiah. According to Nehemiah, the latter's kinship to the priest Eliashib (though not the high priest) allowed for Tobiah's installment in a large room, previously used for the storage of gifts for the clergy "by commandment"—an arrangement that had been agreed by the community already in 10:37–39. Assuming this Tobiah to be Nehemiah's inveterate opponent last encountered in Neh 6, Nehemiah's cause for concern is entirely understandable. Quite apart from the misuse of the temple's estate, Tobiah's presence at the heart of the community's sacred space seems likely to have been an attempt to integrate Jewish concerns within the wider network of Ammonite, Moabite, and Samarian interests. That this could happen at all is then excused by Nehemiah with reference to his absence from Jerusalem (13:6–7), which lasted long enough for the return trip and the passing of "some time" (lit., "the end of the days") in the Persian court. Whether the brevity of Nehemiah's absence is meant to heighten the sense of Tobiah's impropriety, Nehemiah's outraged response ("very angry"; 13:8) leads to the apparently immediate and unceremonious ejection of Tobiah's offending furnishings from the room. The room's purification and the restoration of its rightful contents ("vessels," "grain offering," and "frankincense") complete Nehemiah's decisive intervention on this front.

---

84. While Kellerman and Mowinckel argue that "before this" refers to the situation Nehemiah found on his initial arrival in Jerusalem, this is unlikely; Williamson, *Ezra, Nehemiah*, 382–84.

Nehemiah 13:4–31

13:10–13 Next Nehemiah discovers that the collection of the Levitical tithe, the system for which was agreed by the community in 10:35–39, has ceased to function, resulting in the exodus of the Levites from the capital toward the country (cf. 11:20). While the nature of Nehemiah's initial observation ("did not give"; 13:10) and the role fulfilled by those he appointed (13:13) may point toward a lack of distribution as part of the problem, the conspicuous absence of the Levitical tithe (cf. 13:5, 10, 12) in the gifts restored to the room following Tobiah's ejection suggests that there may have been very little to distribute. As the latter chapters of Nehemiah are currently arranged, Nehemiah's indignant response here, "Why is the house of God forsaken [נֶעֱזַב/*neʿĕzab*]?" (13:11), throws the community's words, "We will not neglect [נַעֲזֹב/*naʿăzōb*] the house of God" (10:39), back at them in no uncertain terms, but the action Nehemiah takes suggests a change of approach. Instead of attempting to restore the earlier system, evidently unimplemented—in which storage in regional depots was linked to subsequent temple delivery—Nehemiah recalls the temple functionaries to their posts (13:11) and resumes the collection of contributions (13:12) centrally in Jerusalem under the supervision of a trusted team composed of a priest, a Levite, a scribe, and an assistant (13:13). It seems likely that the note of a similar set of unnamed appointments on the day of the dedication of the wall (12:44) was an official confirmation of those mentioned here and the gifts mentioned there (12:47) somehow related to those mentioned here (13:12).

13:14 That we have returned to the Nehemiah memoir in Neh 13 is confirmed by the interjection of a prayer not on this occasion for the divine remembering of Nehemiah's enemies' evil or sins (cf. 6:14; 4:4–5) but rather for a preservation of Nehemiah's "faithfulness/loyal love" (חֶסֶד/*ḥesed*). Evidently interpolated after the initial penning of the memoir, this prayer surely reflects Nehemiah's anxieties about a legacy less easily preserved than the wall (cf. 5:19), but there seems little reason to doubt that it also manifests a genuine concern for the worship of his God, which he has worked so hard to reform and whose preservation his prayer now entrusts to God himself.

13:15–22a A third issue confronted by Nehemiah on his return relates to the observance of the Sabbath, on which the community had committed itself to not buying from foreigners (10:31). It is not improbable (nor, however, entirely certain) that it is the returnees themselves whom Nehemiah finds violating the Sabbath by treading the winepresses, harvesting, and burdening their beasts with produce (13:15)—the sale of which Nehemiah warns strenuously against, in keeping with his primary concern regarding commerce on the Sabbath (10:31). In spite of what are presented as these earlier commitments not to purchase from foreigners, Nehemiah finds the people of Judah in Jerusalem doing precisely that, aided and abetted by Tyrian traders with no interest in Sabbath observance (13:16). Having hurled an initial accusatory question at the nobles of Judah (13:17), Nehemiah's subsequent approach appears to draw inspiration from the prophetic example of Jer 17, where Sabbath desecration is also linked explicitly to the apostasy of "your fathers" (אֲבֹתֵיכֶם/'ăbōtêkem; Jer 17:22; Neh 13:18) as well as the potential (Jer 17:27) and past (Neh 13:18) punitive destruction of the city.[85] While not understood to be the sole cause of the destruction of the city, the centrality of the Sabbath observance for those returning from exile (see Isa 56:1–8) suggests that Nehemiah's accusation will have been understood as more than mere rhetoric. As for Jeremiah, so too for Nehemiah, a willingness to prevent the bearing of burdens (מַשָּׂא/maśśā'; Neh 13:15, 19; cf. Jer 17:21, 22, 24, 27) through the gates of Jerusalem (שַׁעַר/ša'ar; Neh 13:19 [twice], 22; cf. Jer 17:19 [twice], 20, 21, 24, 27) due to the undesirable interference of this activity with Sabbath observance suggests an expansion of the range of prohibited activities beyond those stipulated by the Torah. Exercising his authority as governor, Nehemiah has his own servants close and patrol the very gates he had had rebuilt, to safeguard the city from a threat to its holiness as real as any Samarian or Moabite. Having sought to stem the ingress of goods and the creeping commercialization of the Sabbath (13:19), Nehemiah also recounts his apparently successful efforts to frighten off those traders whom he felt or knew to be loitering with intent on Friday night, with the promise of apprehension or worse (13:21). That the Levites, normally trusted with guarding the temple's gates, should be charged with guarding the city gates, specifically "to keep the Sabbath day holy" (13:22a) suggests a final echo and identification with the prophetic purposes of Jeremiah (17:22, 24, 27).[86]

13:22b A further prayer for divine remembrance implores God to spare (i.e., prolong) Nehemiah's life, now not because of Nehemiah's own "loving-kindness" (see 13:14) toward God, but rather because of God's love toward Nehemiah. That the former should be expected to elicit the latter is presupposed in 1:5, where mention is also made of the divine loving-kindness (חֶסֶד/ḥesed). Nehemiah offers his plea to God by celebrating the "abundance of your loving-kindness/mercy" (רֹב חַסְדְּךָ/rōb ḥasdəkā), an expression found also in the prayer of Ps 5:7.

13:23–27 The centrality of the issue of intermarriage with those outside the community is further established when—despite the community's blanket commitment to avoid such attachments (10:30)—Nehemiah returns to discover Jewish men with wives of "Ashdod, Ammon, and Moab" (13:23) and children

---

85. For more detailed discussion of Nehemiah's relationship to Jeremiah, see Shepherd, "Is the Governor Also among the Prophets?"

86. Contra J. L. Wright, *Rebuilding Identity*, 232n34.

whose "mother tongue" appears not to have been Hebrew (or Aramaic) (13:24), but rather that of Ashdod and others. That the violence of Nehemiah's reaction, first merely verbal and then even physical (13:25), relates not to the linguistic situation itself, but the foreign marriages of which they are but a natural symptom, is made clear by his reference to Deut 7:3–4: "Do not intermarry with them, giving your daughters to their sons or taking their daughters for your sons, for that would turn away your children from following me, to serve other gods. Then the anger of Yhwh would be kindled against you, and he would destroy you quickly" (NRSV).

As at Ezra 9:2, the practice of Deut 7 (there applicable to "Canaanites") appears to be extended to preclude marriages to those historically outside the land (Ammon, Moab) on the basis of the principle of Deut 23:3. That it is not, again, the consequent loss of language per se, but the far more lamentable abandonment of God foreseen by 7:4 that is truly exercising Nehemiah is established by his invocation of the case of Solomon (1 Kgs 11:1–6). Emphasizing the latter's privileged status as "beloved by God," Nehemiah underlines the close connection between Solomon's sin and the latter's relations with foreign women both at the beginning and end of Neh 13:26, before rhetorically querying the doing of "this great evil" in Nehemiah's own time as a betrayal of God (13:27). Though Nehemiah mentions in passing the securing of an oath (13:25), his failure to include the oath itself or supply other confirmation of his success stands in sharp contrast to the previous cases as reported already in this chapter. If this omission is not a hint that no oath was in fact uttered, the most plausible explanation for it is that it is assumed in the report of the people's further renewal of its commitment to separation, secured as part of the wall-dedication celebrations with which Nehemiah's governorship is presented as ending (13:1–3).

13:28–31 The topic of intermarriage prompts Nehemiah to report his intervention in a specific case—especially egregious because it involves not merely the people or even the priesthood, but a grandson of the sitting high priest, Eliashib. Not only were high priests (and presumably prospective ones) required to marry within the community (Lev 21:13–15), but the marriage of Eliashib's grandson to a daughter of Nehemiah's old enemy Sanballat (Neh 6) will have opened up the real prospect of Horonite influence on the uppermost echelons of the community's religious establishment. Nehemiah's predictable response is to remove the offending man from the corridors of power (13:28). This action and the notion that "foreign" influence on the clerical ranks was seen by Nehemiah to be specifically "defiling" (גֹּאֲלֵי/*goʾŏlê*) sits comfortably with the note in 7:64 that some priests were seen as defiled (וַיְגֹאֲלוּ/*wayəgōʾălû*) precisely because of questions regarding genealogy. It is little wonder then that Nehemiah feels compelled to report that "I cleansed them [וְטִהַרְתִּים/*wəṭihartîm*] from everything foreign" (13:30) on his return. Such a need would have been all the more pressing if the (impending) dedication of the wall depended on the clergy's ability to purify themselves (cf. 12:30) and if the clerics that he had appointed over the stores (13:10–13; 12:44) were also involved in the task of purification mentioned there (12:45, plural) having been (re)established by Nehemiah here (13:30, singular). Nehemiah's mention of the provision of the "wood offering, at appointed times" recalls the community's earlier commitment in 10:34—a pledge for which Nehemiah may be taking credit at this point due to its association with others dealt with here, rather than because the community had also lapsed in this respect in his absence. Finally, a resumption of prayers has increasingly punctuated these final chapters. Here Nehemiah prays for divine remembrance against his clerical opponents (13:29)—presumably specifically those in the upper reaches of it—and in his final words, for divine remembrance of himself.

Summary of Nehemiah 13:4–31

There can be little doubt that the final chapter of Ezra-Nehemiah serves to confirm the reputation of the book as a whole and its chief individual protagonists (Ezra and Nehemiah) for a radical adherence to its own understanding of Torah and an equally rigorist (and not unrelated) separation from those who would not or could not comply with its requirements. As the book stands, the practices flowing from these convictions and foregrounded by Nehemiah in his interventions in Neh 13 are largely those to which the community had already committed itself in Neh 10. While the precise nature of these practices and the means by which they were derived from Torah may be (and clearly were) debated, they are hardly unexpected in a community whose memory included the further conviction, fully "evidenced" in the historiographical writings (i.e., the Deuteronomistic History), that the material, social, and religious upheaval of the exile stemmed from a lack of religious fidelity that in turn could be connected with a failure to maintain the ethnoreligious boundaries (and identity) of the preexilic community.

If Nehemiah's interpretation of the Sabbath seems rigorist and his response to its violation vigorous, it is hardly more so than that of Jeremiah, whom Nehemiah clearly seems to emulate. Indeed, given Jeremiah's evident influence on Nehemiah's recounting of the debt crisis and his handling of it, and the resonance of Nehemiah's earlier prayers with the prophet, it will hardly be surprising if the influence of the Jeremianic tradition appears too in the prayers that punctuate the end of this chapter. In fact, Nehemiah's request that God "remember" both him (13:31) and his enemies (13:29) finds a unique precedent in Jeremiah's own imprecation of others (Jer 18:21–23) in the same breath as the prophet explicitly appeals to God to "remember" him and his work (18:20; cf. also 15:15).[87] At the heart of Jeremiah's prayer is his deep concern for "good" (טוֹבָה/ṭôbâ) and evil and his experience of injustice: Jeremiah prays that because the good he has done his enemies (by speaking "good" for them; 18:20) has been repaid with evil, so God in his justice should repay their evil with evil in return (18:21–23). At the same time, because the good that Jeremiah has done has been not only for "them," but also before "you" (i.e., God; 18:20), God's willingness to repay his enemies' evil is an act of "goodness" to Jeremiah—and proof that God does indeed remember and care for him (cf. 15:15).

That Nehemiah himself viewed his activities in the same terms (i.e., as good) is confirmed by his report of the people's response to his proposal to rebuild the wall: "So they strengthened their hands for [the] good [טוֹבָה/ṭôbâ] [work]" (Neh 2:18). It is thus not surprising that when the recounting of Nehemiah's activities is supplemented with prayers for his own remembrance, they are offered in terms of the divine repayment of good. Following Nehemiah's return to Jerusalem, his eviction of Tobiah from the temple chamber, its cleansing, and Nehemiah's restoration of the cultic infrastructure and resourcing, his prayer is that "my good deeds" (rather than his enemies' sins; cf. 4:4–5) would not be blotted out (i.e., would be remembered; 13:14).[88] Again, after describing his intervention in the debt-slavery crisis and his seeming resolution of it, Nehemiah prays, "Remember for [my] good [טוֹבָה/ṭôbâ], O my God, all that I have done for this people" (5:19). Finally, at the conclusion of his account and with the prayer that God would remember those who have desecrated the sacred offices still ringing in the reader's ears, Nehemiah concludes a note of his good work in relation to the provision for worship with the by-now-familiar prayer for a divine righting of the scales of justice: "Remember me, O my God, for good [טוֹבָה/ṭôbâ]" (13:31). While Nehemiah's memoirs clearly illustrate his recognition of the divine superintending of his ministry, his interpolated prayers evidence his awareness, perhaps arrived at in later life, that the things he had striven to accomplish in his ministry within the community were themselves in the hands of God. While such prayers will inevitably prompt accusations of overweening self-concern, Nehemiah's identification with the prophetic pur-

---

87. "You understand, O YHWH; remember me and care for me. Avenge me on my persecutors. You are long-suffering—do not take me away; think of how I suffer reproach for your sake" (Jer 15:15).

88. Here the terminology used is חֲסָדָי/ḥăsāday, "my good deeds." In 13:22, Nehemiah prays: "Remember this also in my favor, O my God, and spare me according to the greatness of your steadfast love" (NRSV).

poses and indeed prayer practices of Jeremiah and those of the Psalms suggest that he should be judged no more harshly than the prophet from Anathoth, whose passion and theological convictions are often and rightly praised in the highest terms.

A positive appreciation of Nehemiah's ministry is also encouraged by the climax of the book. The first words of Neh 13 (13:1–3) and the dedication of the wall (12:27–47) to which they are attached report the last "acts" of Nehemiah and, in narratival terms, the end of Nehemiah's story.[89] It is here, beginning in 12:27, in the report of the preparation and then procession, dedication, and other accomplishments of that day, that we find the public celebration of the restoration of the wall—that final component of the capital's reconstruction that would allow for its full repopulation. Given that it is the wall that not only prompts Nehemiah's return to Jerusalem but dominates his account of his own activities as governor (6:15), the narration of its celebration can hardly be gainsaid as the fitting culmination and celebration of Nehemiah's own gubernatorial legacy. Moreover, from the perspective of Nehemiah and the editor, the narrative's insistence that, following the dedication of the wall, the community respond to the reading of the law by embracing an even more widespread policy of separation from those deemed to be inimical to the community's godly interests (13:1–3) can only have added to the luster of Nehemiah's legacy.

While the above observations caution against dismissing too quickly Ezra-Nehemiah's presentation of Nehemiah's contribution to the restoration of Jerusalem in the Persian period, the editor's insistence on ending the book of Nehemiah in the way that he does is noteworthy. Instead of ending with Nehemiah's story (i.e., the dedication of the wall and commitment of the people; 12:27–13:3) the book of Nehemiah and Ezra-Nehemiah as a whole conclude with the lapses of the people and the interventions of Nehemiah (13:4–31), which are now narrated as taking place prior to the rededication of the wall. Even if this presentation of Nehemiah's final return allows him to be credited with the recognition that remedial intervention was required, that he had to return to remedy the situation inevitably leaves the reader with questions not only regarding the people's commitment, but also Nehemiah's leadership.

While it might be argued that the account of the rededication of the wall (12:27–13:3) was not sufficiently *about* Nehemiah to have served as the last word in a book that was very much concerned with him, this seems insufficient on its own to warrant ending instead with Nehemiah's remedial intervention in the

---

89. This is very much in keeping with the observation of Williamson, *Ezra, Nehemiah*, 384, that 12:27–13:3 forms the "abiding climax" of the work and 13:4–31, the "pluperfect."

face of the people's recalcitrance.[90] In fact, given the memory of the community's exilic traumas and its recent commitments to avoid them in the future (Neh 10), the ending of the book inevitably invites the reader to consider how the community could have been so quickly compromised. The attentive reader of the book might well point to the answer supplied already by Neh 9 itself, with its extended recitation of the people's repeated recidivism, in which the prayer includes the people of its own day. However, the final editor's presentation of the end of Nehemiah's ministry seems also to raise questions about the legacy of his and perhaps even Ezra's leadership, while acknowledging their real and lasting contributions to the restoration of God's people.[91]

---

90. Williamson, *Ezra, Nehemiah*, 383, notes that the editor may have been induced to end with 13:4–41 to ensure that Nehemiah's contributions to cultic reform were not forgotten. This may well be, however, as Williamson himself recognizes in judging this ending "anticlimactic" (383, 384); whether these passages end up reminding the reader more about Nehemiah's contribution than the cost of his absence seems questionable.

91. For reflection on the implications of this reading for an analysis of the presentation of Ezra and Nehemiah as leaders, see the chapter "Leadership and Ezra-Nehemiah."

Reading Ezra-Nehemiah Canonically

BY CHRISTOPHER J. H. WRIGHT

Tracing the amount of attention given to the theological significance of Ezra-Nehemiah in works of Old Testament theology over the past century is an interesting exercise (which I cannot claim to have attempted with any pretense of completeness). In earlier classic works, such as Eichrodt and von Rad, there is a somewhat negative assessment, in which the postexilic period is seen as one of general decline from the high point of Israel's prophetic faith in general, and Ezra is seen as the source of the alleged legalism of later Judaism in particular. Perhaps that is why Ezra and Nehemiah get scarcely any mention at all in the Old Testament theologies of Vriezen, Zimmerli, Jacob, and Clements—at any rate, not with any theological reflection in their own right, beyond citation in illustration of theological points derived from other Old Testament contexts. And this is the case even with an explicitly Christian reading of the Old Testament, where one might have expected a more intentional engagement with the faith and practice of Israel in the postexilic period that eventually ushered in the New Testament.[1] A more satisfying treatment comes with Brueggemann's fresh attention to the multiple voices of testimony and countertestimony in the Old Testament. As we shall see, he challenges the negative "Protestant" charge of embryonic legalism against Ezra and appreciates the socioeconomic and political aspects of Nehemiah's leadership. But his major discussion of the books is in the context of their contribution to the Old Testament's understanding of the foreign nations as "Yahweh's partners."[2] Waltke gives commendable space to a theological discussion of Ezra-Nehemiah,[3] but by far the most theologically rich, textually attentive, and satisfyingly comprehensive treatment of the mes-

---

1. Knight, *Christian Theology of the Old Testament*.
2. Brueggemann, *Theology of the Old Testament*, 515–18.
3. Waltke, *Old Testament Theology*, 795–802.

sage of the two books, in my view, comes from Goldingay, in the first volume of his trilogy, significantly entitled *Israel's Gospel*.[4]

To organize our discussion in this chapter, the theological concerns of Ezra-Nehemiah may be viewed as an ellipse around two poles—two poles that represent two fundamental questions that arise in every episode of the two books:

- **Who is this God**—this God who features in multiple ways in every chapter?
- **Who is this people**—this insignificant fragment of a nation, the fragile survivors of the clash of empires and the wars of a previous century?

The **God** of the text is acknowledged on all sides, both by those who worship him exclusively as Yhwh the covenant God of Israel and also by those who, from a pagan standpoint, merely refer to him as the god of that people (Ezra 6:7; 7:14–15). Indeed, this God is acknowledged even by those who end up obstructing and threatening the projects of the former (4:2; 5:8).

And then there are the **people** whose struggles, plans, frustrations, joys, and failures fill the narrative. They claim to be "the servants of the God of heaven and earth" (5:11), yet they scarcely manage to hold on to their precious plot of land and rubble, never mind matching up in any way to the universal claims of their God. Who then are these people, and why is their very local story, which was clearly never more than peripheral to the majestic history of the Persian Empire, told within the grand sweep of God's purposes revealed in the whole Bible?

The answer to both questions—the identity of God and the identity of the people—is to be found in the story. Not just in the story of the books themselves, but in the great overarching biblical story (of which these books are a tiny part) that spans the long-distant past, gave courage to the people in their present, and sustained future hope for them and the reader. Since the events narrated in Ezra-Nehemiah occur after the exile and toward the end of the historical sweep of Old Testament canonical history, there is more of that biblical story "behind them," so to speak, as the prayer in Neh 9 shows clearly. There is a lot of history to look back on.

The canonical story is explicitly summarized in Neh 9, but there are hints and echoes all over the rest of the books. We are reminded of Abraham (9:7–8),

---

4. Goldingay, *Old Testament Theology*, 1.707–72. In an earlier book, Goldingay helpfully presented the postexilic community as a worshiping, waiting, obeying, and questioning community; *Theological Diversity and the Authority of the Old Testament*, 76–80.

the exodus (Ezra 1:6; 6:19; Neh 1:10; 9:9-12), the giving of the law and covenant through Moses at Sinai (Ezra 3:2; Neh 9:13-18), the wilderness experience (9:19-20), Joshua and the entry into the land (Ezra 2:1; Neh 9:22-25; 11:20, 30), the judges (9:27-28), David (Ezra 8:20; Neh 12:24, 36, 45), Solomon (12:45; 13:26), and the prophets (Ezra 5:1; 9:11). The great historical trajectory of Israel's Old Testament faith and journey is the strong and influential background scenery for the twin narratives of Ezra-Nehemiah.

Yet the books are not morbidly obsessed with a dead past. Rather, they use the past as an affirmation of the legitimacy of the tasks of the present and as an assurance for a secure future. Within that big story, as it is either echoed or explicitly recalled in Ezra-Nehemiah, we see **God** from many angles, from the opening scene of creation to the climax of the worship of God in the temple, microcosm of the new creation. And within that story also we see **Israel** portrayed in a variety of colors, from the underlying foundation of election in Abraham to a hope-filled future that survives beyond past judgment and present failure. In both cases (God and people), it is the underlying biblical metanarrative—both preceding Ezra-Nehemiah and following them—that provides the context and canonical coherence for the theological themes that are threaded through the text of both books. In the sections to follow we shall try to see these core themes in Ezra-Nehemiah within the wider context and light of that whole canonical framework.

Who Is This God?

The Creator God

The prayer in Neh 9 begins (9:5-6) with language that echoes many of the Psalms. He exalts Yhwh as the only God, as the maker of all the great magnitudes of the visible universe—the heavens, the earth, and the seas (cf. Ps 33:6-8). He is the giver and sustainer of all life on earth and the only true object of worship—human and heavenly.

This is the most explicit affirmation of God as creator in the two books, but it is supplemented by the commonest descriptor for God (other than by his personal name Yhwh)—as "the God of heaven" (Ezra 1:2; 6:10; 7:12, 21; Neh 1:4-5; 2:4, 20) or (once) as "the God of heaven and earth" (Ezra 5:11). At one level, this description of God might be seen as cultural accommodation to the pagan/secular context in which the Israelites lived. The idea of the "God of heaven" might mean different things to a Babylonian or Persian, but at least the Israelites shared with them the belief in the transcendent power of a supreme deity. In the mouth of Israelites, however, the double expression "God of heaven and earth" (5:11) could mean nothing other than the God of Gen 1:1—Yhwh God, creator of all things in heaven and earth.

Perhaps it is significant that the confessional prayer in Neh 9 begins with creation, before moving on to the redemptive history of Israel, since it follows the weeklong reading of the Torah by Ezra in Neh 8. The two events (the reading of the Torah in Neh 8 and the confession and agreement of the people in Neh 9) happened in the same month. So, clearly the first provided the scriptural foundation and motivation for the second. We do not know, of course, the precise scope and content of "the Book of the Law of Moses, which Yhwh had commanded for Israel" (8:1). But it is likely that it included much of what now constitutes our Pentateuch. Ezra's reading of the Torah, then, would have included the grand opening narratives of creation in Genesis. The story of the creation of the earth and all humanity and the subsequent narrative of the election and redemption of Israel are woven together into a continuum in the Pentateuch. So whatever our version of the redaction history of that monumental literary whole, it is very likely that this combination of creation and redemption was already there in the scroll from which Ezra read.

So the community listening to Ezra and learning from the Levites was encountering the creator of heaven and earth and all nations of humanity, as well as the redeemer and covenant Lord of Israel. They were, indeed, participating in a small slice of the biblical story by which the one and same God of creation and redemption would ultimately bring all nations and the whole earth to a unity of knowledge and worship of the God of heaven and earth.

That perspective, however, introduces one of the tensions in the book. If God is known to be the universal God, the source and giver of all life on earth (Neh 9:6), and if (as we know from other strong notes in Israel's symphony of tradition and praise, such as the Psalms that Ezra and Nehemiah must have known), it is the ultimate mission of this God to bring people from all nations into covenant blessing along with Israel—what then are we to make of the elements of exclusion and differentiation that permeate both books? If the creator-redeemer God intends ultimately to include all, why do Ezra and Nehemiah zealously exclude some? We shall return to this question below.

The Sovereign God

The sovereignty of Yhwh over all kings and empires on the one hand, and over very local situations on the other hand, is a theme throughout both books. It is assumed, and affirmed, and illustrated. It is, of course, a natural implication of the previous point: if the God of Israel is creator of the whole earth and all nations, then he is the sole Lord of all histories. Ezra-Nehemiah does not quite rise to the explicit rhetoric of Jer 27:4–5: "This is what Yhwh the God of Israel says: 'Tell this to your masters: With my great power and outstretched arm I made the earth and its peoples and the animals that are on it, and I give it to anyone I please.'" Nor does it exclaim with Dan 4:17: "The Most High is sovereign over the kingdoms on earth and gives them to anyone he wishes and sets over them the lowliest of people" (NIV modified). But Ezra-Nehemiah assumes that same theology as a simple corollary of the claim that Yhwh is the God of heaven and earth.

This is the theology that launches the narrative in the opening verse: "Yhwh moved the heart [lit., spirit] of Cyrus king of Persia to make a proclamation" (Ezra 1:1). God has a way with human hearts—especially the hearts of those in power, as Pharaoh learned to his ultimate destruction. Human beings make their choices and declare their plans. But God ensures that sooner or later it is God's will that is done on earth as it is in heaven.

In Ezra-Nehemiah, the interplay of divine sovereignty and freely chosen human decisions and actions is also drawn in more subtle colors. The "moving of hearts" is not confined to heads of states, but operates among heads of families as well. God moves their hearts to return, but they make the preparations to do so (Ezra 1:5). Nehemiah also knows what God had put on his heart, and he plans accordingly (Neh 2:12; 7:5). Ezra sees the hand of God, while Nehemiah turns frequently to prayer in the midst of events and plans. Both men thereby show their discernment of God's sovereignty without lessening their personal responsibility in decisions and actions.

Ezra's awareness of the "hand of God"—a powerful metaphor for dramatic divine intervention—is mentioned five times. The exodus and conquest were the work of God's "mighty hand and outstretched arm" (Deut 4:34 and frequently). God's hand, in the Psalms, saves, protects, provides, shields, and guides his people. God's hand was heavy in the life of Ezekiel and could carry him by the hair in his visions (Ezek 8:1–3). But Ezra discerns the sovereign hand of God in some very mundane matters. By the hand of God, he finds favor with the pagan king and obtains his visa and funding (Ezra 7:6, 27–28). By the hand of God, he makes a successful journey (7:8–9), with no trouble from enemies and bandits (8:22, 31–32). By the hand of God he is successful in gathering a squad of Levites and temple servants (8:18–20). In other words, Ezra trusts the sovereignty of God, but he takes steps and makes decisions, as any other human leader must. God's sovereignty works in the midst of human planning. Nehemiah shared the same conviction (Neh 2:8, 18). Conscious though he was of doing the work of the King of heaven, he still needed and sought the human king's permission for his final visit to Jerusalem (13:6–7).

Nehemiah perfected the art of the "arrow prayer" (2:4; 4:4–6; 6:9), as well as more prolonged intercession (1:4–11; 9:5–37). Few verses in the whole Bible express more succinctly the combination of faith in God (in prayer) and practical preparation (in action) than 4:9—"We prayed to our God and posted a guard." Neither contradicts the other. And in a similar way, Ezra 6:14 simply puts together, with full affirmation of both dimensions, "the command of the God of Israel" and "the decrees of Cyrus, Darius and Artaxerxes" as the key factors in the completion of the rebuilding of the temple. The two sources of "causation" are simply set side by side, but it is clear that God's sovereignty is prior: "They finished building the temple according to the command of the God of Israel and the decrees of Cyrus, Darius and Artaxerxes, kings of Persia" (6:14).[5] This conviction, rather than causing theological controversy, is simply a matter of celebration, joy, and praise (6:22; 7:27).

This balanced theology that affirms the overarching sovereignty of God in all human life, alongside the inescapable moral responsibility that attends all human action, is found throughout the Bible. Joseph affirms it to his brothers in the climax of Genesis. Their action against him had been culpably evil in intent and execution. But God overruled it to bring about good—the saving of lives (Gen 50:20; cf. 45:7). Jesus accepts the power that Pontius Pilate is free to wield at his own discretion, but sets it within the context and permission of the superior power of God (John 19:10–11). And as so often, it is at the cross where both sides of the matter are most clearly focused. For those who crucified Jesus did so entirely out of their own evil intentions and freely chosen decisions and actions. Yet what happened, according to Peter, was within the sovereign foreknowledge and purpose of God (Acts 2:23) and resulted in the outpouring of redemptive blessing.

The Redeeming God

Within the scope of God's universal sovereignty lies his exercise of sovereignty in the redemption of Israel. The exodus stands, of course, as the great Old Testament demonstration and model of what God does when he acts as redeemer. And by the time of Ezra-Nehemiah it was a deeply embedded cornerstone of Israel's historical theology (or theological history). The Psalms and preexilic

---

5. Brueggemann makes the additional point that "the cruciality of Persian support for the reconstructive work of Yahwism is indicated by the fact that in much of this literature, time is reckoned by Persian royal chronology, a concession not granted by Israel to any other superpower"; *Theology of the Old Testament*, 517.

prophets are replete with exodus language and themes. And Isa 40–55 envisions the return from exile in the soaring imagery of a new exodus, a repeated but more glorious crossing of the wilderness, and a triumphant reentry to the land.

It had not quite worked out in all the ways Isaiah's poetry portrayed, but the returned exiles still knew where to turn when circumstances called for the God of the exodus to show up again. The exodus was a repeatable pattern, sustaining prayer and hope. And the God of the exodus was, as Ezra calls him three times, "the God of our/your ancestors"—the ancestors to whom God had proved his redeeming power (7:27; 8:28; 10:11).

Echoes of the exodus narrative are there in the opening chapter of Ezra—though with some ironic twists. The Israelites have been in captivity in a foreign land for several generations. A new king has arisen. But whereas the Pharaoh who "knew not Joseph" changed the policy of Egypt from hospitality to oppression and then refused to release the Israelites, hardening his heart against God's word, Cyrus by contrast turns Babylonian oppression to liberation for captive peoples and decrees the release of the Israelites, having his heart moved by God in accordance with the prophetic word of Jeremiah. And whereas the people of Egypt thrust their gold, silver, and clothing on the departing Israelites in the wake of devastating plagues, the neighbors of the Israelite exiles seem to have plied them with generous parting gifts, not only because Cyrus decreed that they should. Return from exile is unmistakably a new exodus. God is doing it again.

When Ezra first appears in the narrative, it is emphasized that he is a direct descendant of Aaron, brother of Moses, who jointly led the people of Israel out of Egypt (7:1–5). There may be an echo of the crossing of the sea and the crossing of the Jordan in the three-day camp at the Ahava Canal (8:15; cf. Exod 14; Josh 1:11). But apart from such textual hints, there is the much clearer liturgical reenactment of the wilderness period in the way the people followed the reading of the law in Neh 8 by observing the festival of booths or tabernacles. "The people were deliberately reenacting the Israelites' wandering in the wilderness after the Exodus (cf. Lev 23:43) and understood their own return from 'captivity' as a second Exodus."[6]

In both Ezra and Nehemiah the exodus-wilderness theme is reflected in both its positive and negative dimensions. On the one hand, there is the constant protection of the people by God. All the attempts of their enemies to frustrate the work of Ezra and Nehemiah are defeated. Those who stand against God are thwarted. God leads his people from exile to the land, from rubble to rebuilding of temple and city. The story recapitulates the whole earlier historical narrative from exodus to Solomon.

---

6. Kelly, "Ezra-Nehemiah," 197.

But on the other hand, the exodus had been followed by the tragic double failure of the golden calf at Mount Sinai (Exod 32–34) and the rebellion of the people at Kadesh Barnea (Num 14). And on both occasions, only the intercession of Moses saved Israel from destruction, as he vividly recollects in Deut 9. Three prayers—one by Ezra and two by Nehemiah—bear strong resemblance to the intercession of Moses and indeed use some of his phraseology. When the extent of mixed marriages confronts Ezra, the issue is framed in the language of Deut 7 (Ezra 9:1–2, 10–12), and Ezra prays in the language of Deut 9 (Ezra 9:14). Nehemiah, confronted with the news of broken Jerusalem, prays the words of Moses from Deut 30 (Neh 1:8–9) and Deut 9 (Neh 1:10). The appeal to the God of the exodus is very emphatic.

Later however, on two occasions, Nehemiah portrays the condition of Israelites as slaves—even in their own land—slaves in need of exodus redemption. In Neh 5, ironically, the oppressors are fellow Israelites, enslaving the poor of the land with the burden of interest on top of the taxes to be paid to the Persian king and the loss of land and family members for debt. As we saw in the commentary, the "outcry" that this raises (Neh 5:1, 6) is the same word as the crying out of the Israelites in their hard labor in Egypt (Exod 2:23), and the passion with which Nehemiah responds matches the compassion of Yhwh that sent Moses down to Egypt. The people of Israel (or some among them) stand yet again in need of redemption. They had returned to the land, but in some senses were still in exile.

In the great prayer of Neh 9, the whole exodus-wilderness-Sinai sequence is recounted in detail (9:9–12), but once again the prayer ends with the theme that the Israelites—even though they have returned from exile—are slaves in their own land. The appeal to the God of exodus liberation is implicit, but unmistakable.

So in a variety of ways the historical-redemptive tradition is harnessed to the challenging situation the exiles faced on their return. The past is drawn into the present through the conviction that Yhwh is the same yesterday, today, and forever. So although we do not hear of any direct divine answer to the great confession and prayer of Neh 9, we are left confident that the God of past deliverance will not abandon his people now. Redemption will be the song of the future as it was of the past. And that is an expectation that the rest of the biblical canon will assuredly fulfill.

The books of Ezra and Nehemiah, then, take their place within the redemptive trajectory of the biblical canon. They point far back to the archetypical redemption of the exodus from Egypt. They live in the immediate glow of the more recent "exodus"—the redemption from exile in Babylon. But they also portray a redeemed community that stands still in need of redemption at various levels—sinners still, and quickly failing even to live up to the commitments they fervently make. The covenant is renewed, but it does not yet match the contours of the "new covenant." The fulfillment of that hope lies beyond the horizon of these books and will depend for its realization on "the exodus" (ἔξοδος) that Jesus would accomplish in Jerusalem, as discussed on the Mount of Transfiguration (Luke 9:31). And that climactic achievement will bring redemption to people from every tribe, language, people, and nation, when the vision of Exod 19:5–6 is ultimately fulfilled and Christ reigns with his people on the earth (Rev 5:9–10). That is a missional theme to which we will return.

The God Who Speaks in the Scriptures

The canonical story (both in its original record in the Pentateuch and in the summary of it in Neh 9) moves forward from creation, through the election of Abraham and the redemption out of Egypt, to the making of the covenant and gift of the law at Sinai. There is a pervasive emphasis throughout Ezra-Nehemiah on "the Book of the Law of Moses, which Yhwh had commanded for Israel" (Neh 8:1). Without entering the minefield of Pentateuchal source and redaction criticism, there seem to be no compelling reasons to doubt that the "book" referred to would have been, by the postexilic period, substantially in the form we now have it—the scroll or scrolls of the canonical Torah, "the Teaching."[7]

Although the first major section of the book of Ezra is taken up with the rebuilding of the temple after the return from exile (Ezra 1–6), when Ezra himself is introduced in Ezra 7, the repeated emphasis is on his role as teacher of the Torah. He is a man with a history (a priestly genealogy stretching back to Aaron—the priestly heritage of teaching the law to Israel). He is a man with the hand of God upon him (7:6, 9). But above all he is a man who "set his heart *to study, and to do, and to teach*" the law of Yhwh. Those simple verbs describe his commitment in 7:10. And indeed, the grammar of that verse suggests that Ezra's commitment to God's law, in theory and in practice, was the reason why the hand of God was upon him, utilizing his history and heritage for the needs of the present and future.

Ezra's professional competence in handling and teaching the law was recognized by the secular authorities. In the record of King Artaxerxes's letter,

---

7. For the use of the Pentateuch in Ezra-Nehemiah, see the commentary on Ezra 9–10; Neh 1; 5; 8–10.

authorizing Ezra's work in Jerusalem, mention is made repeatedly of his learning, his teaching ability, and his educational role in the community, based on the written law of "the God of heaven" (7:11, 12, 14, 21, 25). From the Persian government's point of view, this was simply a matter of good order and imperial administration. Where subject populations had systems of law and codes of practice of their own, let them be governed accordingly, through authorized persons with the necessary cultural affinity, academic training, and administrative competence. Ezra fitted the role perfectly.

However, in characteristic fashion, God's sovereign "moving of the heart" of the Persian king to appoint Ezra to this role (which Ezra acknowledged with praise; 7:27–28) served a larger agenda than the needs of the Persian Empire. Artaxerxes's letter authorized Ezra to play a role in establishing a tiny community in a small corner of his empire—a minor moment in world history, no doubt. But in God's purposes, it would be that community, the covenant people of the God of heaven, that would ultimately evolve into a multinational community of faith that would long outlast the Persian Empire, or any other empire the world will ever see.

Ezra's deep grounding in the Scriptures qualified and equipped him for the task that the God of those Scriptures now laid upon him. God chose not only to be encountered in the rebuilt temple, but also to be known through his word. God chose not only to enable Nehemiah to rebuild the city's walls for the physical protection of his people, but also to rebuild the community around hearing and obeying the Scriptures.

It is noticeable that in both books, when each major initial physical task is accomplished in the face of many challenges (first rebuilding the temple and then rebuilding the walls), the next event in the narrative each time has to do with the teaching of the Scriptures. After the narrative of the geographical return from exile and the rebuilding of the temple (Ezra 1–6) comes the arrival of Ezra—student, teacher, and practitioner of the law of his God. After the narrative of the rebuilding of the city walls (Neh 1–7), and even before the grand celebration and dedication event (Neh 12), comes the reading and teaching of the Scriptures, followed by confession and fresh commitment (Neh 8–10). And it is also significant that all three elements in the narrative (rebuilt temple, rebuilt walls, reading and obeying Scripture) are accompanied by outpourings of resounding and very great joy (Ezra 3:11–13; 6:22; Neh 8:12, 17; 12:27, 43). The law is not even remotely perceived as a burden of legalism, but as a precious gift of God's grace. The law becomes just as much the focus of gratitude and joy (in understanding and obeying it) as was the gift of God's presence in the restored temple or the gift of God's protection in the rebuilt city.

This helps to dispel the idea that reading "the law" was an exercise in legalism, enforcing obedience to rules as the heart of Israel's religion. This way of perceiving postexilic Judaism is rightly challenged. Restoration, forgiveness, grace—all come first: then obedience with gratitude and joy as a response.[8] Even the structure of the Torah shows this. Redemption comes before law in the structure of the book of Exodus and in its explicit theology (Exod 19:3–6):

> Ezra does not read the law in order to reform Israel into becoming the people of God. Rather, the reverse move obtains. It is the reformed people to whom the law is read. The reading of the law does not function to evoke a confession of guilt. Indeed, when the people weep, the Levites admonish them to put away sorrow and to be joyful. The observation to be made is that the reading of the law in Neh 8 is a part of the liturgical celebration by the people of God. The attempt to shift the reading of the law to Ezra 8 derives from a typical Protestant misunderstanding of Old Testament law. Far from being a legalistic system which seeks to dictate religious behavior by rules, the tradition assigned the law a liturgical function which had been reserved for the restored and forgiven community.[9]

Of course, the Torah was not the only vehicle for God's word. The living voice of prophecy was still to be heard in the early postexilic community. Twice Ezra refers to the encouraging effect of the preaching of Haggai and Zechariah in the task of rebuilding the temple (Ezra 5:1; 6:14). But the strong impression one gains from the great ceremonies described in Neh 8–10 is that God now speaks primarily through his inscripturated word. Even "the word of Y<small>HWH</small> *spoken* by Jeremiah," which launches the narrative (Ezra 1:1), would have been, for the returning exiles, the written and edited scroll of Jeremiah that may have been the work of Baruch, or at least based on the original scroll of Jeremiah's first two decades of oral preaching (Jer 36).

The remarkable event described in Neh 8 deserves closer attention. It opens up powerful insights into the dynamic interplay between the word of God and the people of God. Interestingly, the people take the initiative in requesting

---

8. "There is one sure sign that the Chronicler has not succumbed to a mere formalism in religion: his emphasis on joy in the performance of the divine will (Ezra 3:11, 13; 6:16, 22; Neh 12:27; cf. Neh 8:10, 17; 12:43). That is what marks off obedience to God's law from legalism"; Clines, *Ezra, Nehemiah, Esther*, 29.

9. Childs, *Introduction to the Old Testament as Scripture*, 636. His critique of "Protestant misunderstanding" may be aimed at Old Testament theologians such as Eichrodt, who attribute a rigidly legalizing agenda to Ezra that was allegedly "a threat to moral understanding"; e.g., *Theology of the Old Testament*, 342–49.

Ezra to bring out "the Book of the Law of Moses, which Yhwh had commanded for Israel" (8:1). And in that simple phrase is summed up the dual reality of the Scriptures as a whole. They are the work of human authors (the attribution to Moses), but they are simultaneously the word of the divine author, Yhwh himself. The narrative then oscillates between referring to the scroll as the law of Moses and the law of God, or both (8:1, 8, 14, 18; 9:3, 14; 10:29). Accordingly, before Ezra begins to read, he and the people bow in worship and praise to God, whose word they will now hear (8:5–6).

The chapter moves through a sequence of actions, intensifying both the means of communicating the word and the response of the people to it:

1. There is simple *reading and listening*, as the word touches their ears and focuses their attention (8:1–6). Twice we are told that the whole community was present (8:2, 3; cf. Deut 31:10–13). And Ezra made sure that he was visible and the word was audible (Neh 8:4–5). God's word was for all, not an elite few (Deut 30:11–14).
2. There is *explaining and teaching*, as the word touches their minds and feeds their understanding (Neh 8:7–8, 13). Since it was the word of God, they listened with worship and praise. But since it was also the words of human authors from many centuries past in the classical Hebrew language that was giving way to Aramaic as the language of ordinary people, it could not be understood by reading alone. And God wants his word to be not only heard but also understood by all. For that purpose Ezra enlisted those best trained in such a task—the Levites (teaching was supposed to be one of their primary roles; Lev 10:10–11; Deut 33:10; Jer 18:18; 2 Chr 15:3; 35:3; Mal 2:4–9). There was translating (Neh 8:8a) and explaining (8:8b)—essentially the functions of exegesis, interpretation, and application. But there was also extended training of those who would teach others. When "the heads of all the families" gathered together with the priests and Levites (8:13), it was undoubtedly so that they could learn the meaning of the law and then teach it in turn to their households (Deut 6:4–9). Nehemiah 8 stands as the first great program of theological education by extension. The cascading effect of training those who will teach others also was fully appreciated and applied by the apostle Paul (2 Tim 2:2).[10]
3. There is *weeping and rejoicing*, as the word touches their hearts and stirs their emotions (Neh 8:9–12). There was an emotional response to the

---

10. Goldingay provides a fascinating survey of other parts of the Old Testament where applied preaching of earlier texts occurs; *Old Testament Theology*, 1.733–34.

Scriptures, following upon the intellectual understanding of them (8:12). We are not explicitly told the reason for the weeping, but it is likely that the word was having its effect on their consciences, exposing sin and failure, and arousing conviction and penitence. While that is a very valid response, Nehemiah redirects the emotion to "the joy of Y{HWH}"—that is, he reminds them of the covenant grace of God, which is also abundantly revealed in all its forgiving power in the Torah.

4. Finally, there is *finding and doing*, as the word touches their hands and generates their obedience (8:14–18). Like Ezra himself, the people study (lit., "search") the law purposefully, with the intention of doing whatever they find it to require of them in response. On this occasion, the calendar itself called on them to put into practice a festival that was prescribed for that month. The precise details of their obedience is not the issue here, but simply they were determined to obey what they found the Scriptures taught. The passage closes on a note of abundant joy—they hadn't had so much joy for a thousand years (8:17!). Significantly, joy is mentioned twice: when the people *understood* the Scriptures (8:12) and when the people *obeyed* the Scriptures (8:17).

It is a powerful precedent and model for those who lead God's people. Their primary task is to ensure that all God's people, of every age, hear God's word taught with faithfulness, clarity, and relevance and are urged to be not hearers only but doers also. We shall return to this in the following chapter.

The God Who Gives

After Exodus and Sinai, in the foundational narrative, came the gift of the land. And sure enough, the recapitulation in Ezra-Nehemiah of the primal narrative of Israel's election and redemption includes their return to the land—given back to them by the same God who had driven them out of it into exile several generations earlier. The description of the return echoes the story of Joshua at several points. They return "each to their own towns" (Ezra 2:1, 70—the language of land division in Josh 13–21; cf. Neh 11:20). And the historical recital in the great confession prayer of Neh 9 stresses the generosity of God's gift of the land, in spite of the sin and rebellion of the wilderness generation (9:22–25). God fulfilled his word in relation to this item (land-gift) in his great original promise to Abraham (9:7–8).

The gift of land was the most monumental and tangible of all God's gifts in the Old Testament (9:22–25, 35), but God's inclination and capacity for giving is seen in many other items of his generosity. Neh 9 is a catalog of divine giving:

- God gives life to everything in creation (9:6).
- God gave his law at Sinai (9:13, 34), and then went on to give them guidance (9:19), food, and clothing (9:20–21).
- God gave them deliverers (9:27) and prophets (9:30).
- God gave his Spirit. Interestingly, this gift is mentioned twice—in relation to God's instruction (9:20; presumably referring to the law given by Moses) and in relation to the warnings of the prophets (9:30). Sadly the people had paid attention to neither of these gifts of God's Spirit.

And then in the rest of Ezra-Nehemiah, the list of giving goes on:

- God gives answers to prayer, frequently. He is the God of constant attentiveness to every twist and turn of human life and needs.
- God gives access to kings and favor with authorities—when it coincides with his own sovereign agenda for the world and his people.
- God gives resources for tasks he approves—whether rebuilding the temple or the walls of Jerusalem—in both cases, making resources available from secular authorities. Of course, all that kings and governors own belongs to God the creator in the first place anyway, so God is simply releasing his own resources for his own purposes, through the hands of those whose hearts he moves.
- God gives success in the projects that he calls and equips his agents to accomplish.

The God Who Keeps His Promises

It could be argued that the whole canonical arch of the Bible is built around the theme of the faithfulness of God to his promise. From the promise to fallen Adam and Eve in Gen 3:15 that the seed of the woman would crush the head of the serpent to the final destruction of Satan and lifting of the curse in Revelation, the story moves steadily from promise to fulfillment, through many layers of partiality and temporality, but with ever accumulating power and hope.

And Ezra-Nehemiah finds its own historical place in that great arch of biblical theology. The narrative opens with reference to God's promise through Jeremiah and thus interprets the return from exile as God's faithfulness to that prophetic word. Jeremiah, of course, was not the only prophet to articulate God's promise that, in the wake of the catastrophic judgment of 587 BCE—the destruction of the city and temple and the exile of the people—there could still be hope for the future. The people would return. Normal agricultural life in the land would be resumed (Jer 32–33). Isaiah portrayed it as a new exodus and named Cyrus as God's "Moses" for the new reality. Ezekiel portrayed it as nothing less than national resurrection from the grave of dry bones (Ezek 37). But under whatever precedent or metaphor, the promise was clear. And God keeps his promise.

So the opening verses of Ezra-Nehemiah constitute a testimony to a fundamental characteristic of the God of the Bible—a characteristic upon which, indeed, the whole history of salvation depends. Were it not for the faithfulness of God in keeping his promise, the Bible would be a very thin book indeed and the history of humanity a very short story. The story had already gone on for centuries, however, by the time of Ezra-Nehemiah, and so the proven faithfulness of God in the past becomes a motivation for prayer that he would demonstrate it again in the present—even in the midst of the people's continuing unfaithfulness to the God who had done so much for them. That is the burden of Ezra's prayer (Ezra 9:8–9). It is also the launch pad for Nehemiah's introductory prayer (Neh 1:5) and the climax of the confessional prayer (9:32–33).[11]

Ezra and Nehemiah affirm the faithfulness of God as much in his righteous judgment as in his merciful deliverance. That is to say, God is faithful to the explicit threats that were intrinsic to the covenant, as well as to the covenantal promises. God keeps his word either way. So Ezra affirms God's righteousness (Ezra 9:15, in a context that seems to include both his righteous judgment on Israel's sin and yet the hope of his righteous salvation in response to Ezra's appeal), and Nehemiah stresses repeatedly that "in all that has happened" God has been just and faithful, while the people did wrong (Neh 9:33). In these sentiments they echo the theology of many Psalms, where God's character (just, righteous, faithful, merciful) is held up both as the shining backdrop that exposes the opposite characteristics of human sin and also as the source of hope for a future beyond judgment.[12]

So, the immediate circumstances (that the exiles had returned after the devastating judgment of exile) are interpreted in terms of God's faithfulness in keeping his promise expressed in the words of the prophets. However, although the return from exile and the rebuilding of temple, city, and community are seen in promise-fulfillment terms, the outcome is somewhat ambiguous.

---

11. For detailed reflection on the theological import of the prayers of Ezra and Nehemiah, see Balentine, *Prayer in the Hebrew Bible*, 109–17.

12. "Both sides of the nature of God—righteousness and grace—constitute key themes in this prayer [Neh 9]"; ibid., 111.

When the temple foundations are laid, there is praise and joy. But comparison with the past evokes weeping as well (Ezra 3:12–13). We are not explicitly told why some wept. Perhaps they found it hard to believe that any new building—even on the very same site and with the same dimension—could be an adequate replacement for the splendor of the old. God may have kept his promise, but it may have *appeared* to be a disappointing, second-best, kind of fulfillment. Perhaps. The text is not explicit.

Into this confused context, the words of Haggai were needed to bring fresh hope: the future glory of God's purposes for his people and his world were not dependent on the physical architecture of the new temple alone (Hag 2:3–9). Even a superficially unimpressive fulfillment of God's promise in the immediate present could become the focal point for ongoing confidence in God's ultimate promise for a transcendently glorious future. Conversely, when the disciples of Jesus were inordinately impressed with the physical grandeur of the temple in their day, Jesus points beyond that to a much greater reality that would be inaugurated through his own death and resurrection (Mark 13:1–2; John 2:12–22). God's faithfulness could find provisional expression in physical realities like a rebuilt temple—and they were good in themselves. But ultimately the accomplishment of God's purpose was not dependent on such things, but on God's own faithfulness.

And what of the people themselves? They have experienced the faithfulness of God in fulfillment of his promise. They are once again the beneficiaries of his liberating power, provision, and protection. They acknowledge all this and enter into fresh commitments to obey God's requirements. And yet Ezra-Nehemiah ends with the gloomy picture of a pattern very familiar from the centuries of preexilic history—from the wilderness to the exile itself. They once again fail to keep their promises and fall into their habitual covenant-breaking ways.

So again, we are compelled to realize that the future of Israel, and through Israel the future of the nations and the world in the great biblical plan of God, did not depend on human constructs (the temple or the city walls), however successfully completed with royal authorization and divine assistance. Nor does the future depend on human commitments, however sincerely intended and publicly agreed. These human realities (temple, city, community) are all good things. They are all the cause of legitimate celebration and thanksgiving to God (on various occasions within Ezra-Nehemiah). They are all accomplished within the realm of God's acknowledged sovereignty over believers and unbelievers alike. Nevertheless, the only firm foundation for ultimate hope lies in the positive truth that Yhwh "is good; his love [faithfulness, חֶסֶד/*ḥesed*] to Israel endures forever" (Ezra 3:11), and in its negative corollary that he would therefore never ever utterly abandon his people.

Ezra mentions that God had not deserted his people even in their bondage (Ezra 9:9; the verb עָזַב/'āzab is sometimes translated "desert," and mostly "abandon" or "neglect"), but Nehemiah turns it into a refrain. God had not abandoned his people at the great apostasy of the golden calf (Neh 9:17). God had not abandoned them in the blighted wilderness years (9:19). And even in the cataclysmic judgment of exile, God had not utterly abandoned them, such was his grace and mercy (9:31). And so, although the prayer ends with no explicit petition other than asking God to look and see the distress the people are in once again, the implied appeal is: "Do not abandon us now!" And of course, God did not. The story went on and goes on still.

There is a tension here, however. For the Old Testament affirms both that God would *never* abandon his people, and yet that on some occasions he *did* abandon them—to suffer his judgment at the hand of their enemies. The promise that he would not abandon them is made explicitly in the strongly covenantal context of Deut 4:31. And it is repeated significantly at the time of the building of the first temple, in a word from God to Solomon (1 Kgs 6:11–13). However, what if God's people abandon him? That is the scenario that Deut 29:25 envisages and portrays the horror of the destruction and suffering that would be caused when God's judgment falls. And that judgment could indeed be described as God abandoning his people, or his temple, or his inheritance (Jer 12:7; Lam 2:7). "What happens [in the exile] issues from moral and relational principles. Yhwh's abandoning the people is a reaction to their abandoning Yhwh. What else could Yhwh do? Would it be relationally appropriate to act as though their abandoning Yhwh did not matter, made no difference to the relationship?"[13] So they were abandoned, but yet not abandoned. Or as Isa 54:7 expresses it: "For a brief moment I abandoned you, but with deep compassion I will bring you back." This dual truth is reflected at a personal level in the urgent intimacy of the psalmists' relationship with God. They knew that abandonment was the experience of someone deemed to be suffering God's displeasure (Ps 22:1–8). But they also knew that abandonment could never be the final destiny of someone faithful to God (16:10).

Such reflections bring us to the New Testament. At the cross, Jesus knew both the reality of abandonment by God as he bore the consequences of the sin of the world on himself and also the assurance that his destiny was secure in the Father's hands. His "cry of dereliction," quoting the first verse of Ps 22, "My God, my God, why have you forsaken me?," expresses the deepest mystery of the cross, as God the Son experiences the agony of separation from God the Father, something unprecedented in all eternity or in his earthly life. Yet his

13. Goldingay, *Old Testament Theology*, 1.706.

final breath, "Father, into your hands I commend my spirit," demonstrates that although Jesus died in agony, he did not die in despair. The psalmist's words, later quoted by Peter, sustained his hope of ultimate vindication: "You will not abandon me to the grave, nor will you let your faithful one see decay" (Ps 16:10; Acts 2:25–32).

Why was Jesus so confident of his own resurrection that he predicted it several times to his disciples before his death? It was not mere bravado. It was because Jesus knew who he was, and he knew the story he was in. As Messiah, as Son of Man, as Servant of Yhwh, he embodied the identity and mission of Israel. Their story, in a sense, became his—except that where they had proved rebellious and disobedient, he would remain faithful and obedient. So if God had never abandoned his disobedient firstborn son Israel, how much less would God ever abandon his faithful Son, obedient unto death?

In the story of the exile and return—the story, in other words, of the outpouring of God's judgment followed by the life-restoring power of God's restoration—there lies the pattern and paradigm of the cross and resurrection. Except that, whereas Israel bore the consequences of their own sin, Jesus who knew no sin was made sin for us. God himself, in the person of his Son, took upon himself the consequences of the world's sin. And so, in the depth of his suffering on the cross, Jesus experienced abandonment under judgment, as Israel had, but to an infinitely greater degree. And in the victory of his resurrection, he proved the truth of the scriptural promise—God would never abandon his people and would therefore not abandon the one who embodied and represented them.

And that same hope, which sustained Jesus in his agony, also sustained Paul in his agony for his own people. Could it possibly be the case that, because so many of his contemporaries had rejected Jesus as Messiah, God had abandoned his people? Could it be that, because Gentiles were coming to faith in Christ and being assured by Paul that they were thereby children of Abraham and inheritors of the great scriptural promises, God had somehow rejected those to whom those promises had been made in the first place—"Israel after the flesh," ethnic Jews? Or to put it bluntly (and in terms that are rendered more toxic by current controversy), had the arrival of a "Christian church" (though that phrase is not found in the New Testament) that even in Paul's day was becoming predominantly Gentile, simply *replaced* or "superseded" the Jews? By no means! Not at all! That is Paul's reaction to such a thought.

It ought to be ours also. The idea that God has permanently rejected the Jews and replaced them with others, which has led to the horrors of anti-Semitism, is itself rejected by Paul. Paul's is not replacement theology but fulfillment theology. It was not that the Christian church has replaced the Jews, but that Israel has expanded to include the Gentiles—as the Old Testament Scriptures promised in multiple places[14] and as had now begun to happen through the Messiah Jesus. Paul wanted the Gentile believers in Rome particularly to be very clear about this point (in preparation for his exhortations in Rom 14–15). That some Jews were resisting the gospel message and its implications for the inclusion of the Gentiles meant that, in that one respect, they were "enemies"—*not* enemies of the Gentiles, but enemies of God's mission to bring the good news of salvation to the nations. But in relation to God's ultimate purpose of election, the purpose for which they had been chosen, they are loved by God "because of the ancestors"—that is, because of the promises God made to Abraham that will never be broken. God will never take away his calling and love for the Jews or the precious gifts they had received from him (Rom 11:28–29; 9:1–5).

Paul's language in Rom 9–11 is emphatic and unequivocal. God had neither *failed* in keeping his promise to Israel (9:6; on the contrary, the ingathering of the Gentiles *fulfilled* the promise made to Abraham), nor had God *abandoned* his ancient people (11:1–2). *Some* of those people had indeed cut themselves off from their own "olive tree," because of their unbelief. But even for them the possibility of being grafted into that olive tree through repentance and faith in Messiah Jesus remained open.[15]

Paul's ultimate vision and hope for "all Israel"[16] rested in God alone—in God's severity and God's mercy, both of which were expressions of God's faith-

---

14. I explored in depth and detail the great variety of Old Testament texts (in every section of the Hebrew canon) that address the sovereign purpose of God for the nations in relation to his purpose for Israel, and the way the New Testament portrays their fulfillment in C. J. H. Wright, *Mission of God*, 454–530.

15. It should be added that that grafting into the one olive tree of God's people is conditional on faith in Jesus the Messiah, according to Paul's phrasing in Rom 11:23—"and if they do not persist in unbelief, they will be grafted in." So, if Paul's argument in these chapters excludes the one extreme of "replacement" supersessionism, it also excludes the opposite extreme of a "two-covenant" theology that denies the need for Jews to come to faith in Jesus as Messiah for salvation and denounces any attempts (however sensitive and respectful) to bear witness to the messiahship of Jesus among Jewish people. This is discussed further in the chapter "Reading Ezra-Nehemiah Theologically Today."

16. This is not the place for an extended discussion of the complex exegetical debate over exactly what Paul means by those words in Rom 11:26. Those who take them as implying Jewish people as an ethnic solidarity, stress the word "until" in 11:25, and by implication they then envisage a large-scale eschatological turning of Jews to Jesus. Others point out that the opening words of 11:26 (*kai houtōs*) mean "and that is *how*" (not "when"). So 11:26 carries no temporal (future) implication but rather speaks of the *process* that Paul has just been describing as already taking place and that will continue to do so until complete—namely the engrafting of Gentiles into the "stock" of Israel, so that "all Israel" means all those (Jews and Gentiles) who will constitute the redeemed people of God in the Messiah Jesus.

fulness to his promises. And in that regard, Paul would have certainly joined Ezra in singing, YHWH "is good; his love to Israel endures forever" (Ezra 3:11), and so should we. And Paul would also have joined Nehemiah in affirming, "You have kept your promises because you are righteous" (Neh 9:8). Indeed, the strength of Paul's conviction on that very point—the amazing righteousness of God demonstrated in faithfulness to his covenant promises in paradoxical and surprising ways beyond human imagination—led him inevitably to doxology too (Rom 11:33–36). Which is where we need to go next.

The God Who Is Worthy of Worship

Apart from the final chapter (Neh 13), which brings us back down to a fallen and failing people just like ourselves, Ezra-Nehemiah begins and ends in outpourings of worship and praise that are loud and long.[17] After the account of the return of the exiles, the first recorded act is the restoration of "the altar of the God of Israel" on its original foundation and the resumption of worship there through burnt offerings (Ezra 3:2–6). And the next recorded act is the laying of the foundation of the temple itself. When that was completed, there is celebration, "with praise and thanksgiving," "a great shout of praise," along with weeping and joy (3:10–13). Although many obstacles would intervene before the temple itself was fully rebuilt, the community is united from the start in affirming the goodness of God in worship and praise. And then, when the community is united around the hearing and obeying of the Scriptures, there is another outpouring of worship and rejoicing (Neh 8:9–12).

When the temple has been fully restored and the walls of the city have been rebuilt, then Nehemiah organizes a mammoth celebration with massed choirs (the singers needed whole villages to live in; Neh 12:29!) and full orchestras. But after the ceremonial procession around the walls in opposite directions, the service of thanksgiving itself takes place in the temple courts. Once again, it is stressed that the whole community participated in the worship and shared the God-given joy (12:27–43). "Thus, a movement of spiritual and social revival that begins in Jerusalem with the repair of the ruined altar of Solomon's temple (Ezra 3:2) extends, in time, to encompass the city, literally and figuratively. At each point the ideals of the leaders are adopted by the people, in a context of joyful worship and commitment (3:4; 6:22; Neh 8:12; 12:27)."[18]

---

17. As the commentary on Neh 13 reminds us, while these failings are described at the end of the books of Ezra-Nehemiah, it is the celebration and commitment that represent the "end" of the story.

18. Kelly, "Ezra-Nehemiah," 196.

It is unmistakably clear from the commentary how the narrator builds multiple connections between this postexilic restoration of the worship of God and the traditions, institutions, and arrangements of Israel's preexilic history. Lists of priests and Levites and other temple servants dominate the rosters of returning exiles (Ezra 2; Neh 7). Indeed, Ezra takes special measures to ensure there is an adequate supply of Levites and temple servants to assist in his task of carrying substantial funding to the temple in Jerusalem (Ezra 8:15–36). Likewise, links are made not only with the regulations laid down in the law of Moses (3:2; 6:18), but also with the arrangements that had been put in place by David and Solomon (8:20; Neh 12:24, 36, 45–46). Indeed, the whole account of the dedication of the walls in Neh 12 is redolent of the memory of David bringing the ark of the covenant into Jerusalem (2 Sam 6) and of Solomon's dedication of the temple (1 Kgs 8). The worship of God, even by this tiny community of returned exiles, must be worthy of the God of Sinai and Zion.

Within the great arch of canonical biblical theology, however, the temple (whether preexilic or postexilic) held more significance than as a place for gathered worship and sacrifices only. "In the beginning God created the heavens and the earth" (Gen 1:1). "Then I saw a new heaven and a new earth" (Rev 21:1). The biblical narrative spans the arch between creation and new creation. In the account of the new creation in Rev 21–22, John emphasizes that there was no literal physical temple in the city of God. Rather, the whole redeemed creation has now become the place of God's dwelling with humanity. This is not just Eden restored, but the ultimate temple, with the river of God flowing from its heart—as in the vision of Ezekiel. By analogy, the portrayal of creation in Gen 1:1–2:3 can be seen as God creating a temple for himself. Creation is the temple in which God installs his image—the living human being. And creation is where God "rests"—in the sense of settling down to govern the earth from his temple.

However, human sin and rebellion results in a fracture. The integrated unity of heaven and earth is broken. Heaven becomes the realm of God's dwelling, where God's will is done and from where God's sovereign government is exercised. The earth is the place of human dwelling, where God's will is resisted, yet ultimately will be carried out.

So how can God dwell with humankind? It was to be Israel's greatest privilege and distinguishing reality that the living God of the universe chose to dwell in their midst. Indeed, without that residence of God in the midst of his people, what difference was there between Israel and any other nation, pleads Moses in persuading God to go with them, even in their stubborn sinfulness (Exod 33:15–16). And where would God dwell? Initially in the tabernacle, or tent, during their wilderness wanderings. It is emphasized that this structure would be the focal point of God's dwelling in the midst of his people, made visible by the presence of the cloud of God's glory that filled it (25:8; 29:44–46; 40:34–35). The tabernacle, then, and later the temple become the place where heaven and earth meet, the place where there was a symbolic reintegration of what sin had separated. The temple was, in a sense, God's address on earth.

The heaven and earth dimension of the temple appears again when Solomon comes to dedicate it. His great prayer begins by acknowledging that even the heavens are too small to be (literally) God's dwelling place—so how much less the little house that he had built on earth (however grand it appeared in its pristine splendor). Nevertheless, he boldly asks that when people pray in or toward this earthly building where God has put his name, God should hear in "heaven, your dwelling place"—and then act in response (1 Kgs 8:27–30). In other words, the temple is portrayed as the hub that connects the power and resources of heaven with the realities and needs of earth. The God of all creation chooses to make the temple a symbol of his reign on earth.

And for that reason, the temple itself needed to be kept in perspective—for the temptation was always to give it more importance than it intrinsically had, simply as a building, however holy. This is not merely to point out (as successive prophets did) that it could become corrupt and a "den of robbers," nor merely to add that God had never really needed or commanded a building and could very happily do without one (as Stephen rubbed in before he was stoned [Acts 7]). It is rather to observe that *even at its best* the temple was only a *microcosm*—in a literal sense of that word. It was a tiny model of the cosmos—of the whole creation that was filled with the presence of God. The temple, indeed, was in itself nothing more than the footstool of Yhwh (1 Chr 28:2). God was not being sarcastic, but simply pointing out theological reality, when he exposes the absurdity of thinking he would actually "live in a house" (as Solomon realized [1 Kgs 8:27], but his successors tended to forget).

This is what Yhwh says:

"*Heaven* is my throne,
    and *the earth* is my footstool.
Where is the house you will build for me?
    Where will my resting place be?
Has not my hand made all these things
    and so they came into being?"
    declares Yhwh. (Isa 66:1–2, italics added)

The whole cosmos—heaven and earth—constituted the royal residence of creation's king, with his seat in heaven and his feet on the earth, and his hands having created everything contained therein. What a tiny speck the temple was by comparison!

So when God allowed the temple of Solomon to be destroyed, the sky did not fall in. God was still on the throne. God was still YHWH of heaven and earth. Perhaps that is why Book 4 of the Psalms, coming immediately after the agonized questions hurled at God in the second half of Ps 89 after the destruction of Jerusalem's temple and throne, points the worshipers repeatedly to know that *YHWH reigns* and that his kingship is universal over all the earth. They need not fear life without a physical king, city, or temple. Let them put their trust in the God who reigns over heaven and earth.

The restoration of the temple, then, as recorded in Ezra-Nehemiah could certainly be a legitimate cause for thanksgiving and renewed worship. Naturally. But the temple itself—original or restored—pointed beyond itself to the presence of "the God of heaven" on the earth (even pagan kings refer to it as "the house of the God of heaven"; Ezra 6:1–12) and to his sovereignty over the affairs of earth. And that was, and is, a theological truth that transcended not only Solomon's Temple, but also the Second Temple and Herod's Temple. It points us to the New Testament affirmation that God, Immanuel, now dwells with his people in Christ, and they have become that temple, the dwelling place of God by his Spirit (Eph 2; 1 Pet 2). And even beyond that, it points to the day when the whole creation will once again be God's temple, filled with his presence and glory and beauty, with redeemed humanity from every tribe and language and nation serving as kings and priests on the redeemed earth.[19]

But if the temple had such universal significance, and if even Solomon prayed at its dedication that it should be the place where God's blessing would be enjoyed even by foreigners (1 Kgs 8:41–43), how can we reconcile that grand, missional perspective with the apparent narrowness of the measures Ezra and Nehemiah took to exclude foreigners from God's people? That leads us to the second pole of our enquiry.

Who Is This People?

A People with Historical Identity

When we consider the cataclysmic severity of what happened to the small state of Judah in 587 BCE, it ought to be a matter of greater amazement to us than

---

19. For a very rich and thorough survey of the creational significance of the temple in biblical theology as a whole, see Beale, *Temple and the Church's Mission*.

it usually is that the nation survived at all. The kingdom of Judah (with Benjamin), the two-tribe rump of the short-lived greater Israel of the twelve tribes under David and Solomon, was ripped apart and trampled underfoot: its king and governing classes executed or exiled; the city of David and the temple of Solomon both burned to rubble; the leading classes of its population carried off into exile in Babylon; its territory abandoned. It should have been The End. Some thought it was. But God had other plans. And the people had their memories. They remembered who they were (their identity), and they remembered the story they were in (their history and their mission).

So when at last the opportunity came for the descendants of those original exiles to return, they rebuilt not only their temple and city. They rebuilt themselves as a community who knew their *identity* and their *history*. They established identity mainly through the claims of kinship or territory or both. And they reenacted history as a legitimation of the present—sometimes by interpreting current events by analogy with the classic contours of their own redemptive history, and sometimes by reconstituting institutions of the preexilic period as closely as possible to their original patterns.

In preexilic Israel, membership in the covenant community was to a large extent legitimated by kinship and land. If you belonged to an Israelite family living on its inherited portion of the land given to your tribe, then you had secure membership in all the affairs of the community. If you were (or became) familyless (widows and orphans) or landless (foreigners, immigrants), then you were much more vulnerable and insecure. That is why the laws repeatedly urge Israelites to take special care of those categories of people in their midst.

The genealogies in Ezra 2 and Neh 7 perform this vital function. Significantly they are a mixture of kinship genealogies with territorial links (i.e., towns; Ezra 2:1, 59, 70). The emphasis on genealogical authenticity and documentation may seem to us either quaintly antiquarian or exclusionary. At least, it might seem like that to those of us who are Western; more traditional societies immediately resonate with the kinship dimension. But for the returning Israelites, this was vital information that established a family's membership in the covenant community, with the combination of rights and responsibilities that involved.

Turning from their identity to their history, Ezra-Nehemiah shows thorough acquaintance with the whole preexilic story—from the creation of the world through the election of Abraham, redemption from Egypt, covenant at Sinai, years in the wilderness, gift of the land, judges, kings, and prophets. There are hints of most of these at various points in both books, but they all come together in Neh 9. This is a people who know their own story.

At one level, the past was being used to justify and authenticate the present. The little community struggling desperately to establish itself on the site of their ruined city and temple may not have looked remotely like the kingdom of Judah in its glory years under, say, Uzziah and still less like the mini-empire of the united kingdom under Solomon. Yet they kept reminding themselves: "We are that people. We are the heirs of that history. We may be only a remnant. But we *are* the remnant of Israel, the covenant people of the living God. We are Yhwh's people in Yhwh's land once again." The present might have only the slenderest connection to the past, but the connection was there, visible, legible, and tangible in kinship and turf. And it was that solid, ineradicable past that reassured them that the present, however grim, was bearable as a work in progress.

But at another level, even if not so explicitly in our text, the past was being used to build hope for the future. We can see this in the implied plea contained in both prayers in Ezra 9 and Neh 9. The assumption is that, although the people have sinned (again), the historical record clearly and repeatedly affirms that God can follow judgment with grace and bring restoration out of successive disasters. So, provided the people can be brought to repentance and fresh commitment, and provided the intercession of Ezra and Nehemiah reaps the same response as the intercession of Moses and Samuel, then there could be hope—hope both for the people in the story (even though we do not see into the immediate future beyond the story itself) and for the readers of the story. For as we read the books of Ezra-Nehemiah within the canonical sweep of the rest of the Bible, we know that the little community of fifth-century BCE Judah did survive. We know something of the traumas that lay ahead for them, in the centuries between the ending of Old Testament prophecy and John the Baptist's stunning entrance on the stage of biblical history. But the very fact that we can turn the page in our Bibles from Malachi to Matthew is proof that the hope implicit in the prayers of Ezra-Nehemiah was not disappointed. This people with a history was a people with a future—a future we encounter theologically in its emerging Christian form in the New Testament. And that history and future generated a missional dimension of Israel's existence, to which we will turn later.

On this point, therefore, we disagree with and are puzzled by von Rad's interpretation of the alleged swing of Israel toward an identity entirely shaped by the law itself as something "outside history"—thus giving birth to "Judaism":

> Up to now the commandments had been of service to the people of Israel as they made their way through history.... But now Israel had to serve the commandments.... We do not as yet see any legal casuistry proper. But when the law was made absolute, the path to such casuistry, with its intrinsic consequences, had to be followed out. But the most serious aspect of this whole process was that in understanding the law in this way

> Israel parted company with history, that is, with the history which she had hitherto experienced with Jahweh. She did not part company with her relationship to Jahweh. But once she began to look upon the will of Jahweh in such a timeless absolute way, the saving history necessarily ceased moving forward. This Israel no longer had a history, at least a history with Jahweh.[20]

Although von Rad exonerates Ezra-Nehemiah from "casuistry," it seems he is adopting the same negative attitude toward the Old Testament law (perceived as legalistic and "timeless" imposition) that we noticed above. On the contrary, if (as we think likely) the "book of the law" that Ezra read in Neh 8 was more than just the "law code" sections of the Pentateuch, but something much more substantially like the Pentateuch as we know it, then the redemptive history and its ongoing potential for shaping Israel's covenantal relationship with YHWH within history was very much part of what they celebrated that week. If in some sense the whole affair was a reenactment of the Sinai covenant (Exod 24), then it was *not* the case that Ezra-Nehemiah were calling for legalistic submission to the law so that God would be pleased and save them and take them as his people. Rather—just as in the book of Exodus—this is a community of those whom God had already redeemed, who had reentered God's land, and who knew themselves already as "the servants of the God of heaven and earth" (Ezra 5:11).

Reading and obeying God's law was not a means of earning God's favor but the right response to the experience of God's grace. The same historical-theological dynamic is at work here as much as ever before. In whatever ways it may be alleged that Judaism developed a legalistic tendency (itself a tendentious allegation), that charge should not be laid at the door of Ezra and Nehemiah. Brueggemann rightly comments:

> In a Christian discernment of the Old Testament and of emerging Judaism, what most needs to be resisted is the conventional Christian stereotype of

---

20. Von Rad, *Old Testament Theology*, 1.91. A somewhat similar, and surprising, negative assessment of Ezra-Nehemiah comes from Provan, "Hearing the Historical Books." The negativity, however, comes not from seeing Ezra-Nehemiah as in bondage to legalism, but simply because they do not voice the missional eschatology and universality of the Abrahamic tradition: "They [Ezra-Nehemiah] represent a disappointing cul-de-sac within the biblical story, in which the main stream of theology is running elsewhere from now on. In Ezra-Nehemiah, the great onward movement of the redemptive history is stalled, as it were; and when it gets going again, it will not be the inheritors of the Ezra-Nehemiah tradition who move it onwards, but the great inheritor of the prophetic tradition, Jesus of Nazareth. It is Jesus who picks up the same Abrahamic (and indeed Isaianic) vision that Ezra-Nehemiah ignores and calls out a people in which there is neither Jew nor Gentile, male nor female, slave nor free; in which all distinctions of such kinds, maintained in Old Testament Law for particular reasons, are now seen to belong to an age past" (273–74).

legalism. In any serious commitment to obedience, to be sure, zeal may spill over into legalism. But in any attempt to set as antithesis "Christian grace" and "Jewish law," Israel's sense of itself will be distorted and caricatured. Israel, in these interpretive maneuvers and acts of self-discernment led by Ezra, is with considerable daring seeking to order its life in a way that is commensurate with the God who creates, saves, and commands.[21]

A People Called to Unity

Israel never lost a sense of wonder at the sheer improbability of their existence as a people. The strangeness of their origins is captured (celebrated almost) in the creedal affirmation of the Israelite farmer at harvest time: "A wandering Aramean was my father," referring no doubt to Jacob (Deut 26:5). A band of nomads had nearly perished in famine, but were rescued by economic asylum in Egypt. Then, generations later, they were the target of state-sponsored genocide under an Egyptian Pharaoh. But God brought them out of that and into a land of their own (though not before a whole generation perished in the wilderness). There again, they almost destroyed themselves in the anarchic intertribal strife of the era of the judges. The national unity of all the tribes accomplished under David lasted only one more generation before falling apart in the rebellion of five-sixths of the nation and centuries of intermittent civil war between two kingdoms, both of which claimed Israelite identity though only one took the formal name. And that kingdom, the ten northern tribes, had then been smashed, scattered, and erased from history by Assyria. Finally, the rump kingdom of Judah had suffered a similar fate under Babylon. And now, under yet another victorious external empire, it was only a remnant of a remnant that had straggled back to just a small sliver of the land once taken by Joshua and ruled by David and Solomon. And yet, and yet.

In spite of their tiny fragility and vulnerability, they laid claim to their past, their land, and their historic identity as the covenant people of Yhwh. They made every effort to reaffirm who they were and to connect even such a limited and inglorious present to a past narrative that was rich in theological significance and divine promise.

A significant element in that historic identity was the conviction that, in origin and in covenantal ideal, there was truly only one Israel. There was one God, and there was one people of God. Even in the worst days of the divided

---

21. Brueggemann, *Theology of the Old Testament*, 446.

kingdoms, there are plenty of hints in the prophets of this ideal unity. Even though prophets had to be sent, of necessity, either to Israel in the north or to Judah in the south, and even though their messages were targeted at the citizens and governments of those political entities, it is clear that some of the prophets still thought of "Israel" as the one covenant people of God—in spite of political division on the ground. The Chronicler's presentation of the reforms of Hezekiah and Josiah, and their attempts to draw back "into the fold" the people living in the defunct northern kingdom (2 Chr 30; 35:3, 18; 2 Kgs 23:19–23), indicate an awareness even in Judah that "Israel" was greater than either kingdom alone.[22]

And as we read through Ezra-Nehemiah we find the same kind of "all-Israel" perspective. Even if this tiny community was a fragment of two tribes—Judah and Benjamin, along with the service of the Levites—it considered itself to be a reconstituting of Israel, ideally and liturgically represented as a twelve-tribe whole. They were one people again. And wherever possible, they would engage in events as "all the people." The following passages illustrate this perspective.

Ezra 3:1	After the return, the people gather in Jerusalem, "as one man."
Ezra 5:11	There is something exalted and united in the claim they make to the Persian government: "We are the servants of the God of heaven and earth."
Ezra 6:16–17	At the dedication of the rebuilt temple, among the proliferation of sacrifices, they offered "as a sin offering for *all Israel, twelve* male goats, one for *each of the tribes of Israel*" (italics added)—even though ten of those tribes were no longer physically present.
Ezra 8:35	This action was repeated by the exiles who accompanied Ezra on his return: "*twelve* bulls for *all Israel*" (italics added).
Neh 1:10	Nehemiah's first prayer appeals to God in language drawn from Deuteronomy, going right back to when there was only a single people whom God had redeemed from Egypt, reminding God that even now—centuries later and after generations of division, destruction, and dislocation—"they are your servants and your people, whom you redeemed."

22. See also Williamson, *Israel in the Books of Chronicles*.

Neh 3	The whole chapter, with its lovingly recorded details of all those who helped rebuild the wall of Jerusalem, is calculated to carry the message: "this was a task accomplished by the whole people for the sake of the whole people."
Neh 5:5	This chapter is a negative illustration. The people who should have been united in meeting the challenge of survival in tough economic circumstances had in fact allowed themselves to be divided yet again, with all the preexilic deformities of oppression and debt bondage. Nehemiah's strong appeal is to their status as "brothers"—one people who should fear God and deal justly with one another.
Neh 8:1–3	"All the people" gathered for the reading of the law. This chapter emphasizes the unity of the whole people by specifying men, women, children, and all who could understand, and then repeating the word "all" in varying contexts twelve times.
Neh 9	Another negative point, in that the recollected preexilic history, though it mentions many of the great moments of sin and rebellion in that history, omits completely the tragic division of the kingdom after Solomon. All the evil that has encompassed them has simply come upon "all your people" (9:32).
Neh 10:28–29	The covenant renewal is undertaken by "all the people"—with the same detailed listing as at 8:2–3.
Neh 12	Although the familiar phrase "all the people" is not used, the description of the dedication of the rebuilt walls clearly portrays it as a national celebration, bringing joy to the whole united community.

Flowing through all this, then, is a sense of purposefulness. There is a determination to reconstitute the one people of God, Israel. And this has missional significance. For although there is no direct reference to the wider purpose of Israel's existence—namely to be the vehicle of God's blessing and salvation reaching the ends of the earth—the "background music" of texts like Isa 40–66 has not been rendered inaudible. This people needed to be restored so that God could get on with God's own mission in God's own time.

When we widen the theme of the unity of God's people out further, it stands as an important element in biblical theology—and as a major factor in the fulfillment of God's mission. It is, in other words, part of a missional reading of the Bible. The emphasis on one whole people that we see in Ezra-Nehemiah could almost be a commentary on the fulfillment (partially at least) of the vision of Ezek 37:15–28. Following hard on his vision of a restored Israel that would be nothing short of a national resurrection accomplished by the power of God's Spirit (37:1–14), Ezekiel is told to join together two sticks—representing the divided kingdoms of Judah and Ephraim. Significantly, the name "house of Israel" is attached to both nations (37:16–17). The vision then goes on to expand on the theme of restored unity, under one king, one God, one covenant, and one dwelling place for God, with division and idolatry consigned to the past. This unification of God's people will be a significant moment—not just for them, but through them for God's wider purpose of making himself known to the nations. *The God of Ezekiel is the God who wills to be known.* The phrase "then you/they/the nations will know" occurs more than eighty times in the book, as here at the climax of the whole chapter: "Then the nations will know that I Yhwh make Israel holy, when my sanctuary is among them forever" (37:28)—that is, when God is to be seen dwelling in the midst of his unified, sanctified people.

Unity and sanctification go together also in the great high priestly prayer of Jesus in John 17. The influence of Ezekiel on the Johannine tradition is acknowledged to be strong, and this may be one such echo. After praying for his Father to sanctify his disciples, Jesus prays (twice) that they may be one—one in the indwelling unity of the Father and the Son. And significantly, this prayer for unity is also missional, since the whole purpose of the church's unity is "so that the world may believe that you have sent me. . . . The world will know that you sent me" (17:21–23). The revelation of the identity, deity, and mission of Jesus is bound up with the oneness of the people who are his disciples.

Paul likewise may have Ezek 37 in mind when he transposes the reunification of the two kingdoms of Israel into the uniting of Jew and Gentile in Christ—at the very heart of his gospel. The great accomplishment of the cross is that God "has made the two one . . . creating one new humanity out of the two, thus making peace" (Eph 2:14–16). And, in another echo of Ezekiel, the privilege of this unified people of God from Jews and Gentiles is that they both become not only citizens of God's people, not only members of God's family, but also the place of God's dwelling. "The nations will know . . . when my sanctuary is among them forever," Ezekiel had said (37:28). Not only the nations, but "the rulers and authorities in the heavenly realms" will know, says Paul, when the multinational people of God are united as "a holy temple in the Lord . . . a dwelling in which God lives by his Spirit" (Eph 2:21–22; 3:10).

The unity of the Israel of God, accomplished in such a partial and provisional way, though with clear intentionality, in Ezra-Nehemiah reaches its final fulfillment in the portrait of the redeemed people of God in the new creation.

The city of God in John's "virtual reality" tour, transcending the rebuilt Jerusalem of Nehemiah, will have twelve gates bearing the names of the twelve tribes of Israel, and foundations bearing the names of the twelve apostles of the Lamb. Here is the one united people of God in the complete totality of Old and New Testaments (Rev 21:12–14). Redeemed humanity can be pictured as the twelve tribes of Israel, even though in reality they will be drawn from every nation on earth—a great multitude whom no one could number (7:4–10).

Within a canonical perspective, then, the unity of God's people may be seen to have both a horizontal dimension (in that it will ultimately embrace people from all nations, tribes, and languages) and a vertical dimension (in that it will bind into one those from every historical era who have belonged to God as his redeemed people—within Old Testament Israel and the New Testament church). This double dimension of unity seems core to Paul's understanding of his own mission. On the one hand his apostolic mandate to the Gentiles was creating communities of both Jews and Gentiles, whom he affirmed, on the foundation of faith and baptism in Christ, to be "all one in the Messiah Jesus" (Gal 3:28). The messianic community is as diverse as humanity itself, yet one people. And on the other hand, he insists on an organic spiritual continuity among all who have believed God's promises, beginning with and including Abraham himself. The messianic community includes within the fellowship of Christ all who share the faith of Abraham, in Old and New Testament eras. Indeed, Paul uses clearly Abrahamic language in his definition of his own apostolic mission, to bring about the "obedience of faith among all nations" (Rom 1:5; 16:26).

A People Called to Distinctiveness

Returning to our text and to the tiny community that embodied that hope in scarcely more than embryonic form, we cannot miss the emphasis on the need for this community to maintain its distinctiveness from the surrounding "peoples of the lands" (the literal phrase that the NIV translates "the neighboring peoples"). That expression is used for the population that had settled in abandoned Judah during the generations of the exile. Judah had been a backwater of the Babylonian Empire, and now it was a small province of the Persian Empire. Local rulers in the region proved themselves occasionally helpful but mostly obstructive and hostile to the returning exiles and their reconstruction projects. The call for distinctiveness and separation comes on several occasions (Ezra 4:1–3, 9–10; Neh 10:30–32; 13:23–28).

How should this dimension of postexilic Israel's life and faith be evaluated? It can be viewed in two ways—one positive and the other more problematic. On the one hand, it was the outworking of a principle that had been at the core of Israel's faith from the beginning and formed part of their missional identity in the world. But on the other hand, the specific practical implementation of the principle that Ezra supervised (divorcing foreign wives) is open to some cautious critique.

First, the positive. When God brought Israel out of Egypt, he brought them "to himself" at Mount Sinai. And there, having gotten their full attention, so to speak, he addressed them in a classic text: "You yourselves have seen what I did to Egypt, and how I carried you on eagles' wings and brought you to myself. Now if you obey me fully and keep my covenant, then out of all nations you will be my treasured possession. For[23] the whole earth is mine, and you will be for me a kingdom of priests and a holy nation" (Exod 19:4–6 NIV modified).

Significantly, God points first of all to his own initiative of redemption ("you have seen what I have done"). All that will follow (including the giving of the law) is founded on the grace of God that had intervened in their bondage and liberated them. Only on the basis of that prior grace does God then call for obedience and covenant-keeping. Obedience is not a condition of salvation. But it is a condition for what God has in mind for Israel as they face the future. Israel is called to *be something* for God in the midst of "all nations" in "the whole earth." In other words, Israel now has an *identity* and a *mission*: "You will be for me a priestly kingdom and a holy nation."

The precise meaning and significance of Israel being a "priestly kingdom" is much discussed. But at the very least, it seems to me, it means that Israel will occupy a comparable kind of mediatorial role between God and the nations as their priests do between God and the rest of the Israelites. Priests stood in the middle. They were called to teach God's law (Lev 10:11; Deut 33:10). So, through the priests God would be known to the rest of the people. And they were ordained to offer the sacrifices of the people at the altar before God. So, through the priests, the people could come back into covenant fellowship with God in the worshiping assembly. Now God says to Israel as a whole people: "You will be for me to the rest of the nations of the world what your priests are for you. Through you, I will become known to the nations; and through you ultimately I will draw the nations to myself in covenant relationship."

---

23. I am certain that Hebrew כִּי/*kî* should be translated in its normal sense: "for" or "because"—not "although," as in so many English versions. Israel is to be God's holy priesthood in the midst of all the nations, *not* as something set in contrast to, or in spite of, Yhwh's owning the whole earth (as is implied by the concessive "although"), but rather precisely *because* of that. In the framework of Yhwh's universal ownership of the whole earth and all nations, Israel will have a particular identity and role to play in God's purposes for the world.

Both of these dimensions of Israel's existence among the nations (centrifugal and centripetal) are found in the prophets and Psalms. And this is part of a missional understanding of Old Testament Israel. The Israelites were not (in my view) expected to go out to the nations or to send out "missionaries" in our sense of the word. They were to live among the nations as witnesses to the one true living God. They were called not to *go*, but to *be*. To live as the people of God.[24]

In order to be that kind of *priestly* people, they must necessarily also be a *holy* people. That did not mean they were to be specially "religious." Rather, holiness meant distinctiveness. God had set them apart from the nations. Fundamentally, Israel was to be a different kind of people from the nations around them. The most succinct summary of that distinctiveness comes in Lev 18:3-4, in that section of the book often referred to as the Holiness Code: "You must not do as they do in Egypt, where you used to live, and you must not do as they do in the land of Canaan, where I am bringing you. Do not follow their practices. You must obey my laws and be careful to follow my decrees. I am YHWH your God." They were not to imitate the idolatry of Egypt—with its gods of imperial splendor and state power. Nor were they to imitate the idolatry of Canaan—with its gods of fertility, sex, and material prosperity. No, "you must be holy because I, YHWH your God, am holy" (Lev 19:2). Israel must be a different, distinctive people, because YHWH is distinct among all the so-called gods of the nations.

Israel's separation/holiness was then reflected in myriad ways in their laws and customs—including the distinction between clean and unclean food. That distinction in the animal kingdom is explicitly said to mirror the distinction between Israel and the nations (Lev 20:25-26). That symbolism was representative of something theologically significant—the demand that God's people should be, and be seen to be, different.[25]

But the difference was not merely ritual. Far greater emphasis is laid in the law on the *ethical* dimensions of Israel's holiness. That is what would raise interest and questions among the nations. Deuteronomy gives many motivations for Israel to obey God's law. But one of the earliest, in the key orientation chapter (Deut 4), is that if Israel would live in the way God intended (in the whole range of social, economic, political, judicial, and familial contexts that

---

24. For detailed discussion of the missiological significance of Exod 19:4-6 and related texts throughout the Old Testament, see my *Mission of God*, 114-27.

25. That the distinction between clean and unclean foods was symbolic of the distinction between Israel and the other nations is confirmed by the way, in the New Testament, the abolition (for those in Christ) of the distinction between Jew and Gentile meant the end of the need to maintain the clean-unclean food distinction that symbolized it.

are addressed in the book), then the nations would take note. This is a major missional text that binds together biblical ethics and biblical mission:

> Observe [these laws] carefully, for this will show your wisdom and understanding to the nations, who will hear about all these decrees and say, "Surely this great nation is a wise and understanding people." What other nation is so great as to have their gods near them the way Yhwh our God is near us whenever we pray to him? And what other nation is so great as to have such righteous decrees and laws as this body of laws I am setting before you today? (Deut 4:6–8)

The people of God do not live in vacuum-sealed isolation. They are to be separate and distinct from the nations, yes. But the whole point of that is to bear witness to the nations as to what it means to live under the nearness of God and in a society of justice and compassion.

So then, there was a missional dimension to the holiness of Israel. Paradoxically, their separation from the nations was part of an agenda that was ultimately for the blessing of the nations. And to that extent, when we see the emphasis in the postexilic community to maintain their distinctiveness from the surrounding peoples, we can understand the theology that lay behind it—even if, in the circumstances, it was not practiced with a particularly mission-minded attitude toward those other nations. Distinctiveness from the nations had become hostility toward the nations—although, to be fair, it has to be said that the hostility was experienced in both directions.

When we pursue the theme of holiness and separation on into the New Testament, two things happen. On the one hand, the distinction between Jew and Gentile, which had been symbolically represented in the distinction between clean and unclean food, is abolished in Christ through the cross. Through Christ and the gospel, God opened the door for people of any and all nations to become, in Paul's language, "heirs together with Israel, members together of one body, and sharers together in the promise in Christ Jesus" (Eph 3:6). On the other hand, the concept and vocabulary of holiness and separation is not nullified altogether. Rather, it is transformed into the call for distinctively *Christian* holiness of life. Just as Old Testament Israel was called to avoid the ways of the surrounding nations, so with equal rhetoric and authority, Paul urges Christians no longer to live "as the Gentiles do." Interestingly, Paul transposes the Old Testament distinction between *Israelites* and the other nations (Gentiles) into a New Testament distinction between Christian believers (many of whom were Gentiles in the Old Testament sense) and pagans. Holiness and separation does not mean withdrawal from the world into sacred isolation. It does mean living *in* the world, but living *by* the standards of the kingdom of God as taught by Christ and his apostles.

Turning now, however, to the specific issue on which Ezra and Nehemiah found Israel's distinctiveness from the nations to be compromised—marriages involving foreign wives—we face a more difficult hermeneutical challenge. We may well understand and even appreciate their motives, but are we required to approve of their actions? It may help to address the question in three parts: we should appreciate how serious the issue was; we should look carefully at how the Scriptures are used in responding to the problem; and we should ask whether the solution proposed requires our approval or has any prescriptive force.

The Importance of the Issue

There can be no doubt that the complaint raised by "the leaders" in Ezra 9:1 was perceived as a serious threat to the small community seeking to establish itself after the exile, and indeed it was exactly that. This was a vulnerable and fragile community that needed to define its own identity and preserve it.

At a purely social level that identity would be compromised by intermarriage with surrounding peoples. Cultural assimilation would inevitably follow within a generation or two. This probability is all the greater if, as some scholars think, one of the motives for taking these foreign wives was for social and/or economic advantage. The "peoples of the lands" were already well established long before the exiles of Judah began to return. Some of them may have become quite wealthy landowners. They had strong political leaders (as we see in the opposition to the rebuilding of both the temple and the walls). For some Israelite men, the temptation to gain advantages by "marrying up" was too strong to resist. And that would only increase the pressure to accommodate to the culture and religion of their new spouses. Indeed, if Mal 2:10–16 refers to the same issue around the same time, then it seems some Jewish men had compounded their sin by divorcing the Jewish wives of their youth in order to enter into these foreign marriages. Cultural assimilation would produce other undesirable effects, as Nehemiah encountered. The next generation could even lose the language of Israel (Neh 13:24). Not only did that spell loss of Israelite culture (given that language and culture are so symbiotically connected), it meant they would lose the ability to hear and understand the Scriptures—the very foundation of the community itself. Furthermore, at a political level, the mandate of the Persian king, Artaxerxes, was specifically to frame and order the returning community according to "the laws of your God." His decree was specific and repeated on that point, with severe sanctions (Ezra 7:11–26). Ezra was accountable not just to God but to the secular government for preserving the separate identity of the community.

But the primary issue was clearly one of preserving the distinctiveness of Israel's faith and worship from the contamination of the worship of other gods and the accompanying degrading practices that went along with that. That not only constituted "unfaithfulness" (Ezra 9:2; 10:2; Neh 13:27)—a serious word signifying disloyalty to the covenant and its fundamental monotheistic requirement—it would also lead to the adoption of the "detestable practices" of the Canaanites (with whom the present "peoples of the land" are equated; Ezra 9:11). That is the key factor in Nehemiah's appeal to the bad example of Solomon and how marrying foreign wives led him into sin and unfaithfulness (Neh 13:26–27).

So then, we need to understand that the underlying rationale for the prohibition on marrying the Canaanites (in the first place) was not racial but religious.[26] It was not the foreignness of these wives that was the problem in itself, but that, being foreign, they were importing pagan gods and polluted practices into the heart of Israelite families. And as the history of preexilic Israel had so graphically demonstrated—that was a path that could only end in tears. Or rather, in death—as indeed it had in the "death" of exile. Recognition of this explains the threefold action of Ezra on hearing the news: tearing his clothes, tearing his hair, and sitting on the ground (Ezra 9:3) were combined symbols of the mourning of bereavement. Israel, on this course, was in deadly danger. This was serious.

The Use of Scripture

The problem was that there is no direct instruction in the laws of Moses about what to do in such circumstances. The law clearly prohibited Israelites from marrying Canaanites (Exod 34:11–16; Deut 7:1–4). But the law did not prescribe what should be done if Israelites *had already* married Canaanites (or their equivalents). So the leaders come to Ezra with a speech that shows they have done some fascinating scriptural interpretation, presenting the problem in the light of several Scriptures that they have drawn together. And in applying those texts to the current situation, they actually extend them beyond their original target. But then, that's what all scriptural application has to do.[27]

26. "Both Ezra and Nehemiah cast the danger of intermarriage with foreigners as one of apostasy driven by the pagan beliefs of the foreign spouse. Ethnic or racial issues, other than religion, are not at all related to the prohibition"; Hays, *From Every People and Nation*, 79.

27. The discussion here is heavily dependent on the fine exegesis and comment of Williamson, *Ezra, Nehemiah*, 129–38.

They begin from Deut 7:1–4. The first thing they "extend" is the list of names of the old Canaanite nations. None of them were now living in the land, but the leaders apply their status as banned nations to their current "neighboring peoples." But then they also add "Ammonites and Moabites"—who are not in the list of Deut 7, but do appear in 23:3, as nations to be excluded from Israel's worshiping assembly. But 23:3 says nothing about marriage—so once again, a text is being stretched. Finally, they include "Egyptians," which possibly hints at Lev 18:3, where Israel was told not to do as the Egyptians do, but not to refrain from marrying them. So, these leaders are comparing and combining Scriptures to strengthen their case for coming to Ezra (renowned as an expert in the law) with a perception of the problem that they consider to be, as we might put it, "unbiblical."

Their primary choice of text (Deut 7) is important because it forbids intermarriage with the *Canaanite* nations living in the land, and the leaders feel that the "neighboring peoples" can legitimately be equated with those listed in the text. They have to do this because, in fact, there was no blanket ban on Israelites marrying foreigners. Some of the most famous Israelites had done so, including Joseph (Gen 41:45), Moses (Exod 2:21; Num 12:1), and Boaz (ancestor of David; Ruth 4). Indeed the law of Deuteronomy permitted an Israelite soldier to take a wife from among the captives of a foreign defeated city (presumably outside the land; Deut 21:10–14).

But the scriptural application of these leaders takes a more questionable turn when they interpret these foreign marriages in these terms: "they have mingled the holy race [lit., seed] with the peoples around them" (Ezra 9:2). There is nothing about "seed" or race in Deut 7. The marriage ban there is to preserve religious and ethical distinctiveness, not to preserve racial purity. Possibly they are using and applying the precedent of Lev 19:19, which prohibits the mixing of different kinds of animals, seeds, or clothing. The meaning of that law is almost certainly symbolic of Israel's separation from the nations in holiness of faith and behavior. But it is being applied by these leaders to *racial* separation per se. Interestingly, in the other place where "mingling" or "mixing" is used to describe Israel's accommodation to the culture of Canaan, the emphasis is entirely on the religious and moral dimensions of that mingling (idolatry, child sacrifice, shedding innocent blood, defiling behavior; Ps 106:35–39)—and not at all on any racial dimension as such.

It feels as if these leaders are focusing on the simplest way of dealing with the issue. The *real* problem is the sin of unfaithfulness and polluted worship and life, along with, probably, the selfish ambition of the men involved. But that is connected to the foreign wives. So their response concentrates on the *foreignness* itself, as the easiest thing to identify and deal with. Blame the foreigners.

It is a well-trodden path in human history. I find myself, therefore, agreeing with Williamson's assessment: "It is thus difficult to avoid the conclusion that the community here regards itself as racially distinct from its neighbors. The concept of the seed of Abraham, elect by God as a 'holy people' not because of any superiority but in order to be his servant for the blessing of the nations (e.g., Gen 12:1–3, 7; Deut 7:6–7) has now been twisted by the misapplication of a quite separate law into an ideal of racial, as distinct from religious, separation."[28]

The Solution: Right or Wrong?

Having said that, we are still left with this being a seriously threatening problem, and the leaders rightly felt that they had to do something about it. So they come up with a radical solution: those who had married foreign wives must be summoned to "send them away" along with their children, or face some severe penalties (Ezra 10:3). This was indeed a severe, somewhat surgical, action. Not even Nehemiah repeated it. When he encountered men who had married foreign wives, he berated them with rhetorical and physical abuse. But he did not insist that they divorce those wives. He simply quoted the Scriptures that said such things should not happen (Neh 13:23–28).

So how are we to evaluate this, the concluding scene of the book of Ezra? It is not at all easy to give a clear answer to that question, but the following considerations can be taken into account:

- The proposal comes from Shecaniah son of Jehiel (Ezra 10:2).[29] It does not come from Ezra (though he accepts it). It did not emerge from the mouth of a prophet speaking on behalf of God. The narrator does not say that God told Shecaniah, or Ezra, or the Israelites, to do this. So although we have the record in the Bible of what was proposed and what was done, simply as a matter of reported fact, we are not necessarily compelled to see it as a divinely mandated or approved strategy. Still less can we see it as an "example to follow." In fact, Paul, while he urges Christians not to "be yoked together with unbelievers" (2 Cor 6:14; which probably, though not exclusively, refers to marriage), tells those with unbelieving spouses *not* to divorce, unless the unbelieving partner chooses to do so (1 Cor 7:12–16).

---

28. Ibid., 132.

29. If, as seems likely, this is the same Jehiel who is listed among those who had married foreign wives (Ezra 10:21), then Shecaniah is himself the son of a foreign wife. This makes his leadership of the group who propose the divorce policy all the more remarkable, since it was taking a stance against his own parents.

- Having said that, the overall feel of the passage is that the narrator approves of this action as one sign among others of the determination of Ezra and his community to turn away from unfaithfulness and return to biblical obedience as they perceived it.
- We may well think that the action was unfair on the women and children involved, effectively punishing them for the sins of their Israelite husbands, retrospectively so perceived. We have no way of knowing if Ezra and the other leaders had the same qualms and if so, what they did with their consciences on that matter. The law of Deuteronomy *permitted* divorce, of course (Deut 24:1–4), but as Jesus sharply pointed out, it did not *command* divorce. Perhaps, if they did reflect on the suffering caused by their action, they took the view that for the sake of the whole community and its future, this was the lesser of two evils. And we know that in a fallen world, that is sometimes a choice we cannot avoid.
- What happened to the wives and children who were "sent away"? Again, we have no way of knowing, but if the law of Deut 24:1–4 was applied then they would have had certificates of divorce and been free to remarry. Some of them may have taken the "Orpah option" and returned to their fathers' houses and found other husbands, within the "kindness of Yhwh" (Ruth 1:6–14). We might also imagine that Ezra, since he was so committed to thoroughly practicing the law of Moses, would take seriously the frequent injunctions in the law to take care of widows and orphans—which was what the foreign wives and their children effectively became.
- We might still question if mass divorce was the only option open to the leaders. As mentioned above, there was no prohibition on marrying foreign wives, *if the wives in question accepted Israel's faith and exclusive worship of Yhwh*. That is manifestly the case with Ruth. But such an option (conversion) was not offered to these women, as far as we know. Indeed, given the complexity of the postexilic situation, it is very likely that some foreign wives had effectively already converted to Israel's faith, and equally plenty of native-born Israelite wives who had abandoned theirs. But the leaders found "foreignness" to be the easiest criterion to apply and made that the sole criterion, a policy that might bear legitimate criticism.
- In any case, "mass divorce" may be a wrong perception of the whole affair. The list of those who had married foreign women (and presumably agreed to divorce them) is relatively small. "The list includes 27 clergymen [*sic*] and 84 laymen, a total of 111 persons altogether. That is a very small proportion of the population of almost 30,000 returned exiles. Several possibilities have been suggested to explain this. Some maintain that it may be only a partial listing, others that it may indicate that only a small

percentage of people really did reform. Others suggest that the problem was not in actuality as serious as it appears on the surface."[30] Again, we have no way to be certain on this either way, but it is at least an aspect that we should not overlook.

Perhaps at the end of our pondering, we may conclude that while we can understand why Ezra and the leaders took the action they did, and while we can appreciate the seriously threatening potential of the situation they were seeking to rectify, we must leave an open verdict on whether it was the right thing to do, or the only option available. They did it. And we can understand why. And they did it with serious attention to the Scriptures as they interpreted them in their situation—applying Scriptures to a situation for which there was no actual specific command to simply quote and obey. Shecaniah urges Ezra to take the action he proposes, "in accordance with the counsel . . . of those who fear the commands of Yhwh. Let it be done according to the law" (Ezra 10:3). But as pointed out, there was no command of Yhwh in the law to do what they were proposing. He would have more accurately said, "Let it be done according to the way we think the law should be interpreted, extended, and applied to this situation." He was not wrong to seek to apply the Scripture to a new situation. We all have to do that. Perhaps he was claiming too much in presenting his proposed action as being simply "according to the law." It is worth remembering that accepting the authority of the Scriptures does not guarantee right interpretation and application of the Scriptures. Nor can we guarantee that those who sincerely accept the authority of the Scriptures will agree on whose interpretation and application is right or better than others. But the absence of such guarantees does not excuse us from the challenging task of exegesis and application, along with the responsibility of mutual and respectful critique.

But let's return to the primary issue in this section: Israel's distinctiveness. This is how Williamson appropriately concludes his discussion of these chapters:

> Finally, if we may overlook for the moment the details of how Ezra worked out the principle of Jewish distinctiveness, his underlying concern was absolutely right. Israel's mission could only make headway if she maintained the servant identity that separated her from the nations to whom she should mediate the revelation of God. In just the same way, Christians individually and collectively as the Church are called to be "light" and "salt," elements

---

30. Howard, *Introduction to the Old Testament Historical Books*, 295.

that function effectively precisely because of their difference from the setting in which they are placed; "But if the salt has lost its savor" (cf. Matt 5:13–16).[31]

A People Prone to Failure—Past, Present, and Future

The historical location of the whole narrative of Ezra-Nehemiah presupposes and points to past failure. The story begins with the edict of Cyrus allowing the descendants of the Israelites exiled by Nebuchadnezzar to return to their land and rebuild their temple. But why had their ancestors had to leave their land, and why had their temple been destroyed? The answer of course requires the whole preexilic history of Israel from Solomon to Zedekiah. And that, we know, is a story of repeated rebellion and unfaithfulness, incorrigible idolatry, individual wickedness, social corruption, and royal arrogance. We trace it through the Deuteronomistic History, accompanied by the preexilic prophets. The axe of God's judgment finally fell in 587 BCE, and two generations of Israelites had lived in a far country.

But that was then, and this is now. The return to the land spoke of God's forgiveness and restoration, with all the eloquence of Isa 40–55 or Jer 30–31. The old has gone, the new has come. Failure is the story of the past. A new day has dawned, has it not? Well, yes and no.

Certainly, the restoration after exile was a fresh start for the nation of Israel (or at least the tiny leftovers of it) and, in that sense, also a fresh start for the purposes of God for humanity. The soaring visions of Isaiah and the more tender compassion of Jeremiah were not inappropriate. God was indeed "on the move" again in the history of this people. But just as the generation that experienced God's first great act of redemption out of Egypt failed in faith and obedience, so this generation, redeemed again through a new exodus, failed to live up either to the law of God that was read to them (as it had been to their ancestors at Sinai) or to the promises they made on various occasions (as their ancestors had at Sinai and in the land itself; Exod 24; Josh 24). History repeats itself, not only in positive redemptive dimensions, but also in classic past failures. "If Ezra is a second Moses, he, like the first Moses, has not produced and cannot produce a change in the heart of the people. That awaits some future day. The exile continues even though Israel is in the land."[32]

The three great confessional prayers (Ezra 9; Neh 1; 9) show that Israel's

---

31. Williamson, *Ezra, Nehemiah*, 162.
32. Dempster, *Dominion and Dynasty*, 224.

sins and failures could not be cheerfully consigned to the past. Postexilic Israelites were as fallen and sinful as preexilic Israelites and could default into very similar patterns of behavior, as the crisis of Neh 5 illustrates. So the history lesson of Ezra 9 and Neh 9 especially—apart from their primary purpose in pleading for God's mercy in the midst of the current specific failure—was to remind this and every subsequent generation that Israel lived solely by the forgiving grace and mercy of God—and always had done. The recital of Israel's history of past failure, then, was both humbling and encouraging. Their history gave them no reason to boast, but every reason to trust.

This must also be the rationale for the otherwise enigmatic ending of the book of Nehemiah. We would love it to end with Neh 12, with the whole countryside resounding to the songs of massed choirs in Jerusalem at the dedication of the walls. Surely that note of exuberant joy would be the place to end the book. But no. Even after such a climax of worship and praise we have the sorry tale of yet another episode of disobedience, as some of the people renege on the very things they had so recently promised to observe (Neh 13). The story of God's people seems like a never-ending rollercoaster. No matter what heights of praise and promise they attain, there always follows the sickening plummet into sin and disobedience.

'Twas ever thus, we may say, as we scan the whole Bible story. Genesis 3 follows Gen 1–2. Noah's sin follows hard on his experience of salvation. The golden calf follows the exodus redemption and Sinai revelation. Achan and Ai follow Rahab and Jericho. The chaos of Judges follows the covenant renewal at Shechem (Josh 23–24). Adultery and murder follow David bringing the ark of the covenant into Jerusalem. Foreign wives, idolatry, and oppression follow Solomon building the temple for YHWH. And even when we come to the New Testament, Peter's denial of Jesus follows his profession of loyalty even unto death. And even after the birth of the eschatological community of the Messiah and the outpouring of God's Spirit, Ananias and Sapphira follow Pentecost. God's redeemed people are sinners still.

'Twas ever thus, but *will it be* forever thus? Is it in fact a *never-ending* rollercoaster? Are we doomed to repeat the past *ad infinitum*, or *ad aeternitatem*? A hint that the cycle of failure will eventually be broken "for good" lies in Nehemiah's closing words in his book. After his attempt yet again to purify the service of the priests and Levites in the temple, he appeals to God: "Remember me, O my God, for good" (Neh 13:31 NRSV). "For good" is the final word of the book. "Good" was God's first word about creation, and it will be God's last word too. Ultimately all will be good and for the good of those who are called and redeemed for God's purpose and glory (Rom 8:28).

However, much stronger than mere verbal hints of that sort are the explicit promises of the prophets that the day will come when God's people will love and serve God in perfect righteousness and obedience and with joy untarnished by any further sin or failure. In fact, that hope was entertained by Deuteronomy. Knowing full well Israel's story of past and future failure, Deuteronomy looks forward to the day when "Yhwh your God will circumcise your hearts and the hearts of your descendants, so that you may love him with all your heart and with all your soul, and live" (30:6). God's grace will give what God's law demands: "Then will all your people be righteous," promises Isaiah, when the light of God brings an end to the darkness of Israel and the whole world (Isa 60:21). Jeremiah expands the theme of a renewed covenant, including an end to all apostasy: "They will be my people, and I will be their God. I will give them singleness of heart and action, so that they will always fear me for their own good and the good of their children after them. I will make an everlasting covenant with them: I will never stop doing good to them, and I will inspire them to fear me, so that they will never turn away from me" (Jer 32:38–40).

Ezekiel foresees a radical heart surgery through the spirit of God that will enable God's people to live in perfect obedience: "I will give you a new heart and put a new spirit in you; I will remove from you your heart of stone and give you a heart of flesh. And I will put my Spirit in you and move you to follow my decrees and be careful to keep my laws" (Ezek 36:26–27). Ultimately then, the cycle of repeated commitment followed by repeated failure will be broken. John's picture of the new creation includes a catalog of things that will be "no more" or "no longer." They include death, mourning, sin, impurity, deceit, curse. Then, and for eternity, God's "servants will serve him" (Rev 22:3). But until then?

It would be easy to surrender to cynicism in reaction to a reading of Ezra-Nehemiah from beginning to end. Here we see people who, on several occasions, make solemn promises to obey God in various particulars of his law. And these promises are accompanied by public occasions that include considerable amounts of formal ritual and emotional expression—of weeping and celebration. And yet with breathtaking regularity, they break those very same promises and repeat the pattern of failure that is so familiar from their long history. What then, we might well ask, was the point of those great ceremonies of commitment? If covenant commitments are so relentlessly followed by covenant failures, is there ever any value in making or renewing such commitments at all?

The question hits us much earlier than Ezra-Nehemiah, though those books are a stark illustration of it. Deuteronomy is a book that, remarkably, begins and ends with failure and yet includes the most solemn of covenant renewals. It begins, in a manner reminiscent of Nehemiah, with a searing reminder of the failure and rebellion of the previous generation (Deut 1:19–46). And it ends with relentless predictions of the failure and apostasies of the generations to come (29:22-28; 31:16-18, 21, 27; 32:1-52). And yet the thrust of the whole book is a repeated appeal and challenge to Israel to renew their covenant commitment to Yhwh, to love and obey him exclusively and wholeheartedly. Even those closing chapters, with their predictions and curses for failure, include the mutual affirmation of covenant commitment: "You have declared this day that Yhwh is your God and that you will walk in his ways, that you will keep his decrees, commands and laws, and that you will obey him. And Yhwh has declared this day that you are his people, his treasured possession as he promised" (26:17-18). Such covenant commitment is not blind or naïve on either side. It is made in full realization of the sinful fallibility of the human party. Failure is anticipated. But equally, such covenant commitment is not rendered irrelevant or invalid by the awareness of future failure. On the contrary, that failure is foreseen makes the regularity of renewed commitment all the more necessary. Since the covenant was founded on the past grace of historical redemption, it must be renewed on the basis of future grace that will be experienced through confession, repentance, and forgiveness. And renewed commitment to *obedience* is the proper response to grace. Obedience, of course, in both Old and New Testament, is never the means to earn or deserve God's blessings (material or spiritual). Rather, it is the appropriate response to the grace of God already received in election, redemption, and covenant. Obedience is founded on forgiving and sustaining grace and mercy.[33]

Perhaps no one knew this better than Peter. He had made his great confession of faith in Jesus as the Messiah. He had vowed never to desert Jesus, even at the cost of his life. Yet he failed abysmally when the test came. He denied even knowing Jesus at all. But, in a replay of Deuteronomy, Jesus had warned the disciples that this would be the case (Luke 22:31-34; John 13:37-38). Peter's failure was foreseen! And in a further replay of Deuteronomy, how did Jesus restore Peter? By calling for his love. Jesus, who had endorsed Deut 6:5 as the first and greatest commandment in the law, that we should love Yhwh our God with all our heart and soul and strength, adopts the Yhwh position with the simple covenantal question: "Do you love me?" And with Peter's renewed confession of love, his failure was forgiven and his future ministry assigned (John 21:15-19).

It is the testimony of the whole Bible, from Gen 3 until the arrival of the new creation, that failure is a fact (not only by humanity at large but also within

---

33. Brueggemann deplores the suspicion of obedience within the Western Protestant church where it is strongly influenced by the Augustinian-Lutheran dichotomy of grace and law: "The result ... has been a remarkable aversion to 'works,' as though obedience to the commands of God, that is, performance of 'works,' is in and of itself a denial of the gospel"; Brueggemann, "Duty as Delight and Desire," 35.

the people of God), that failure is foreseen, and that failure can be forgiven. And in that great truth of the biblical narrative lay Israel's future and Israel's hope—and ours, and the world's.

A People with a Hope and a Future

Ezra-Nehemiah, then, is ruthlessly realistic about the past and the present:

> The people of God, who were constituted at Sinai, have passed through all the vicissitudes of the monarchy and the catastrophe of the exile, to be gathered once more, in chastened circumstances around the temple and under the mosaic Torah. They have been restored as God promised, but the achievement is only partial and in no sense does the restored community represent the fulfillment of God's purposes for his people. The earlier Davidic-Messianic hope of the prophets, which promised a glorious and peaceful future for the people (cf. Isa 9:6–7; Jer 33:15–22; Ezek 37:24–28), is apparently dormant in a period preoccupied with the survival and consolidation of the covenant community. It is clear that many things are far from ideal in the community's present circumstances.[34]

Nevertheless, in spite of all that being true, the overall conclusion is one of hope. This people will survive. They have a city, a temple, a renewed covenant, and (for a time at least) godly leaders. There is a sense that, if God can bring them this far, he will not abandon them even if the future is uncertain and even if future failures will echo the past. God can be trusted. And in that alone lies the hope of God's people.[35] That we meet the same people four centuries later in the pages of the New Testament proves the point.

There is more to this than mere passage of time, of course. We are not talking only about the historical resilience of the Jewish people. We must set all this (memory of the historical past and reassurance for the future) within the overall biblical framework of God's promise (as noted in the section "The

---

34. Kelly, "Ezra-Nehemiah," 198.

35. "The future, moreover, is not to be determined by Israel's obedience; the future . . . is in the hands of the One who is sovereignly faithful and faithfully sovereign. . . . The God who commands continues to command and Israel must obey in the present. And the God who saves is resolved to save in the largest scale of all creation. . . . Israel as a holy people refuses to doubt the promises, which assert that the future is dependent on nothing in this world, not even on Israel's obedience, but only on Yahweh's good intention, which is more reliable than the world itself"; Brueggemann, *Theology of the Old Testimony*, 447.

God Who Keeps His Promises"). And that generates a *missional* dimension to the discussion.

After all, why did it matter whether this tiny refugee fragment of a nation would survive or not? What difference would it have made if they had never returned from exile? Or if, having returned, they had simply withered away under the external hostility of surrounding peoples or the internal acids of cultural assimilation and covenant disobedience? Why was it so important that they should reconstitute themselves as a community of covenant faith in continuity with the nation to whom God had made such promises and done such great things in the past?

We cannot answer those questions directly from within the books themselves. Our texts show a people who were preoccupied with affirming their past, authenticating their present, and assuring their future—amid all the immediate pressures of their historical location. But when we set that limited story in the context of the wider biblical narrative, we immediately see that it did matter very much whether they survived. For this was the people to whom God had made a promise—a promise not for them alone, but through them for the whole world.

Nehemiah 9:7–8 recalls God's promise to Abraham. Now at that point, Nehemiah mentions only the promise of land and God's faithfulness to that promise—which is hardly surprising since the return to the land was uppermost in their minds at that point. But the full scope of that foundational Abrahamic covenant always remains close to the surface: the promise of blessing, of posterity (a great nation), of land, and (bottom line) of *all the nations on earth* blessing themselves, or in some sense being blessed, through Abraham and his descendants.

In other words, Israel existed as one nation in the world for the sake of God's mission of blessing all the rest of the nations in the world. The purpose of their election, redemption, and covenant relationship with Yhwh was not so that they would be the only people who would enjoy God's blessing and salvation. Rather their election and existence was instrumental in God's salvation going to the ends of the earth. Indeed, the promises received before and during the exile that there would be a return and a restoration include that element of universality. The rhetoric of Isa 40–66 especially sees Israel's return from exile as much more than a continuation of the preexilic nation. It envisages the event as a new act of Yhwh in his ultimate purpose of revealing his identity, glory, and saving power to "all flesh." That is the good news that the ruins of Jerusalem must hear. And that is the salvation that will be seen by the ends of the earth (52:7–10).

Nehemiah speaks of Abraham's "faithful heart" (Neh 9:8)—which must be a way of summarizing the double truth of Genesis, that Abraham both believed

God and obeyed him, or rather (as James would put it) that he proved his faith by his actions. That "obedience of faith" is what Paul sought to accomplish among all nations. It was indeed Paul's missionary agenda (Rom 1:5; 16:26). Paul's goal was to see the Abrahamic model, centered now on the saving work of God through Jesus the Messiah, replicated to the ends of the earth in communities of covenantal faith and transformed living. And in that great goal of the biblical drama, the story of Ezra-Nehemiah was one short but significant chapter.

The books of Ezra-Nehemiah, then, portray a very provisional and proximate hope (the partial and fractured fulfillment of great prophetic promises in a fallen and struggling community of mixed faith and failure). But in the context of the rest of the Bible story, they point to a greater hope that lies beyond not only their own horizon, but also beyond the gospel horizon of the New Testament, to the ultimate and eternal horizon of new creation.

So, with all their historically situated particularity and the detailed granularity of the problems they faced, Ezra and Nehemiah fit within the wider hope-filled story of biblical theology. Ultimately, this story of a redeemed people of single ethnicity returning to their own land, worshiping in a rebuilt temple within the restored walls of a ravaged city, is a microcosm of the story that looks forward to the redeemed people of God from all nations worshiping God in the temple of his new creation, free from the fear of their enemies, protected by the walls of the new Jerusalem, and enjoying the fruit of work that has been freed from the curse, and with the splendor of all nations, kings, and empires—purged of all evil—brought into the city of God. But for *that* story, and for that ending (or new beginning), we need our whole Bible, with its center in the person and work of Jesus Christ, through whom God was reconciling the whole world to himself.

Reading Ezra-Nehemiah Theologically Today

BY CHRISTOPHER J. H. WRIGHT

Community building is the heart of the books of Ezra and Nehemiah. The single narrative of both books portrays the restoration and reformation of God's covenant community, in its ideals and in its continuing fallibility. As Williamson shows, four major sections straddle both books, each of them describing different dimensions of the rebuilding of the postexilic community:[1]

Ezra 1–6: restoration of the temple
Ezra 7–10: restoration of the community
Neh 1–6: restoration of the city and its walls
Neh 7–13: restoration of covenant commitment

So as we reflect on the theological message of Ezra-Nehemiah for today, we can collect our thoughts around what kind of community they wanted to be and how the various dimensions of their aspirations and accomplishments can inform our own theological and practical efforts for the sake of the life and mission of the Christian church. Indeed, whereas the earlier Old Testament narratives highlight charismatic individual leaders—Abraham, Moses, Joshua, Samuel, David, and so on—the books of Ezra-Nehemiah make a subtle shift from leaders to community.[2] The role of Ezra and Nehemiah is crucial and catalytic, of course. Nevertheless we are clearly meant to be impressed that it is the community working together who rebuilds the wall; it is the community that rejoices at the completion of both temple and wall; it is the community that calls Ezra to read the law; it is the community that makes professions of collec-

---

1. Williamson, *Ezra, Nehemiah*, xlix–lii.
2. Though for a more precise analysis of "charisma" in relation to leadership in Ezra-Nehemiah, see the chapter "Leadership and Ezra-Nehemiah."

tive obedience.[3] There is even an argument that, with the failure of the Davidic monarchy (ethically and now also historically—there is no king in Jerusalem), the community itself "has become the heirs of the promises to David."[4]

This is not to reduce all theology to ecclesiology. Rather it is to acknowledge that all our theological understanding, assumptions, affirmations, and their implications have to be worked out within the community of God's people and in relation to our mission in God's world. So then, in the light of Ezra-Nehemiah, what kind of community are we called to be?

A Community of People Who Know Their Own Identity

The returning exiles knew precisely who they were. Not only were they from the tribes of Judah, Benjamin, and Levi, they also knew their genealogies and their geography. They had, so to speak, mental maps of their kinships and their townships. So although they had lived out of the land for two generations (so that only the very oldest had a memory of the original temple; Ezra 3:12), they still knew where and to whom they belonged. And so they were able to claim authenticated membership in the restored people of God.

It was a secure claim, but a humble one also. They could not forget (and Ezra's and Nehemiah's prayers would never let them forget) that they were, collectively, a prodigal child returning from a far country. Only by the grace and mercy of God were they restored to their land, their city, their temple, and their God. They knew that the decree of Cyrus, which had given them freedom to return, was the work of God in the king's heart and that he had been raised up by God for that purpose, in fulfillment of God's promises through Jeremiah (Ezra 1:1) and Isaiah (Isa 44:24–45:8).

So the identity of this community was a paradoxical mixture of unshakeable assurance and profound humility. They could hold their heads up and claim, "We are the servants of the God of heaven and earth" (Ezra 5:11). Yet they could also weep on the ground with Ezra, saying to God, "Here we are before you in our guilt, though because of it not one of us can stand in your presence"

---

3. Provan, Long, and Longman, *Biblical History of Israel*, 302; citing the insights of Eskenazi, *In an Age of Prose*. See also Birch et al., *Theological Introduction to the Old Testament*, 424–28.

4. Clines, *Ezra, Nehemiah, Esther*, 29. This did not mean, of course, that the wider and more long-term hopes attached to God's covenant with the house of David were forgotten; as Clines adds: "A more satisfying future realisation of those promises is not excluded." But in the immediate context of the community being restored and reformed by Ezra and Nehemiah, the core elements of Israel's identity, faith, and life could be enjoyed and exercised quite satisfactorily by the community without the presence of a king in the line of David.

(9:15). A redeemed people, but a repentant people. Secure in their inheritance but sober in their self-estimation.

The apostle Paul took the good news of what the God of Israel had done to bring salvation to the world through his Son, the promised Messiah Jesus of Nazareth, to the Gentile nations beyond the borders of Israel. In response to his mission, new communities of believers sprang up in towns around Asia Minor and then in Greece. How should they think of themselves? They were no longer pagan worshipers of the multiple gods of Greece and Rome. But neither were they native-born Jews practicing a *religio licita* (lawfully permitted religion within the Roman Empire), though some of them certainly had been among the Gentile "Godfearers" who were attracted to the monotheistic worship of the synagogue. Even at a sociological level, if they were to survive as viable communities they needed a sense of distinct identity—the dignity of belonging to something more than just a local club or sect. And that is exactly what Paul gave them through his constant teaching. He made sure they knew who they were, what people they now belonged to.

To the extent that Paul's letters reflect and reinforce the teaching he would have previously done in person, it is remarkable how much knowledge of the Old Testament Paul assumes in his letters. Clearly, although those Gentile believers had been converted from a background of total ignorance of Israel's Scriptures (apart from those who would have been observers of synagogue worship), Paul lost no time in teaching them "the whole counsel of God" (Acts 20:27)—a phrase that I take to mean the whole plan of God as revealed in the Old Testament, beginning at creation and including the story of the fall, the election of Abraham, the exodus redemption of Israel, and the covenant and promises that followed. And the purpose of all that teaching was precisely to give these small communities of believers a new identity, a new belonging. But, like the identity of the exiles returning to Jerusalem, this was not something new and unprecedented. Those who had put their faith in Jesus Christ were not crazed followers of some newfangled religion (even if the nickname *Christianoi*—"Christ-fans"—may have arisen with that sort of mocking assumption). On the contrary, they had been grafted into a people with an identity stretching back nearly two thousand years.

This was the direct implication of Paul's missional theology based on the universality of God's promise to Abraham. The gospel, in Paul's understanding, began in Genesis, when "Scripture foresaw that God would justify the Gentiles by faith, and announced the gospel in advance to Abraham: 'All nations will be blessed through you.' So those who have [i.e., rely on] faith are blessed along with Abraham, the man of faith" (Gal 3:8–9). But it was not merely that these Gentile believers in Jesus were "blessed *along with* Abraham"—while remaining somehow *outside* Abraham's people. No, faith in the Messiah Jesus gave them the same spiritual ancestry. They now belonged to this very people. It was the privilege of Israel to be called "my firstborn son" (Exod 4:22) and to call God "our Father" (Isa 63:16; 64:8). But now, Paul tells the Galatians, "in Christ Jesus" you (i.e., Gentile believers) "are all children of God through faith." Not only that, but you are counted among Abraham's descendants. And your inheritance is secure, not by genealogy, like the returning exiles, but by grace through faith. For "if you belong to Christ, then you are Abraham's seed, and heirs according to the promise" (Gal 3:26–29).

Genealogy, kinship, and citizenship—so important in Ezra-Nehemiah—were never far from Paul's mind, however. The original criteria for membership in God's people, Old Testament Israel, could still have metaphorical and spiritual content for these new believers. They too belonged—just as securely as any exiled Israelite returning to the land with genealogical documents intact. Indeed, Paul seems to draw from the imagery of coming back from far away (exile and return) in describing the transformation that the Gentile believers have experienced. Writing to the churches in the great metropolitan area of Ephesus, he reminds them of their former alienation and present inclusion: "Remember that formerly you who are Gentiles by birth . . . at that time you were separate from Christ, excluded from citizenship in Israel and foreigners to the covenants of the promise, without hope and without God in the world. But now in Christ Jesus you who were once far away have been brought near through the blood of Christ" (Eph 2:11–13). The language of "far and near" is another hint of the return from exile. Paul picks up a passage of Isaiah that pictures the messenger proclaiming peace (Isa 52:7) and combines it with the promise of peace to those "far and near" (57:19). In the context of Isaiah, those "far away" would have meant the exiles in Babylon, and those "near" would have meant those who had remained in the land. But Paul picks up the "return from exile" theme and applies "you who were far away" to the Gentiles and "those who were near" to believing Jews like himself. Christ "came and preached peace" to both (Eph 2:17).

So then, just as the exiles who returned could prove by their genealogies recorded in Ezra-Nehemiah that they were not "foreigners and strangers" (and distinguished themselves rigorously from those who were), so, says Paul, Gentiles who believe in the Messiah Jesus are no longer in that category either. On the contrary, they are now "fellow citizens with God's people and members of God's household" (2:19)—a description that the community of Ezra-Nehemiah would have claimed and accepted with relish. And in a final echo of that story, Paul recalls what had been the very first thing the returning exiles had done: they laid the foundations for the rebuilding of the temple. Even so, says Paul, these new communities of believers—Gentiles and Jews together—are being constituted as "a holy temple in the Lord" (2:21), with scriptural foundations (prophets and apostles), and the messianic cornerstone of Christ Jesus himself.

Any Gentile believers then who were taught by Paul and those of his team who shared his deeply rooted scriptural theology (as presumably did Timothy, Titus, and Apollos, for example) were left in no doubt at all about their new identity in Christ. They knew who they were. They knew the people they now belonged to. Through the gospel first announced to Abraham they had become the fulfillment of the promise first made to Abraham. Drawn from different nations, they were "all one in Christ Jesus" (Gal 3:28), "heirs together with Israel, members together of one body, sharers together in the promise in Christ Jesus" (Eph 3:6).

It is a challenging question, however, whether most Christians in today's churches are as aware of these biblical truths as they ought to be. Are new believers being taught to know their identity, to know the people they belong to, to understand their deep roots in the Scriptures (Old as well as New Testaments), to realize what God has done for them when they put their faith in the Messiah Jesus, to rejoice (but not boast) in being grafted into the olive tree of God's chosen people? I have no empirical evidence, but I suspect not. Most evangelistic and discipling programs seem to place their emphasis on solving the problem of the immediate present (my personal sin and need for forgiveness) and the ultimate future (being sure to "go to heaven" when I die). The questions of who I have now become in Christ and the people to whom I now belong for the sake of God's mission in God's world seem to be ignored. The church, to the extent that it features in such teaching at all, is simply the helpful company of others who are also on their way to heaven or a place to meet up, celebrate our future hope, and find strength for our challenging present.

People who are thus deprived of knowing the people to whom they belong according to the Bible—the spiritual descendants of Abraham, inheritors of both his blessing and his mission—are likely to have limited understanding and appreciation of the Old Testament. If it is read, preached, or taught at all, it will be only for moral lessons from the heroes of faith; or for warnings about the dangers of legalism; or worst of all, for obscure calculations and predictions about "the end times," from which, unfortunately, it is possible to make a great deal of money to enhance the plausibility of the predictions.

Some parts of the Old Testament will seem tediously irrelevant, or be mentioned only with dismissive humor. All those genealogies in Chronicles, Ezra, and Nehemiah! What are they there for? All those tribal boundaries and town lists in Joshua? What have they got to do with anything? Once we recognize, however, that kinship and land were primary criteria for membership in the covenant people of God—and that we belong to that people through faith in the Messiah Jesus—then we will not be so dismissive. We no longer depend on biological kinship and geographical turf, but we do share kinship in the family of God, and we have an inheritance transcending a single land.

Identity matters. Christians who do not know the people to whom they belong will similarly fail to see the relevance of Rom 9–11, as is evident from the way those chapters are so often ignored or sidelined in preaching on that letter. Romans 1–8 seems to say all we need to know about our salvation, and Rom 12–15 gives us good practical advice. Enough, surely. So Rom 9–11 is seen as a minor parenthesis dealing with an issue that troubled Paul but need not detain us today. Whereas the truth is that for Paul those chapters are theologically (and ecclesiologically) essential. Why should Gentiles put their faith in the God of Israel, if the God of Israel had failed to keep his promise to his own people? Paul argues emphatically that God had not done so, but on the contrary had kept his promise to Abraham by bringing blessing to the Gentiles. So God had been faithful, but had Israel been rejected? Again, Paul argues no. Israel is God's original olive tree, and the Gentiles are being grafted in. So the Gentiles (to whom he was writing) needed to know precisely where they stood. Included, yes, but with no grounds for boasting or superiority over their Jewish fellow believers. Again—identity matters. There is only one olive tree. We all belong to this one people of God. And that becomes precisely the foundation for Paul's imperative on mutual acceptance within that one united people of God, in Rom 14–15.

In the same way, Paul follows his teaching on the oneness of Jew and Gentile in Christ in Eph 2–3 with the immediate imperative to "make every effort *to keep the unity of the Spirit* through the bond of peace. There is one body and one Spirit—just as you were called to one hope when you were called—one Lord, one faith, one baptism; one God and Father of all, who is over all and through all and in all" (4:3–6, italics added). Paul's total conviction about the oneness of God's people in Christ echoes the point made in the previous chapter about the aspirational unity of the people of Israel as perceived by the returning exiles in Ezra-Nehemiah. Though only a fragment of the original whole nation, they still acted, worshiped, and prayed as "all Israel." Though a "remnant," they considered themselves to be the spiritual heirs of the "twelve tribes"—erasing the hoary historical and political division of the two kingdoms. One God, one people of God.

The unity of God's people is a significant theme in the Bible, as seen in the previous chapter. It is not simply that "it's nice when we can all get on well together." It is the profoundly missional truth that, out of the fractured nations of humanity, scattered and divided since the tower of Babel in Gen 11, God has created one new, reconciled people among whom the old barriers and divisions have been broken down. That is why unity among Christians is such a powerful engine of effective mission, and disunity is such a blight on our witness. *The Cape Town Commitment* of the Lausanne Movement recognizes this missional element of the unity of God's people:

> A divided church has no message for a divided world. Our failure to live in reconciled unity is a major obstacle to authenticity and effectiveness in mission.... Three times Jesus repeated, "A new command I give you: Love one another. As I have loved you, so you must love one another" (John 13:34; 15:12, 17). Three times Jesus prayed "that all of them may be one, Father" (John 17:21–23). Both the command and the prayer are missional. "By this everyone will know that you are my disciples, if you love one another." "May they be brought to complete unity so that the world will know that you sent me." Jesus could not have made his point more emphatically. The evangelization of the world and the recognition of Christ's deity are helped or hindered by whether or not we obey him in practice.... When Christians live in the reconciled unity of love by the power of the Holy Spirit, the world will come to know Jesus, whose disciples we are, and come to know the Father who sent him.[5]

Two wider theological issues—the "two-covenant" theory and the phenomenon of Messianic Judaism—arise in this context and need continuing reflection and resolution.

If what we explored above is true—about the identity and unity of the people of God, spanning both Old and New Testaments, and created by the gospel through the cross and resurrection of the Messiah Jesus—then it excludes the so-called two-covenant theory of the relationship between Jews and Christians. That is the view that Jews have their own covenant with God by which they have salvation, while Jesus is offered as Savior for Gentile Christians. Christian evangelism among Jewish people is excluded, on this view, both for reasons of sensitivity in the wake of the Holocaust and for the theological reason that it is unnecessary anyway. I cannot see how such a theory can survive exposure to the teaching of the apostle Paul—himself a faithful Jew. For him, and on his whole reading of the Scriptures, if Jesus of Nazareth were truly the Messiah of Israel, then of necessity he was also Savior of the Gentiles (as Simeon also perceived; Luke 2:28–32), since it was for their sake that Israel existed as God's people. And indeed, Jesus could be the Savior of the world of nations only if he were in truth the Messiah of Israel, the one who fulfilled God's promise to Abraham

---

5. *Cape Town Commitment*, §II.F1 and conclusion.

and who, through his death and resurrection, opened the way for people of all nations to be grafted into the one people of God, the new humanity in Christ.

Paul was a Jew who had encountered Jesus of Nazareth and had acknowledged him as Messiah, Savior, and Lord. So were the rest of Jesus's apostles, and many within the Jewish communities around the Mediterranean who gladly received Paul's word that "what God promised our ancestors he has fulfilled for us, their children, by raising up Jesus" (Acts 13:32–33 NIV modified). By God's grace there have been Jews down through the centuries who have found the fulfillment of their scriptural faith and hope in Jesus Christ in the same way. Today, communities of Messianic Judaism are to be found in the state of Israel and many other countries of the world. It is a growing and vigorous movement.

One of the challenges that Messianic Jews face, however, is theological. As Jews committed to the truth and authority of the whole canon of Scripture—Torah, Prophets, Writings, and the apostolic documents of the New Testament—how are they to understand their own identity in relation to God's primal election of Israel, now that they share the Messiah (so to speak) with Gentiles of all nations? And how is that election of Israel to be understood and articulated in relation to the Jewish people as a whole today—whether Messianic believers or not?

As I understand the matter from conversations with close friends in the Messianic Jewish community, there are two fundamental theological pillars of their identity: first, the messiahship and lordship of Jesus of Nazareth and the necessity of faith in him for salvation; and, second, the ongoing election of the Jewish people in accordance with God's promises to Abraham, as affirmed by Paul. Exactly what that second conviction implies for Jews who do not yet believe in Jesus as Messiah, or for the relationship between synagogue and church, seems to me to be a "work in progress" still in Messianic Jewish theological reflection and writing.

This question of identity for Messianic Jewish believers is both profoundly important and potentially troubling. It can produce division and conflict among themselves and with Gentile Christians, since it naturally carries with it affections and loyalties to their own Jewish people, as well as to the land and modern state of Israel. They frequently find that their identity is questioned (even denied) *both* by nonbelieving Jews *and* by unsympathetic Gentile Christians. This is not the place to survey those issues, since it has been well done elsewhere.[6]

---

6. One of the best available guides to the whole movement and theology of Messianic Judaism is provided by Harvey, *Mapping Messianic Jewish Theology*. An excellent survey of some key theological and historical issues in the relationship between Messianic Jews and Palestinian believers is provided in a book jointly authored by one from each community: Munayer and Loden, *Through My Enemy's Eyes*.

But Gentile Christians ought to be much more aware of this contemporary community of sisters and brothers in Christ than they are, as well as understand their own theological and spiritual roots in Israel of the Scriptures. We need to know the people we belong to, with the same diligence and affirmation as those returning exiles of Ezra-Nehemiah.

A Community of People Who Know the Story They Are In

The returning exiles knew who they were because they knew their own story. In the previous chapter we explored the strong emphasis in Ezra-Nehemiah on connecting with their historical roots and precedents—either by simply recalling them or by seeking to re-create them in the present. The return from bondage to new life in the land combined the exodus and Joshua. The reading of the law and covenant renewal echoed Sinai. The rebuilding of the temple revived memories (painful for some) of Solomon. The restoration of worship was explicitly in accordance with what was attributed to David's choreography. And the great prayer of Neh 9 rehearses history from creation to their immediate present. In other words, this was a people with memory.

And because they had *memory*, they had *hope*. Even the awareness and confession of past sins and failures functioned to remind them of the recurring forgiveness of God, even through and beyond acts of God's righteous judgment. God could therefore be trusted to carry them into the future with the same forgiving faithfulness, the same saving righteousness, provided they responded with renewed penitence and reform. The future was secure because the past was proof. And the promises of God spanned both past and future.

And because they had memory and hope, they had a *mission*. As pointed out in the previous chapter, the books of Ezra-Nehemiah do not articulate the wider purpose of Israel's existence, which other Old Testament books exploit fully (especially Isaiah and many Psalms). Survival and reconstitution was their immediate priority. However, within the sweep of the biblical narrative, the missional nature of Israel is explicit. They were created by God for the sake of his ultimate goal of bringing Abrahamic blessing to all nations. The launch of the story of Israel, with the election of Abraham and God's covenant with him and his descendants, in Gen 12 is God's response to the crisis of humanity—the whole world of nations—that has escalated through Gen 3–11.

That the returned Israelites remember (or were reminded of) their history so forcefully in Ezra-Nehemiah is significant, given that the preexilic prophets so often lamented that it was when Israel *forgot* their story that they went astray from YHWH their God and began to live like the nations around them. That is the point of the great historical psalms: Pss 105-7. They lost their distinctiveness when they forgot who they were and what story they were in. That indeed had been precisely the warning that Deuteronomy had given them from the start (4:23, 32-35; 6:12, 20-25). Conversely, since Ezra and Nehemiah were striving to create a faithful and obedient community, after the searing object lesson of 587 BCE and the exile, they revive the people's memory and powerfully rehearse and affirm their history.

An example from the exilic period of one who knew the story (past and future) is Daniel. The narratives of the book place him among the first of those who were taken into exile in Babylon. He and his friends settle down in Babylon, perhaps in obedience to the advice of Jeremiah's letter (Jer 29:4-7), accepting Babylonian names, education, and careers. Yet they remain faithful to the living God of their people and refuse total allegiance to the king they serve (the probable meaning of refusing to eat the "meat from the king's table"). Daniel remains a man of prayer.

We get a very instructive little glimpse into his daily habit of prayer when we are told that he had a "room where the windows opened toward Jerusalem" (Dan 6:10). I do not think Daniel was dreaming nostalgically of the homeland he had left as a boy. Nor do I think the window was open to let his prayers out. Rather, the window was open toward the city of God, from which Daniel drew his faith, his ethical values, and his future hope. Daniel had forcibly become part of the story of Nebuchadnezzar and Babylon. But he was still living in the story of the God of Zion. Not only did he know the story of the past that shaped him and his Jewish companions from their youth in Jerusalem, he also knew, by divine revelation through the prophecies of Jeremiah and the dreams of Nebuchadnezzar, where the future lay. He himself might die in Babylon. But the story he lived in would not die there. For the future belonged not to the city Nebuchadnezzar had built, but to the city Nebuchadnezzar had destroyed.

When we move through to the New Testament, we meet people again and again who know the story they are in and what time it is in that story. Simeon, for example, was assured that he would not die till he had seen Yhwh's Messiah. That is to say, he knew that the story of Israel was coming to its scripted climax. But he also knew that the story would not end with that coming. For when he held the infant Jesus in his arms, he knew (again from his immersion in the Scriptures) that the salvation embodied in that little bundle was not for Israel alone, but for "all nations": "a light for revelation to the Gentiles and for glory to your people Israel" (Luke 2:32). The story would go on, to the ends of the earth. And that indeed is how Luke ends his Gospel, with Jesus summarizing the story so far and pointing ahead to the story to come—insisting that this is precisely the meaning of the whole story of the Old Testament Scriptures: "This is what is written: The Christ will suffer and rise from the dead on the third day, and repentance and forgiveness of sins will be preached in his name to all nations, beginning at Jerusalem. You are witnesses of these things" (24:46–48). Jesus provides his disciples (then and now) with a *messianic* and *missional* understanding of the Scriptures. The Old Testament story leads to Christ and points beyond the historical events of his life, death, and resurrection to the ongoing mission of the church to all nations in fulfillment of God's promise to Abraham. That is the story that governs Acts, which takes the story as far as Rome and climaxes in Revelation, when God's people redeemed from every nation will worship him in resurrection bodies in the new creation.

Paul reminds the elders of the churches in Ephesus that he had taught them "the whole plan/purpose/will of God." That almost certainly means the whole scriptural story in which the purpose of God is revealed, as he says in his letter to them, "to bring unity to all things in heaven and on earth under Christ (Eph 1:9–10). Paul's use of the word *mystērion* to describe this (in Colossians and Ephesians especially) probably does not quite mean what our English "mystery" has come to mean, but rather refers to the meaning of the (Old Testament) story whose climax and purpose has now been revealed. And even when Paul does not explicitly refer to that story, it seems that it constantly shapes the way he understands and teaches the gospel—even to Gentile believers. The narrative of Old Testament Israel shapes the order of his thinking—perhaps subconsciously. He speaks of the Christians in Thessalonica, for example, as loved by God, chosen, saved, sanctified, and sharing in Christ's glory (2 Thess 2:13–14). That is the story of Israel, from the election of Abraham, through exodus redemption, called to be holy at Sinai, and seeing the glory of God in the tabernacle and later the temple. That is the story we are in, now recapitulated and "realized" in Christ.

Once again we have to ask: are Christians in today's church as aware as they should be of the people they belong to and the story they are part of? And again, I fear not. It is sad, to say the least, that many Christians have very little knowledge of *church* history—the great river of faith and tradition in which we stand with saints down the ages. But it is more than sad, it is seriously detrimental, that so many have little awareness of *biblical* history. The Bible has become merely an object to which we have to give some attention, for its promises and rules. It is not perceived as a whole canon from creation to new creation, as *the story* within which we live and participate as the people whom God has called into existence for the sake of his mission to bring salvation to the ends of the earth and ultimately restoration and unity to the whole creation (Eph 1:10). Yet that, of course, is what the Bible is. This is God's story. This is our story. This is the people to whom we belong. This is the future to which God leads us. This is the task entrusted to us in every generation till Christ returns.

The returning exiles under Ezra and Nehemiah were a people with memory and hope. Whether they were conscious of it or not at the time, that was what enabled them to survive and continue as the people participating in the long-term mission of God for the nations, in accordance with the prophetic vision and promise. The challenge for today's church is to recognize that a significant factor in the loss of missional effectiveness is our loss of biblical memory and hope. That is to say, we invite people to accept an instrumental Jesus who can solve their sin problem and assure them of heaven beyond death, but in the meantime we leave them living in the story of this world (or escaping from it). We have forgotten who we are and why we are here. We fail to know our own true identity as the biblical people of God, and we fail to live in, by, and for the biblical story we are part of. And, as the prophets tearfully reminded Israel, when God's people forget who they are and forget their own story, then they bring grief and anger to God's heart and render themselves useless in the very task for which they were created, to be a light to the nations that God's salvation should reach to the end of the earth.

A Community of People Who Exalt the Scriptures

Sustaining memory and hope and mission is built upon sustaining the knowledge of God's word, from which all three are derived. So it is not surprising to note that the community of Ezra-Nehemiah prioritized the reading, explaining, and practicing of the Scriptures. And it is also noteworthy that this was not something imposed upon them. The great occasion of Ezra's reading of the book of the law of Moses was initiated by the request of the people (Neh 8:1). Like a collective embodiment of Ps 119, they reach out and long for God's word to be brought to them (119:40, 48). Indeed, many of the personal emotions, desires, struggles, and commitments cataloged in Ps 119 find community expression in Neh 8, just as Ezra himself is an embodiment of Ps 119:30: "I have set my heart on your laws."

The importance of this occasion of public reading, and celebration, of the Scriptures can be further assessed by the way the text of Neh 8 echoes (surely intentionally) the celebration that occurred at the laying of the foundation of the temple. The wording of 7:73–8:1 is almost identical to Ezra 3:1. The celebration of God's word in Scripture is equivalent to the celebration of God's presence in sacrifice and worship at the altar and in the temple. "The similarity makes the obvious point that this reading of the law is to be understood in the same way as the rebuilding of the altar and temple foundation some ninety years earlier. They were both great, significant, and happy occasions. This is supported, e.g., by the prominence of the 'rejoicing' motif in both contexts" (Ezra 3:10–13; Neh 8:6, 12, 17).[7] And, we might add, by the combination of weeping with rejoicing on both occasions.

Assuming the probability that "the Book of the Law of Moses" was substantially what we now call the Pentateuch as a whole, then the people were being reminded of, and nourished and challenged by, the whole foundational narrative that in many ways programs the rest of our canonical Bible: creation, fall, promise, redemption, covenant, inheritance, ethical response. Ezra and Nehemiah knew that the restored community needed more than the physical protection of walls and the physical presence of the temple in their midst. They needed to be grounded and built up in knowledge of, and obedience to, the Scriptures.[8] That was the soil in which their memory and hope, as well as their worship and mission, were rooted. Churches today that are not substantially nourished by the faithful reading, preaching, and teaching of the Bible are severely handicapped in the depth of their worship and the effectiveness of their mission.

In the previous chapter I noted some features of that great occasion in Neh 8. Here I reflect on some dimensions of it that warrant reflection and emulation in today's church, particularly in the work of Christian education in general (including the preaching and teaching work of pastors and others entrusted with the task in a local congregation) and theological education in particular.

Ezra's Personal Example

Ezra's actions and posture on the day itself were a model to the people, to which they responded with echoing reverence. But they were indicative of the orientation of his whole life. Once we have been introduced to Ezra and have marveled at his personal direct descent from Aaron (so his priestly credentials

---

7. Howard, *Introduction to the Old Testament Historical Books*, 308.

8. "The initial work of Ezra (7–10) as well as the building of the wall by Nehemiah (Neh 1–6) receive their significance only in the light of the religious reordering of the community of faith in Neh 8–12. The explicit intent of the author is to describe this event as one shared by both Ezra and Nehemiah. Thus Nehemiah participates with Ezra in the instruction of the people, and conversely Ezra shares in the dedication of the wall build by Nehemiah (12:27). Clearly the author envisions the political and religious work of the two men as functioning together in the reconstitution of the community"; Childs, *Introduction to the Old Testament as Scripture*, 635.

were impeccable) and have read (twice) that the hand of God was on him, the first thing we are told about him is that "Ezra had set his heart to study the law of YHWH, and to do it, and to teach the statutes and ordinances in Israel" (Ezra 7:10 NRSV). He stands as a model for pastors and theological educators in all three of those verbs on which he had "set his heart": "study ... do ... teach." You cannot teach what you have not studied, and you should not teach what you don't practice. Sadly all around the global church, there are many leaders, pastors, and theological educators who do not study, or teach, or live in accordance with the Bible. Churches inevitably languish in immaturity, vulnerable to false teaching and unbiblical practices.

Practical Preparation

Although we are told that Ezra's reading of the law was at the request of the people (Neh 8:1), it was clearly not a spontaneous and unplanned gathering. The place was carefully chosen so the maximum number of people could gather and hear. A "wooden platform" had been built (the first pulpit?) so that Ezra could be clearly seen and heard (8:4–5). Associate helpers had been briefed and prepared beforehand and strategically positioned to make sure the reading was understood throughout the crowd. The engagement of God's people with God's word was clearly something to be taken seriously, carefully planned, and systematically delivered over a significant period of time. Contrast that with the thin diet (if any) of biblical teaching in many churches today, where thoughtful engagement with the Bible (in whatever form—reading, preaching, group study, etc.) has been severely decentered in favor of more entertaining kinds of consumerist "worship experience." Even the visual symbolism of Ezra's pulpit and reverently opened scrolls has been replaced by a flimsy music stand for the Bible preacher (if you're lucky).

Reverent Acknowledgment of the Book of Moses as the Word of God

Ezra led the people in a moment of worship before the reading began. This does not mean, of course, that they were engaged in what is scathingly called "bibliolatry." They were not worshiping the scrolls. Rather, they were acknowledging that these scrolls, filled with the words of "the Book of the Law of Moses" (and therefore fully human in origin, editing, and transmission), also constituted "the law ... that YHWH had given to Israel ... the law of God ... that YHWH had commanded by Moses" (8:1, 8, 14). They were listening to a human voice reading human words; they were at the same time hearing the word of God. This deliberate combining of the dual authorship of Scripture (human and divine) is significant not only in underlining the solemnity and joy of that occasion itself, but also for our own ongoing theological appreciation of what we have in our hands every time we open the Scriptures and read, preach, or teach from them.

Use of Trained Teachers

It had always been one of the responsibilities of the Levites and priests to be teachers of God's law (Lev 10:11; Deut 33:10; cf. Jer 18:18; Mal 2:1–9). Although the prophets accuse them of failing in that task, there were some occasions when reforming kings made use of the training of these men in inculcating the requirements of Israel's law and worship among the population (2 Chr 17:7–9; 19:8–11; 29–31; 35). So here, Ezra reinforces his own authority and training by sharing the task of teaching the people with those who lived among them and would know exactly how to explain and interpret the sacred texts.

One of the priorities of the Protestant Reformers was to restore to the church an educated clergy. Whether the plethora of theology departments in universities, and of theological colleges and seminaries, has fulfilled their vision in the way they hoped for would be an interesting question, but the principle seems generally accepted in the Western church at least—that those whom God gives to the church as pastor-teachers to equip the saints for works of service should themselves be equipped for the task (Eph 4:11–12; 2 Tim 2:2). In many parts of the world church, however, the training of pastors—especially in the basic skills of how to preach and teach the Scriptures with simplicity, faithfulness, and relevance—is feeble or nonexistent, to the great detriment of the church's maturity and mission.

Simplicity of Process—Reading, Translation, Explanation, Application

Though it was an occasion of great solemnity and emotional power with significant practical preparation and outcome, the actual process of communicating the book of the law was relatively simple. It was read aloud. Probably this was done with sufficient pauses to allow for each section to be translated and explained, "so that the people could understand what was being read" (Neh 8:8). That is a straightforward description of the fundamental task and purpose of the exegetical and hermeneutical work that should underlie all effective teaching and preaching of the Bible in the community of God's people. It sounds very much like what Paul had in mind when he urged Timothy to "devote yourself to the public reading of Scripture, to preaching and to teaching" (1 Tim 4:13) and to do so as a worker "who does not need to be ashamed and who correctly handles the word of truth" (2 Tim 2:15).

Involvement of the Whole Community and Whole Families

This is emphatic. Who were present for the reading and teaching of the Scriptures? We are told twice in Neh 8:1–3: "All the people . . . men and women and all who were able to understand [presumably children beyond infancy] . . . men, women and others who could understand . . . all the people." This inclusiveness is characteristic of the instructions in Deuteronomy concerning the dissemination of the knowledge of the law among the people. The law that God gave them was not too difficult, not too high, not too far away, for ordinary people to know and understand. On the contrary it was "very near you; it is in your mouth and in your heart so you may obey it" (Deut 30:11–14). Accordingly, when it was to be read to the people as part of the sabbatical year, "all Israel" must be there: "men, women and children, and the foreigners residing in your towns. . . . Their children, who do not know this law, must hear it and learn to fear Yhwh your God as long as you live in the land you are crossing the Jordan to possess" (31:10–13). As Ezra and Nehemiah prepared the people who had metaphorically "crossed the Jordan" once again to live in the land, they made sure that the whole community was conscious of, and committed to, the scriptural foundation of their life and future.

Once again, we find interesting comparisons with the small communities of faith that Paul founded. He urged them to practice a rich and deeply grounded community engagement with the Scriptures: "Let the word of Christ dwell among you richly as you teach and admonish one another with all wisdom through psalms, hymns, and songs from the Spirit, singing to God with gratitude in your hearts" (Col 3:16, my translation). And to the extent that his written letters were to be received as Scriptures, it is significant that he expected that the whole community would be there to hear them read—husbands *and* wives, parents *and* children, masters *and* slaves—"all who could understand," as Nehemiah might have said. And all who could be expected to respond in practical obedience.

With such scriptural precedents it is surely a major responsibility of the leader or leaders in any church to ensure that the whole community is being summoned to pay attention to the word of God—in whatever way that can be done, at whatever level is appropriate for their age, and in whatever cultural form that may take.

Balance of Understanding, Emotion, and Obedience

Ezra and Nehemiah could not be accused of emotionalism. There was no attempt to stir up or play on the people's emotions (something Nehemiah could do very effectively when confronting people with their injustice in Neh 5). Yet neither did they attempt to stifle the emotions that surfaced that day. The simple reading and explanation of the Scriptures produced first weeping and then rejoicing. Weeping, one presumes, because their consciences were being challenged and convicted as they heard the purity of God's word impacting their history of failure. Rejoicing, we are explicitly told, "because they now understood the words that had been made known to them" (8:12). There was no contradiction between intellect and affections. On the contrary, it was because of their intellectual grasp of the teaching of the Scripture that their hearts were filled with joy, expressed in jubilant celebration. Joy comes when God's word is understood.

Sadly, in today's church the two are frequently set in opposition. Some churches have a diet of worship (so-called, usually referring exclusively to singing) that is predominantly subjective and emotionally charged, but reduce or eliminate the time available for any mental engagement with the word, competently preached and willingly heard.[9] Some churches place great stress on preaching and teaching the word, but it remains stiff and cerebral with very little warmth of the heart and affections,[10] either in the preaching or the worshiping response. Surely we need both, just as both were engaged in the great Scripture-fest of Ezra-Nehemiah.

But they did not stop with listening (however attentive and purposeful; 8:13) and rejoicing (however socially inclusive; 8:10–12); they were committed to do whatever they found in their study of the law that they ought to do. Prompt obedience was proof of the effectiveness of the whole teaching project (8:15–17). And pointedly, the narrator returns to the theme of rejoicing (8:17). And what rejoicing! The reference to Joshua, however, is doubtless telling us more than simply that the Israelites had the most enjoyable festival of booths they'd had

---

9. African friends tell me that in some churches there, by the time the first hour or more of energetic dancing and singing is over, people are so exhausted they fall asleep during any preaching that follows.

10. Moody and Weekes, *Burning Hearts*, address this tendency.

for a thousand years. The echo is surely that just as Joshua called the people to covenant loyalty and obedience after they had entered the land, so here the returning exiles are summoned to hear and obey the word of God in the law of Moses. And in both hearing with understanding (8:12), and in obeying with enthusiasm (8:15–18), they found joy abundant (8:17).

What makes a church joyful? In the midst of the plethora of patented and published recipes, schemes and strategies for building churches filled with joy and "success," are we in danger of forgetting the simplest biblical principles? Happy are those who hear God's word and obey it. Blessed are churches that have leaders who teach and encourage them to do both.

A Community of People Committed to Worship

In the previous chapter we noticed how God is deemed worthy of worship—in many moods: gratitude, praise, confession, supplication, and sheer celebration. The commitment of the postexilic community to sustain the worship of God can be gauged from several reports in the text:

- freewill offerings given for the rebuilding of the temple (Ezra 2:68–69), echoing the giving of the people for the tabernacle in the wilderness and for the temple of Solomon
- resumption of sacrificial worship as soon as the altar alone was rebuilt, in spite of fear of the surrounding people (3:2–6)
- immediate outburst of praise and thanksgiving when nothing more than the foundations for the new temple were laid (3:10–13)
- additional celebration when the temple was finally finished, celebrating God's sovereignty over the attitudes of the imperial government (6:16–22)
- ensuring that there were sufficient Levites in Ezra's group of returning exiles for the service of the temple (8:15–20)
- celebration of the Festival of Booths, during the reading of the law (Neh 8:13–18)
- commitment to provide all that was necessary for supporting the priests and Levites in their service in the temple (10:32–39), even if it was short-lived (13:10–11)
- willingness of the people to have 10% of the population live in Jerusalem, presumably to support the economy and the work of the temple there; that it was seen as a commendable act probably means that it was a costly one, when so much depended on restoring the productivity of the farmland and villages (Neh 11)

- restoration of Davidic arrangements for choirs and musicians in the final mass celebration, with emphasis on giving thanks and praise (Neh 12)

What was the focus and content of all these costly practical arrangements and commitment to be a worshiping community? The clue is given in the very first text in the books that describes their worship: "They sang with praise and thanksgiving to Yhwh, 'For he is good [טוֹב/*ṭôb*], for his faithful love [חַסְדּוֹ/*ḥasdô*] is forever'" (Ezra 3:11, my translation). That phrase is an unmistakable indication that they were singing Ps 136, in which those words form the repeated refrain. The everlasting goodness and loving faithfulness of Yhwh are the constant theme of the praise of Israel and should be for God's people everywhere for all time. As we join in singing the psalms of Israel, so too would they no doubt echo words such as those in a eucharistic prayer from the Anglican Communion:

> It is indeed right,
> it is our duty and our joy,
> at all times and in all places
> to give you thanks and praise,
> holy Father, heavenly King,
> almighty and eternal God,
> creator of heaven and earth,
> through Jesus Christ our Lord.[11]

Psalm 136, of course, repeats those phrases precisely in the context of remembering God's great acts of salvation and blessing in their past history, something that characterized this community in many ways. Praise rises when people look back and think what God has done. In a more subtle way, looking to the future, Nehemiah uses the same two words at the end of his book. The context is not one of public praise but personal prayer. Nehemiah asks that God should remember him, according to "the greatness of your faithful love" (רֹב חַסְדֶּךָ/*rōb ḥasdekā*) and for "good" (טוֹבָה/*ṭōbâ*) (Neh 13:22, 31).

Asking questions about the state of worship in today's churches would likely prompt as many opinions as there are churches. But it is a matter of concern to many. Israel's worship was rich in praise of God, filled with content drawn from the history of redemption and the great affirmations of its faith. It was filled with truth—historical and confessional truth, revealed and experiential truth. One wonders if some of today's "worship" is not so much "three

---

11. Church of England, *Alternative Service Book 1980*.

chords and the truth,"¹² as three notes and a cliché. Worship should always be "contemporary" and should be expressed and explored in the modes and moods of every culture and generation. But when obsession with the "contemporary" ends up overlooking the vast treasury of the church's hymnody and liturgy of two thousand years, there is surely a grievous loss of memory—and with it the same dangers noted above: the loss of deep-rooted maturity, well-grounded hope, and historically informed mission.

The worship we encounter in Ezra-Nehemiah includes not just praise and thanksgiving, but also confession of sin, reading and explanation of Scripture, prayer (both personal and communal), and affirmations of commitment to God and trust in him. I have been in many churches around the world. I have been in some where there was no reading of the Bible, apart from my own during the preaching. I have been in churches where there is scarcely any prayer, and what little there is focuses on the personal needs of the congregation and ignores the world (in disobedience to Paul's clear instructions in 1 Tim 2:1–3). I have been in many churches where there is no confession of sin or declaration of God's forgiveness. And there are churches everywhere in which there is little or no regular, faithful, and relevant preaching of the Bible. The community of Ezra-Nehemiah raises some challenges and provides a more rounded and nourishing model of worship.¹³

A Community of People Committed to Justice

Nehemiah built the walls of Jerusalem. That is what he is known for, and that is often the limit of any series of preachings or Bible studies that are based on the book. Nehemiah 5, however, shows another side to this deservedly famous leader, in which both his passion and his public authority are exercised to the full. His people needed protection not only from external enemies, but from internal oppression and injustice.

The situation described in jarring detail in 5:1–5 sounds many echoes from the earlier history of Israel. The opening words, "there was an outcry," use a powerful and emotive word, צְעָקָה/ṣəʿāqâ (5:1; cf. זְעָקָה/zəʿāqâ in 5:6). The word means a cry for help, a yell of pain under cruelty or violence—most graphically of a woman being raped (Deut 22:24, 27). We encounter it first applied to Sodom

---

12. This phrase, added by Bono to U2's cover of a song by Bob Dylan, "All Along the Watchtower" (in U2's album *Rattle and Hum*), is first attributed to Harlan Howard's definition of a great country song.

13. Worship can have missional power also. See C. J. H. Wright, *Mission of God's People*, chap. 14.

and Gomorrah—an outcry that came up to God (Gen 18:20–21). People were suffering there, as the later characterization of the cities, or comparison of them with Jerusalem, colors in with graphic detail (Isa 1:10, 21–23; Ezek 16:49–50). It is what God heard from the Hebrews suffering under the cruelty and oppression of the Egyptians (Exod 2:23–25). It is the word that Isaiah chooses to describe what God finds among Israel, outcry when he sought righteousness—צְעָקָה/ṣəʿāqâ when he was looking for צְדָקָה/ṣədāqâ—because the land was filled with all the effects of widening social and economic inequality (Isa 5:7). So when Nehemiah opens a chapter with such a word, our hearts sink. We've been here before with Israel.

And as before, the Old Testament not only exposes and deplores poverty and its debilitating effects, but also recognizes and analyzes the causes of it.[14] The explanation that the men and their wives[15] give for their suffering rehearses familiar realities. The primary one is debt. But the debt has, in part, natural causes—famine. A time of acute need, however, often brings out the worst in people, as prices rise and those with limited resources are forced to borrow at high cost in order merely to survive. So the most destitute poor were borrowing grain simply to stay alive (5:2). Others who had some property were having to mortgage "fields ... vineyards ... homes" as security for loans—which further reduced their ability ever to pay off the debt (5:3). And on top of all that, being a vassal state to the Persian Empire, there were taxes to be paid. So not only material goods were being used as security, family members also were being sold into debt servitude. Social chaos and family breakup are among the symptoms of a society where inequality and poverty have taken root.

And the cumulative effect? Powerlessness. The closing words of 5:5 are poignant and utterly true—today as much as in ancient times. Poverty—especially debt-based poverty—produces powerlessness. "The borrower is slave to the lender" (Prov 22:7). The sage never spoke a truer word, magnified not only in the staggering levels of personal debt in Western economies, but the astronomical levels of institutional and national debt that seem to drive Western economies and bedevil majority world ones. And at the bottom of the pile in either place lie the powerless poor. Nehemiah's response is remarkably frank and detailed. It can be summed up in four words: passionate, public, practical, and personal.

It was *passionate*. Nehemiah is not embarrassed to say that the poverty and injustice he witnessed made him "very angry" (5:6). As it should. Anger

---

14. See C. J. H. Wright, *Old Testament Ethics*, 146–81, and the extensive bibliography there cited. For even greater detail, see also Baker, *Tight Fists or Open Hands?*

15. Goldingay, *Old Testament Theology*, 1.721–24, notes how mothers, wives, and daughters play a significant role in Israel's self-understanding and how the narrative of Nehemiah highlights this in several ways, seeing Israel itself as a restored "family community."

is the right and proper response to the social evils of gross inequality that are caused by greed, exploitation, profiteering, and callous neglect of the needs of families. And that anger was in part aroused by the ugly fact that people who should have seen themselves as equals within one family ("your brothers") were treating each other with the same kind of jagged inequality that characterized other societies that had never had the teaching and ideals of God's law (such as the stress on equality under God in Lev 25:39–43). "This swelling volume of complaints begins to sound like a speech on equality: . . . *we are of the same flesh and blood as our countrymen and . . . our sons are as good as theirs* ([Neh] 5:5). The Bible did not wait for the Universal Declaration of Human Rights to announce the equality of all."[16] Like the preexilic prophets who reflected the emotions of God in the emotions they themselves felt and expressed, Nehemiah here feels what God feels. Anger against injustice is the proper human reflection of the anger of God himself. Pity and compassion were surely present also (as they are for God), but by themselves they are not enough. Anger energized Nehemiah and drove him back into the public arena.

Nehemiah's response was also immediately *public*. He did nothing behind closed doors, but summoned "a large meeting" of the people who had responsibility for the economy and the power to do something about it. In that context he shamed them into accepting the reality of what their policies and actions were causing (5:8), challenged them with the fear of God and the reproach of the watching world (5:9). That is, he put forward a powerful moral and spiritual case to which there was no answer. There is a value in not confining our passion for justice to private or charitable words and actions. There is a proper place for public advocacy in the political realm. We may stop short of appealing to the fear of Yhwh in a society that does not stand in a relationship of covenant obligation to God, but we can certainly build a serious moral case and "speak truth to power," in defense of values that we know to be derived from the character and will of God. Defense of the poor against the strong remains a public Christian duty.

But Nehemiah did not just verbally criticize. He was *practical*. After some pondering (5:7), he was ready to face them with specific proposals. There should be a return of land and houses that had been mortgaged for debt (which amounted to cancellation of outstanding debts secured by them), and there should be a return to the only legal way of making loans in Old Testament Israel—loans without interest. It was a kind of instant, emergency jubilee.[17]

Finally, Nehemiah led by *personal example*. In contrast to the greed that

---

16. Weanzana, *Africa Bible Commentary*, 549.
17. Williamson, *Ezra, Nehemiah*, 241.

had exploited the need even of fellow Israelites ("brothers"), Nehemiah had not only declined to take advantage of the material perks of his position as governor of a province of the Persian Empire, he had also pursued a policy of personal generosity at his own cost. This was in contrast to previous governors who had exploited their office and power for personal gain (5:14–19). Generosity instead of greed was the hallmark of Nehemiah's leadership—even if he did say so himself. His claim in Neh 5, however, considered as a whole and seen as his "submitting his accounts" to the divine auditor, should not be criticized as boasting. In the context of the standards of Old Testament law and the frequent demands of the prophets, Nehemiah is a perfect illustration of the qualities of the righteous person "who fears Yhwh, and finds great delight in his commands," as described in Ps 112:1. In that psalm, the marks of righteousness include grace, compassion, and justice, mirroring God's (112:4); generosity and free lending; giving to the poor; no fear of enemies; and (significantly, in view of Nehemiah's closing request in Neh 5:19) being remembered forever (Ps 112:6). Psalm 112 could have been written as a portrait of Nehemiah.

In the flow of thought so far in Neh 5, when God's people remember who they are and why they exist (they know their *identity* and the *story* they are part of), they will be committed to participate in God's mission in the world, with their eyes fixed on the *hope* that is generated by God's historical action and God's promise for the ultimate future. Such a community will likewise be committed to the *Scriptures* in which these truths are revealed and where the great story of God's mission (past, present, and future) is recorded. For the same reason they will be committed to *worship* this living God for all he is, all he has done, and all he purposes to do. And a community that knows and worships the God of the Scriptures cannot but be committed to *justice*, for justice and compassion are definitive of Yhwh in all his works and ways (Ps 145).

There is, then, an eloquent integration in Ezra-Nehemiah of enthusiastic spiritual worship and engaged social action, of reverent attention to the word of God and passionate action for economic justice, of repentant confessional prayer and determined efforts to amend past failures with present practical obedience. Their obedience was by no means perfect or permanent, but the integrated intentionality of the community and the two prime leaders is striking.

Unfortunately some churches and mission agencies today still quarrel over the biblical integration of the different dimensions of mission, preferring to assign priority or primacy to one or another in theological conviction or practical allocation of resources, or even asserting that only one kind of mission can be considered "real" mission. Since 1984, however, many have come to accept, as an integrated group of missional tasks, the so-called five marks of mission proposed by the Anglican Communion: evangelism, teaching, love and compassion, seeking justice, and creation care.[18] And since 1974 the Lausanne Movement has stood for an integrated understanding of the global mission of the church, holding evangelism and social action together, and now also acknowledging creation care as a third biblically missional responsibility at the Third Lausanne Congress in Cape Town in 2010. Two quotations from *The Cape Town Commitment* make the point clearly and biblically:

We love the world's poor and suffering. The Bible tells us that the Lord is loving toward all he has made, upholds the cause of the oppressed, loves the foreigner, feeds the hungry, sustains the fatherless and widow.[19] The Bible also shows that God wills to do these things through human beings committed to such action. God holds responsible especially those who are appointed to political or judicial leadership in society,[20] but all God's people are commanded—by the law and prophets, Psalms and Wisdom, Jesus and Paul, James and John—to reflect the love and justice of God in practical love and justice for the needy.[21]

Such love for the poor demands that we not only love mercy and deeds of compassion, but also that we do justice through exposing and opposing all that oppresses and exploits the poor. "We must not be afraid to denounce evil and injustice wherever they exist."[22] We confess with shame that on this matter we fail to share God's passion, fail to embody God's love, fail to reflect God's character and fail to do God's will. We give ourselves afresh

---

18. Anglican Consultative Council, *Bonds of Affection*, 49; and Anglican Consultative Council, *Mission in a Broken World*, 101. Since 1984 there has been ongoing debate around the "five marks," with some modification of the terminology. But the essential thrust of them remains, even under different expressions. For example, the Anglican Board of Mission in Australia recently reframed them as follows: (1) witness to Christ's saving, forgiving, reconciling love for all people; (2) build welcoming, transforming communities of faith; (3) stand in solidarity with the poor and needy; (4) challenge violence, injustice, and oppression and work for peace and reconciliation; and (5) protect, care for, and renew life on our planet. See anglicancommunion.org/ministry/mission/fivemarks.cfm and anglicannews.org/news/2013/01/abm-welcomes-change-to-the-marks-of-mission.aspx.

19. Ps 145:9, 13, 17; 147:7–9; Deut 10:17–18.

20. Gen 18:19; Exod 23:6–9; Deut 16:18–20; Job 29:7–17; Ps 72:4, 12–14; 82; Prov 31:4–9; Jer 22:1–3; Dan 4:27.

21. Exod 22:21–27; Lev 19:33–34; Deut 10:18–19; 15:7–11; Isa 1:16–17; 58:6–9; Amos 5:11–15, 21–24; Ps 112; Job 31:13–23; Prov 14:31; 19:17; 29:7; Matt 25:31–46; Luke 14:12–14; Gal 2:10; 2 Cor 8–9; Rom 15:25–27; 1 Tim 6:17–19; Jas 1:27; 2:14–17; 1 John 3:16–18.

22. *Lausanne Covenant* §5.

to the promotion of justice, including solidarity and advocacy on behalf of the marginalized and oppressed. We recognize such struggle against evil as a dimension of spiritual warfare that can only be waged through the victory of the cross and resurrection, in the power of the Holy Spirit, and with constant prayer.[23]

It is not hard to imagine Nehemiah heartily endorsing those affirmations and aspirations.

> *Our participation in God's mission.* God calls his people to share his mission. The church from all nations stands in continuity through the Messiah Jesus with God's people in the Old Testament. With them we have been called through Abraham and commissioned to be a blessing and a light to the nations. With them, we are to be shaped and taught through the law and the prophets to be a community of holiness, compassion and justice in a world of sin and suffering. We have been redeemed through the cross and resurrection of Jesus Christ, and empowered by the Holy Spirit to bear witness to what God has done in Christ. The church exists to worship and glorify God for all eternity and to participate in the transforming mission of God within history. Our mission is wholly derived from God's mission, addresses the whole of God's creation, and is grounded at its center in the redeeming victory of the cross. This is the people to whom we belong, whose faith we confess and whose mission we share.
>
> *The integrity of our mission.* The *source* of all our mission is what God has done in Christ for the redemption of the whole world, as revealed in the Bible. Our evangelistic task is to make that good news known to all nations. The *context* of all our mission is the world in which we live, the world of sin, suffering, injustice, and creational disorder, into which God sends us to love and serve for Christ's sake. All our mission must therefore reflect the integration of evangelism and committed engagement in the world, both being ordered and driven by the whole biblical revelation of the gospel of God.[24]

Once again, had Nehemiah known the gospel of the Lord Jesus Christ, he could have endorsed all that is affirmed in that statement. The "good news" that he *did* know was that Yhwh reigned sovereign over all nations, including

---

23. *Cape Town Commitment* §1.7.c. The biblical references in the footnotes above are an integral part of the text of *Cape Town Commitment*.
24. *Cape Town Commitment* §1.10.a–b.

the hearts of pagan kings, and that Yhwh would be faithful to his promise to Israel and would establish his kingdom in their midst as they worshiped him with faith, repentance, and obedience. And that is at the core of the gospel of the kingdom of God as preached by Jesus and Paul.

A Community of People Served by Godly Leadership

The personal qualities of Ezra and Nehemiah—their characters, commitments, and accomplishments—shine through the dual narrative to such an extent that they have been extensively studied, preached, and taught as classic models of leadership.[25] So we need to do little more here than summarize the key points, while being well aware that the characteristics of the postexilic community were generated in great measure by the quality of leadership these two men provided in their generation.[26]

They Prayed

The text records that both leaders prayed on many occasions and with varying kinds of prayer: petition, thanksgiving, praise, confession. Their prayers, however, were not an alternative to practical action, but accompanied it. They prepared, planned, and programmed their work, and they reacted to events with intelligence, prudence, and emotions. But in the midst of all that was the presence of God, constantly sought in prayer.[27]

---

25. The validity of such popular books as "models of leadership" is critically evaluated in the next chapter. Shepherd's perceptive analysis there and his reading of the possible intention of the editors in their portrayal of the nature of leadership exercised by Ezra and Nehemiah (in its success and failure) need to be set alongside the more conventional points below.

26. Some of the most perceptive theological insights on Ezra and Nehemiah, paying close attention to the text of both books and particularly focusing on the power of their praying, are to be found in Goldingay, *Old Testament Theology*, 1.760–72.

27. An interesting African perspective on this double reality (prayer and practical means) comes from a native of the Democratic Republic of Congo, Weanzana, *Africa Bible Commentary*, 532: "Though God has the power to do anything by simply speaking the word, he will not come down in person to build hospitals, repair roads, bring an end to tribal conflicts and wars, stop the HIV/AIDS epidemic, and so on. God needs men and women of this continent who will take the initiative in his name to mobilize the entire community to work to rebuild Africa. A theology that simply waits to see miracles is harmful. Ezra and Nehemiah were men of prayer and men of faith and holiness . . . but they were also and especially men of action. The African church needs men and women of their caliber today."

They Trusted in God

Both men refer often to "the gracious hand of God" upon their lives and doings. And they discern this not just in the grand projects such as the rebuilding of the temple and the wall, but in the everyday and ordinary events of life, such as making a journey safely and arriving on schedule. Again, faith in God did not rule out practical prudence. "We prayed to our God and posted a guard," sums it up (Neh 4:9). So when the wall was completed, for example, even their enemies had to acknowledge that "this work had been done with the help of our God" (6:16).

They Heeded the Word of God

Ezra had set his heart to study, practice, and teach the law of Yhwh (Ezra 7:10). As a descendant of Aaron, that was "in his blood," we might say. Nehemiah, however, knew his Scriptures too. His very first prayer is soaked in the language of Lev 26 and Deut 30 and even appears familiar with Jer 14:20–21 (Neh 1:5–11). Together they arranged a weeklong "Scripture festival" and followed it up with practical implementation. Theirs was a leadership style that modeled, practiced, and inculcated biblical faithfulness and obedience. And for that reason—their scriptural faithfulness—they also modeled biblical integration of worship, prayer, teaching, and practical engagement in the social, political, and economic arenas.

They Demonstrated Integrity and Trustworthiness

This is apparent both in their accountability to the secular government by whom they were appointed and in their dealings with local people. And in Nehemiah's case, it extended to the quality of people he appointed and entrusted with major responsibility, such as Hananiah whom he appointed alongside his own brother (perhaps to avoid any accusation of nepotism and corruption). He was, Nehemiah notes, "a man of integrity and feared God more than most people do" (Neh 7:2). Nehemiah's integrity, like Samuel's, kept him from using public office for personal gain, whether by oppressive tax demands or by excessive consumption (cf. 1 Sam 12:1–5).

They Were Courageous

Ezra showed his courage, based on prayerful faith in God, by choosing not to ask the Persian king for military protection for his journey to Jerusalem (Ezra 8:21–23), though Nehemiah was happy to accept such precautions (Neh 2:9). Nehemiah's steadfast resistance to all the attempts of his enemies to frustrate the rebuilding of the walls is well known. It called not only for practical measures to fortify the will of the people (Neh 4), but also for personal shrewdness and courage in the face of cunning conspiracies against him (Neh 6).

They Coped with Failure as Well as Success

We see, of course, their passionate commitment to the success of their respective missions and the measure of success God did indeed grant them. Yet both of them also had to contend with degrees of failure and disappointment. There were broken promises (on the part of the people). And there were only partially fulfilled promises (on the part of God), inasmuch as the struggles of the early postexilic community could not be seen to match up to the rhetorical expectations found in the second half of the book of Isaiah, for example. There is a fascinating blend of strongly made resolutions and commitments, on the one hand, with confessions of failure and sin, on the other hand. Ezra and Nehemiah were leaders who knew how to inspire people to the highest ideals and intentions, but also knew how to lead them back to the footstool of God's mercy in repentance and confession—and renewed commitment.

God's people still need leaders, and God has given leaders to his people. At least, that is how Paul saw the roles that he lists in Eph 4:7–13. It is not so much that some people are naturally gifted leaders. Rather it is that leaders such as Paul describes are themselves gifts of the risen Christ. And leadership, on the single occasion that it is mentioned, is simply one of the gifts of God's grace (Rom 12:6–8). Some of the qualities of Ezra and Nehemiah mentioned above would fit with the criteria Paul and Peter set out for those who exercised oversight in the churches they wrote to (e.g., 1 Tim 3:1–10; 1 Pet 4:10–11; 5:1–4). There is a great need in today's church worldwide for leaders who are men and women of prayer, faith, biblical faithfulness, integrity, courage, and balanced realism:

> The rapid growth of the Church in so many places remains shallow and vulnerable, partly because of the lack of discipled leaders, and partly because so many use their positions for worldly power, arrogant status or personal enrichment. As a result, God's people suffer, Christ is dishonoured, and gospel

mission is undermined.... Authentic Christian leaders must be like Christ in having a servant heart, humility, integrity, purity, lack of greed, prayerfulness, dependence on God's Spirit, and a deep love for people. Furthermore, some leadership training programs lack specific training in the one key skill that Paul includes in his list of qualifications—ability to teach God's Word to God's people. Yet Bible teaching is the paramount means of disciple-making and the most serious deficiency in contemporary Church leaders.[28]

A Community of People of Ethical Distinctiveness

Few things stand out more in Ezra-Nehemiah than the sense of separation between the returning community of Israelite exiles and the neighboring "peoples of the lands." This took on the form of social and political obstruction and hostility during the building of both the temple and the walls of Jerusalem. But the impact was most keenly felt internally over the issue of marriages between Israelite men and foreign women. The response that Ezra and Nehemiah made to the problem occupies half of that part of the book of Ezra in which Ezra himself is present (Ezra 9–10) and it colors the final chapters of the book of Nehemiah, leaving a somewhat sour taste at the very end (Neh 10:30; 13:23–27).

As seen in the previous chapter, although their motives were valid (seeking to preserve the purity of Israel's worship and avoid the temptation of worshiping false gods), the resolution (summoning men with foreign wives to divorce them) is neither necessarily commended in the text nor offered for emulation by the church today. However, the basic principle remains valid, theologically and missiologically. God's people are called to a way of life that will be significantly different from the surrounding pagan culture—whatever that may be, and even if it claims to be "Christian." Holiness in its New Testament dress may look different from the way it was symbolically enacted in the Old Testament (in the laws of ritual purity, clean and unclean food, etc.), but it retains the same strongly ethical force. From the call of Jesus on his disciples to be salt (in a world of corruption) and light (in a world of darkness), to the clear teaching of Paul and Peter that Christians must no longer live in the ways of their own pagan past and the surrounding pagan present, the New Testament insists that the gospel is a transforming power that is to be obeyed in this life, not just a saving formula guaranteeing safe entry to the next life.

Of course, in every era and in every culture, holiness (in the sense of distinctiveness from the world around) will take on different "clothes." Each genera-

---

28. *Cape Town Commitment* §II.D.3.

tion of believers needs to think very carefully in order to discern what elements of its own cultural surroundings are to be resisted or rejected, and not merely repeat whatever assumptions and expectations were placed upon Christian behavior in previous generations. Nevertheless, there will be core elements of Christian living that remain constant. The behaviors that are condemned or commended in Eph 4–5, for example, have a perennial ethical relevance, based as they are on the very essence of what the gospel is and does. As Paul put it, we are to "walk worthy" of our calling as God's reconciled people. "Walking" is the strongly Old Testament image for the whole of life lived before God. Once again, the *Cape Town Commitment* points out the missional importance of Christian distinctiveness:

> The people of God either walk in the way of the Lord, or walk in the ways of other gods. The Bible shows that God's greatest problem is not just with the nations of the world, but with the people he has created and called to be the means of blessing the nations. And the biggest obstacle to fulfilling that mission is idolatry among God's own people. For if we are called to bring the nations to worship the only true and living God, we fail miserably if we ourselves are running after the false gods of the people around us.
>
> When there is no distinction in conduct between Christians and non-Christians—for example in the practice of corruption and greed, or sexual promiscuity, or rate of divorce, or relapse to pre-Christian religious practice, or attitudes toward people of other races, or consumerist lifestyles, or social prejudice—then the world is right to wonder if our Christianity makes any difference at all. Our message carries no authenticity to a watching world.
>
> (a) We challenge one another, as God's people in every culture, to face up to the extent to which, consciously or unconsciously, we are caught up in the idolatries of our surrounding culture. We pray for prophetic discernment to identify and expose such false gods and their presence within the church itself, and for the courage to repent and renounce them in the name and authority of Jesus as Lord.
>
> (b) Since there is no biblical mission without biblical living, we urgently recommit ourselves, and challenge all those who profess the name of Christ, to live in radical distinctiveness from the ways of the world, to "put on the new humanity, created to be like God in true righteousness and holiness."[29]

To which, one can easily imagine, both Ezra and Nehemiah would have said a hearty "Amen."

---

29. *Cape Town Commitment* §II.E.1.

Leadership and Ezra-Nehemiah

BY DAVID J. SHEPHERD

The preceding chapter points to a variety of important ways in which the books of Ezra and Nehemiah might inform a more practical theology, including one concerned with cultivating Christian leadership. Indeed, those surveying more popular Christian treatments of Nehemiah over the last several decades might be forgiven for coming to the conclusion that the sole purpose of the book of Nehemiah especially is to furnish readers with a model for contemporary leadership.[1]

In considering what factors contributed to Nehemiah's recent popularity in this connection, it is worth noting that in comparison with other leading figures of the Hebrew Bible/Old Testament like Moses and David, Nehemiah's story of leadership is more concise and focused on a definable task or set of tasks, as we have seen. Thus while Solomon, like Nehemiah, is a builder, the accounts offered of the construction of the temple in 1 Kgs 6–8 and 2 Chr 1–8 (cf. 1 Chr 22–29) are more focused on details of procurement, architecture, furnishings, and dedication than the dramatic detail of initiating and managing a process found in the book of Nehemiah. Perhaps unlike Solomon, who, as king, inherits both his position and his project, the manifestly nonroyal Nehemiah resonates with readers whose contemporary models and circumstances of leadership are less traditional.

Of course, the book of Ezra offers less memoir material than does the book of Nehemiah, and Ezra's association with the teaching of the (Jewish)

---

1. See, for instance, Redpath, *Victorious Christian Service*; Barber, *Nehemiah and the Dynamics of Effective Leadership*; Swindoll, *Hand Me Another Brick*; Campbell, *Nehemiah*; Taylor and Hawkins, *When Revival Comes*; Rendall, *Nehemiah*; Getz, *Nehemiah*; White, *Excellence in Leadership*; Boice, *Nehemiah*; Jacobs, *From Rubble to Rejoicing*; Wiersbe, *Be Determined*; McCutcheon, *Rebuilding God's People*; Packer, *Passion for Faithfulness*; Stanley, *Visioneering*; and Page, *Nehemiah Factor*.

law may well have played a part in twentieth-century Christian preference for Nehemiah as exemplary leader. However, given that Nehemiah is presented as no less Jewish than Ezra, this preference may be less related to Ezra's perceived Jewishness than to his status as priest and Nehemiah's as layperson.[2] That this is so may well be suggested by Nehemiah's popular presentation as exemplary leader being largely (although not exclusively) a product of an evangelical Protestantism resistant to clericalism and enthusiastic about the activity and empowerment of the laity. Yet that Nehemiah's popularity as leader has burgeoned only toward the latter half of the twentieth century even within largely Protestant evangelical traditions suggests that the wellsprings of such interest are to be found elsewhere, at least in part.

Nehemiah as a Model of Leadership

While conscious and explicit reflection on leadership principles and practices is to be found already in antiquity,[3] there can be little doubt that the twentieth century witnessed an extraordinary explosion of interest in the theory and practice of leadership generally. The seeds of this growth were sown already in the nineteenth century by those such as Thomas Carlyle who espoused the view that history is shaped first and foremost by "great men."[4] Perhaps predictably, research that followed focused particularly on what made such men great including especially those personality traits that were thought to be characteristic of leaders. Despite the early and enduring popularity of research that focused on the personality traits of leaders (including, for instance, cognitive ability, confidence, sociability, etc.),[5] the limitations of such an approach were highlighted early on and confirmed in subsequent studies. Indeed, persistent disagreement regarding which traits are more universally characteristic of leaders highlights the subjectivity of the approach and the weakness of the methodology. Even more importantly, approaches that focus solely on leaders and their traits fail to account for the importance of the situation/context of leadership. In other

---

2. For the early "afterlives" of Ezra and Nehemiah, see Blenkinsopp, *Ezra-Nehemiah*, 54–59; and Bergen, "Ezra and Nehemiah Square Off," and the literature listed there.

3. For what appears to be presented as advice specifically for prospective leaders in the Hebrew Bible, see Prov 28–29, 31 and discussions in Malchow, "Manual for Future Monarchs"; and Yoder, "On the Threshold of Kingship."

4. For a useful discussion of theories of leadership in the late nineteenth and twentieth centuries, see Bass and Stogdill, *Handbook of Leadership*, 37–58.

5. For discussion and critique of trait theories of leadership and research, see Northouse, *Leadership*, 19–42.

words, traits that might well contribute to a leader's success in certain situations might not necessarily be as important, useful, or determinative in another situation.

Dissatisfaction with a focus on largely fixed personality traits as the determining factor in leadership toward the end of the 1940s led to an interest in leadership styles or behaviors that might be learned. Such behaviors included organizing work, defining role responsibilities, scheduling, as well as relationship behaviors such as building trust and respect. Further refinements of this approach generated a variety of "leadership styles," including so-called authority-compliance leadership that is heavily task-oriented and "team management" in which the leader stimulates participation and behaves open mindedly. By looking at behaviors that may be learned and styles that may be (potentially) adopted, this approach offered more potential than the trait approach to account for the variables involved in leading in different situations.[6]

In reviewing discussions of Nehemiah and leadership over the last several decades it becomes clear that the approach most often adopted is that of highlighting in the books of Ezra and Nehemiah personality traits and/or behaviors that constitute what a given author considers to be good or exemplary leadership. While it is not possible here to review the volume of literature and the variety of insights generated, it is, for example, common to see the presentation of Nehemiah as exemplifying leadership behavior in his planning and preparation, his prayer, and his dealing with opposition.[7] While there is no doubting the practical appeal of such an approach, closer attention to the text of Nehemiah itself nevertheless points to the complexities of adopting Nehemiah as a model for leadership, let alone for Christian leadership.

To take but one example, as we saw in the commentary, Neh 13:25 presents the reader with Nehemiah's encounter with those of Yehud who had married women of Ashdod, Ammon, and Moab—an encounter in which Nehemiah claims to have "confronted them and cursed them and beat some of them and pulled out their hair." This passage is treated in various ways by those who wish to appropriate Nehemiah as a model for contemporary leadership. Some interpreters, while noting that physical violence can hardly be adopted as a leadership behavior, seek to extract the principle of a robust confrontation of sin.[8] Others simply prefer to omit any mention of Nehemiah's tactic.[9] Still others attribute Nehemiah's act of violence to the personality trait of extroversion as

---

6. For more on such approaches, see ibid., 43–98.

7. See Barber, *Nehemiah and the Dynamics of Effective Leadership*; Swindoll, *Hand Me Another Brick*; McCutcheon, *Rebuilding God's People*; Stanley, *Visioneering*; Wiersbe, *Be Determined*.

8. See Stanley, *Visioneering*.

9. Wiersbe, *Be Determined*, who finishes his commentary on Nehemiah at 13:22.

a means of contrasting it with Ezra, whose mere tearing out of his own hair (Ezra 9:3) suggests a more introverted personality.[10] Of course, Nehemiah does not present his physical punishment of those who intermarried as any (more or) less exemplary of his leadership than for instance his nighttime ride on his arrival in Jerusalem, taken by some to illustrate the importance of a leader's initial, independent review of his situation. What the ignoring or spiritualizing of Nehemiah's physical intervention as leader seems to suggest is that most who appropriate Nehemiah as an exemplary leader have some externally derived notion of leadership that does not include the use of physical violence or coercion. What this also suggests is that interpreters who appear to be *extracting* leadership behaviors or skills *from* the book of Nehemiah may well instead be simply or largely *illustrating* them *by means of* the book of Nehemiah. Theoretically, the leadership behaviors being illustrated may be drawn from an interpreter's personal experience of leadership, from other secular research on effective leadership, or perhaps even, nominally at least, from some specifically Christian notion of leadership. In practice, however, most treatments of Nehemiah as a model for Christian leadership are simply presented as the results of unadulterated exegetical reflection on the book itself.

The suggestion that Nehemiah's violent intervention as leader might reflect his extroversion offers a neat illustration of the tendency to extract personality traits typically identified with leadership in the popular literature. However, quite apart from the difficulty of justifying a leader's verbal and physical abuse of followers as the (excusable?) result of a personality trait, it seems doubtful that the book of Nehemiah really offers sufficient grounds for making a judgment regarding Ezra's introversion and Nehemiah's extroversion. Even if it did, is it safe to assume that Nehemiah's tearing of the offenders' hair out and Ezra's tearing of his own hair out reflect purely or primarily a difference of personality?[11] The difficulty with this assumption is that trait studies appear ill-equipped to account for the specifics of a particular situation. While Ezra's actions (Ezra 9:3) and Nehemiah's (Neh 13:25) represent their respective responses as leaders to the problem of Yehudite intermarriage with outsiders, the narrative situations differ in at least one important way: while Ezra's response is the first sign within Ezra-Nehemiah that the question of intermarriage with foreigners is a problem, the same cannot be said by the time Nehemiah responds. In fact, within the book as it stands, when Nehemiah responds to the intermarriage crisis in 13:25,

10. See Allen and Laniak, *Ezra, Nehemiah, Esther*, 166.
11. If so, contemporary Christian interpreters' preference for what they perceive to be Nehemiah's style of leadership generally might tell us more about their own preferences for extroverted leadership than what kinds of behavior are necessarily likely to contribute to successful leadership in any given situation.

he appears to be responding to the people's violation of a solemn and binding agreement (10:30) to not do precisely what he finds them now doing (again). Indeed, even if we think it likely that Nehemiah's intervention in Neh 13 takes place before (despite its current presentation after) the people's agreement not to intermarry in 10:30, Nehemiah is still not responding to a first offense but rather to recalcitrance following the covenant to avoid intermarriage secured by Ezra's earlier intervention. Whichever the case may be, if the behavior to which Nehemiah responds is presented as more egregious than that encountered by Ezra, how can we be sure that Nehemiah's greater aggression should not be understood as reflecting not a more assertive personality or a more domineering leadership style but rather a more aggravated situation, to which Ezra might well have responded in the same more aggressive and physical fashion?[12]

While the above comparison of Nehemiah and Ezra highlights the challenges of attributing the particular activities of leaders as represented in Ezra-Nehemiah to personality traits or leadership styles (exemplary or otherwise), it also illustrates incidentally what may be missed when Nehemiah becomes the primary or exclusive focus of those seeking a model for leadership. That Ezra and Nehemiah at the end of their respective books are portrayed as grappling with similar (though not, as we have seen, identical) issues in their leadership points toward the unity of Ezra-Nehemiah reflected in their fusion in the Hebrew canon and evidenced in various ways. While there are a variety of reasons for Nehemiah's greater popularity as a model for those interested in contemporary leadership, the literary unity of Ezra-Nehemiah as we now have it leaves those interested in leadership models few obvious reasons for limiting their attention to Nehemiah.[13] Indeed, Tamara Cohn Eskenazi's analysis of Ezra and Nehemiah as characters in Ezra-Nehemiah suggests that an understanding of the depiction of Nehemiah's leadership might well be enhanced by an analysis of Ezra's.[14] By means of a careful comparison of their respective characterizations, Eskenazi argues that the leadership of Ezra as the "self-effacing teacher of Torah" is intentionally juxtaposed and contrasted with that of Nehemiah as the "self-glorifying entrepreneur."[15] There is much to be admired in Eske-

---

12. As noted in the commentary on Neh 10:28–29 and 13:1–3, it is also possible that Nehemiah was advocating for a broader separation that extended beyond the exclusion of intermarriage.

13. More popular treatments of Nehemiah as exemplary leader may be contrasted with the commentaries on Ezra-Nehemiah by, for instance, Blenkinsopp, *Ezra-Nehemiah*; Clines, *Ezra, Nehemiah, Esther*; and especially Williamson, *Ezra, Nehemiah*, in which an interest in leadership in Ezra-Nehemiah is evident throughout and is rooted in and related to an awareness of wider literary and historical issues.

14. Eskenazi, *In an Age of Prose*.

15. Ibid., 127–54. While her preference for Ezra's style is clear, Eskenazi does in the end (154)

nazi's analysis, in her dismantling of previous denigrations of Ezra's portrayal as leader, and in her highlighting of apparently intentional contrasts between the depictions of Ezra and Nehemiah. Yet, if Eskenazi's contrasting of leadership styles in Ezra and Nehemiah is indeed illuminating, might her reluctance to recognize the possible fallibilities of Ezra's approach and her own largely disparaging characterization of Nehemiah's leadership reflect in part her own personal preference for the leadership style she finds in Ezra, and her lack of sympathy for the leadership style that so many popular Christian interpreters detect and resonate with in Nehemiah?

One further benefit of a broader analysis of leadership in Ezra-Nehemiah as a whole (including not merely Ezra and Nehemiah, but Zerubbabel and others) is that it might place interpreters in a better position to analyze how success or outcomes of leadership are represented in these books. The unfortunate consequence of popular interpreters focusing on and appropriating only what they find to be exemplary in the presentation of Nehemiah's leadership is that while those behaviors that they associate with what they deem to be his leadership successes are highlighted, behaviors or tactics that may reflect failures or inadequacies may be neglected, even if they might offer their own insights regarding the presentation of leadership within Ezra-Nehemiah. For example, while our journey through the books of Ezra-Nehemiah suggested that Nehemiah is presented (in large part by his own memoirs) as successful insofar as the rebuilding and dedication of the wall was concerned, the final presentation of the book leaves some doubt regarding how successful his reforming of temple and people were. Indeed, if the report of Nehemiah's return to find his earlier reforms neglected and his increasingly frequent pleas to be remembered very much create the impression that his remedial efforts are not likely to have had a much greater impact than his earlier ones, one might well wonder how this reflects the final editor's view of the success of Nehemiah's leadership.

An Alternative Approach to Leadership in Ezra-Nehemiah

While conventional efforts to extract or illustrate exemplary leadership traits or behaviors will undoubtedly continue to be attractive, it is worth considering whether an alternative approach might avoid at least some of their limitations and advance our understanding of how leadership is represented in Ezra-Nehemiah as a whole. In searching for such an approach, it may be recalled that

---

suggest that Ezra-Nehemiah's presentation of the memoirs of both Ezra and Nehemiah points toward the necessity of both types of leaders for the restoration of the community.

alongside the development of trait theories of leadership in the early twentieth century, a quite different way of conceptualizing leadership was articulated by Max Weber.[16]

Weber's interest was less in the particular traits or behaviors associated with particular leaders than in the ways in which leaders were recognized by others as entitled to rule or exercise authority as such. In an important essay, Weber outlined three pure types of legitimate(d) authority: traditional authority, legal-rational authority, and charismatic authority.[17] Traditional authority is "based on the belief in the sanctity of orders and powers of rule which have existed since time immemorial."[18] Weber points toward heads of families, clans, and feudal lords as examples of those exercising traditional authority, but his emphasis on traditional authority as a genealogically inherited authority means that hereditary kings and priests also exercise traditional authority.[19] By contrast, legal-rational authority commands obedience of those governed by virtue of a legally defined office, which is itself subject to rules within a bureaucratic system, even if the head of that system and the ultimate authority is a monarch whose rule is inherited. Finally, and most famously, charismatic authority is defined in Weber's own words as follows:

> The term "charisma" will be applied to a certain quality of an individual personality by virtue of which he is considered extraordinary and treated as endowed with supernatural, superhuman, or at least specifically exceptional powers or qualities. These are such as are not accessible to the ordinary person, but are regarded as of divine origin or as exemplary, and on the basis of them the individual concerned is treated as a "leader."[20]

Given this description, is it hardly surprising that while various qualities might qualify a leader as extraordinary, Weber finds examples of charismatic author-

---

16. Weber's influence on the study of the Hebrew Bible both directly and as mediated through the subsequent development of sociological approaches to religion is significant, but its exploration lies far beyond the scope of our interest here. For discussion see Petersen, "Max Weber and the Sociological Study."

17. English translation of the original German essay is from Whimster, *Essential Weber Reader*, 133–45.

18. Ibid., 135.

19. Weber's differentiation of prophet as called and priest as office holder in his *Economy and Society*, 1.440, seems to point toward the charisma of office characteristic of the consecration of priests in the Christian tradition rather than the inheritance of priestly status associated with the Hebrew/Jewish tradition, a distinction that seems not to be fully appreciated by Hendel, "Prophets, Priests and the Efficacy of Ritual," 186.

20. Weber, *Economy and Society*, 1.241.

ity among religious leaders including Jesus and the Old Testament prophets who claimed some kind of supernatural license.[21] Among the many and varied observations Weber makes regarding the features of charismatic authority are the following.

First, it is most likely to be exercised in times of crisis of almost any sort including situations of political, economic, ethical, or religious distress.[22] The charismatic leader "seizes the task for which he is destined and demands that others obey and follow him by virtue of his mission."[23] However, because it is often related to extraordinary times and people, charismatic authority is also inherently unstable and indeed likely to dissolve with the charismatic leader's death or departure or the perception that their work has failed or powers have waned. In order therefore to preserve its values or accomplishments, charismatic authority may be routinized in a variety of ways, including the appointment of a successor or the institution of structures of authority. If, for instance, a successor to a charismatically established king (i.e., David) is chosen on the basis of blood descent from that king, this is likely to inaugurate a transformation of charismatic authority into traditional authority. In the process of such a transformation, any remaining element of charismatic authority will be extinguished by the requirement that the crown be inherited by the firstborn, who may of course possess none of the extraordinary qualities that allowed the progenitor to seize power in the first place.[24] Again, a failure to routinize charismatic authority in the direction of traditional or legal-rational authority will result in its dissolution.

Of the three types of rule, it is the latter, charismatic authority that has proven much the most popular, both in reflection on organizational leadership[25] and within biblical studies itself, including those focused on the Hebrew Bible/Old Testament.[26] In the significant treatment of the biblical traditions in Weber's *Ancient Judaism*, his classification of the authority of Samson and other judges (84–98), King David (184, 260), and the prophets (286, 297) as

---

21. See ibid., 1.440, and the distinction between prophet and priest.
22. Ibid., 2.1112.
23. Ibid., 2.1112.
24. Ibid., 2.1135, where Weber clarifies that "we are justified in still speaking of charisma in this impersonal sense only because there always remains an extraordinary quality that is not accessible to everyone and that typically overshadows the charismatic subjects."
25. For more on the significance of Weber's notion of charismatic leadership in the development of recent leadership theory (including especially transformational leadership), see Bryman, *Charisma and Leadership in Organizations*, 91–114.
26. For discussion of some of the literature, see Overholt, "Thoughts on the Use of 'Charisma.'"

charismatic prompted subsequent scholarly exploration in relation to all three of these types of leaders.[27] While more recent studies sustain the judgment of early commentators that the bulk of the figures in Judges answer well to Weber's understanding of charismatic leadership,[28] the situation is more complicated in the case of kings and certainly prophets. For example, as hinted at by others, the emphasis on divine revelation to Solomon in 1 Kings and his elevation at the expense of Adonijah hint at a properly charismatic authority beyond merely the hereditary charisma bestowed upon him by virtue of being a son of the king.[29] So too, while prophets like Hosea or Elijah might seem to offer an even clearer example of a properly charismatic leader who stands apart from and is inherently critical of traditional authority, the Hebrew Bible also knows prophets who are no less charismatic for their support of traditional authority.[30] Of course, Weber himself recognized that the three types of authority would almost certainly coexist in particular historical contexts and that charismatic leadership was not entirely incompatible with a traditional or bureaucratic regime.[31]

While Weber's own comments are suggestive at various points and will be considered below, his discussion of the returnees from Babylon in *Ancient Judaism* does not include any explicit mention of which of his three types of authority are displayed by Ezra or Nehemiah or other leading figures of the return such as Zerubbabel, Sheshbazzar, or Jeshua the priest. Nevertheless, it seems likely that the basic type of authority exercised by these figures is a particular species of traditionalism that Weber termed "patrimonialism."[32] In patrimonial rule, the (patriarchal) rule of the father over his house becomes the model for an exercising of authority over those beyond his household.[33] In the

---

27. See, for instance, the bibliography offered by Overholt, ibid., to which may be added the literature cited in Clements, "Max Weber, Charisma, and Biblical Prophecy."

28. See Malamat, "Charismatic Leadership in the Book of Judges"; and Weisman, "Charismatic Leaders in the Era of the Judges," 401, 410.

29. Ahlström, "Solomon the Chosen One." See also the discussion in Overholt, "Thoughts on the Use of 'Charisma,'" 293–97.

30. So Overholt, "Thoughts on the Use of 'Charisma,'" 298–99, who notes however that prophets and the cult may not be as closely linked as is assumed by Berger's trenchant and influential critique of Weber's notion of prophet as charismatic authority in "Charisma and Religious Innovation."

31. So Bryman, *Charisma and Leadership in Organizations*, 29. For Weber's writings relating to charisma and analysis of them, see Eisenstadt, *Max Weber on Charisma and Institution Building*.

32. So Weber, *Ancient Judaism*, 359: "The political prerogatives rested always in the hands either of the Persian satrap and later of the Hellenistic regent and their officials or in those of a special commission of the king, as Nehemiah was de facto. Ezra's position, likewise, rested formally, solely on the authority invested in him by the Persian king.... Ezra's position, opposite the high priest, is inconceivable without far-reaching royal authorization."

33. For the application of Weber's notion of patrimonialism to hierarchies of authority

patrimonial state, this extends to areas and regions that are established as de facto personal dependencies of the king. In fact, such patrimonial rule was for Weber exemplified by the empires of the Near East, of which the Persian was the last and greatest.[34] More recent studies of Bronze Age Canaan suggest the appropriateness of patrimonial rule to this earlier era,[35] and there is some reason to think that it may indeed be no less appropriate to the Achaemenid Empire.[36]

Jeshua, Zerubbabel, Sheshbazzar

We see Weber's patrimonial rule exemplified in the book of Ezra as we have it, when Ezra 4:3 presents the authority of Zerubbabel, Jeshua, and the "heads of the houses of the fathers" as being derived from the Persian crown, which is itself underlined by the substance of the imperial correspondence in Ezra 1–6. In these letters, it is not correct bureaucratic procedures that are at stake, but rather issues of loyalty and contribution to the royal coffers (4:13)—which are reinforced by the accusers' justification for their warning of the king out of loyalty (we "eat the salt of the palace"; 4:14) and the king's eventual insistence that royal revenues be diverted (6:8–9).

Yet the figures exercising patrimonial authority on behalf of the crown in relation to the reestablishment of the temple and worship in Yehud are far from randomly chosen. Already in 1:8 the reader is informed that Sheshbazzar is "a prince" (נָשִׂיא/nāśîʾ), which while it does not necessarily imply royal descent, almost certainly does suggest he was a tribal leader among the exiles (cf. Num 2:3–31) and perhaps for that reason made governor by Cyrus (Ezra 5:14). As evidenced by his descent from Shealtiel (3:2; cf. Hag 1:1), Zerubbabel seems much more clearly to be of the house of David (cf. Zech 12), which again seems unlikely to be unrelated to his appointment as Sheshbazzar's successor as

---

in the Hebrew Bible, see Stager, "Archaeology of the Family"; and idem, "Forging an Identity," 149–51, 171–72.

34. Weber, *Economy and Society*, 2.1010–13.
35. See Schloen, *House of the Father as Fact and Symbol*.
36. See, for instance, Root, "From the Heart," 4, who cites Weber explicitly. While there is much to admire in the basic argument of Fried's *Priest and the Great King* that Yehud enjoyed no greater autonomy than other corners of the Achaemenid Empire (and considerably less than some suggest), her insistence on the latter as a straightforward example of Eisenstadt's "historical bureaucratic empire" seems doubtful. While the much later Sassanid Empire bore all the hallmarks of other historical bureaucratic empires, Eisenstadt's very limited treatment of the Achaemenid period includes his acknowledgement (*Political Systems of Empires*, 10–11) that the first great Persian Empire was in large part patrimonial in character with only incipient signs of the bureaucracy that would later be manifest in the Sassanid regime.

governor (Hag 2:21). For his part, Jeshua's presentation as not merely priest, but high priest, is likewise underlined by the mention of his descent from Jozadak (Ezra 3:2; Hag 1:1). While it is impossible to be certain to what extent personal charisma may have played a part in the choice and recognition of these leaders, the presentation of them in Ezra-Nehemiah itself offers no grounds for assuming their possession of anything more or less than the hereditary charisma that their descent from particular leading and priestly families automatically conferred upon them. All (including the heads of the houses of the fathers) are thus presented by Ezra-Nehemiah as basically traditional in the type of authority/leadership they exercise, by virtue of the patrimonial quality of both the golah community itself and the Persian royal authority structure to which it was subordinate.

If Ezra 1–6 appears thus far to present the human leaders who exercise leadership as doing so on the basis of a patrimonial type of traditional leadership, it is worth considering how this relates to the theological interests of these chapters. First, the writer makes it clear that Cyrus, whose extraordinariness (and thus charismatic leadership) is chronicled in other ancient sources, is presented here as being "stirred up" by YHWH (1:1) to restore the Jewish cult in Jerusalem.[37] A few verses later, this same language is used to describe the divine impetus for the heads of the fathers' houses (as well as the priests and Levites) to begin the preparations to return. Recalling that Cyrus's divine inspiration is noted in 1:1 as linked to prophetic activity (Jeremiah), it is interesting to note that in 5:1–2, the prophesying of Haggai and Zechariah is reported as prompting and supporting the resumption of the rebuilding of the temple by Zerubbabel and Jeshua (despite their patrilineal descent being emphasized). The note in 5:5 that "the eye of their God was on the elders of the Jews" seems to invite the interpretation that the prophetic activity is seen as efficacious in some measure (cf. also 6:14).

Yet if Weber's own recognition that types of authority might be mixed in practice means that a charismatic flavor to the presentation of otherwise traditional leadership is not entirely unexpected, it should be acknowledged that the assessment of the initial leaders discussed above is that of the writer of Ezra/Nehemiah and/or their sources rather than the self-presentation of the leaders themselves (of which there appears to be none in these chapters). Moreover, if the writer/editor of Ezra 1–6 does acknowledge the divine inspiration of the elders, a large part of the credit is ascribed to prophetic figures—Weber's archetypal expression of the charismatic leader—rather than Jeshua, Zerubba-

---

37. Cf. Isa 45:1. For a recent and insightful analysis of the presentation of Cyrus as a charismatic (and traditional) leader, see Lincoln, *Religion, Empire, and Torture*, 33–50.

bel, or Sheshbazzar, whose traditional leadership/authority is not substantially or explicitly qualified as charismatic.[38] What this does suggest is that if, as suggested elsewhere, the writer/editor has indeed played down Zerubbabel's Davidic descent and political connections in Ezra 1-6 in order to emphasize the divine grace of the restoration,[39] there seems to be conspicuously little interest in emphasizing the charisma (in a Weberian sense) bestowed upon Zerubbabel or either of the other two patrimonial leaders of the time.

Ezra

Ezra 7 introduces readers to a new leader during the reign of Artaxerxes, namely Ezra himself. If, as with Jeshua, the original introduction of Ezra here was limited to an immediate ancestor, Seraiah (7:1),[40] this is nevertheless a first and important indicator of the priestly authority vested in Ezra—an authority clarified and reinforced by the extension of the lineage back to the first or chief priest Aaron (7:2-5).[41] As was the case with Jeshua, the introduction of Ezra makes clear that this priest is empowered or authorized to undertake a particular set of tasks under the patrimonial authority of (local governors ultimately answerable to) the Persian crown. Like Jeshua and the others in the opening chapter of the book, Ezra's royal patrimonial authority is reinforced by the inclusion of an edict (7:12-26) that is, however, much more focused on the personal nature of Ezra's authority (7:12, 25) than the earlier edict of Ezra 1. That the authority exercised by Ezra is a matter of royal patrimony is underlined further by the editorial note in 8:36 confirming both the delivery of the royal commissions to the "king's satraps" and to the governors of the province "Beyond the River" as well as the efficacy of these commissions in securing local support.

Thus far, the traditional type of authority that Ezra is presented as exercising seems to differ very little from that of Jeshua, but the text offers a series of hints that its presentation of Ezra's claim to authority is rather more nuanced. More specifically, while Ezra 1-6 offers no suggestion of personal charisma attached to Jeshua apart from the hereditary charisma of being (perhaps first) born of a high priestly house, the portrayal of Ezra appears to reflect something more approximating a degree of pure or personal charisma in the Weberian sense.

---

38. The issue largely hinges on whether Ezra 1:5 and 5:5 are meant to be understood as including these figures, even if they are not explicitly mentioned.
39. As plausibly suggested by Japhet, "Sheshbazzar and Zerubbabel."
40. Williamson, *Ezra, Nehemiah*, 91 (cf. also Blenkinsopp, *Ezra-Nehemiah*, 135-36).
41. Williamson, *Ezra, Nehemiah*, 91.

This is first evident in the part of the memoir of Ezra (7:27–28) in which he himself notes that the courage required of him to recruit leaders to return to Yehud was inspired and justified by "the hand of Yhwh" upon him. While we cannot pretend to know whether Ezra communicated his own perception of his possession of this charism to these leaders at the time, the sanction of the king is supplemented here by the claim of the kind of extraordinary grace that Weber would undoubtedly associate with charismatic leadership. That this particular expression of supernatural empowerment ("the hand of Yhwh") is also to be found in the verses that introduce Ezra (7:6, 9) may well support the suggestion that Ezra's memoir lies behind 7:1–10 and indeed 8:18, 22, 31.[42] As in 7:28, so too in these other verses, divine overshadowing is claimed as a means of explaining actions or outcomes that might otherwise appear humanly improbable, including royal acquiescence to Ezra's requests (7:6), recruitment of a man of discretion (8:18), and safe journey to Yehud (7:9; 8:22, 31).[43] To the extent that Ezra's readers shared his view of these improbabilities (as he must have assumed they would), we may expect that they will also have agreed with his assessment of the charismatic quality of his own authority in leading the returnees back to Yehud. While the royal exhortation for Ezra to appoint judges/magistrates using a wisdom that is God-given (7:25) lacks the phraseology "hand of Yhwh," the sentiment seems nevertheless not dissimilar.[44]

If the above illustrates Ezra's claim to charismatic authority in supernatural terms reminiscent of prophets and judges, it is worth noting that for the editor at least, Ezra's claim includes extraordinary qualities that are in some sense more mundane, though no less a marker of his charisma. Reference to Ezra as not merely a scribe (so 7:12, 21) but a "skilled" one (7:6) enhances the portrait of a leader whose royal authorization and hereditary charism are supplemented by an evidently extraordinary capacity for interpretation and application of Jewish law.[45] The mention of such a capability might well be related to the claim by the editor (or Ezra himself originally) that Ezra "had set his heart"[46] to interpret, apply, and teach the law (7:10)—an interest or passion that seems unlikely to have been mentioned had it not been deemed in some way exceptional.

---

42. Williamson, *Ezra, Nehemiah*, 89–90.

43. For a comparable use of this phraseology for the same purposes, see 1 Kgs 18:46.

44. Agreeing with Clines, *Ezra, Nehemiah, Esther*, 106, that this is more likely the intention of "the wisdom of God" than an identification of the latter with the "law of God" in 7:14.

45. Seeing this as more likely than a reference to Ezra's superior ability as a statesman, as would be implied if "scribe" was a political office in the Persian bureaucracy; so Schaeder, *Esra der Schreiber*, 39–59.

46. For the notion of "setting one's heart" (לְבָב/*lēbāb* + כּוּן/*kwn*), see 1 Sam 7:3; 2 Chr 12:14; 19:3; 20:33; 30:19.

If, as seems most likely for a variety of reasons, an earlier version of Ezra's memoirs included his teaching of the law (Neh 8) immediately after the account of Ezra's arrival in Jerusalem (Ezra 8:32), the people's summoning of him (rather than he them) in Neh 8:1 may be less suggestive of a particular style of leadership than of the people's recognition of Ezra's imperial and priestly authority to fulfill his commission to teach the law, regardless of whether his reputation as a skilled scribe preceded him or not. In any event, the extent of the people's recognition of Ezra's authority in this matter is illustrated by Neh 8's account of the reading of the law itself. It is not some but "all" of the people who gather (8:1), both men and women and "all who could understand" (8:2–3), and it is the ears of "all" of them that are attentive to the reading of the law. When Ezra opens the book in the sight of "all" the people, not some but "all" stand up (8:5), and when Ezra blesses YHWH they "all" answer "Amen" and engage in worship. "All" the people weep when they hear the law (8:9), "all" of them put into practice the commands they have had interpreted for them (8:12), and finally "all" the assembly of those who had returned from the captivity celebrate Sukkot (8:17). While it is impossible to delineate precisely where Ezra's patrimonial authority ends and his charismatic authority begins in his reading of the law, the presentation of the collective and inclusive quality of the people's response suggests an intention to present Ezra's authority to read and teach the law as one that was firmly and widely recognized.

Assuming that Ezra's reading of the law (Neh 8) was originally followed by his confrontation of the intermarriage issue described in Ezra 9–10, this latter episode too illustrates the nature of Ezra's authority/leadership and the people's response to it. As was the case in the reading of the law, Ezra does not take the initiative but is approached, not this time by "all" the people but by the "officials" who proceed to describe in highly charged language the problem of intermarriage (9:1–2). If the royal edict in 7:14 authorizing Ezra to "make inquiries about Judah and Jerusalem according to the law of your God" relates to an issue like intermarriage,[47] then the approach of the people to Ezra (rather than vice versa) may again be an indication by the writer/editor that Ezra's authority to adjudicate such matters was specifically recognized by the leaders of the community. Yet, what is striking is how what follows is different in various ways from the reading of the law by Ezra, whose patrimonial authority to do so seems to have been based on royal fiat and the inherited charisma of priestly status.

First, it is worth noting that we do not find at this point in the narrative Ezra simply ordering the dissolution of the offending marriages. Instead, Ezra's response is extremely animated and highly expressive, both emotionally and

---

47. Williamson, *Ezra, Nehemiah*, 101.

physically. In fact, leaving aside the extent to which the representation of Ezra's personal grief may be intended here, there can be little doubt that the tearing of the garments, the plucking of the hair and beard, and the sitting appalled should be primarily understood as serving a representative and symbolic function of the sort elsewhere associated with prophets such as Ezekiel.[48] While this is not to suggest that Ezra is being presented here as a prophet per se, it highlights the possibility that in comparison with the previous episode, Ezra's authority/leadership here is being portrayed as less patrimonial and more charismatic in nature. If the officials' initial approach to Ezra (9:1) may still reflect their recognition of Ezra's patrimonial authority, the subsequent gathering of "those who trembled at the words of the God of Israel" (9:4) around Ezra here seems to be represented as arising from actions that are, in keeping with Weber's own understanding of charismatic authority, both extraordinary and exemplary: extraordinary in that we do not read of those drawn to Ezra replicating the more extreme aspects of his behavior, but exemplary in that they do gather round him while he sits.

In his confronting of this issue, it is perhaps not surprising that Ezra the teacher might display qualities of charismatic authority, in light of Weber's own difficulty in distinguishing between the "prophet" and the "teacher of ethics," not least because, according to Weber, the latter often gathers disciples about himself by means of a new or recovered ancient wisdom, sometimes with a view to establishing a new ethical order.[49] Indeed, if we recognize that the extraordinary qualities of the charismatic leader may not be limited to the divine revelation claimed by the prophet, then Weber's only means of distinguishing between the teacher of ethics and the prophet is the "vital emotional preaching" that for Weber makes the prophet closer to the popular leader than a teacher.

Yet, if what follows in Ezra 9 is in formal terms a penitential prayer, there can be no denying that the emotion of Ezra's initial response is picked up in the prayer itself that strikes a note of heartfelt confession even as it recites the history of Israel's infidelity. Indeed, as noted by others, this prayer of confession is at points quite clearly hortatory, reflecting a consciousness of the audience that surrounds Ezra in the present literary context.[50] Given the importance of oratory in construals of charismatic authority,[51] here again we find an indication that the authority that Ezra is presenting himself as exercising, the influence

---

48. Clines, *Ezra, Nehemiah, Esther*, 120, suggests that Ezra here "enacts a typical piece of prophetic symbolism," citing Isa 20:1–4 and Ezek 4–5 as examples of the same. Blenkinsopp, *Ezra-Nehemiah*, 177, compares Ezra's "catatonic" state to that of Ezekiel, encouraged by the appearance of "appalled" (מְשׁוֹמֵם/mašômēm in Ezra 9:3; מַשְׁמִים/mašmîm in Ezek 3:15).

49. Weber, *Economy and Society*, 1.444–46.

50. Williamson, *Ezra, Nehemiah*, 129.

51. See, for instance, Bryman, *Charisma and Leadership in Organizations*, 58–62.

that he is presenting himself as wielding, has a distinctly charismatic quality, not obviously reflected in the episode in which he teaches the law. More than that, Ezra within the public prayer explicitly invokes the prophets (9:11) whose frenzied physicality he continues to emulate before the temple (10:1). However culturally determined, the recognition of the behavior of the charismatic leader as such is confirmed by the note of the size and comprehensive complexion of the crowd that now gathers ("a very great assembly of men and women and children"; 10:1), and, as Ezra weeps, so too do they weep "very sorely." Here then is perhaps the beginning of the formation of Weber's charismatic community, which he sees as being based on an "emotional form of communal relationship."[52] The force of Ezra's charismatic authority is reinforced by the representative confession articulated in 10:2–3 and the people's invitation to Ezra to bind them in a solemn covenant separating themselves from the "foreign wives" and "children." Here Ezra's charismatic authority is supplemented by an invoking of the royally authorized sanctions for noncompliance (cf. 7:14). Finally, in due course and after an investigation by the leaders (rather than Ezra) the matter is concluded, and the women and children apparently sent away.

While the leadership exercised by Ezra in teaching the law in Neh 8 appears to reflect a patrimonial authority arising from his royal commission and priestly position, his engagement with the issue of intermarriage in Ezra 9–10 seems to reflect a greater exercising and recognition of the charismatic authority alluded to in Ezra 7. Yet if Ezra presents himself as a largely successful leader, the displacement of his reading of the law in Neh 8 by the editor of Ezra-Nehemiah inevitably complicates such an assessment. Not surprisingly, the delay created by this displacement in Ezra's fulfillment of his commission to teach the law some years after his arrival strikes most readers as odd and implies for others that Ezra's authority or position was somehow compromised, soon after he arrived.[53] Perhaps more importantly, despite Ezra's confrontation of the problem of intermarriage with foreigners, this issue recurs in some form at least once (and perhaps twice) in the time of Nehemiah (Neh 10, 13). While the presentation of such a recurrence seems to be intended to point to the recalcitrance of the people, it would also seem to cast doubt on the efficacy of Ezra's intervention as leader and perhaps hint at his inability to institutionalize the reforms he initiated.[54] Such doubts become more intelligible in view of the charismatic quality of Ezra's leadership.

---

52. Weber, *Economy and Society*, 1.243.
53. Williamson, *Ezra, Nehemiah*, 282–83, 287.
54. Ibid., xlvii. The seeds of such doubts may well be seen in the mention of dissenters in Ezra 10:15.

The unstable and extraordinary quality of charismatic authority thus requires that it be routinized eventually in some fashion, often through the agency of the charismatic leader's successor and/or followers and through the implementation of a system to preserve and enshrine the values established initially by that leader. Indeed, precisely such a process of routinization seems to be intended and authorized toward the end of the royal edict in Ezra 7:25, where Ezra is instructed to appoint "magistrates and judges" to ensure compliance with the law of his God. The absence of any mention of Ezra appointing such authorities is conspicuous and begs a variety of questions. Might Ezra's original memoir materials have included a note of his appointment of these authorities? If so, then why has this not been included in Ezra-Nehemiah as we now have it? Were these judicial authorities intended to be part of Ezra's charismatic staff or his successors, and if so, on what basis were they to be appointed? Finally, if Ezra did in fact fail to make such appointments, why did he fail to do so? Whatever the answers to these questions might be, it seems likely that one of the chief responsibilities of such judicial authorities might have been to ensure that the marital separation from foreigners initially secured by Ezra's charismatic authority was routinized by policing the community's compliance with the covenant to which they agreed.

It thus seems quite plausible that the presentation of Ezra's authority and leadership within the books of Ezra-Nehemiah as a whole is intended to suggest that while the community fully recognized his exercising of patrimonial authority (on the basis of royal fiat and priestly position) in teaching the law and his charismatic authority in confronting the issue of foreign intermarriage, Ezra's failure to routinize these values by appointing magistrates/judges should be seen as leading ultimately to the dissolution of his charismatic authority in this respect.[55]

Nehemiah

The book of Nehemiah wastes little time in introducing us to its protagonist, Nehemiah son of Hacaliah. Unlike the lineage of Ezra, which in its present form confirms his status and hereditary charisma as priest, Nehemiah's patronym, "Hacaliah," sheds little light on his status or connections. Yet, what-

---

55. There may even be an intentional contrast drawn between the lack of routinization in this area and the beginning of routinization of Ezra's teaching authority if we are meant to understand his delegation of duties to the Levites in this manner. For a helpful focus on Ezra's tendency toward empowerment and delegation, see Eskenazi, *In an Age of Prose*, 136–44.

ever Nehemiah lacks in terms of markers of traditional Yehudite authority or status is more than made up for by the office of cupbearer he claims to hold within the Persian court (Neh 1:11). By all accounts, the cupbearer enjoyed considerable status and informal influence within the royal household and is an archetypal example of Weber's "patrimonial office," whether the holder is recruited from among free peoples or subject peoples, as was clearly the case with Nehemiah.[56] For the purposes of Nehemiah's work in Jerusalem it was, however, his possession of the office of governor that ensured that he enjoyed a patrimonial authority derived directly from the royal crown (5:14). The mention of correspondence from the Persian crown to the governors of the satrapy "Beyond the River" to ensure Nehemiah's safe passage and to procure timber from the "king's forest" (2:7–9) underlines the royal authorization of Nehemiah's mission to rebuild Jerusalem. Apart from making him eligible to receive a royal allowance, it is however far from clear precisely what else Nehemiah was authorized to do *as governor*, in large part because of the way in which Nehemiah's leadership is presented, especially in the memoir materials.

First, given Weber's observation that charismatic authority is often exercised in situations of political, economic, ethical, or religious distress, it is interesting to note that Nehemiah presents his mission as arising not from a deputation or commission but rather from his own emotional response (1:4) to a report of great trouble and shame thanks to the sorry state of the wall in Jerusalem (1:3). Indeed, as his account unfolds, Nehemiah will report encountering and addressing all of Weber's species of distress. Yet, Nehemiah's presentation of his mission hints at his interest in underlining that his leadership is based on something more than merely the power associated with his patrimonial office(s). So, for instance, royal permission to return to Yehud (as governor) is presented by Nehemiah as an "act of God" thanks to both his explicit insistence that he "prayed" for the favor of the king (1:11; 2:4) and his acknowledgment that this favor was finally forthcoming because "the gracious hand of my God was upon me" (2:8). That this supernatural grace is not merely instrumental but inspirational is confirmed by Nehemiah's assurance to the reader in 2:12 that this was not *his* idea but rather "what my God had put in my heart to do for Jerusalem."

If Nehemiah's presentation of himself to the reader as the beneficiary of supernatural charism is similar in this way to Ezra's, it is worth noting that, unlike Ezra, Nehemiah also reports his claim to charismatic authority to the people themselves (2:18): "I told them that the hand of my God had been gra-

---

56. Weber, *Economy and Society*, 2.1025–26.

cious upon me, and also the words that the king had spoken to me" (NRSV). Without knowing precisely what words Nehemiah claims to have shared with the people, one might assume that they will have alluded to both the king's pleasure in sending Nehemiah (2:6) and his provision (2:7–8). It is clear, however, that in Nehemiah's report of his communication at least, the royal pleasure is quite literally a secondary concern when compared with the divine power that has secured it.

Whether Nehemiah possessed the patrimonial authority to simply conscript labor for the reconstruction of the wall in Jerusalem or not, his report of his own appeal and of the people's positive response ("they committed themselves to the common good"; 2:18 NRSV) suggests a desire to present the community of builders that now gather round Nehemiah as a charismatic community rather than a conscripted one. A final illustration of Nehemiah's presentation of himself as possessor of supernatural charism is offered by his report that "my God put it in my mind to assemble the people" (7:5) whether for the purposes of genealogical enrollment and/or the repopulation of the city. Taken together, the above appears to offer clear evidence that Nehemiah's presentation of his own authority in his memoir (at least) and perhaps before the people is inflected more in charismatic terms than patrimonial ones.

Such an emphasis is also reinforced, in a more mundane way, in Nehemiah's account of his resistance to the threat of armed opposition faced by him and his community (Neh 4). Prominent among the defenders of the wall are Nehemiah's own "servants" (4:16), who if they arrived with him from Susa may have been assigned to him by the crown as part of his entourage. If, however, he means to imply that these servants were drawn to him after his arrival in Jerusalem, they may well reflect a group of men formed by their personal devotion to Nehemiah—the heart or nucleus of Nehemiah's charismatic community. If Ezra acts like a prophet in his confrontation of the intermarriage issue, Nehemiah appears to do likewise in rousing the community to resist potential attack from outsiders by reminding them that their God will fight for them, echoing the divine-warrior language of the archetypal prophet Moses (Deut 1:30). Moreover, like the judges, Nehemiah acts the part of the charismatic warlord by orchestrating, if not the actual deliverance of the people, then at least their armed defense.

While Nehemiah reports his patrimonial entitlement to a royal allowance (perhaps as a portion of the royal levy) he does so only as a means of making clear that he did not personally profit from his mission to Yehud by "acquiring land" (Neh 5:16) and was even himself out of pocket thanks to his refusal of the "food allowance" that he was patrimonially authorized to take. The charismatic quality of Nehemiah's leadership is underlined by his own presentation of such forbearance as both exceptional (unlike former governors; 5:15) and exemplary (his brothers joined him in this refusal; 5:14). In this respect, Nehemiah's self-presentation resonates clearly with Weber's observation that "in its pure form, charisma is never a source of private income; it is neither utilized for the exchange of services nor is it exercised for pay, and it does not know orderly taxation to meet the material demands of its mission."[57] While provision for the temple by means of a kind of taxation will be a concern for Nehemiah, his emphasis on his own sponsorship of his mission without drawing on such imperial provision would seem to offer further evidence of his desire to present the charismatic quality of his leadership.[58]

That this is so is finally suggested by the observation, offered in this commentary and elsewhere, that while Nehemiah does not present himself as a prophet per se, various aspects of his self-presentation suggest his desire to identify himself and his behavior with the purposes of a prophet like Jeremiah. Thus Nehemiah seems intent on presenting himself to his readers as one "acting like" a prophet, not only in his confrontation of false prophets (Neh 6), but also in his exhortations to Sabbath observance and nonabusive economic practices (Neh 10, 13) and, perhaps at a later date, even in his prayers to God to be remembered for various actions. When considered alongside the ample evidence of Nehemiah's presentation of himself as the possessor of supernatural charisms, such quasiprophetic resonances can hardly but contribute to a self-portrait of Nehemiah that evokes Weber's charismatic authority despite the patrimonial rule devolved to him by the Persian crown.

It seems most likely that an earlier presentation of Nehemiah's detection and confrontation of problems such as intermarriage with foreigners, lack of provision for the Levites and the cult generally, and Sabbath abuse (13:10–27) preceded the account of the covenant secured by Nehemiah to avoid such practices (10:28–39). If so, then as we saw with Ezra's memoir prior to its inclusion in Ezra-Nehemiah, Nehemiah's memoir in this more original form will have of-

---

57. Ibid., 2.1113.
58. North, "Civil Authority in Ezra," 380, eliminates (by means of emendation) any reference to Nehemiah as governor in the Masoretic Text of 5:14 and argues that Nehemiah was merely a "charismatic building contractor" (though the term "charismatic" is not used in the Weberian sense). However, Williamson, "Governors of Judah under the Persians," shows that it is probable that Nehemiah was indeed a governor, being preceded in the office by Zerubbabel and Sheshbazzar and followed by Elnathan. He also shows (61–63) how extrabiblical sources from the Achaemenid period substantiate the suggestion that Nehemiah forewent an allowance or salary to which he was entitled as governor, a practice that appears to have been more generous than his predecessors in the post.

fered evidence of the success/effectiveness of Nehemiah's charismatic authority and leadership not only in rebuilding the wall and repopulating Jerusalem, but also in reforming certain aspects of communal and religious life and observance in Jerusalem and Yehud. As with Ezra, however, it is clear that here, too, Nehemiah's presentation of the success of his charismatic leadership is complicated by its ultimate presentation in Ezra-Nehemiah. Whether or not in their present form these books imply that Nehemiah's exercising of charismatic authority in addressing these issues (13:10–27) takes place before or after the dedication of the wall (12:27–47), it is clear that Nehemiah's intervention is presented as taking place following his return after an absence of some twelve years. Instead of representing Nehemiah's initial detection of these social and religious problems on his arrival, the problems described in 13:10–27 now appear to reflect a persistent recidivism and recalcitrance on the part of the community, discovered by Nehemiah on his return, despite the community's solemn agreement to avoid such practices. As such, insofar as the final word (and chapter) of the editor requires a very different assessment of the success of Nehemiah's charismatic leadership, Weber's analysis of charismatic leadership and routinization again proves instructive.[59]

On Weber's account, the charismatic leader's succession is a key element in the routinization of charisma and a determining factor in whether their values will be perpetuated and achievements secured. Nehemiah's account may illustrate both this point and some of the relevant processes. In granting his brother Hanani authority over Jerusalem (7:2), Nehemiah reflects the introduction of hereditary charisma, in which the extraordinary qualities of the charismatic leader are assumed to be found in a member of his kin group (usually a son, but in this case a brother).[60] In appointing the presumably separate figure of Hananiah as governor of the citadel, Nehemiah discloses a means of selection not based on kinship but rather on the basis that "he feared God more than many." Given Nehemiah's own "fear of God" (5:15), this appointment appears to reflect the recognition of a shared charism of piety that distinguishes both Nehemiah and Hananiah from others and qualifies the latter for charismatic leadership. Crucially, however, the text gives no indication that these appoint-

---

59. While he does not name it as such in his commentary on the final chapter of Nehemiah, the treatment of the end of Nehemiah in Williamson, *Ezra, Nehemiah*, 391–402, points clearly to the relevance of routinization—a point that he explicitly mentions in passing in Williamson, "Belief System of the Book of Nehemiah," 280.

60. For succession and charismatic staff, see Weber, *Economy and Society*, 1.246–51. Fried, *Priest and the Great King*, 199, notes that Nehemiah's gubernatorial appointment of his brother as garrison commander over the city of Jerusalem is paralleled in Elephantine, where a father and son take these two roles.

ments singly or taken together are meant to replace Nehemiah as governor of Yehud as a whole. They are therefore presented not as successors to the charismatic leadership of Nehemiah himself so much as appointments to his charismatic staff.

In fact, in the absence of any other notification of succession in Ezra-Nehemiah, the reader of Nehemiah is left with the impression that while some authority may have been delegated in some areas, Yehud was either left without a governor during Nehemiah's twelve-year absence, that he attempted to govern from Mesopotamia, or that Hanani and Hananiah along with others attempted to exercise authority on Nehemiah's behalf in his absence. In any case, the lack of notification of succession and admission of a prolonged absence of the charismatic leader point toward precisely the failure to routinize that seems to be evidenced in the final chapter of Nehemiah. Indeed, given what appears to be the final editor's condemnation of Ezra's failure to routinize aspects of his charismatic leadership, it seem entirely possible that an editor may well have passed a similar judgment on Nehemiah's failure to routinize his own reforms (which in the case of foreign marriage simply reinforce his earlier judgment of Ezra). By ending the book in such a fashion, the editor's praise of Nehemiah's return to Jerusalem must be reckoned to be very faint indeed and his damning of Nehemiah's failure to routinize his charismatic authority rather deafening.

Ezra-Nehemiah: Learning from the Failures of Leadership?

While it would be simplistic indeed to suggest that the composition of Ezra-Nehemiah was exclusively shaped by an interest in notions of leadership, the prominence within these books of the figures of Ezra and Nehemiah especially and what are presented as their reflections on their own leadership make it not at all improbable that an interest in saying something about their leadership influenced the final editor's efforts in shaping these books.[61] If the final editor preserved Ezra's and Nehemiah's own characterizations of their leadership in charismatic terms, but presented this memoir material in such a way as to qualify their success by passing judgment on their ultimate failure to routinize their authority, what might have encouraged him to do so?

---

61. While Eskenazi, *In an Age of Prose*, 170–71, contrasts 1 Esdras's emphasis on "great man" leadership with the book of Ezra's focus on the community's initiative, the depiction of leadership remains central to Ezra-Nehemiah. See the careful critique of Grabbe, *Ezra-Nehemiah*, 100–101, 115, 186.

Acknowledging that any answer to such a question belongs firmly and probably indefinitely to the realm of speculation, it is nevertheless stimulating to juxtapose the picture offered by Ezra-Nehemiah with the one presented in 1–2 Maccabees. Leaving aside the possibility (suggested by others) that Ezra-Nehemiah in its final form may have been shaped during the Hasmonean period, there can be little doubting the interest of 1–2 Maccabees in legitimating the royal and priestly status of the Maccabees, whose initial authority was apparently and manifestly charismatic.[62] In doing so, 1–2 Maccabees illustrate and indeed serve as instruments of the very sort of routinization of authority/leadership that the books of Ezra-Nehemiah suggest was lacking in Yehud during the Persian period. However much the books of Maccabees identify their protagonists' activities with the real and supposed work of Nehemiah,[63] one might well imagine the final form of the books of Ezra and Nehemiah being read in the early days of the Maccabees as, among other things, a compelling argument for taking the crucial steps of routinization (by dynastic means) necessary to ensure that the Maccabean values and achievements as charismatic leaders would be more fully secured than those of Ezra and Nehemiah.

Of course, one of Weber's parade examples of the routinization of charismatic leadership in the religious realm is that of Jesus, his early followers, and the eventual development of the church hierarchy and bureaucracy that preserved the original values of the charismatic leader.[64] While the presence of the institutional Christian church in its many forms and denominations up to the present day confirms the success of this process, it seems unlikely to be a coincidence that interest in what Nehemiah (in particular) might illustrate or exemplify by way of leadership has been especially widespread in Protestant traditions that resist clericalism, value the empowerment of the laity, and in some cases reflect leadership that is charismatic in both the spiritual and popular senses of this word.

Despite the patrimonial authority bestowed upon leaders in Ezra-Nehemiah, it is clear that for both Ezra and Nehemiah and the subsequent editors, the authority that they wish to be remembered exercising was one largely inflected by charisms, both supernatural and more mundane. Given the current and probable future growth of church traditions resonant with this type of leadership, it will not be surprising at all if Ezra-Nehemiah remains especially

---

62. See, for instance, Weitzman, "Plotting Antiochus's Persecution." For the recognition of the charismatic quality of the presentation of Maccabean military leadership in 1 Maccabees 5:62, see Yarbro Collins, *Cosmology and Eschatology*, 199.

63. On this identification see Blenkinsopp, *Judaism*, 171–75.

64. For recent discussion, see, for instance, Taylor, "Max Weber Revisited."

popular for what these church traditions may glean from Ezra's and Nehemiah's own recollections of the manner and means of their successes as charismatic leaders. Whether the lessons to be learned from the final editor's view of the failures of Ezra's and Nehemiah's charismatic leadership and the importance of routinization will be equally appreciated by these theological traditions remains to be seen, but may well be even more important in ensuring that the values of these particular Christian traditions are preserved and continue to be preached in the days to come.

Bibliography

Ackroyd, P. R. "Chronicles-Ezra-Nehemiah: The Concept of Unity." Pp. 344–59 in Ackroyd's *The Chronicler in His Age*. Journal for the Study of the Old Testament Supplement 101. Sheffield: Sheffield Academic Press, 1991.
———. *I and II Chronicles, Ezra, Nehemiah*. Torch Bible Commentaries. New York: Harper & Row, 1973.
Ahlström, G. W. "Solomon the Chosen One." *History of Religions* 8 (1968–69): 93–110.
Allen, L. C., and T. S. Laniak. *Ezra, Nehemiah, Esther*. New International Bible Commentary. Peabody: Hendrickson, 2003.
Andrews, D. K. "Yahweh the God of the Heavens." Pp. 45–57 in *The Seed of Wisdom*. Edited by W. S. McCullough. Toronto: University of Toronto Press, 1964.
Anglican Consultative Council. *Bonds of Affection*. Proceedings of the Anglican Consultative Council 6, Badagry, Nigeria, 1984. London: Anglican Consultative Council, 1984.
———. *Mission in a Broken World*. Proceedings of the Anglican Consultative Council 8, Wales, 1990. London: Anglican Consultative Council, 1990.
Baker, D. L. *Tight Fists or Open Hands? Wealth and Poverty in Old Testament Law*. Grand Rapids: Eerdmans, 2009.
Balcer, J. "The Athenian Episkopos and the Achaemenid King's Eye." *American Journal of Philology* 98 (1977): 252–63.
Balentine, S. E. *Prayer in the Hebrew Bible: The Drama of Divine-Human Dialogue*. Minneapolis: Fortress, 1993.
Balzer, K. "Moses Servant of God and the Servants: Text and Tradition in the Prayer of Nehemiah (Neh 1:5–11)." Pp. 121–30 in *The Future of Early Christianity*. Edited by B. A. Pearson. Minneapolis: Fortress, 1991.
Barber, C. J. *Nehemiah and the Dynamics of Effective Leadership*. Neptune: Loizeaux, 1976.
Bartholomew, C., and M. W. Goheen, *The Drama of Scripture: Finding Our Place in the Biblical Story*. Grand Rapids: Baker, 2004.
Bass, B. M., and R. M. Stogdill. *Handbook of Leadership: Theory, Research, and Managerial Applications*. New York: Free Press, 1990.
Batten, L. W. *A Critical and Exegetical Commentary on the Books of Ezra and Nehemiah*. International Critical Commentary. Edinburgh: T&T Clark, 1913.

Bautsch, R. J. *Developments in Genre between Post-Exilic Penitential Prayers and the Psalms of Lament.* Leiden/Boston: Brill, 2003.

Beale, G. K. *The Temple and the Church's Mission: A Biblical Theology of the Dwelling Place of God.* Downers Grove: InterVarsity/Leicester: Apollos, 2004.

Becker, J. *Esra/Nehemiah.* Neue Echter Bibel. Würzburg: Echter, 1990.

Bergen, T. "Ezra and Nehemiah Square Off in the Apocrypha and the Pseudepigrapha: Some References to the Fate of Ezra-Nehemiah in the Jewish and Christian Traditions." Pp. 340-66 in *Biblical Figures outside the Bible.* Edited by M. Stone and T. Bergen. Harrisburg: Trinity, 1998.

Berger, P. "Charisma and Religious Innovation: The Social Location of Israelite Prophecy." *American Sociological Review* 28 (1963): 940-50.

Bickerman, E. J. "En marge de l'Écriture, I. Le comput des années de regne des Achéménides (Neh. i,2; ii,1 et Thuc. viii,58)." *Revue biblique* 88 (1981): 19-23.

Birch, B. C., W. Brueggemann, T. E. Fretheim, and D. L. Petersen. *A Theological Introduction to the Old Testament.* Nashville: Abingdon, 1999.

Blenkinsopp, J. *Ezra-Nehemiah: A Commentary.* Old Testament Library. Louisville: Westminster, 1988.

———. *Judaism: The First Phase: The Place of Ezra and Nehemiah in the Origins of Judaism.* Grand Rapids: Eerdmans, 2009.

Boda, M. *Praying the Tradition: The Origin and Use of Tradition in Nehemiah 9.* Beihefte zur Zeitschrift für die alttestamentliche Wissenschaft 277. Berlin: de Gruyter, 1999.

———. "Redaction in the Book of Nehemiah: A Fresh Proposal." Pp. 25-54 in *Unity and Disunity in Ezra-Nehemiah: Redaction, Rhetoric, and Reader.* Edited by M. Boda and P. Redditt. Sheffield: Sheffield Phoenix, 2008.

Boda, M., et al., eds. *Seeking the Favor of God*, vol. 1: *The Origin of Penitential Prayer in Second Temple Judaism.* Society of Biblical Literature: Early Judaism and Its Literature. Atlanta: Society of Biblical Literature/Leiden: Brill, 2006.

———. *Seeking the Favor of God*, vol. 2: *The Development of Penitential Prayer in Second Temple Judaism.* Society of Biblical Literature: Early Judaism and Its Literature. Atlanta: Society of Biblical Literature/Leiden: Brill, 2007.

———. *Seeking the Favor of God*, vol. 3: *The Impact of Penitential Prayer beyond Second Temple Judaism.* Society of Biblical Literature: Early Judaism and Its Literature. Atlanta: Society of Biblical Literature/Leiden: Brill, 2008.

Boice, J. M. *Nehemiah: Learning to Lead.* Grand Rapids: Revell, 1990.

Botterweck, G. J., H. Ringgren, and H.-J. Fabry, et al., eds. *Theological Dictionary of the Old Testament.* Grand Rapids: Eerdmans, 1977-.

Bowman, R. A. "The Book of Ezra and the Book of Nehemiah (Introduction and Exegesis)." Vol. 3, pp. 551-822 in *The Interpreter's Bible.* Edited by G. A. Buttrick. Nashville: Abingdon, 1954.

Brockington, L. H. *Ezra, Nehemiah, and Esther.* New Century Bible Commentary. London: Oliphants, 1969.

Brueggemann, W. "Duty as Delight and Desire: Preaching Obedience That Is Not Legalism." Pp. 35-47 in Brueggemann's *The Covenanted Self: Explorations in Law and Covenant.* Minneapolis: Fortress, 1999.

———. *Theology of the Old Testament: Testimony, Dispute, Advocacy.* Minneapolis: Fortress, 1997.

Bryman, A. *Charisma and Leadership in Organizations.* London: Sage, 1992.
Burt, S. *The Courtier and the Governor: Transformations of Genre in the Nehemiah Memoir.* Göttingen: Vandenhoeck & Ruprecht, 2014.
Campbell, D. K. *Nehemiah: Man in Charge.* Wheaton: Victor, 1979.
Cape Town Commitment. 2011. lausanne.org/content/covenant/lausanne-covenant (accessed 9/29/2016).
Childs, B. S. *Introduction to the Old Testament as Scripture.* Philadelphia: Fortress, 1979.
Church of England. *The Alternative Service Book 1980.* London: SPCK/Beccles: William Clowes/Cambridge: Cambridge University Press, 1980.
Clements, R. E. "Max Weber, Charisma, and Biblical Prophecy." Pp. 89–108 in *Prophecy and Prophets: The Diversity of Contemporary Issues in Scholarship.* Edited by Yehoshua Gitay. Atlanta: Scholars Press, 1997.
Clines, D. J. *Ezra, Nehemiah, Esther.* New Century Bible Commentary. Grand Rapids: Eerdmans/London: Marshall, Morgan & Scott, 1984.
Dempster, S. G. *Dominion and Dynasty: A Theology of the Hebrew Bible.* Downers Grove: InterVarsity/Leicester: IVP, 2003.
Driver, G. R. "Forgotten Hebrew Idioms." *Zeitschrift für die alttestamentliche Wissenschaft* 78 (1966): 1–7.
Dumbrell, W. J. "The Tell el-Maskhuta Bowls and the 'Kingdom' of Qedar in the Persian Period." *Bulletin of the American Schools of Oriental Research* 203 (1971): 33–44.
Eichrodt, W. *Theology of the Old Testament,* vol. 2. London: SCM, 1967.
Eisenstadt, S. N. *Max Weber on Charisma and Institution Building.* Chicago: University of Chicago Press, 1968.
———. *The Political Systems of Empires.* 2nd ed. New Brunswick: Transaction, 1993.
Eskenazi, T. C. *In an Age of Prose: A Literary Approach to Ezra-Nehemiah.* Society of Biblical Literature: Monograph Series 36. Atlanta: Scholars Press, 1988.
Fensham, F. C. *The Books of Ezra and Nehemiah.* New International Commentary on the Old Testament. Grand Rapids: Eerdmans, 1982.
Fried, L. S. *The Priest and the Great King: Temple-Palace Relations in the Persian Empire.* Winona Lake: Eisenbrauns, 2004.
———, ed. *Was 1 Esdras First? An Investigation into the Priority and Nature of 1 Esdras.* Ancient Israel and Its Literature 7. Atlanta: Society of Biblical Literature, 2011.
Gelston, A. "The Foundations of the Second Temple." *Vetus Testamentum* 16 (1966): 232–35.
Getz, G. A. *Nehemiah: A Man of Prayer and Persistence.* Ventura: RLG, 1981.
Gibson, J. C. L. *Syrian Semitic Inscriptions.* Oxford: Clarendon, 1973.
Goldingay, J. *Old Testament Theology,* vol. 1: *Israel's Gospel.* Downers Grove: InterVarsity, 2003.
———. *Theological Diversity and the Authority of the Old Testament.* Grand Rapids: Eerdmans, 1987.
Grabbe, L. *Ezra-Nehemiah.* London: Routledge, 1998.
Gunneweg, A. H. J. "Zur Interpretation der Bücher Esra-Nehemia." Pp. 146–61 in *Congress Volume Vienna 1980.* Vetus Testamentum Supplement 32. Edited by J. A. Emerton. Leiden: Brill, 1981.
Harvey, R. *Mapping Messianic Jewish Theology: A Constructive Approach.* Milton Keynes: Paternoster, 2009.

Bibliography

Hays, J. D. *From Every People and Nation: A Biblical Theology of Race*. Downers Grove: InterVarsity/Leicester: Apollos, 2003.

Hendel, R. S. "Prophets, Priests, and the Efficacy of Ritual." Pp. 185–98 in *Pomegranates and Golden Bells: Studies in Biblical, Jewish, and Near Eastern Ritual, Law, and Literature in Honor of Jacob Milgrom*. Edited by David P. Wright, David Freedman, and Avi Hurvitz. Winona Lake: Eisenbrauns, 1995.

Hossfeld, F. L., and I. Meyer. *Prophet gegen Prophet*. Fribourg: Schweizerisches Katholisches Bibelwerk, 1973.

Howard, D., Jr. *An Introduction to the Old Testament Historical Books*. Chicago: Moody, 1993.

Jacobs, D. R. *From Rubble to Rejoicing: A Study in Effective Christian Leadership Based on Nehemiah*. Pasadena: William Carey Library, 1991.

Japhet, S. "Postexilic Historiography: How and Why?" pp. 144–73 in *Israel Constructs Its History: Deuteronomistic Historiography in Recent Research*. Edited by A. de Pury et al. Journal for the Study of the Old Testament Supplement 306. Sheffield: Sheffield Academic Press, 2000.

——— . "Sheshbazzar and Zerubbabel—Against the Background of the Historical and Religious Tendencies of Ezra-Nehemiah." *Zeitschrift für die alttestamentliche Wissenschaft* 94 (1982): 66–98; 95 (1983): 218–29.

——— . "The Supposed Common Authorship of Chronicles and Ezra-Nehemiah Investigated Anew." *Vetus Testamentum* 18 (1968): 330–71.

Jaubert, A. "Le Calendrier des Jubilés et de la Secte de Qumrân: Ses Origines Bibliques." *Vetus Testamentum* 3 (1953): 250–64.

Jones, D. R. *Jeremiah*. New Century Bible Commentary. Grand Rapids: Eerdmans, 1992.

Kellerman, U. *Nehemia: Quellen, Überlieferung und Geschichte*. Beihefte zur Zeitschrift für die alttestamentliche Wissenschaft 102. Berlin: Töpelmann, 1967.

Kelly, B. E. "Ezra-Nehemiah." Pp. 195–98 in *New Dictionary of Biblical Theology*. Edited by T. Desmond Alexander and Brian S. Rosner. Leicester: IVP and Downers Grove: InterVarsity, 2000.

Kidner, D. *Ezra and Nehemiah: An Introduction and Commentary*. Tyndale Old Testament Commentaries. Downers Grove: InterVarsity, 1979.

Knight, G. A. F. *A Christian Theology of the Old Testament*. London: SCM, 1959.

Koch, K. "Ezra and the Origins of Judaism." *Journal of Semitic Studies* 19 (1974): 173–97.

Lausanne Covenant. 1974. lausanne.org/content/covenant/lausanne-covenant (accessed 9/29/2016).

Levering, M. *Ezra-Nehemiah*. London: SCM/Brazos, 2007.

Lincoln, B. *Religion, Empire, and Torture*. Chicago: University of Chicago Press, 2007.

Lipschits, O., G. N. Knoppers, and M. Oeming, eds. *Judah and the Judeans in the Achaemenid Period: Negotiating Identity in an International Context*. Winona Lake: Eisenbrauns, 2011.

Long, V. P. *The Art of Biblical History*. Foundations of Contemporary Interpretation 5. Grand Rapids: Zondervan, 1994.

Malamat, A. "Charismatic Leadership in the Book of Judges." Pp. 152–68 in *Magnalia Dei, The Mighty Acts of God: Essays on the Bible and Archaeology in Memory of G. Ernest Wright*. Edited by F. Cross, W. Lemke, and P. Miller. Garden City: Doubleday, 1976.

Malchow, B. V. "A Manual for Future Monarchs." *Catholic Biblical Quarterly* 47 (1985): 238–45.

Mason, R. *Preaching the Tradition: Homily and Hermeneutics after the Exile Based on "Ad-*

dresses" in Chronicles, the "Speeches" in the Books of Ezra and Nehemiah, and the Post-Exilic Prophetic Books. Cambridge: Cambridge University Press, 1990.

McCutcheon, M. *Rebuilding God's People: Strategies for Revitalizing Declining Churches Based on Nehemiah*. Camp Hill: Christian Publication, 1993.

McKay, H. A. *Sabbath and Synagogue: The Question of Sabbath Worship in Ancient Judaism*. Leiden: Brill, 1994.

Moody, J., and R. Weekes. *Burning Hearts: Preaching to the Affections*. Fearn: Christian Focus, 2014.

Munayer, S., and L. Loden. *Through My Enemy's Eyes: Envisioning Reconciliation in Israel-Palestine*. Milton Keynes: Paternoster, 2013.

Myers, J. M. *Ezra, Nehemiah*. Anchor Bible. Garden City: Doubleday, 1965.

North, R. "Civil Authority in Ezra." Vol. 6/pp. 377–404 in *Studi in Onore di Edoardo Volterra*. Milan: Giuffré, 1971.

Northouse, P. *Leadership: Theory and Practice*. 6th ed. London: Sage, 2012.

Olmstead, A. T. "Tattenai, Governor of 'Across the River.'" *Journal of Near Eastern Studies* 3 (1944): 46.

Oppenheim, A. L. "The Eyes of the Lord." *Journal of the American Oriental Society* (1968): 173–180.

Overholt, T. W. "Thoughts on the Use of 'Charisma' in Old Testament Studies." Pp. 287–303 in *In the Shelter of Elyon: Essays on Ancient Palestinian Life and Literature in Honour of G. W. Ahlström*. Edited by B. Barrick and J. A. Spencer. Sheffield: Sheffield Academic Press.

Packer, J. I. *A Passion for Faithfulness: Wisdom from the Book of Nehemiah*. Wheaton: Crossway, 1995.

Page, F. *The Nehemiah Factor: 16 Characteristics of a Missional Leader*. Birmingham: New Hope, 2008.

Pakkala, J. *Ezra the Scribe: The Development of Ezra 7–10 and Nehemiah 8*. Beihefte zur Zeitschrift für die alttestamentliche Wissenschaft 347. Berlin: de Gruyter, 2004.

Petersen, D. L. "Max Weber and the Sociological Study of Ancient Israel." Pp. 117–49 in *Religious Change and Continuity: Sociological Perspectives*. Edited by Harry Johnson. San Francisco: Jossey-Bass, 1979.

Pritchard, J. B. *Ancient Near Eastern Texts*. 3rd ed. Princeton: Princeton University Press, 1969.

Provan, I. "Hearing the Historical Books." Pp. 254–76 in *Hearing the Old Testament: Listening for God's Address*. Edited by Craig G. Bartholomew and David J. H. Beldman. Grand Rapids: Eerdmans, 2012.

Provan, I., V. P. Long, and T. Longman III. *A Biblical History of Israel*. Louisville: Westminster John Knox, 2003.

Rad, G. von. *Old Testament Theology*. 2 vols. Edinburgh: Oliver & Boyd/New York: Harper, 1962–65.

Redpath, A. *Victorious Christian Service: Studies in the Book of Nehemiah*. Grand Rapids: Revell, 1958.

Reinmuth, T. *Der Bericht Nehemias: Zur literarischen Eigenart, traditionsgeschichtlichen Prägung und innerbiblischen Rezeption des Ich-Berichtes Nehemias*. Orbis Biblicus et Orientalis 183. Freiburg: Universitätsverlag Schweiz/Göttingen: Vandenhoeck & Ruprecht, 2002.

Rendall, T. S. *Nehemiah: Laws of Leadership (24 Ways to Build God's Work Today).* Three Hills: Prairie, 1980.

Root, M. C. "From the Heart: Powerful Persianisms in the Art of the Western Empire." Pp. 1-29 in *Achaemenid History VI: Asia Minor and Egypt: Old Cultures in a New Empire.* Edited by A. Kuhrt and H. Sancisi-Weerdenburg. Leiden: Nederlands Instituut voor Het Nabije Oosten, 1991.

Schaeder, H. *Esra der Schreiber.* Tübingen: Mohr Siebeck, 1930.

Schloen, J. D. *The House of the Father as Fact and Symbol: Patrimonialism in Ugarit and the Ancient Near East.* Winona Lake: Eisenbrauns, 2001.

Shepherd, D. J. "Is the Governor Also among the Prophets? Parsing the Purposes of Jeremiah in the Memory of Nehemiah." Pp. 209-28 in *Prophets and Prophecy in Ancient Israelite Historiography.* Edited by M. Boda and L. Wray-Beal. Grand Rapids: Eisenbrauns, 2013.

———. "Prophetaphobia: Fear and False Prophecy in Nehemiah vi." *Vetus Testamentum* 55 (2005): 232-50.

Southwood, K. *Ethnicity and the Mixed-Marriage Crisis in Ezra 9-10: An Anthropological Approach.* Oxford: Oxford University Press, 2012.

Stager, L. "The Archaeology of the Family in Ancient Israel." *Bulletin of the American Schools of Oriental Research* 260 (1985): 25-28.

———. "Forging an Identity: The Emergence of Ancient Israel." Pp. 123-75 in *The Oxford Handbook of the Biblical World.* Edited by M. D. Coogan. New York: Oxford University Press, 1998.

Stanley, A. *Visioneering: God's Blueprint for Developing and Maintaining Personal Vision.* Colorado Springs: Multnomah, 1999.

Swindoll, C. R. *Hand Me Another Brick: Building Character in Yourself and Others.* Nashville: Nelson, 1978.

Taylor, J. "Max Weber Revisited: Charisma and Institution at the Origins of Christianity." *Australian Journal of Theology* 19.3 (December 2012): 195-208.

Taylor, J. R., and O. S. Hawkins. *When Revival Comes.* Nashville: Broadman & Holman, 1980.

Van der Kooij, A. "Nehemiah 8:8 and the Question of the 'Targum'-Tradition." Pp. 79-90 in *Tradition of the Text: Studies Offered to Dominique Barthélemy in Celebration of His 70th Birthday.* Edited by G. J. Norton and S. Pisano. Orbis Biblicus et Orientalis 109. Göttingen: Vandenhoeck & Ruprecht, 1991.

Walsh, J. T. *Style and Structure in Biblical Hebrew Narrative.* Collegeville: Liturgical Press, 2001.

Waltke, B. K. *An Old Testament Theology: An Exegetical, Canonical, and Thematic Approach.* Grand Rapids: Zondervan, 2007.

Weanzana, N. *Africa Bible Commentary.* Edited by Tokunboh Adeyemo. Nairobi: Word Alive/Grand Rapids: Zondervan, 2006.

Weber, M. *Ancient Judaism.* Edited and translated by H. H. Gerth and D. M. Martindale. New York: Free Press, 1952 (originally 1920).

———. *Economy and Society.* 2 vols. Edited and translated by G. Roth and C. Wittich. Berkeley: University of California Press, 1968-78 (originally 1921).

Weisman, Z. "Charismatic Leaders in the Era of the Judges." *Zeitschrift für die alttestamentliche Wissenschaft* 89 (1977): 399-411.

Weitzman, S. "Plotting Antiochus's Persecution." *Journal of Biblical Literature* 123 (2004): 219-34.

Whimster, S. *The Essential Weber Reader*. New York: Routledge, 2004.

White, J. *Excellence in Leadership: The Pattern of Nehemiah*. Leicester: IVP, 1986.

Wiersbe, W. *Be Determined: Standing Firm in the Face of Opposition*. Wheaton: Victor, 1992.

Williamson, H. G. M. "The Belief System of the Book of Nehemiah." Pp. 271-81 in Williamson's *Studies in Persian Period History and Historiography*. Tübingen: Mohr Siebeck, 2004 (originally 1999).

———. *Ezra and Nehemiah*. Old Testament Guides. Sheffield: Sheffield Academic Press, 1996.

———. *Ezra, Nehemiah*. Word Biblical Commentary 16. Waco: Word, 1985.

———. "The Governors of Judah under the Persians." Pp. 46-64 in Williamson's *Studies in Persian Period History and Historiography*. Tübingen: Mohr Siebeck, 2004 (originally 1988).

———. *Israel in the Books of Chronicles*. Cambridge: Cambridge University Press, 2007.

———. "Nehemiah's Walls Revisited." *Palestine Exploration Quarterly* 116 (1984): 81-88.

Wright, C. J. H. *The Mission of God: Unlocking the Bible's Grand Narrative*. Downers Grove: InterVarsity/Nottingham: IVP, 2006.

———. *The Mission of God's People: A Biblical Theology of the Church's Mission*. Grand Rapids: Zondervan, 2010.

———. *Old Testament Ethics for the People of God*. Leicester: IVP/Downers Grove: InterVarsity, 2004.

Wright, J. L. *Rebuilding Identity: The Nehemiah-Memoir and Its Earliest Readers*. New York: de Gruyter, 2004.

Wright, N. T. *New Testament and the People of God*. Minneapolis: Fortress, 1992.

Yarbro Collins, A. *Cosmology and Eschatology in Jewish and Christian Apocalypticism*. Leiden: Brill, 2000.

Yoder, C. R. "On the Threshold of Kingship: A Study of Agur (Prov 30)." *Interpretation* 63.3 (2009): 254-63.

Zadok, R. "Notes on the Biblical and Extrabiblical Onomasticon." *Jewish Quarterly Review* 71 (1980): 107-17.

Author Index

Ackroyd, P. R., 7n12, 73n38
Ahlström, G. W., 196n29
Allen, L. C., 191n10
Andrews, D. K., 12n2

Baker, D. L., 178n14
Balcer, J., 25n37
Balentine, S. E., 125n11
Balzer, K., 50n4
Barber, C. J., 188n1, 190n7
Bartholomew, C., 9n21
Bass, B. M., 189n4
Batten, L. W., 11n1, 74n43, 76n49
Bautsch, R. J., 43n85
Beale, G. K., 133n19
Becker, J., 74n40
Bergen, T., 189n2
Berger, P., 196n30
Bickerman, E. J., 49n1
Birch, B. C., 159n3
Blenkinsopp, J., 3n3, 12n3, 13nn5–6, 15n10, 28n45, 29nn46,48, 32n56, 34n61, 37n71, 38n75, 55n10, 68n31, 64n82, 84n69, 89n74, 90n76, 93n80, 98n81, 189n2, 192n13, 199n40, 202n48, 210n63
Boda, M., 4n4, 5n7, 51n5, 86n70, 87n71, 91n77
Boice, J. M., 188n1
Bowman, R. A., 34n62
Brockington, L. H., 73n38

Brueggemann, W., 111, 116n5, 136–37, 154n33, 155n35
Bryman, A., 195n25, 196n31, 202n51
Burt, S., 4n6

Campbell, D. K., 188n1
Childs, B. S., 121n9, 170n8
Clements, R. E., 111, 196n27
Clines, D. J., 12n3, 19nn20,22, 23n31, 55n10, 64n23, 68n30, 89n73, 91n78, 93n80, 98n82, 102n83, 121n8, 159n4, 192n13, 200n44, 202n48

Dempster, S. G., 151n32
Driver, G. R., 80n55
Dumbrell, W. J., 56n11

Eichrodt, W., 111, 121n9
Eisenstadt, S. N., 196n31, 197n36
Eskenazi, T. C., 82n62, 159n3, 192–93, 204n55, 209n61

Fabry, H.-J., 74n41
Fensham, F. C., 81n61
Fried, L. S., 7n15, 197n36, 208n60

Gelston, A., 18n18
Getz, G. A., 188n1
Gibson, J. C. L., 43n84
Goheen, M. W., 9n21

Author Index

Goldingay, J., 8–9, 112, 122n10, 127n13, 178n15, 183n26
Grabbe, L., 209n61
Gunneweg, A. H. J., 80n59

Harvey, J., 165n6
Hays, J. D., 146n26
Hendel, R. S., 194n19
Hossfeld, F. L., 78n52
Howard, D., Jr., 150n30, 170n7

Jacobs, D. R., 188n1
Japhet, S., 6n10, 27n42, 31n51, 199n39
Jaubert, A., 39n77
Jones, D. R., 51n5

Kellerman, U., 73–74n39, 103n84
Kelly, B. E., 117n6, 130n18, 155n34
Kidner, D., 8, 76n49
Knight, G. A. F., 111n1
Koch, K., 30n50, 31n53

Laniak, T. S., 191n10
Levering, M., 9n20
Lincoln, B., 198n37
Loden, L., 165n6
Long, V. P., 6n11, 7n16, 159n3
Longman, T., III, 159n3

Malamat, A., 196n28
Malchow, B. V., 189n3
Mason, R., 43n86
McCutcheon, M., 188n1, 190n7
McKay, H. A., 92n79
Meyer, I., 78n52
Moody, J., 174n10
Munayer, S., 165n6
Myers, J. M., 36n68

North, R., 207n58
Northouse, P., 189n5

Olmstead, A. T., 25n35
Oppenheim, A. L., 25n37
Overholt, T. W., 195n26, 196n27, 196nn29–30

Packer, J. I., 188n1
Page, F., 188n1
Pakkala, J., 30n49
Petersen, D. L., 194n16
Pritchard, J. B., 21n25, 27n44
Provan, I., 136n20, 159n3

Rad, G. von, 8, 111, 135–36
Redpath, A., 188n1
Reinmuth, T., 69n33
Rendall, T. S., 188n1
Root, M. C., 197n36

Schaeder, H., 32n56, 200n45
Schloen, J. D., 197n35
Shepherd, D. J., 51n6, 62n19, 70n35, 75n46, 78n51, 105n85, 183n25
Southwood, K., 2n1
Stager, L., 196–97n33
Stanley, A., 188n1, 190nn7–8
Stogdill, R. M., 189n4
Swindoll, C. R., 188n1, 190n7

Taylor, J., 210n64
Taylor, J. R., 188n1

Van der Kooij, A., 83n67

Walsh, J. T., 6n9
Waltke, B. K., 111
Weanzana, N., 179n16, 183n27
Weber, M., 194–200, 202–3, 205, 207–8, 210
Weekes, R., 174n10
Weisman, Z., 196n28
Weitzman, S., 210n62
Whimster, S., 194n17
White, J., 188n1
Wiersbe, W., 188n1, 190nn7,9
Williamson, H. G. M., 2n2, 4n5, 7nn13–14, 8, 11n1, 12n3, 13n4, 14nn7–8, 15n11, 16n13, 16nn15–16, 19n19, 19nn21–22, 22n30, 23n31, 25n34, 27n43, 30n49, 31n54, 32n55, 34n60, 35n66, 37n70, 38n75, 39n78, 41n80, 41n82, 47n95, 53n9, 55n10, 58n13, 61n17, 64nn22–23, 65n27, 68n31, 73nn37–38, 74n39, 75n45, 77n50,

80nn57–58, 81n60, 103n84, 109n89, 110n90, 138n22, 146n27, 148, 150–51, 158, 179n17, 192n13, 199nn40–41, 200n42, 201n47, 202n50, 203nn53–54, 207n58, 208n59
Wright, C. J. H., 129n14, 177n13, 178n14
Wright, J. L., 50n4, 105n86

Wright, N. T., 9n21

Yarbro Collins, A., 210n62
Yoder, C. R., 189n3

Zadok, R., 16n12

Subject Index

Aaron, 31, 36, 117, 119, 170–71, 184, 199; line of, 17; and other priests, 46
Abraham, 14, 41, 112, 158; expansion of blessing, 128–29, 136n20, 141, 148, 156–57, 160–66, 168; God's covenant with, 87, 113, 123, 129, 134, 141, 148, 156–57, 160–68
Achaemenid Empire. *See* Persian/Achaemenid Empire
altar, temple: building/restoration of, 2, 18, 20, 28, 35, 100, 130, 170; use of, 93, 142, 169, 175
ancestors. *See* Aaron, line of; community: and connection with past; David, line of; exodus, the; exile(s): and continuity with past; Ezra, ancestry of; genealogy; generations; Nehemiah, ancestry of; sin: of ancestors; tribes; Zerubbabel, ancestry of
anger: concerning intermarriage, 40, 106; of enemies, 61–63, 68; of God, 62, 106, 169, 179. *See also* Nehemiah, anger of
Anglican Communion, 176n11, 181
Aramaic, 3–4, 22, 32, 106, 122
Artaxerxes I, 2–3, 22, 26, 28, 30–34, 34n63, 35, 39, 45, 49, 53, 53n8, 56, 63, 70, 116, 119–20, 145, 199
Artaxerxes II, 2, 30
authority, charismatic. *See* leadership: charismatic

Babylon, 22–23, 30–31, 36, 38n75, 42, 52, 68, 81, 102–3, 137, 196; and exile, 2, 17, 26, 117–18, 134, 141, 161, 167; religion of, 12, 113–14
Bible: and Christianity, 9, 66, 135, 162, 168–73, 177; and ethics, 144, 179; God in, 112, 116, 124–25, 139–40, 155–56; Hebrew, 31, 64, 66, 69, 74, 170, 188, 189n3, 194n16, 195–96, 196–97n33; missional reading of, 139–41, 144, 163–64, 169, 180–83 (*see also* mission); narrative of, 8–9, 14, 34, 112–18, 123–26, 131, 135, 137, 152–58, 166–70 (*see also* Ezra-Nehemiah: narrative of); and obedience, 149, 184–85; and theology, 8–9, 111, 116, 121n9, 124–25, 131–33, 135–37, 139, 157–59, 162–63, 170–71 (*see also* Ezra-Nehemiah: and theology); unbiblical, 147, 148–49, 171. *See also* exegesis; hermeneutics; Scripture
blessing: from God to Israel, 25, 89, 114, 116, 139, 144, 154, 156, 162–63, 166, 176; from God to all people, 114, 116, 133, 139, 144, 156, 160, 162–63, 166; from Israel to God/other Israelites, 87, 95, 99, 160, 201; and obedience, 154. *See also* Abraham; Ezra: blessing God
Booths, Festival of. *See* Sukkot
building, rebuilding: altar (*see* altar, temple); and Cyrus the Great, 1, 11–12; community, 103, 120, 125, 158, 175, 181n18, 206, 208; opposition to, 24–25,

222

56, 61–67, 72–74; Second Temple, 1–4, 19–20, 23–28, 53–54, 60–61, 64n25, 116–17, 119–21, 124–26, 145, 151, 161, 170, 17, 184, 186, 198; support for, 16–17, 19, 21, 25, 27, 56–61, 175; (First) Temple, 17, 19, 24, 127, 132, 152, 161, 175, 188; wall of Jerusalem (*see* wall)

Cambyses, 2
celebration. *See* joy
census, 80
charisma: and Ezra, 198–203, 209–11; and Nehemiah, 55, 198, 203–11. *See also* community: charismatic; leadership: charismatic
children: and covenant, 32, 43, 128, 153, 159, 161, 165; included in community, 44, 68, 82, 101, 139, 173, 203. *See also* debt; intermarriage
Christ, Jesus, 116, 119, 126–29, 133, 136n20, 140–41, 144–45, 149, 152, 154, 157, 160–69, 173, 176, 181n18, 182–83, 185–86, 195, 210. *See also* cross; resurrection
Christian/Christianity, 128, 144–45, 148, 158, 160, 163–70, 179, 186–87; education, 170 (*see also* Bible: and Christianity); and Ezra-Nehemiah, 9–10; and leadership, 188–91, 193, 194n19, 210–11; and Old Testament, 111, 121, 135–37, 141, 144, 160–62, 167–68, 186–87. *See also* Christ, Jesus; community: Christian; Abraham: expansion of blessing; cross; distinctiveness: Christian; Messianic Judaism; New Testament; Paul; Peter
Chronicler, the, 25, 43, 51n5, 121n8, 138
citizen/citizenship, 138, 140, 161
commandments, 18, 31–33, 43, 50–51, 68, 82, 84, 88, 92, 94, 114, 119, 135, 149–50, 154, 164, 171, 180, 201
commitment: of Artaxerxes, 33; of the community, 16, 45, 56, 58–60, 63, 90–95, 99–101, 104–10, 119–20, 126, 130, 135, 137, 153–54, 158, 165, 169, 173–77, 180, 185, 206; of Ezra (*see* Ezra: and commitment); of Nehemiah (*see* Nehemiah: and commitment)
community, 4, 30, 32–34, 38, 40, 50, 67–72, 80–81, 84, 86, 101, 103–4, 107–8, 112n4, 118–19, 121, 177–78, 193n15, 209n61; and building, 55–61, 63–68, 77–78, 125–26, 158–59, 206; charismatic, 203–6; Christian, 141, 152, 157, 160–61, 173–74, 180–83, 186–87; and connection with the past, 9, 17, 21n24, 24, 27–28, 48, 50, 52, 57, 84–85, 110, 134–38, 156, 159–60, 166–67; and exclusion, 29n47, 44–46, 69, 92, 94–95, 101–2, 105–7, 109, 144–46, 148, 186–87; golah, 25, 79, 85, 89, 198; and inclusion, 15–16, 29n47, 40–41, 85, 89, 134, 173–74; and justice, 139, 144, 174, 177–81; and outsiders/enemies, 23–25, 55–56, 63–67, 76–79, 89–90, 186–87, 206; and repentance, 41–42, 43n85, 44–46, 48, 90, 94, 208; and Scripture, 90–91, 94–95, 114, 120–23, 128–30, 145–50, 160–62, 165, 169–75, 180, 184; and worship, 16–18, 20, 27, 30, 37–38, 63, 90, 93–95, 101, 112, 122, 130–31, 139, 142, 146–47, 163, 169–70, 173–77, 180, 201, 208. *See also* children; distinctiveness; Ezra: as leader; intermarriage; Nehemiah: as leader; women
confession, 5, 22, 42, 44–46, 48, 50–52, 68, 87, 90n76, 94, 114, 118, 120–21, 123, 151, 154, 166, 175, 177, 180, 183, 185, 202–3
covenant/covenantal, 112, 114, 120, 140, 170, 175, 179; Abrahamic (*see* Abraham); Davidic, 51n5, 159n4; and disobedience, 89, 125–27, 146, 156, 192; and Ezra (*see* Ezra: and covenant); Mosaic, 50–51, 88, 95, 113, 119, 124, 134, 136, 142, 151–52, 166, 168; and Nehemiah (*see* Nehemiah: and covenant); people, 17, 134–38, 158; renewal of, 80, 90–93, 95, 97–98, 103, 119, 139, 142, 152–55, 158, 166; two-covenant theology, 129n15, 164
Creator/creation, 87, 113–15, 119, 124, 131–34, 152, 154, 160, 166, 170, 176, 181; new, 113, 131, 133, 140, 153, 157, 168
cross, 116, 127–28, 140, 144, 164
cult(ic), 27, 33, 90; calendar, 18, 20, 74; leadership of, 17, 32, 35n65, 69, 108, 110n90; 196n30; foreign, 12, 21, 24; personnel of, 28, 33, 60, 79, 91, 96, 108; restoration of, 16, 18, 27n41, 29–30, 33,

Subject Index

47, 95, 101–2, 108, 198; support of, 18, 33, 45n92, 60, 93, 95, 108, 207
Cyrus II, "the Great," 1–3, 11–13, 28, 30, 32–33, 40, 53n8, 197; edict of, 14n1, 26–28, 42, 115–16, 151, 159; positive biblical portrayal of, 11n1, 14, 117, 125, 159, 198, 198n37

Daniel, 167
Darius I, 2, 18–19, 22, 24, 26–28, 30, 33–34, 53n8, 97, 116
David, 6, 15, 18, 23, 31, 50, 51n5, 54–55, 59, 102, 113, 134, 137, 152, 158, 188, 195; line of, 19, 36, 73, 73n39, 147, 155, 159, 159n4, 195, 197, 199; and the (First) Temple, 19, 24, 37n72, 98, 101, 131, 166, 176
debt, 92, 95, 178; debt servitude crisis, 67–70, 71, 74, 77, 86, 93, 107–8, 118, 177–79
dedication: of altar, 2, 100; of Jerusalem's walls, 58, 99–104, 106–7, 109, 120, 131, 139, 152, 170n8, 193, 208; of precincts, 29; of Second Temple, 28, 30, 100, 102, 138; of tabernacle, 28–29; of (First) Temple, 18, 26, 28, 131–33, 188
Deutero-Isaiah, 11, 11n1, 185
Deuteronomistic History, 41, 107, 151
Deuteronomy, 34n61, 66, 69, 78, 89, 95, 143, 147, 149, 153–54, 167, 173; Deuteronomic, 28, 50–51, 78, 92; and Ezra, 43, 43n85, 44, 118; and Nehemiah, 50, 64, 66, 76, 78–79, 89, 118, 138
disobedience, 88–89, 128, 152, 156, 177. *See also* unfaithfulness
distinctiveness: Christian, 160, 186–87; Israelite, 141–48, 150, 167, 186. *See also* separation
divorce, 44, 145. *See also* intermarriage

earth: and Christ, 119, 127, 141, 157, 167–69, 176; God's sovereignty over, 1, 12–14, 26, 30–31, 56–57, 79, 87, 112–15, 131–33, 136, 138–39, 142, 156, 159, 176. *See also* Creator/creation
ecclesiology, 159, 163
economy, 14, 93n80, 95, 111, 137, 143, 145, 175, 184, 195, 205; and injustice, 71–72, 139, 178–80, 207. *See also* debt; firstfruits; Jubilee; sabbatical; tithes
Egypt, 22n29, 27, 40, 54, 56n11, 143, 147; and exodus, 12, 31, 33–34, 67, 87–88, 115, 117–19, 134, 137–38, 142, 151, 178
enemies. *See* community: and outsiders/enemies; Ezra: opposition to; Nehemiah: opposition to
ethics/ethical, 90, 102, 143–44, 147, 159, 167, 170, 186–87, 195, 202, 205
exclusion. *See* community: and exclusion; distinctiveness
exegesis, 122, 129n16, 150, 172, 191
exile(s), 21, 31, 36–37, 41–42, 92, 107, 112, 120, 130, 141, 145; and Babylon, 2, 17, 26, 117–18, 134, 141, 161, 167; and continuity with past, 14, 16–17, 26, 36, 48, 80, 83, 110, 117–18, 123–27, 131, 134, 138–39, 146, 151–52, 159–61, 163, 166–67, 169; and Persia, 11–12, 14, 26–28, 42, 49, 81, 85, 87–88, 117–18, 125, 141, 151; and prophecy, 11, 19, 25, 78n52, 116–17, 121, 124–25, 151, 156, 161, 185
exodus, the, 12–14, 17, 34, 113, 116–18, 152, 160, 168; allusions to, 15, 29, 31, 36–37, 40, 45, 51, 85, 87, 96, 98, 115, 117–18, 125, 136, 151, 166; and Christ, 119, 168; generation of, 12, 18
eye: of God, 25, 30, 50, 198; of historiography, 6
Ezekiel (as prophet), 69, 78, 115, 125, 131, 140, 153, 202
Ezra (person): ancestry/name of, 30–31, 35–36, 90, 117, 119, 170, 184, 199, 204; blessing God, 34–35, 82, 117; character of, 191; and commitment, 31–32, 119–20, 149, 183, 185; commonality with Nehemiah, 50–52, 55, 60, 98, 107, 114, 125, 158, 170, 173–74, 185, 205, 208; and covenant, 203–4, 44, 48, 50–51; and Deuteronomy, 43, 43n85, 44, 118; as example, 148, 170–71, 193, 202; and intermarriage, 40–46, 48, 69, 94, 118, 133, 142, 145–49, 186, 191–92, 201–3, 206, 109; and Jeremiah, 11, 51, 121; as leader, 15, 30–46, 48, 57, 81–82, 87, 94, 100, 110, 114–15, 120, 131, 145–46, 148–50, 167–68, 172, 183n25, 185–87,

191–93, 196, 200–205; 208–11; memoir of, 5–8, 36–37, 38n74, 43, 51, 60–61, 81, 91, 188, 192–93n15, 200–201, 204, 207, 209; and Moses, 32, 135, 151; opposition to, 25, 60, 46, 117, 203n54; and Persian/Achaemenid Empire, 32–35, 38–40, 42, 54–55, 115, 119–20, 185, 197, 199–200; and prayer, 5–7, 35, 35n65, 38–40, 42–45, 48–50, 52, 87, 118, 125, 127, 130, 135, 151, 159, 183, 185, 202–3; as priest, 30–34, 119, 170–71, 189, 199, 201, 203–4; return from exile of, 2–3, 11–14, 17, 31, 35–40, 54, 115, 138, 175, 185, 200–201; as teacher, 32–35, 81–82, 84, 114, 119–20, 122–23, 170, 172, 184, 188–89, 192, 200–201, 203; and Torah, 31–35, 40–48, 81–82, 84–85, 107, 114, 119–23, 136, 147, 149, 158, 169–72, 184, 188–89, 192, 200–201, 203

Ezra-Nehemiah, 1–10, 21, 24–26, 48, 60, 69, 73–74n39, 98, 107, 109, 111–13, 115–16, 119, 123–26, 130, 133–36, 138, 140, 155, 158–59, 161, 163, 166, 169, 174, 191–92, 198, 208–9; and historiography, 1, 6–7; and Jeremiah, 115; and memoir, 4–8, 38n74, 193, 207–8; and narrative, 2, 4, 8–9, 25, 112–15, 117, 120–24, 131, 137, 151, 153, 157–58, 183, 191–93, 210; and New Testament, 9, 111; and Old Testament, 8–9, 111; and prayer, 5–7, 177, 180

failure: of Christians, 163, 169; of God, 24, 129, 163; of individuals, 106, 154, 159, 183n25, 193, 195, 204, 209–11; of Israel, 26, 45, 91, 107, 112–13, 118–19, 123, 126, 130, 151–55, 157, 159, 166, 172, 174, 180, 185
faithfulness, 18, 39, 87, 89, 104, 123–30, 156, 163–67, 170, 172, 176–77, 183–85
faithlessness. *See* unfaithfulness.
family, 15, 36, 47, 67, 79, 91, 96, 98–99, 103, 118, 134–35, 159, 161–62, 178–79, 208; of Ezra (*see* Ezra: ancestry of); firstborn of, 93; of God, 140, 163 (*see also* Abraham: expansion of blessing); of Nehemiah (*see* Nehemiah: ancestry/family of). *See also* debt: debt servitude crisis; genealogy; generations; leadership: patrimonial; tribes

fasting, 38, 40, 42, 45, 50
fear: of enemies, 18, 20, 23–24, 52, 64, 66, 75–79, 157, 175; of God, 51, 68, 70–72, 77–79, 139, 150, 153, 160, 173, 179–80, 184, 208; of other gods, 33–34
firstfruits, 93, 95
foreigners. *See* community: exclusion, outsiders/enemies; distinctiveness; separation
future, 6, 9, 11, 110, 112–13, 118–19, 125–26, 129n16, 135, 142, 149, 151–56, 162, 166–69, 173, 176, 180

gate(s), 50, 54–55, 58–59, 79, 100, 105, 141; Dung, 59; East, 59; Fish, 58; Fountain, 59; of the Guard, 100; Horse, 59; Mishneh, 58; Sheep, 58, Valley, 55, 100; Water, 59. *See also* gatekeepers
gatekeepers, 15, 31–32, 59, 79, 91, 96, 98, 101
genealogy, 15–16, 30–31, 35, 80, 95, 106, 119, 134, 159, 161–62, 194, 206
generations, 117, 123, 137–38, 141, 159, 169, 177, 183, 187; and exclusion, 40, 145; and sin, 26, 42, 151–54; younger, 82n63. *See also* exodus: generation of; genealogy
Gentiles: and Christianity, 128–29, 136n20, 140–41, 143n25, 144, 160–68; in Ezra-Nehemiah, 12–13, 16, 68
gifts, 31, 117, 185; of God, 31, 42, 88, 90, 119–20, 123–24, 129, 134, 185; for temple support, 16–17, 20, 33, 40, 93, 102–4
good/goodness, 60, 71, 108, 126, 160, 190, 206; divine, 20, 22, 25, 54, 88–90, 116, 126, 129–30, 152–53, 156, 176, 182; of land, 31, 43. *See also* hand of God
governor, 124, 134, 138, 146, 175, 194; Ezra as (*see* Ezra: and leadership); God as, 31, 131, 184; Nehemiah as (*see* Nehemiah: and leadership); of specific places, 13, 25, 27, 39, 54, 58, 97, 99, 138, 180, 199, 209
grace, 42, 88, 120–21, 123, 127, 135–36, 142, 152–54, 159, 161, 165, 180, 185, 199–200, 205
gratitude, 20, 101, 120–21, 173, 175
Greece, 160
guards, 38, 63–67, 79–80, 105, 116, 184
guilt, 40–47, 51, 62, 68, 77, 89, 146–47, 149,

151, 159. *See also* community: repentance; sin

Haggai (as prophet), 24, 25n33, 27–28, 74, 87n71, 121, 126, 198
Hanani, 49, 79, 208–9
hand of God, 25, 31, 34, 37–40, 51, 54–57, 108, 115, 119, 127–28, 132, 171, 184, 200, 205–6
heart, 29, 31, 34–35, 39, 55, 57, 74, 77, 80, 115, 117, 119–20, 122, 124, 151, 153–54, 156, 159, 169, 171, 173–74, 178, 183–84, 200, 205
heaven, 1, 12–14, 26, 30–32, 42, 50–51, 53, 56–57, 61, 87, 112–15, 120, 131–33, 136, 138, 140, 159, 162, 168–69, 176
hermeneutics, 48, 83, 145, 172; missional, 9
Hezekiah, 29, 29n48, 54, 85, 138
high priests, 30–31, 30n50, 58, 96–98, 106, 140, 198–99
Holiness Code, 143
holy: God, 66, 176, 182; people, 38, 41, 48, 140, 142–44, 147–48, 162, 168, 186–87; places, 42, 100, 105, 132; times, 83, 105. *See also* community: and exclusion; distinctiveness; intermarriage; purity; race; separation
humility, 38, 159

identity. *See* community: and connection with the past; distinctiveness; exile(s): and continuity with the past; separation
idolatry, 12, 21, 88, 140, 143, 147, 151–52
inheritance: of authority, 22, 188, 194–95, 201; of Christians, 128, 161–63; of Israel, 32, 43, 85, 96, 127, 134, 160–63, 170. *See also* Abraham
intermarriage: children of, 44, 47, 105–6, 148–49, 203; and divorce, 44, 47, 142, 145, 148–49, 186; foreign wives in, 44, 46–47, 105–6, 142, 145–49, 186, 203–4. *See also* Ezra: and intermarriage; Nehemiah: and intermarriage; Shecaniah; Solomon
Isaiah (as prophet), 51, 72, 117, 125, 151, 159, 178

Jeremiah (as prophet), 1, 9, 11, 25, 49, 51, 62, 62n19, 69–70, 72, 78, 105, 107–9, 117, 121, 124–25, 151, 153, 159, 167, 198, 207
Josephus, 7
Joshua (as leader), 37, 39, 45, 85, 113, 123, 137, 158, 174–75
Josiah, 29, 83, 138
joy, 112, 123, 152–53, 158, 162; and celebration, 28–29, 84–86, 99–102, 116, 120, 122–23, 126, 130, 139, 152, 170, 172, 174–75; and grief, 20, 84, 126, 130, 170. *See also* gratitude; thanksgiving
Jubilee, 93, 179
Judaism, 36, 44, 86, 92n79, 111, 121, 135–36; and Christianity, 128–29; Weber on, 195–96. *See also* Paul: and Judaism
Judaism, Messianic. *See* Messianic Judaism
judges, 34, 113, 134, 137, 152, 195–96, 200, 204, 206
judgment, 11, 34, 43, 72, 109, 113, 125, 127–28, 135, 151, 166
justice, 43, 90, 108, 120, 125. *See also* community: and justice; economy: and injustice

king, 22–23, 25, 28, 31–32, 39, 42, 52–53, 55, 72–74, 114–15, 124, 132–35, 137–40, 157, 159, 167, 172, 183. *See also* Artaxerxes I; Artaxerxes II; Cambyses; Christ, Jesus; Cyrus II, "the Great"; Darius I; David; Hezekiah; Josiah; leadership: patrimonial; Nebuchadnezzar; Solomon; sovereignty
kinship. *See* family

lament, 43, 79, 89, 106, 166
land. *See* ancestors; exodus; good/goodness; tribes
laugh/laughter: and weeping 84, 100
Lausanne Movement, 164, 181; *Cape Town Commitment*, 164, 181–82, 185–87
law. *See* covenant: Mosaic; legalism; Torah
laity/laypeople, 5, 15–17, 31–32, 36, 47, 82, 84, 91, 96, 99, 149, 189, 210
leadership: charismatic, 57, 158, 194–96, 198–211; patrimonial, 196–99, 201–7, 210. *See also* Ezra: as leader; Nehemiah: as leader

Subject Index

legalism, 111, 120–21, 136–37, 162

letter(s), 2–3, 54; of Jeremiah, 167; of Paul, 160, 163, 168, 173; from Persian monarchs, 3, 23, 27–28, 32–35, 53, 119–20, 197, 205; to Persian monarchs, 22–23, 25–27, 53, 73, 76n48, 77, 197

Levites: duties of, 15–17, 59–60, 79, 83–84, 87, 90–91, 94, 96–99, 101–2, 104–5, 114–15, 121–22, 138, 172, 175, 204n55; holiness/purification of, 29, 38, 99–100, 152; provision for, 102, 104, 175, 207; return of, 13, 15–16, 28–29, 32, 37–40, 97, 131, 159, 175, 198

lists, 3–4, 124; of people, 4, 14–17, 25, 30–31, 35–38, 46–48, 57–59, 79–81, 89, 91–93, 96–99, 131, 139, 147–49, 185; of places, 17, 40, 97–99, 147, 162; of punishments, 34; temple, 3, 13, 25, 38, 57–59, 61, 91–93, 96–99, 131

liturgy, 20, 82, 86, 117, 138, 177

Maccabees, 210

marriage. *See* intermarriage

memory/memories, 4, 53, 58, 94, 131, 177; of Ezra, 35n65; and hope, 166–70; of Israelites, 9, 94, 107, 110, 134, 155, 159, 166–67, 169–70; of Nehemiah, 4. *See also* community: and connection with past; exiles: and continuity with past

messianic, 72, 74, 77, 155; Jesus as Messiah, 128–29, 141, 152, 154, 157, 160–65, 167–68

Messianic Judaism, 164–66

mission/missional, 9–10, 72, 114, 119, 128–29, 133–35, 136n20, 139–44, 156–64, 166, 168–70, 172, 177, 180–81, 185, 195, 205–7. *See also* Lausanne Movement: *Cape Town Commitment*

mockery, 12, 160; of Israel, 56, 61–63

Moses, 50, 147; and Aaron, 31, 117; covenant of (*see* covenant, Mosaic); law of, 18–19, 31–32, 82–84, 92, 113–14, 119, 122, 124, 131, 146, 149, 169–72, 175; as leader, 34, 118, 125, 151, 158, 188; and prayer, 118, 131, 135; as prophet, 43, 51, 206; and tabernacle, 28–29, 131; as teacher, 83–84, 92

mourning, 41, 45, 50, 83, 86, 146, 153. *See also* weeping

music. *See* singers/song; trumpets

nation(s): Gentile, 20, 24, 40–41, 73, 114–15, 119–20, 126, 129, 131, 133, 140–48, 156–57, 160, 162–65; Israel, 63n21, 112, 125, 131, 134, 137, 139–48, 151, 156, 163. *See also* distinctiveness; intermarriage; separation

Nebuchadnezzar, 2, 13–14, 23, 26, 30, 151, 167

Nehemiah (person): ancestry/family of, 49–50, 52–53, 73, 204–5, 207–8; anger of, 68, 103, 178–79, 190–92; character of, 52, 63, 65, 68, 70, 73, 177–85, 190–93, 205–7; commonality with Ezra, 50–52, 55, 60, 98, 107, 114, 125, 158, 170, 173–74, 185, 205, 208; and covenant, 51, 80, 89–93, 97–98, 103, 123, 146, 207; and debt servitude crisis, 68–73, 107–8, 118, 139, 174, 177–80; and Deuteronomy, 50, 64, 76, 78–79, 118, 138; and intermarriage, 105–7, 133, 145–46, 148, 186, 190–92, 203, 207, 209; and Jeremiah, 62, 69–70, 72, 78, 105, 107–9, 207; as leader, 51, 55–59, 63–81, 84, 93–94, 100–111, 120, 122, 130, 158, 167, 169–70, 173, 177–80, 183–93, 196, 205–11; memoir of, 4–8, 38n74, 49, 51–53, 57, 70, 72, 79–81, 99, 104, 108, 152, 188, 193, 205–7, 209; and Moses, 50–51, 118, 135, 188; opposition to, 54–56, 58, 60–79, 106–7, 117, 185–86, 206; and Persia, 6, 23, 38, 49, 51–57, 78, 102–3, 115, 118, 180, 184–85, 205–6, 209; and prayer, 4–7, 38, 50–53, 56–57, 62–63, 66–67, 71, 75–78, 104–5, 107–10, 112–18, 125, 127, 129, 138, 151, 156, 159, 176, 183–84, 190, 205–7; and rebuilding/rededication, 4, 22–23, 43n84, 53–70, 72–74, 77–80, 99–109, 120, 130, 141, 170, 177–184–85, 188, 193, 205–8; return from exile of, 2–3, 23, 38, 39n78, 49–50, 53–57, 79, 81, 101, 115, 169; and temple management, 79, 93–94, 103–4, 107–8, 152, 207

New Testament, 66, 111, 127–28, 133, 135, 143n25, 144, 152, 154–55, 157, 162, 164, 167, 186; and scriptural canon, 9, 141, 165, 168. *See also* Paul

227

Subject Index

Noadiah, 76, 76n49, 77

oath, 69, 106
obedience, 32, 39, 48, 86, 91, 112n4, 120, 121, 123, 126, 130, 136, 141–43, 149–51, 153–54, 157, 159, 167, 170, 173–75, 180, 183–84, 186, 194–95. *See also* faithfulness
opposition. *See* community: and outsiders/enemies; Ezra: opposition to; Nehemiah: opposition to
oppression/oppressors, 152, 177, 184. *See also* exiles: and Babylon; Egypt: and exodus

Passover, 29–31
Paul, 122, 140–41, 148, 157, 160–63, 168, 173, 177, 181, 183, 185–87; and Judaism, 128–30, 141, 144, 161–65
Pentateuch, 9, 31, 40, 43, 67–69, 72, 86, 88, 114, 119, 136, 170
Persian/Achaemenid Empire, 2–3, 6, 13, 21–22, 26–28, 29n48, 31–33, 35, 42, 51–55, 57, 63, 102–3, 112, 116n5, 118, 120, 138, 196n32, 197, 197n36, 198, 200n45, 207n58. *See also* Ezra: and Persian/Achaemenid Empire; Nehemiah: and Persian/Achaemenid Empire
Peter, 116, 128, 152, 154, 185–86
praise. *See* joy; singers/song
prayer, 5, 26–27, 34–35, 43, 62, 124–25, 132–33, 163, 167, 176–77, 180, 183, 185; confessional/penitential, 5, 12, 87–92, 94–96, 98–99, 112–14, 117, 123, 135, 151, 166; of Ezra (*see* Ezra: and prayer); of Jesus, 140; of Nehemiah (*see* Nehemiah: and prayer)
priests, 13, 15–17, 28, 32, 47, 69, 74, 91, 103, 133, 142, 194, 198, 210; community support of, 93–94, 103–4, 175; and learning/teaching, 84, 122, 142, 172; lineage of, 30–31, 36, 46, 97–98; purity of, 99, 106–7, 152; and rebuilding, 58–60, 98; and worship, 15, 38, 96, 100–102, 131. *See also* high priests; Ezra: as priest; Levites; Nehemiah: and priests
prophets, 24–25, 30, 43, 72–78, 89–90, 111, 113, 124, 132, 134, 138, 143, 148, 153, 157, 162, 169, 172; and Ezra, 200, 202–3, 206; false, 72–78, 207; and Nehemiah, 51, 57, 69, 72–78, 105, 107–9, 180, 207; preexilic, 116–17, 151, 166, 179; Weber on, 194n19, 195–96, 198, 202. *See also* Ezekiel; Haggai; Isaiah; Jeremiah; Moses; Shemaiah; Zechariah
Protestantism, 111, 121, 121n9, 154n33, 172, 189, 210
purity, 30, 41, 48, 58, 100–101, 103, 107, 174, 186; impurity, 39, 153; of Levites, 29, 99–100, 107, 152. *See also* race, separation

race: and holiness, 48; and separation, 146–48. *See also* intermarriage
rebellion: against God, 88–90, 118, 123, 128, 131, 139, 151; political, 137, 139
redemption, 14, 51, 68, 80, 89–90, 93, 98, 114, 116–19, 121, 123, 129n16, 131, 133–34, 136, 138, 140–42, 151–52, 154, 156–57, 160, 168, 170, 176
repopulation, 2, 4, 17, 21, 24n32, 36, 80–81, 94–95, 109, 149, 206, 208
resurrection: of Israel, 125, 140; of Jerusalem, 101; of Jesus, 126, 128, 164–65, 168; of the temple, 19
returnees. *See* community: and connection with past; exile(s)
righteous, righteousness, 43, 72, 87, 125, 130, 153, 166, 178, 180
Rome, 129, 160, 168
Ruth, 149

Sabbath, 88, 91–92, 95, 104–5, 107, 207
sabbatical year, 173
sacrifice, 18–19, 21, 27–28, 33n58, 62, 71, 81, 83, 99, 100, 131, 138, 142, 147, 169, 175
salvation, 32, 125, 129, 139, 142, 152, 156, 168–69, 167; through Jesus Christ, 129n15, 160, 163–65, 167
Samuel (as prophet), 135, 158, 184
Sanballat, 54, 56, 61–64, 68, 72–73, 73n38, 74, 76, 76n48, 77, 106
sanctuary, 19, 140
Scripture, 90–91, 114, 119–23, 128–30, 145–50, 164–70, 172–74, 177, 180, 184; canon of, 66, 112–13, 118–19, 124, 129n14,

131, 135, 165, 170, 192; and Paul, 128–29, 160–62, 164, 168, 173; and prayer, 82, 90–91, 94–95; and story, 9, 91, 168. *See also* Ezra-Nehemiah; New Testament; Pentateuch; Torah

separation, 86, 91–92; from God, 86, 127, 132, 161; and holiness, 29, 94, 101–2, 106–7, 109, 141–48, 150, 186, 192n12. *See also* intermarriage: foreign wives; race

Shecaniah, 36; and intermarriage, 44–45, 148, 148n29, 150

Shemaiah, 76, 76nn48–49, 77

Sheshbazzar, 13–14, 14n8, 27, 196–97, 199, 207n58

sin, 5, 28, 42–45, 52, 76, 90, 119, 125, 127–28, 131, 135, 151–54, 162, 168–69, 177, 185, 190; of ancestors, 26, 42, 50, 52, 88–89, 123, 125, 131–32, 135, 139, 152, 166; of enemies, 62, 104, 108; and intermarriage, 40–45, 106, 145–47, 149; sacrifices for, 28, 28–29n45, 39, 138

Sinai, 46, 118, 123, 131; covenant at, 88, 113, 119, 124, 134, 136, 142, 151–52, 155, 166, 168

singers/song, 15–16, 31–32, 79, 91, 97, 99–102, 130, 152, 173–74, 176, 177n12

Solomon, 18, 23, 50, 51n5, 55, 85, 113, 117, 134–35, 137, 139, 151, 196; foreign wives of, 41, 106, 146, 152; temple of (= First Temple) 16, 18–19, 24–26, 26n39, 28, 127, 130–34, 152, 166, 175, 188

sovereignty of God, 12–13, 26, 32, 57, 114–16, 120, 124, 126, 129n14, 131, 133, 155n35, 175, 182–83

Spirit of God, 12–14, 88–90, 124, 133, 140, 152–53, 163, 173, 179

story. *See* Bible: narrative of

Sukkot, 18, 84–86, 93–94, 117, 174–75, 201

tabernacle, 17n17, 28, 131–32, 168, 175

Tabernacles, Festival of. *See* Sukkot

tax, 184, 207; and Persian/Achaemenid Empire, 23, 33, 34n63, 118, 178; temple, 93, 207. *See also* debt

teach/teaching: *see* Ezra: as teacher; priests: and learning/teaching; Torah: teaching of

temple: complex, 44, 58–60, 102–3, 105, 108, 126, 130 (*see also* gatekeepers); as God's dwelling, 19, 24–25, 26n39, 94, 120, 126–27, 131–33, 140, 152, 157, 162, 168. *See also under* altar; building/rebuilding; David; dedication; gifts; lists; Nehemiah; resurrection; Solomon; tax; vessels

thanksgiving, 39, 45, 96–102, 126, 130, 133, 175–77, 183

tithes, 94–95, 104. *See also* firstfruits

Tobiah, 54, 56, 60–63, 63n21, 72, 77, 100, 103–4, 108

Torah, 20, 28–29n45, 74, 80–89, 99, 119, 121, 123, 165; and Ezra, 31–32, 35, 40, 43, 82–85, 114, 119, 192; observance of, 18, 48, 85–89, 91–92, 95, 101–2, 105, 107; teaching of, 32, 40, 44, 80–85, 87, 91, 94, 119, 192; and "Torah Tremblers," 41–42, 44

translation, 83, 122, 172–73

tribes, 28, 36, 38, 134, 137–38, 159, 163; in Christian eschatology, 119, 133, 141; and land, 96–97, 134, 159, 162; leaders of, 13–15, 28–29, 197

trumpets, 65, 100

unfaithfulness, 125, 146–47, 149, 151

unity: in Christianity, 140–41, 163; communal, 86, 130, 135, 138–41; historical, 135

universality, 112–16, 131, 133, 136n20, 142n23, 156, 160

vessels, temple, 13–14, 27, 33, 38, 103

violence, 63–66, 106, 177, 181n18, 190–91, 206

wall (of Jerusalem): building of, 4, 24, 34n63, 55–67, 72–74, 77–78, 108, 120, 124, 139, 145, 158, 170n8, 184–86, 193, 206, 208; dedication of, 58, 99–104, 106–7, 109, 120, 131, 139, 152, 170n8, 193, 208; and Nehemiah (*see* Nehemiah: and walls); opposition to, 56, 61–67, 72–74, 77–78, 145, 185–86

weep, weeping, 44, 50, 83, 159, 201, 203,

229

Subject Index

and rejoicing, 84, 121–23, 126, 130, 153, 170, 174
wives. *See* intermarriage
women: included in community, 16, 44, 82, 139, 173, 178, 201, 203; foreign (*see* intermarriage; Solomon)
word of God, 1, 31, 41, 51, 117, 125, 127, 169, 171–75, 180, 184, 202; and prophets, 11, 19, 25, 43, 74, 74n42, 117–18, 121–25; Torah as, 84, 120–23, 169, 171–72, 175
worship, 37, 82n65, 87, 152, 166, 170–72, 174–77, 197; and Ezra (*see* Ezra: and worship); and God, 12, 14–15, 20, 30, 87, 113–14, 130–31, 133, 142, 157, 168–69, 175–77, 180, 183–84; and holy days (*see* Passover, Sukkot); and Nehemiah (*see* Nehemiah: and worship); Persian support of, 28, 35, 38; and outsiders, 21, 23, 146–47, 149, 160, 186. *See also* community: and worship; priests: and worship; sacrifice; singers/song

Xerxes, 22, 22n29

Yehud, 2, 3n3, 24, 31, 33, 34n63, 36, 54, 59, 81, 96, 103, 190–91, 197, 200, 205–6, 208–10, 197n36

Zechariah (as prophet), 24, 28, 74, 87n71, 98, 121, 198
Zerubbabel, 2, 18, 28, 36–37, 40, 81, 94, 193, 196–99, 207n58; ancestry of, 15, 197–99
Zion: epithet, 131, 167; hill, 54

Scripture Index

OLD TESTAMENT / HEBREW BIBLE

Genesis	12, 114, 116, 152, 156–57, 160
1–2	152
1	87
1:1	114, 131
1:1–2:3	131
3–11	166
3	152, 154
11	163
12	166
12:1–3	148
12:7	148
12:10	67
15	87
15:3	41
15:19–20	40
17	87
18:19	181n20
18:20–21	178
21:12	41
26:1	67
41:45	147
45:7	116
50:20	116

Exodus	31, 33–34, 67, 93, 98, 117, 121, 123, 136
2:21	147
2:23	118
2:23–25	178
3:7	67
3:8	40
3:9	67
3:15	124
3:21–22	13
4:22	161
6:16	37
8:8	33–34
9:20	12
11:2	13
12:35	34
12:35–36	3, 13
13:9	51
13:13	51
13:15	51
13:16	51
14–15	87
14	117
18:19–24	34
19:3–6	121
19:4–6	142, 143n24
19:5–6	119
20:25	18
22	71
22:21–27	181n21

22:25	69
22:25–26	68
22:27	68n29
23:6–9	181n20
23:10–11	92
23:19	93
24	136, 151
24:3	46
25:2–7	17n17
25:8	132
28:30	16n14
29	29
29:18	28
29:38–42	18
29:40	28
29:44–46	132
32–34	118
33:15–16	131
34:6	88
34:9	12
34:11–16	146
34:19–20	93
35:21–29	17n17
40:34–35	132

Leviticus	41, 43, 43n85, 71–72
1:3	28
1:9	28
1:10	28
6:8–13	93

231

Scripture Index

8	29	16	16	7:9	50		
8:8	16n14	16:28	74n42	7:21	50, 64		
10:10–11	122	18:9–10	16n14	8:4	88		
10:11	142, 172	20	88	8:18	64n24		
18	41n80	21	88	9	118		
18:3	147	24:13	74n42	10:17–18	181n19		
18:3–4	143	26:55–56	95	10:18–19	181n21		
19:2	143	27:21	16n14	12:11	51		
19:19	41, 147	28:17	29	13:15	45n92		
19:33–34	181n21	29:2–6	83	14:1	41		
20:25–26	143			15:1–18	68, 92		
21:13–15	106	**Deuteronomy**	12, 34n61,	15:7–11	181n21		
23	18		43–44, 66,	15:12	68–69		
23:23–25	18		76, 89, 95,	16:18	34		
23:24	83		153–54, 167	16:18–20	181n20		
23:33–36	18	1:5	83	18	76, 78		
23:33–43	84	1:8	88	18:9	43		
23:39–43	18	1:16–17	34	18:21–22	78, 78n52		
23:43	117	1:19–46	153	18:22	76		
25	68, 71, 93	1:30	65, 206	21:10–14	147		
25:17	71	1:38–39	43	22:24	177		
25:35–37	71	3:5	89	22:27	177		
25:36	71	4	143	23	101		
25:39–43	179	4:6	34	23:1	52n7		
25:43	71	4:6–8	144	23:2–7	40		
26	51n5, 184	4:23	167	23:3	106, 147		
26:42	50–51	4:31	127	23:3–5	101		
26:45	50–51	4:32–35	167	23:6	43		
27:21	45n92	4:34	115	24	44		
		5:31	50	24:1–4	44, 149		
Numbers	37, 97	6:1	32	26:5	137		
1–2	15	6:4–9	122	26:7	34		
1:20–45	15	6:5	154	26:17–18	154		
2:3–31	197	6:7	82n63	26:19	41		
3–4	15	6:11	43	28:10	79		
3:17	37	6:12	167	29:12–21	92		
7	28–29, 39	6:20–25	167	29:22–28	154		
7:84–86	13–14	7	94, 106, 118, 147	29:25	127		
8	29	7:1	43	30	118, 184		
8:6–26	29	7:1–3	40	30:1–5	51		
9	29	7:1–4	146–47	30:2	51		
9:14	29	7:3	43	30:3	51		
11	88	7:3–4	106	30:3–4	51		
12:1	147	7:4	106	30:4	51		
14	66, 118	7:6	41	30:6	153		
14:8–9	12	7:6–7	148	30:11–14	122, 173		
15:1–16	33n58	7:8–13	34	31:10–13	85, 122, 173		

31:16–18	154	8	26, 50, 50n4, 51n5, 131	6:1–15	30
31:21	154			6:15	26
31:27	154	8:2	18	8:14	18
32:1–52	154	8:15	34	9	96
32:15	89n73	8:22	26n39, 42	9:28	13
33:10	122, 142, 172	8:23	26n39, 50	15–16	19
34:5	50	8:23–30	26n38	22–29	188
		8:26	50	22:2–4	19
Joshua	14, 66, 89, 96–98, 162, 166	8:27	26nn38–39, 132	23–26	19
		8:27–30	132	23:14	18
1:11	37, 117	8:30	26n39	25:8	37n71
3:1	39	8:32	50	26:14	37
3:2	37	8:36	50	28:2	132
7:19	45	8:41–43	133	28:8	31–32
10:14	65	8:52	50	28:20	24
13–21	123	8:53	50	29:6	17
14:2	95	8:59	50	30:16	18
15:8	97	8:63	28		
15:21–62	17	8:66	28	**2 Chronicles**	
18:21–28	17	10:20	85	1–8	188
23–24	152	11:1	41	2:7–15	19
24	151	11:1–6	106	3:2	19
		12	74	6:42	51n5
Judges	137, 152, 195–96	12:33	74	7:5	28
2	89	18–19	89	7:6	19
3:27	65	18:46	200n43	7:16	25
6:34	65	21:22	62n20	11:1	21n24
7:18	65			11:3	21n24
20:1	18	**2 Kings**		11:10	21n24
		3:27	33n59	11:12	21n24
Ruth		17	21	11:16	21n27
1:6–14	149	17:24	21	11:23	21n24
4	147	17:41a	21	12:14	200n46
		17:41b	21n28	15	21n24
1 Samuel		21:6	62n20	15:3	122
7:3	200n46	22:8–9	83	15:8–15	44
11:7	18	22:11	83	17:7–9	83, 172
12:1–5	184	23:19–23	138	19	34n61
14:29	42	24–25	2	19:3	200n46
		24:13	13	19:8–11	172
2 Samuel		25:12	15	20:6	34
6	131	25:13–16	13	20:33	200n46
7	15	25:23	58	24:4–14	93
				24:13	63n21
1 Kings		**1 Chronicles**		28:10	69n34
6–8	188	5:40	30	29–31	172
6:11–13	127	6	15	29:10	44

233

Scripture Index

30	29, 138	2:1–2	2, 14–15	3:12	159
30:13	29	2:2	28, 36, 38	3:12–13	20, 28, 126
30:15	29	2:3–20	15	3:13	20, 100, 121n8
30:17–20	29	2:14	47	4	21–25, 34n63, 56
30:19	200n46	2:21	15	4:1	24
30:21	29	2:21–28	15n11	4:1–2	21
30:22	37	2:21–35	15	4:1–3	141
30:25	85	2:24–26	15n11	4:2	21, 25, 112
34:25	38n73	2:33	15	4:3	21, 24, 197
35	172	2:36	46	4:4	23–24
35:1–19	29	2:36–39	15	4:4–5	21–22
35:3	29, 37n71, 122, 138	2:37–43	47	4:5	21, 24, 64n25
35:6	29	2:40	15	4:6–24	73
35:17	29	2:40–42	15	4:6–6:12	2–3
35:18	138	2:43–58	16	4:7–23	50
36:10	13	2:59	134	4:8	22
36:17	26	2:59–63	15–16	4:8–11	22
		2:64	16	4:9	22
Ezra		2:64–67	16	4:9–10	141
1–6	3, 119–20, 158, 197–99	2:65	16	4:11	26
		2:66	16	4:12	22
1–2	35	2:68	17–18	4:12–13	22
1	11–14, 16, 20, 28, 34, 199	2:68–69	16–17, 175	4:13	22–23, 34n63, 197
		2:69	93	4:14	197
1:1	2–3, 9, 11, 13, 28, 115, 121, 159, 198	2:70	15, 17, 123, 134	4:14–16	22–23
		3	17–20, 23, 27, 100	4:15	22–23
1:1–3	1	3:1	17–18, 28, 138, 169	4:17	23
1:2	12, 26, 42, 50, 113	3:2	18, 113, 130–31, 197–98	4:17–20	23
1:2–4	2–3, 27			4:17–22	51
1:3	1, 36	3:2–6	19, 130, 175	4:18	23
1:3–4	12–13	3:3	18	4:19	23
1:4	12, 33, 93	3:3–6	28	4:20	23
1:5	36, 115, 199n38	3:4	18, 130	4:21	23, 52
1:5–6	12–13	3:4–6	18	4:21–24	23
1:6	2–3, 13, 33, 93, 113	3:5	18	4:22	23
1:7	13	3:6	18–19	4:23	23
1:7–11	13–14	3:7	18–19, 54	4:24	12
1:8	13, 197	3:7–11	19	5–6	2, 24–30
1:9–10	13	3:8	85	5:1	25, 113, 121
1:9–11	2–3, 16	3:8–9	19	5:1–2	24–25, 28, 30, 98, 198
1:11	13	3:10	19		
2	2, 4, 14–17, 19–20, 25, 29n47, 30–31, 36, 36n67, 46–47, 47n94, 79–80, 91, 97, 131, 134	3:10–11	19–20, 27n43, 28, 69	5:2	12, 25
				5:3	25
		3:10–13	130, 170, 175	5:3–4	26
		3:11	19–20, 35, 121n8, 126, 130, 176	5:3–5	25, 30
				5:4	25
2:1	15, 17, 113, 123, 134	3:11–13	120	5:5	25, 198, 199n38

5:6–10	25–26	6:22	29, 35, 56, 116, 120, 121n8, 130	7:24	33, 34n63
5:8	33n57, 112			7:25	34, 120, 199–200, 204
5:11	26, 30, 112–14, 136, 138, 159	7–10	2, 5, 158, 170n8		
		7	2, 30–35, 40, 119, 199, 203	7:25–26	34
5:11–12	42, 50			7:26	34, 45
5:12	12, 26, 30	7:1	30, 199	7:27	28, 34–35, 39, 55, 116–17
5:13–15	3	7:1–5	117		
5:13–17	26–27	7:1–6	30–31	7:27–28	34–35, 115, 120, 200
5:14	13, 207	7:1–8	2		
5:14 (MT)	207n58	7:1–10	30n49, 32, 200	7:27–9:15	5
5:15	207	7:1–11	5	7:28	34, 36–37, 42, 200
5:17	27	7:1b–5	30	8	2, 5, 31, 35–40, 46–47, 81n60, 121
6	33, 100, 207	7:2–5	199		
6:1–2	27	7:5	36	8:1	35–36, 122
6:1–5	27	7:6	25, 34–35, 37, 54, 82, 115, 119, 200	8:1–6	122
6:1–12	133			8:1–14	35–36
6:3	27	7:6a	31	8:2	122
6:3–5	27, 27n41	7:7	31n52	8:3	122
6:6	27	7:7–10	31–32	8:3–13	38
6:6–12	27–28	7:8	31n52	8:3–14	47
6:7	27, 112	7:8–9	115	8:5–6	122
6:8	27	7:9	25, 31, 31n53, 34–37, 39, 54, 119, 200	8:8	122, 172
6:8–9	197			8:13	36
6:9	27, 93	7:9–10	31n52	8:14	122
6:9–10	12, 42, 50	7:10	31–32, 81, 119, 171, 184, 200	8:15	15, 36, 117
6:10	27, 113			8:15–20	36–37, 175
6:11	27	7:11	32, 120	8:15–36	131
6:12	28	7:11–20	32–33	8:16	37
6:13	3	7:11–26	145	8:17	37
6:13–15	28	7:12	31–32, 42, 50, 113, 120, 199–200	8:18	37, 40, 54, 122, 200
6:14	28, 30, 60–61, 61n16, 116, 121, 198	7:12–26	53, 199	8:18–20	115
6:14a	28	7:13	32	8:20	37, 46, 113, 131
6:15	28	7:14	33–34, 34n60, 120, 200n44, 201, 203	8:21	38, 42
6:16	28, 121n8			8:21–23	185
6:16–17	138	7:14–15	112	8:21–34	31
6:16–18	28–30	7:15	33	8:21–36	38–39, 54
6:16–22	175	7:15–24	28	8:22	38–40, 46, 115, 200
6:17	28–29, 36, 38–39	7:16	33	8:23	38, 42, 50
6:18	29, 131	7:17	33, 39	8:24	38
6:19	113	7:18	33	8:24–30	37
6:19–22	29–30	7:19	33	8:25–27	38
6:20	29n46, 99–100	7:20	33	8:26–27	3
6:20a	29	7:21	31, 33, 42, 50, 93, 113, 120, 200	8:28	38, 117
6:20b	29n46			8:29	38
6:20b–21	29	7:21–24	33–34, 39	8:30	39
6:21	29, 85, 91	7:23	33, 42, 50		

Scripture Index

8:31	39–40, 200	10:4	44–45	1:5–7	26
8:31–32	38, 115	10:5	45–46	1:5–11	5, 50–51, 64, 184
8:32	37, 39, 201	10:5–9	45	1:6	50, 76
8:33	39n78, 59	10:6	38, 45, 45n91, 50	1:7	50
8:33–34	39	10:8	69, 85	1:8	51
8:35	39, 85, 138	10:8–9	40	1:8–9	50, 118
8:35–36	5	10:9	45	1:9	51
8:36	54, 199	10:10–11	45–46	1:10	51, 113, 118, 138
9–10	40–48, 86, 94, 101–2, 119n7, 135, 186, 201, 203	10:11	117	1:11	52–53, 205
		10:12	46, 85	2	52–58, 62, 100
		10:12–15	46	2:1	49
9	5, 41n83, 50, 81n60, 90, 92, 151–52, 202	10:14	46, 85	2:1–2	52
		10:15	46, 60, 203n54	2:1–8	52–54
9:1	40, 45–46, 89, 91, 145, 202	10:16	46	2:2	52, 78
		10:16–17	46	2:4	12, 57, 78, 113, 116, 205
9:1–2	40–41, 118, 201	10:18–19	46–47		
9:1a	40	10:18–44	44	2:4–5	63, 66
9:2	40, 44, 47, 89, 92, 101, 106, 146–47	10:19	47	2:5–7	53
		10:20–24	47	2:6	53, 206
9:2b	40	10:21	148n29	2:7	53
9:3	50, 122, 146, 191, 202n48	10:24	45n91	2:7–8	206
		10:25–44	47	2:7–9	205
9:3–5	41–42	10:26	44	2:8	42, 54–55, 57–58, 115, 205
9:4	41, 50, 202	10:27	45n91		
9:5	43, 50	10:28	45n91	2:9	38, 185
9:6	42	10:29	122	2:9–10	54
9:6–7	42	10:34	47	2:10	54, 63
9:6–15	5, 48	10:36	45n91	2:11	2, 54
9:7	42–43	10:38 (MT)	47n95	2:11–16	54–55
9:8	49	10:44	47	2:12	35n64, 55, 57, 80, 115, 205
9:8–9	42, 125				
9:9	127	**Nehemiah**		2:13	54–55
9:10	43	1–7	120	2:14	55, 59
9:10–12	118	1–6	158, 170n8	2:15	55
9:10–15	43–44	1–2	4, 74n39	2:16	58n13
9:11	43, 89, 113, 146, 203	1	4, 26, 49–52, 56, 103, 119n7, 151	2:16a	55
9:13	22, 43, 49			2:16b	55
9:14	43, 46, 118, 122	1:1–4	49–50, 52	2:17	50, 55
9:15	43, 49–50, 125, 159–60	1:1a	49	2:17–18	55–56
		1:1b	49	2:18	55, 57–58, 108, 115, 205–6
10	5, 48, 83	1:2	49–50		
10:1	44, 50, 82n63, 203	1:2–3	79	2:19	56, 61–63
10:1–2	44	1:3	42, 50, 55, 205	2:19–20	55–56, 61
10:2	44, 48, 146, 148	1:4	50, 205	2:20	12, 56–57, 61, 113
10:2–3	203	1:4–5	12, 113	3–6	71
10:3	40, 42, 57, 148	1:4–11	116	3–4	67
10:3–4	44–45	1:5	50, 64, 105, 125	3	2, 4, 57–61, 65, 67, 139

Scripture Index

3:1	45n91, 57–58	4:11	64, 67	6:1	57, 72, 77
3:1–2	58–59	4:12 (MT)	64–65, 65n26	6:1–7	72–74
3:1–15	58	4:13	42, 64	6:1–13	76
3:3	58	4:14	64, 76, 78	6:1–14	78
3:3–32	58–60	4:14–15	64–65	6:2	73, 76n48, 77
3:4	39n78, 59, 77	4:15	42, 65	6:4	77
3:5	57, 58–60	4:15b	65	6:5	77
3:7	58	4:16	65n27, 206	6:5–7	73, 77
3:8	58	4:16–20	65	6:6	73
3:9	59	4:16b–17	65	6:7	72–73, 75, 75n44
3:10	58	4:17	42, 65	6:8	74
3:12	59	4:18	54, 65	6:8–9	74–75
3:15	59	4:19	42, 65	6:9	54, 74, 78, 116
3:16	59	4:20	65	6:10	54, 75, 76n48
3:16–32	58–59	4:21	65	6:11	77
3:17	59	4:21–23	65	6:11a	75
3:17–18	59	4:22	65, 65n26	6:12	75, 77
3:19	59	4:23	65	6:12–14	77
3:20	45n91	5	67–72, 74, 77,	6:12a	75
3:20–21	59		86, 93, 95, 118, 119n7,	6:12b	75
3:21	39n78, 45n91		152, 174, 177, 180	6:13	76–77
3:22	59	5:1	67, 68n29, 69, 118, 177	6:14	75–77, 104
3:23	59	5:1–5	67–68, 177	6:14 (LXX)	76n49
3:26	17, 59	5:2	67, 70	6:15	77, 99, 109
3:27	59	5:3	67	6:15–19	72, 77
3:28	59	5:4	67	6:16	77–78, 184
3:29	59	5:5	67, 69–70, 139, 179	6:17	77
3:30	77	5:6	67–68, 68n29,	6:17–19	77
3:31	17, 58		118, 177–78	6:18	45n91
3:31–32	60	5:6–13	68–70	6:19	77
3:32	60	5:7	69, 71, 179	7–13	158
4	61–67, 71, 185, 206	5:8	68, 179	7	4, 14n8, 15n11,
4:1	61–63	5:8a	70		78–81, 91, 95–97,
4:1–3	61–62	5:9	70–72, 79, 179		99, 131, 134
4:1–7:5	4	5:10	68	7:1	79
4:2	63	5:11	68	7:1–4	79–80
4:3	61–62, 100	5:12	69	7:2	49, 184, 208
4:4	76	5:13	69	7:2a	79
4:4–5	62–63, 71, 104, 108	5:14	70, 205	7:3	79–80, 80n56
4:4–6	116	5:14–19	70–71, 180	7:3 (MT)	79n54
4:5	62, 62n18, 63	5:15	70–71, 79, 208	7:4	80, 80n56
4:6	63	5:16	70, 206	7:5	35n64, 79–80,
4:6–9	63	5:17–18	70		115, 206
4:7	68	5:18	70–71	7:6–73	80
4:9	63, 116, 184	5:19	75, 104, 108, 180	7:6–73a	80
4:10	63	6	24, 67, 72–79, 99,	7:7	15n9
4:10–13	63–64		103, 106, 185	7:45	79

237

Scripture Index

7:64	106	8:17	85–86, 120, 121n8, 123, 170, 174–75, 201	9:25	89
7:66	80			9:26–31	89
7:73	81	8:18	84–85	9:27	89, 124
7:73–8:1	169	9–10	81, 92	9:27–28	113
8–12	170n8	9	5, 12, 43, 86–92, 95, 98–99, 109, 112–14, 118–19, 123–24, 125n12, 134–35, 139, 151–52, 166	9:28	89
8–10	119n7, 120–21			9:29	89
8–9	88			9:30	92, 124
8	2, 5, 31, 40, 48, 80–86, 90–91, 93, 99, 114, 117, 121–22, 136, 169–70, 201, 203			9:31	89, 127
				9:32	89, 139
		9:1	38	9:32–33	125
		9:1–5	86–87, 91	9:32–38	89–90
		9:2	86, 91–92, 94, 101	9:33	125
8:1	18, 81, 84–85, 114, 119, 169, 171, 201	9:3	82, 82n65, 87	9:34	89
		9:4	87	9:35	89–90, 123
8:1–3	139, 173	9:4–5	83	9:36	90
8:1–8	81–83	9:5	91	9:37	88, 90
8:1–12	82	9:5–6	113	9:38	90
8:2	83, 85	9:5–37	116	10	4, 86, 88, 91–95, 97, 99, 103, 107, 109, 203, 207
8:2–3	139, 201	9:5b	87		
8:3	82–83, 85	9:6	87, 114, 124		
8:4–5	122, 171	9:6–8	87	10:1	4
8:4–7	82	9:6a	87	10:1–27	4, 91
8:5	82, 85, 201	9:7	87	10:2	91
8:6	82, 85, 170	9:7–8	112, 123, 156	10:5	47
8:7	91	9:8	87, 130, 156	10:9–12	91
8:7–8	82, 122	9:9	67, 88	10:20–27	91
8:8	83–84, 171	9:9–10	88	10:28	82, 89, 91–92, 94, 102
8:8a	122	9:9–11	87–88		
8:8b	122	9:9–12	113, 118	10:28–29	91–92, 139, 192n12
8:9	83–85, 201	9:10	88		
8:9–11	83–84	9:12	88	10:28–39	207
8:9–12	83–84, 122, 130	9:12–15	88	10:29	58n13, 92, 94
8:10	83–84, 86, 121n8	9:13	88, 124	10:30	91–92, 94, 102, 105, 186, 192
8:10–11	83	9:13–18	113		
8:10–12	174	9:14	88, 91–92	10:30–32	141
8:11	83	9:15	88	10:31	91–93, 95, 104
8:12	84–86, 120, 123, 130, 170, 174–75, 201	9:16	88–89	10:32–33	93
		9:16–22	88	10:32–39	94, 175
8:13	83–84, 122, 174	9:17	127	10:33	91, 93
8:13–18	84–85, 175	9:18	88	10:34	93, 107
8:14	83–85, 171	9:19	88, 124, 127	10:34–39	93–94
8:14–15	84	9:19–20	113	10:35–37	100
8:14–18	123	9:20	88–89, 124	10:35–39	104
8:15–17	174	9:20–21	124	10:36	93
8:15–18	174	9:22–25	113, 123	10:37	93
8:16	84	9:23–25	88–89	10:37–39	38, 103
8:16–18	84	9:23b–24a	88	10:37b	94

Scripture Index

10:38	94	12:11	97	13:4–31	102–9, 109n89, 110
10:38–39	100	12:12–21	91	13:5	104
10:39	94, 104	12:13	45n91	13:6–7	2, 103, 115
11	80–81, 95, 99, 103, 175	12:16	98	13:7	45n91
11:1	95, 100	12:19–21	98	13:8	103
11:1–3	95–96	12:22	45n91, 96	13:10	104
11:1–12:26	95–99	12:22–23	98	13:10–11	175
11:2	95	12:23	45n91	13:10–13	104, 107
11:3	96–97, 99	12:24	18, 69, 113, 131	13:10–27	207–8
11:3–20	4	12:26	4, 98	13:11	94, 104
11:3a	96	12:27	99, 101–2, 109, 120, 121n8, 130, 170n8	13:12	104
11:3b	96	12:27–30	58, 99–100	13:13	59, 104
11:4	96	12:27–43	100, 130	13:14	71n36, 104–5, 108
11:4–9	96	12:27–47	109, 208	13:15	104–5
11:5	96	12:27–13:3	99–103, 109, 109n89	13:15–22a	104
11:6	96	12:28–29	99	13:16	105
11:9	58n14, 96	12:29	130	13:17	105
11:10	96	12:30	99, 101, 107	13:18	105
11:10–18	96	12:31	99–100, 102	13:19	105
11:11	96	12:31–39	100	13:21	105
11:12	96	12:31–43	4	13:22	71n36, 105, 108n88, 176, 190n9
11:17	96–99, 101	12:36	18, 100, 113, 131	13:22a	105
11:18	96, 100	12:38	100, 102	13:22b	105
11:19	96, 98	12:39	58, 100	13:23	92, 105
11:19–24	96–97	12:40	102	13:23–27	105–6, 186
11:20	96–97, 99, 104, 113, 123	12:40–43	100	13:23–28	141, 148
11:21	17, 96	12:41	100	13:24	106, 145
11:21–24	96	12:42	45n91, 100	13:25	106, 190–91
11:22	97, 101	12:43	100–101, 120, 121n8	13:26	92, 106, 113
11:23	97, 101	12:44	101–2, 104, 107	13:26–27	146
11:24	97	12:44–47	100–101	13:27	106, 146
11:25	96	12:45	101, 107, 113	13:28	45n91, 106
11:25–36	97	12:45–46	131	13:28–31	106–7
11:28	97	12:46	101–2	13:29	107–8
11:30	97, 113	12:47	4, 101, 104	13:30	93, 107
11:36	97	13	4, 44n89, 88, 91, 93, 101–4, 107, 109, 130n17, 152, 192, 203, 207	13:31	93, 108, 152, 176
12	94, 100, 102, 120, 131, 139, 152, 176			**Esther**	
12:1	97	13:1	101	1:21	53
12:1–7	91, 97	13:1–3	101, 106, 109, 192n12	2:4	53
12:7	97			2:9	53
12:8	97	13:3	101	4:3	38
12:8–26	97	13:4	45n91	4:16	38
12:9	97	13:4–9	38, 60, 103	5	53n9
12:10	45n91			5:3	53

Scripture Index

Reference	Page
5:6	53
7	53n9
9:5	88
9:19	84, 84n68
9:19–22	84
9:22	84n68

Job

Reference	Page
1:20	41
2:13	41–42
22:26	42
29:7–17	181n20
31:13–23	181n21
39:11	61n17
42:2	57n12

Psalms 12, 43, 66, 109, 116–17, 125, 166

Reference	Page
2	24
5:7	105
10:14b	61n17
13:3	42
16:10	127–28
22:1	127
22:1–8	127
22:23	41
27:7	62
27:9	38n73
28:6	34
30:10	62
31:21	34
32:1	62n18
33:6–8	113
33:18	25
34:15	25
44	62
51	43
72:4	181n20
72:12–14	181n20
74	62
77	62
82	181n20
89:46–49	133
105–7	167
106	20n23, 87
106:13	88
106:29	62n20
106:35	41
106:35–39	147
107	20n23
109:2	23
109:6–19	62
112	180, 181n21
112:1	180
112:4	180
112:6	180
118	20n23
119	32, 169
119:30	169
119:40	169
119:45	32
119:48	169
119:53	38n73
119:94	32
119:137	43
119:155	32
136	20n23, 87, 176
137	36, 62
143:10	88
145	180
145:9	181n19
145:13	181n19
145:17	181n19
147:7–9	181n19
148:1–6	87

Proverbs

Reference	Page
14:31	181n21
16:33	95
19:17	181n21
22:7	178
28–29	189n3
29:7	181n21
31:4–9	181n20

Isaiah 12, 72, 117, 125, 151, 161, 166

Reference	Page
1:10	178
1:16–17	181n21
1:21–23	178
5:2	178
5:3	178
5:5	42, 178
5:7	178
6:13	41
8:10	66n28
9:6–7	155
11:2	72
11:3	72
11:4	72
20:1–4	202n48
33:20	42
34:16	31
40–55	117, 151
40–66	139, 156
40:3	38
41:2	11n1
41:25	11n1
44:9–20	12
44:24–45:8	159
44:26–28	24n32
44:28	11n1
45:1	11n1, 198n37
45:13	11n1
46:1–7	12
49:16–26	24n32
49:17–22	24n32
52:7	161
52:7–10	156
54:7	127
56:1–8	105
57:19	161
58:6–9	181n21
58:8	63n21
60:13	19
60:21	153
61:4	24n32
62:12	41
63:16	161
63:18	41
64:8	161
66:1–2	132
66:2	41
66:5	41

Jeremiah 9, 11, 11n1, 26, 64, 66, 69–70, 72, 105, 107–9, 117, 121, 167

Reference	Page
1:1	49
8:22	63n21

12:7	127	34:9–10	70	4:17	115
14:8	44n90	34:10	69	4:27	181n20
14:17–21	51n5	34:11	70	5	53n9
14:20–21	184	34:14	69	5:10	52
15:15	108, 108n87	34:16	69	6:10	167
17	105	36	121	9	5, 91n77
17:13	44n90	40:5–12	58	9:4	50n3
17:19	105	41:5	21	12:7	41
17:20	105	44:30	26		
17:21	105	46:26	26	**Amos**	
17:22	105	50:7	44n90	1:1	49
17:24	105	51:11	11	5:11–15	181n21
17:27	105	51:50	64	5:21–24	181n21
18:18	122, 172			8:5	92
18:20	108	**Lamentations**			
18:21–23	108	2:7	127	**Micah**	
18:23	62n18	5:18	62	7:10	25
21:7	26				
22:1–3	181n20	**Ezekiel**	78, 125, 131, 140,	**Haggai**	24, 25n33,
22:25	26		153, 202, 202n48		27–28, 126
23:16	74n42	1:1	36	1:1	197–98
23:26	74n42	3:15	202n48	1:1–11	27
24:6	25	4–5	202n48	1:4	25n33
25:11–12	11	8:1–3	115	1:15	24
26:20–23	89	13:2	74n42	2:1–9	18
27–28	78n52	13:6	78	2:3–9	126
27:4–5	115	13:6–7	78	2:6	26n40
27:6	26	16:49–50	178	2:20–23	74
27:8	26	16:61–63	50–51	2:21	26n40, 198
28	78	18	26, 42		
29:4–7	167	36:10	24n32	**Zechariah**	24, 98
29:7	27n44	36:26–27	153	1:1	98
29:10	14, 28	36:33–36	24n32	6:9–14	74
29:10–11	11	37	125, 140	12	197
29:21	26	37:1–14	140		
30–31	151	37:15–28	140	**Malachi**	135
30	24n32	37:16–17	140	2:1–9	172
30:17	63n21	37:24–28	155	2:4–9	122
31:40	59	37:28	140	2:10–16	145
32–33	125	48:15–35	24n32	3:16	80
32:28	26				
32:38–40	153	**Daniel**	167	**ANCIENT NEAR**	
33:6	63n21	1	52	**EASTERN TEXTS**	
33:15–22	155	2:4	52		
34	72	2:5	28	**Behistun Inscription**	
34:8–22	69	3:9	52	§67	28
34:9	69	3:29	28		

Scripture Index

Cyrus Cylinder	27n44	

GREEK LITERATURE

Ctesias
Persica
14.39 — 53

Herodotus
Histories
3.34 — 52n7
3.91 — 33
9.110–11 — 53

APOCRYPHA / DEUTEROCANONICAL BOOKS

Tobit
1:22 — 52n7

Sirach/Ecclesiasticus
24 — 34n60

1 Maccabees
5:62 — 210n62

2 Maccabees
10:7 — 84n69

1 Esdras — 7n15, 13, 209n61
2:10–14 — 13
4:48 — 54
7:11 — 29n46
8:29 — 36n69
8:69 — 41n80
9:36 — 47
9:48 — 83n66

DEAD SEA SCROLLS

1QS i–ii — 90n76

NEW TESTAMENT

Matthew — 135
5:13–16 — 151
17:24 — 93
25:31–46 — 181n21

Mark
13:1–2 — 126

Luke — 167
2:28–32 — 164
2:32 — 167
9:31 — 119
14:12–14 — 181n21
22:31–34 — 154
24:46–48 — 168

John
2:12–22 — 126
13:34 — 164
13:37–38 — 154
15:12 — 164
15:17 — 164
17 — 140
17:21–23 — 140, 164
19:10–11 — 116
21:15–19 — 154

Acts — 168
2:23 — 116
2:25–32 — 128
7 — 132
13:32–33 — 165
20:27 — 160

Romans
1–8 — 163
1:5 — 141, 157
8:28 — 152
9–11 — 129, 163
9:1–5 — 129
9:6 — 129
11:1–2 — 129
11:23 — 129n15
11:25 — 129n16
11:26 — 129n16
11:28–29 — 129
11:33–36 — 130
12–15 — 163
12:6–8 — 185
14–15 — 129, 163
15:25–27 — 181n21
16:26 — 141, 157

1 Corinthians
7:12–16 — 148

2 Corinthians
6:14 — 148
8–9 — 181n21

Galatians
2:10 — 181n21
3:8–9 — 160
3:26–29 — 161
3:28 — 141, 162

Ephesians — 168
1:9–10 — 168
1:10 — 168
2–3 — 163
2 — 133
2:11–13 — 161
2:14–16 — 140
2:17 — 161
2:19 — 161
2:21 — 162
2:21–22 — 140
3:6 — 144, 162
3:10 — 140
4–5 — 187
4:3–6 — 163
4:7–13 — 185
4:11–12 — 172

Colossians — 168
3:16 — 173

2 Thessalonians
2:13–14 — 168

1 Timothy
2:1–3 — 177

3:1–10	185	James		21:1	131
4:13	173	1:27	181n21	21:12–14	141
6:17–19	181n21	2:14–17	181n21	22:3	153

2 Timothy

2:2	122, 172
2:15	173

1 John

3:16–18	181n21

RABBINIC WORKS

Revelation 124, 131, 140–41, 153, 168

Babylonian Talmud
Megillah

1 Peter

2	133
4:10–11	185
5:1–4	185

5:9–10	119
7:4–10	141
21–22	131

3a	83

www.ingramcontent.com/pod-product-compliance
Lightning Source LLC
Chambersburg PA
CBHW031252230426
43670CB00005B/153